COMMUNICATION ETHICS AND UNIVERSAL VALUES

Edited by

CLIFFORD CHRISTIANS
MICHAEL TRABER

SAGE Publications
International Educational and Professional Publisher
Thousand Oaks   London   New Delhi

For information, address to:

SAGE Publications, Inc.
2455 Teller Road
Thousand Oaks, California 91320
E-mail: order@sagepub.com

SAGE Publications Ltd.
6 Bonhill Street
London EC2A 4PU
United Kingdom

SAGE Publications India Pvt. Ltd.
M-32 Market
Greater Kailash I
New Delhi 110 048 India

Printed in the United States of America

Library of Congress Cataloging-in-Publication Data

Main entry under title:
Communication ethics and universal values / editors, Clifford Christians
   and Michael Traber.
      p. cm.
   Includes bibliographical references (p.) and index.
   ISBN 0-7619-0584-7 (acid-free paper).—ISBN 0-7619-0585-5
(pbk.: acid-free paper)
      1. Communication—Moral and ethical aspects.   I. Christians, Clifford G.
   II. Traber, Michael.
   P94.C5716   1997
   174—dc21   96-51209

97 98 99 00 01 02 03   10 9 8 7 6 5 4 3 2 1

Acquiring Editor:	Margaret Seawell
Editorial Assistant:	Renée Piernot
Production Editor:	Astrid Virding
Production Assistant:	Denise Santoyo
Typesetter/Designer:	Marion Warren
Print Buyer:	Anna Chin
Indexer:	Teri Greenberg
Cover Designer:	Lesa Valdez

COMMUNICATION ETHICS AND UNIVERSAL VALUES

Contents

PART III: Applications

Introduction

Communication ethics faces a monumental challenge at present. It has to respond to both the rapid globalization of communications and the reassertion of local sociocultural identities. It is caught in the apparently contradictory trends of cultural homogenization and cultural resistance. Therefore, ethics must confront these critical questions: Can theoretical models be developed that are explicitly cross-cultural? Can moral principles be identified that are universal within the splendid variety of human life? Will a multicultural comparative ethics replace the dominant canons, most of them North Atlantic and patriarchal? As the field grows empirically and matures conceptually, a new axis is needed to replace its mono-cultural one.

The comparative ethics represented in this book places Western and non-Western cultures, and those North and South, on a level playing field. It presumes that all philosophies of culture can offer unique insights into the fundamental principles of communication ethics and can thus make substantial contributions to normative discourse. Every culture depends for its existence on norms that order human relationships and social institutions.

To foster participation and equality, working sessions on multicultural ethics were held in various locations around the world. These colloquia were organized by the World Association for Christian Communication in London—cosponsor of the Sage monograph series "Communication and Human Values" and editorial home of the international journal *Media Development.* Sometimes, these forums were held alongside the conventions of the International Association for Mass Communication Research, as in Lake Bled, Slovenia, in 1990 and São Paulo, Brazil, in 1992. Other seminars were cosponsored by universities or professional organizations, such as the meetings in Moscow (1991), Seoul (1992), Dar es Salaam, Tanzania (1993), Colombo, Sri Lanka (1994), and Munich, Germany (1994). In such venues, local and regional scholars presented the major discussion papers on the question: What are the fundamental ethical principles of human interaction in general and public communication in particular within one's native cultural tradition? Several of these papers, in revised form, are included in this volume; others were commissioned as a result of the debate.

During this process, it became obvious that the current problems (some would say malaise) of the mass media cannot be resolved by new press or broadcasting codes, let alone legislation, but by in-depth and systematic reflection about the fundamental norms that form the bedrock of ethical reasoning and moral choices. The decision, therefore, was not to study professional ethics in a narrow sense (which is being done by many other institutions) but to discover a normative vision or a broadly based ethical theory of communication. Such a vision transcends the world of mass media practice and makes a contribution to the public ethos, that is, to a more humane and more responsible code of values that society as a whole could and should adopt.

For a comparative communication ethics of this scope to be credible, questions need to be asked on three different levels of abstraction. In foundational terms, what is the rationale for normativity itself in an age of normlessness? Within the domain of particular cultures, are there common values underlying them that are similar to those of other cultural traditions? And, on the level of communication practice and policy, are there master norms that provide direction and boundaries for media morality? These various levels, although discrete for purposes of analysis, mix through one another as components of the whole. In a version of the hermeneutical circle, they serve as entry points into the overall project of systematizing a multicultural communication ethics.

The four chapters in Part I approach the foundational issues from four perspectives. In the face of philosophical relativisim, and contradicting the commonplaces that deny there are common values which transcend ideologies and culture, these chapters defend the possibility of universal moral imperatives. Although such norms are known to us in diverse languages, geography, and history, the general argument in this section is that principles or protonorms, regardless of region and symbolic forms, are essential for maintaining human society.

In Chapter 1, ethics is grounded in being. The primal sacredness of life on earth is identified as the philosophical foundation of the moral order. The rationale for human responsibility is reverence for the organic realm in which human civilization is situated. Nurturing life has a taken-for-granted character; its purpose is embedded in the animate world, evident in its own reproduction. The universal sacredness of human life bonds us into an organic unity and imputes to humankind a privileged ontological status. As with parents' obligation to children, our universal solidarity is unquestioned—stitched into our being as a moral species.

Antonio Pasquali, in Chapter 2, calls for a new morality of intersubjectivity as the prime need of our time. He develops a multicultural model that accounts for shifting East-West relations and the ongoing confrontations between North and South. In his construction, human relations are recovered as nonnegotiable, and distributive justice replaces traditional social contracts constrained by nationalism. Intersubjectivity models situate morality in our everyday experience and locate the conceptual more closely to the way ethical judgments actually occur in the human community. This strategy enables us to be continually self-analytical from within rather than merely critical from the outside.

The discourse ethics of Karl-Otto Apel and Jürgen Habermas enjoy the widest critical attention at present in unearthing the universal structures of communication. Edmund Arens evaluates the concept of communicative rationality in Chapter 3 as a procedure for universally grounding norms of human action. His approach implies three universals for media ethics: orientation toward shared truth, authentic expression free of delusion, and social justice.

Chapter 4 examines moral development theories to understand what constitutes the content and process of moral growth. Moral development theories derive from the observation that people grow and change in their perception of what makes an action good or bad, right or wrong. Just as one's cognition and physical self change through growth and experience, so too does one's moral sense. Because valuing is presumed to be a basic activity in all conscious humans, theories of moral development rest on the assumption of universality. Their validity depends on a credible version of universal values.

Part II enters the field of comparative ethics from the perspective of particular cultures. From six different regions of the world in five continents, authors probe beneath the surface for bedrock values in which their cultures are grounded. In these philosophical reflections of ethicists and academics who analyze social communication within their own contexts, a short list of ethical principles emerges—many of them overlapping one another. Their focus is not on abstract, noncontingent axioms that exist in metaphysical isolation. These reflections center on protonorms or underlying presuppositions that are necessary for ethical reasoning. Proto- can mean first or initial, as in "prototype," where a model is fabricated and engineers reproduce it in a second step in a process. However, Part II understands proto- in terms of lying beneath, as in the proto Indo-European language—a lingual predecessor underlying the actual languages that exist in history and one that can be reconstructed from languages we know.

Truth is one underlying principle about which there is cross-cultural agreement. The most fundamental norm of Arab-Islamic communication is truthfulness. Truth is one of the three highest values in the context of the Latin American experience of communication. In Hinduism, the supreme ideal is the state of *moksha* or liberation, and actions characterized by truth [*satya*] are essential for achieving it. Truth is the highest *dharma* and the source of all other virtues; it is unanimously recognized in all Hindu traditions. Deception destroys the social order. Living with others is inconceivable if we cannot tacitly assume that people are speaking truthfully. Lying, in fact, is so unnatural that machines can measure bodily reactions against it. When we deceive, Dietmar Mieth argues in Chapter 5, the truth imperative is recognized in advance: "otherwise, there would be no need to justify such exceptions as special cases. . . . those who relativize such a norm are indirectly recognizing it by offering reasons to justify their limitation of its categorical validity" (p. 89).

Respect for another person's dignity is a second underlying principle on which various cultures rest. Different cultural traditions affirm human dignity in a variety of ways, but together they insist that all human beings have sacred status without exception. Native American discourse is steeped in reverence for life, an interconnectedness among all living forms so that we live in solidarity with others as equal constituents in the web of life. In communalistic societies, one's own self-respect, by definition, entails a total commitment to the community's reputation as a whole, allowing nothing that would put others in disrepute. A philosophical analysis of Latin

American societies sees in the insistence on cultural identity an affirmation of the unique worth of human beings. One of the features that both religious and secular Arab traditions have in common is insisting on every person's right to honor and a good reputation.

No harm to the innocent is a third protonorm weaving its way through the diversity of Chapters 6 through 10. In some ethical systems, protecting the innocent revolves around the search for a just society and the consequent revulsion if the powerless are abused. In communalistic and indigenous cultures, care for the weak and vulnerable (children, sick, and elderly) and sharing material resources and knowledge are a matter of course. The ability to forgive, to be reconciled and show compassion are also expressions of the principle that the innocent ought not be harmed. In Latin American axiology, this protonorm takes shape in appealing for nonviolence. *Ahimsa* [non-violence] along with truth in *dharma* forms the basis for the Hindu worldview as a whole. *Ahimsa,* closely associated with the virtue of compassion or universal kindness, is applicable to all beings and in all circumstances of life.

The efforts at grounded theory in Part 2 benefit from Kaarle Nordenstreng's extensive work on codes of ethics in an international setting (Nordenstreng & Topuz, 1989; cf. Juusela, 1991).[1] This section shows some similarities to Thomas Cooper's (1989) study of international media ethics, which also identifies three protonorms for universal status.[2] Cooper concluded that one worldwide concern within the apparatus of professional standards and codes is the quest for truth (though often limited in the literature to a concern for objectivity and accuracy; p. 20).[3] A second concern based on the available research data, Cooper defines as "a desire for responsibility among public communicators" for the social mores and cultural features in which they operate (p. 20). This sense of obligation is more diffuse than protonorm three (no harm to the innocent) described earlier. However, Cooper's vision of justice, equality, and protection of privacy overlap with, and arise from, a self-consciousness that the innocent ought not be harmed. Cooper also concludes that freedom of expression is a possible third imperative across the professional media practices that he and his colleagues investigated (p. 21). Although its scope is narrower than the protonorm of human dignity, free speech is an important component of maintaining human uniqueness. The emphasis on cultural identity in Latin America and the concern for a public voice of indigenous integrity in Native American discourse are illustrations of how human dignity and free expression are part and parcel of one another.

Part 3 asks whether protonorms across cultures make any difference in contemporary mass communications practice. Steeped as they are in tradition and social philosophy, do these ethical protonorms have any practical relevance for the urgent media issues of today? Do protonorms help us build a theoretical model that is multicultural but with little chance to influence particular communication systems? Chapters 11 through 16, in fact, argue the opposite; protonorms for them are a vital resource in facing today's media crises and conundrums.

Pedro Gomes in Chapter 11 calls on mass media professionals to break away from established social codes that mask unfairness and to follow instead the demands of a liberating ethics. Journalists, producers, and editors in a complicated world must keep their eyes on the horizon of utopia to serve society effectively. Ethics codes and organizational canons are insufficient; they ordinarily protect the status quo and stultify action. Over the long term, professionals need a moral conscience inscribed by such principles as justice, reciprocity, and human dignity.

In Chapter 12, recent changes in Taiwan offer author Georgette Wang a rare opportunity to examine the relationship between media morality and protonorms. As old political and social taboos collapse, media professionals are prompted to reexamine the codes and behavior that typically have defined acceptable practice. A rich and broad definition of truth-telling as comprehensive understanding of reality is critical, while a new participatory public sphere takes shape and journalistic definitions of accuracy and objectivity are discredited as too narrow for the sea-changes underway.

For Hideo Takeichi, in Chapter 13, the traditional Japanese emphasis on group harmony is too insular and weak for dealing with the globalization of the economy and internationalization of communication. The Japanese challenge for the new age, as he sees it, is reaching beyond its national borders to the ethical principle of human solidarity, transcending the differences of nationality and culture.

Starting with the Solidarity revolution of 1980, Polish society—media practitioners among them—have struggled with the question of what value system to recognize and follow; this is the topic of Chapter 14. Whereas moral values such as justice, equality, truth, and human dignity dominated the agenda during the 1980s, these values have been traded away for a laissez faire system since a Solidarity-led government was elected in 1989. Journalists have tended to retreat to a standard market model. However, if they are to genuinely serve the public interest, they should invigorate their journalistic conventions with such universal principles as truth-telling, free expression, and justice.

In coming to grips with issues of power among visual anthropologists and in ethnographic film making, Keyan Tomaselli and Arnold Shepperson (Chapter 15) turn to global criteria articulated by Agnes Heller. The basic common values in her notion of dynamic justice are freedom and the protection of life. As a communicative practice, ethnographic film is explicitly multicultural and intercultural. The standard appeals for "professionalism" ignore the ideological questions and obscure the oppressive practices. Therefore, a normative system rooted in dynamic justice is necessary to insure that this genre affirms the humanist project.

Chapter 16 examines the welfare debate currently taking place in the United States media. It argues for an ethical approach able to address issues of stereotyping and visual association and of dehumanization and polemical discourse. Morally acceptable welfare coverage requires a theoretical model able to shed light on the discursive formation of social identity, bias, and such practices as scapegoating. The three pillars of this model are the protonorms of human dignity, unconditional acceptance of the Other, and solidarity with the weak and vulnerable.

In conclusion, the atmosphere of the new millenium has temptations and its own challenges. The temptations are to succumb to the pessimism of the *fin-de-siècle* ambience, and to look for scapegoats, including the mass media, that could be blamed for the ills of our time. The final chapter postulates that the current lack of certitude that marks the extraordinary age in which we live should, instead, encourage us to engage in a rigorous analysis of the crises in values around us. As Hans Küng (1991) reminds us, today's complex and fragile world needs "global ethical standards to survive. . . . [It] does not need a unitary religion and a unitary ideology, but it does need some norms, values, ideals and goals to bring it together" (pp. xvi-xvii; cf. Kidder, 1994). The urgency of common values for a sustainable 21st century is especially apparent among the powerful transnational media and information systems.

Needless to say, consensus about ethical principles of communication has broken down in some countries and is under assault in others. This book is not a rescue operation to recover these principles of times past. Its aim is to reintroduce them into the current normative discourse and reconceptualize them as systematically as possible for the modern institutions of mass communication.

The multicultural comparative ethics developed here does not aim at geographic representation. The approach is topical and issue oriented. The study process for this book has demonstrated that cultures in all their differences also reflect common humaneness and humanity. This book thus shows the many different entranceways that can lead to a common ethical discourse on a global scale, centered on truth-telling, human dignity, and no harm to the innocent.

Notes

1. Nordenstreng's (1984) *The Mass Media Declaration of UNESCO* was a pathbreaker in understanding professional ethics internationally through codes of ethics; cf. also Nordenstreng and Topuz (1989). For a summary of the common values expressed in journalistic codes and how they can account for diversity at the same time, see Nordenstreng (1989). Juusela (1991) adds to this analysis from the perspective of human rights with his research on journalistic codes of ethics in the 23 countries of the Conference on Security and Cooperation in Europe; Juusela also lists some of the earlier work on codes of ethics (pp. 5 6).

2. Cooper's *Communication Ethics and Global Change* was the first comprehensive survey of media ethics across cultures by an international network of media professionals and teachers from 13 countries. Nordenstreng, Topuz, and Juusela investigated codes of media ethics empirically, and Cooper evaluated the state of the art in professional morality, whereas *Communication Ethics and Universal Values* is more philosophical in orientation.

3. In his research on human values among indigenous peoples, Cooper (1994, p. 338) identified truthfulness as one of their primary principles. Truth-telling is the moral centerpiece of the Shuswap bands in Western Canada.

References

Cooper, Thomas W. (Ed.). (1989). *Communication ethics and global change*. New York: Longman.

Cooper, Thomas W. (1994). Communion and communication: Learning from the Shuswap. *Critical Studies in Mass Communication, 11*(4), 327-345.

Juusela, Pauli. (1991). *Journalistic codes of ethics in the CSCE countries*. Tampere, Finland: University of Tampere, Department of Journalism and Mass Communication Publications, Series B.

Kidder, Rushworth M. (1994). *Shared values in a troubled world.* San Francisco: Jossey-Bass.
Küng, Hans (1991). *Global responsibility: In search of a new world ethic* (Trans., John Bowden). London: SCM.
Nordenstreng, Kaarle. (1984). *The mass media declaration of UNESCO.* Norwood, NJ: Ablex.
Nordenstreng, Kaarle. (1989). Professionalism in transition: Journalistic ethics. In Thomas W. Cooper (Ed.), *Communication ethics and global change* (pp. 277-283). New York: Longman.
Nordenstreng, Kaarle, & Topuz, Hifzi. (Eds.). (1989). *Journalist: Status, rights and responsibilities.* Prague: International Order of Journalists.

PART I

Foundations and Framework

CHAPTER 1

The Ethics of Being in a Communications Context

CLIFFORD G. CHRISTIANS[1]

Ethical rationalism has served as the prevailing paradigm in Western moral philosophy. Reason made the human species distinctive and only through rationality were moral canons legitimate. The truth of prescriptions could be settled by formal examination of their logical structure. In the Cartesian version, reason was considered "the same for all thinking subjects, all nations, all epochs and all cultures" (Cassirer, 1951, p. 6). By making cognitive processes explicit and combining them with the ancient Western emphasis on reason's universality, basic rules were constructed that autonomous moral agents considered obligatory and against which all counter claims about moral obligation could be measured.

> Just as western science has held there are universal truths about the world, discoverable through reason and accessible in principle to people of all times and places, so western philosophers such as Plato, Aristotle, and Kant have held that there are timeless moral truths, arising out of human nature and

independent of the conventions of particular societies. (Paul, Miller, & Paul, 1994, p. vii)

The idea of a common morality known to all rational beings had its detractors, of course, from within the Western tradition itself. Giambattista Vico (1948; cf. Verene, 1976), professor of rhetoric at the University of Naples (1699-1741), argued for imaginative universals rooted in *fantasia* rather than in linear rationality. David Hume (1739, 1748/1963) took seriously the multiplying discoveries of other cultures in the 18th century, recognizing within the framework of empirical philosophy that these diverse conceptions of the good life might turn out to have nothing in common. But such oppositional voices and trajectories were of limited influence, until in the late 20th century the paradigm of immutable and universal morality has been generally discredited.[2] Though presumably based on shared features of human beings as a whole, it has been exposed as the "morality of a dominant gender and class" (Farley, 1993; Outka & Reeder, 1993, p. 4; Welch, 1985). Postulating an abstract good is no longer seen as beneficent but as imperialistic control over moral judgments; it allows "the tyranny of particular communities . . . to define for us every- thing that can possibly matter in human life" (Outka & Reeder, 1993, p. 24).

The Enlightenment version of common morality has been preeminent in the European and North American context since the 18th century. Deter- mined to remove all external authority except human reason, the Enlight- enment celebrated advances in science and politics founded on rational consent. But now, the curtain is coming down on 300 years of Enlighten- ment modernity. The foundations on which universal norms were built have eroded. The very concept of norms has been destroyed; the Western world has lost its feeling for them. The modernist project to establish reason and truth as being everywhere and always the same has failed.

The West's predicament is typically understood in terms of language theory and global communications.

In Wittgenstein's (1953, 1956) linguistic naturalism, for example, the search for an abstract essence entangles us in a maze of propositions that lead finally to the point where the essentialist turn was taken in the first place. Instead of essentialism, we can only claim in mathematical proofs, "this is what we do. This is use and custom among us, a product of our natural history" (Wittgenstein, 1956, sec. 63, p. 20; cf. 1953, pp. 116-123).

Objects and events situated in time and space contain all the facts there are. Moral standards, therefore, are only intelligible within their own lingual context. In Moritz Schlick's (1949) semantics, "The meaning of a word is solely determined by the rules which hold for its use. Whatever derives from these rules, follows from the mere meaning of the word and is therefore purely analytic, tautological, formal" (p. 285; cf. 1992).

Contemporary technological societies, supercharged with information, have become fragmented by linguistic games. In deconstructionist terms, modern mass-mediated discourse is an arbitrary system of differences, oppositions, and conventions, of sliding signs and signifiers (Derrida, 1984). Proliferating information technologies have created a hyper-reality of simulated images more definitive for contemporary civilization than are political institutions, economics, or the family and the church. In what Jean Baudrillard (1983, p. 2) calls "the precession of the simulacra," we create cybernetic models to organize reality, but a reversal occurs and reality arises from matrices and information banks instead. In the technical artifice, we are uprooted from history and social memory.[3]

There are major paradoxes in these analyses that center on language and communications. But underneath the often overwrought claims, they speak in concert against the totalizing conditions of knowledge that the 18th century fostered—against metaphysics, universal reason, ethical systems, correspondence views of truth, and essentialist theories of human nature. And cultures feeding from the Enlightenment worldview now face a crisis of validation. What still counts as legitimate knowledge for them? There are no widely accepted rational means for people committed to different beliefs to debate them constructively. Transhistorical certitude has been replaced by philosophical relativism, that is, by the presumption that moral principles have no objective application independent of the societies within which they are constituted.[4] Nihilism (no moral truths exist) and skepticism (moral propositions cannot be justified) are prevalent responses as well (cf. Stout, 1993, p. 215).

At this critical juncture in its history, the Enlightenment's progeny needs to examine once again whether a universal moral order is conceivable and intellectually defensible. In fact, it has to recover the very idea of moral universals itself. And this must be done without presuming first foundations, without the luxury of an objective metaphysical reality from which to begin. The only legitimate option is an ethics that is culturally inclusive rather than biased toward Western hegemony. The future of communication

ethics, in Seyla Benhabib's (1992) terms, depends on whether "a post Enlightenment defense of universalism, without metaphysical and historical
props, is still viable" (p. 3). Obviously, as one period of history is left
behind and another begins, our mandate is not an ethics of any sort under
any conditions. A minimalist, limpid, quandary ethics has little contribution to make; parochialism has no credibility whatsoever as the global information society takes shape.

Rather than move uncritically from objectivity to subjectivity or from
correspondence to coherence views of truth, I believe resolution emerges
from philosophical anthropology.[5] The modernist period co-opted moral
issues into epistemology, and when its cognitive system went bankrupt,
moral imperatives were destroyed also. But if normativity is adequately
understood in terms of our human wholeness, an ontological ground for
ethics is once again viable in the contemporary context. Therefore, the
question for metaethics: Are there global principles or a moral order or
master norms that belong to our humanness? The philosophy of communication itself offers the possibility of discovering something ontologically—rather than epistemologically—universal. For communication to
occur beyond mere transmission, the human being

> must be able to recognize in the "otherness" of its representations that which
> is intelligible to itself, that is, what is universal in them. . . . A communicative
> subject must actually know universals, not in the sense of . . . abstract gener-
> alizations, but with the capacity to grasp precisely the universality imminent
> in the particular. . . . The communicative mind must be able to assimilate that
> universality of something "other," without thereby losing self-identity, that is
> to say, without itself becoming something universal. . . . The communicative
> mind comprises both the power of reflection and the potential universality of
> human consciousness. (Henrici, 1983, p. 3)

Sacredness of Life as Protonorm

The German philosopher Hans Jonas illustrates one strategy for establishing the idea of universal norms free of a static, Newtonian cosmology.
He turns to nature rather than to modernist foundationalism for grounding
a responsibility that is global in scope and self-evident regardless of cultures and competing ideologies. Natural reality has a moral claim on us for
its own sake and in its own right. The philosophical rationale for human

action is reverence for life on earth, for the organic whole, for the physical realm in which human civilization is situated.

The Enlightenment worldview assumed that humans alone are conscious and purposeful and that nature is spiritless. Jonas contradicts this dichotomy. In his perspective, purpose is embedded in the animate world and its purposiveness is evident "in bringing forth life. Nature evinces at least one determinate goal—life itself" (Jonas, 1984, pp. 74). Thus, Jonas concludes, "showing the immanence of purpose in nature, . . . with the gaining of this premise, the decisive battle for ethical theory has already been won" (p. 78).

Our duty to preserve life is to be understood as similar in kind to parents' responsibility for their children. It is an obligation "independent of prior assent or choice, irrevocable, and not given to alteration of its terms by the participants" (Jonas, 1984, p. 95). When new life appears, the forbears do not debate their relationship to it as though the offspring is neutral protoplasm and their responsibility a matter of calculating the options. Parental duty to children is an archetype of the natural accountability Jonas thus establishes—an *a priori* ought, grounded ontologically, an obligation that is timeless and nonnegotiable.

Human responsibility regarding natural existence contributes the possibility of intrinsic imperatives to moral philosophy. It demonstrates the legitimacy of concluding that collective duty can be cosmic, primordial, and irrespective of our roles or contracts. Through the preservation of life as the ground for human responsibility, Jonas has established normative discourse to help contradict the postmodern assumptions that metaphysical truths do not exist and that no ought can be derived from being.

Jonas gives the preservation of life a taken-for-granted character. Our human identity is rooted in the principle that "human beings have certain inescapable claims on one another which we cannot renounce except at the cost of our humanity" (Peukert, 1981, p. 11). Rather than generating an abstract conception of the good, the primal sacredness of life is a catalyst for binding humans universally into an organic whole. In Peukert's terms, given the oneness of the human species, our minimum goal must be

> a world in which human beings find ways of living together which enable every individual to work out a lifestyle based on recognition and respect of others, and to do so ultimately in a universal perspective not confined to small groups

or nations. . . . Universal solidarity is thus the basic principle of ethics and the normative core of all human communication. (p. 10)

In other words, there are protonorms that precede their reification into ethical principles. There is at least one primordial generality underlying the logos of systematic thought. And its universal scope enables us to avoid the divisiveness of appeals to individual interests, cultural practices, and national prerogatives.

Application to Communications

The communications context is especially appropriate for understanding the scope and character of reverence for life. Within a symbolic cultural theory of communication, the complex relationships become clear among human interaction, our global oneness, and the web of life as a whole.[6]

Martin Buber (1970) makes the dialogic primal in his famous lines, "In the beginning is the relation" (p. 69) and the relation is "the cradle of actual life" (p. 60). He intends that ontologically as a category of being. Human relationships, not individuals per se, have primacy. "Persons appear by entering into relation to other persons" (p. 112). "The one basic word is the word-pair I-Thou" (p. 3).[7] Rather than arguments and concepts, this embodied connection gives moral anchorage. For Emmanuel Levinas, as quoted by Olthius (in press),

> the face of the Other commands me not to kill. . . . The face is the epiphany of the nakedness of the Other, a visitation, a coming, a saying which comes in the passivity of the face, not threatening, but obligating. My world is ruptured, my contentment interrupted. I am already obligated. Here is an appeal from which there is no escape, a responsibility, a state of being hostage. It is looking into the face of the Other that reveals the call to a responsibility that is before any beginning, decision or initiative on my part. (p. 139; cf. Levinas, 1979, 1981)

Moreover, in Levinasian terms, when I turn to the face of the Other, I see not only flesh and blood but the whole of humanity—dialogic communication understood as intersubjective universalism. Defining humans as communicative beings within the fabric of everyday life applies "both to the ontogenesis of the individual human being . . . and to the hominization of the human species" (Henrici, 1983, p. 2).

Paulo Freire (1969/1973) insists on the same integrated unity: "I cannot exist without a not-I; in turn the not-I depends on that existence." "There is no longer 'I think' but 'we think,' " he writes. It is the "we think" that establishes the "I think" and not the contrary. "This co-participation of Subjects in the act of thinking is communication. . . . Communication implies a reciprocity which cannot be broken"—giving and receiving, comprehending and creating, teaching and learning (pp. 137-139). Communication is a process with a double function—I-Thou or I-It—but never one element in isolation. Communication is not the transference of knowledge but a dialogic encounter of subjects creating it together. Freire's approach to communications presumes and articulates an explicit ontology of radical humanness.

Buber, Freire, and Levinas categorically reject the Enlightenment's dichotomies, its dualisms between self and language, the isolation of the individual from society, and its rupture of subjective and objective. The centerpiece of Buber's I-Thou and I-It modalities is human-to-human relationships (cf. Theunissen, 1984). But this horizontal plane also turns on a vertical axis, with human-divine bondedness understood in terms of personhood: "Extended, the lines of relationships intersect in the eternal You. Through every single You the basic word addresses the eternal You. The mediatorship of the You of all beings accounts for the fullness of our relationships" (Buber, 1970, p. 123). And concrete human existence is embedded in the vitalistic order as a whole; we nurture I-Thou relationships with the natural world as a dimension of our corporality in general and through our sense perception in particular. Although he does not attribute consciousness to trees, for example, Buber speaks of a mutuality that occurs in the ongoing oscillation of I-Thou and I-It relations: "It can happen, if will and grace are joined, that as I contemplate a tree I am drawn into a relation, and the tree ceases to be an It" (p. 58). "Relation is reciprocity . . . and there are three spheres in which the world of relation arises: life with nature . . . life with men . . . life with spiritual beings" (pp. 56-58). This is an incarnational worldview—one explicitly social, which extends the personal to the supreme reaches of the universe and embraces a land ethic as well. It is the only counter-Enlightenment philosophy of communication that explicitly meets the challenge of J. B. Lotz (1963):

> The ontology of Being dominated by the person differs greatly from an ontology of being dominated by the thing. . . . Ontology must be rescued from submersion in things by being thought out entirely from the viewpoint of person and thus of Being. (pp. 280, 294)

In dialogic theory, humans—in contrast to the rest of the animal kingdom—are not only situated in the natural world but live alongside it. Their symbolic capacity separates them from other life forms through their consciousness. In fact, humans range from a nearly spontaneous response to reality, on the one hand, to a critical process of intervention, on the other. We can even objectify ourselves within our existential experience. The dialogic tradition sweeps epistemology into anthropology. We understand reality when we get inside the self that is bonded-in-relation and embedded in purposive nature.

This is a philosophy of communication not limited to hermeneutics and semantics but one that is decidedly

> anthropological or more exactly anthro-ontological. For one thing, language presupposes corporeality for vocal utterances to be articulated and pronounced. For another, language necessarily refers to a world perceptible to the senses and common to the speaker; it implies their common being-in-the-world. (Henrici, 1983, p. 2)

Mediated systems, from this perspective, are inescapably human creations as well. In literary works or cinema, the indispensable features of their inner dialectics—the point of departure, plot, setting, overall tone, and resolution of conflicts—all are value driven and either engage a culture's value system or they cannot be understood.

Contrary to another Western dualism—humans as body and mind—the dialogic worldview is trinitarian, that is, including the spirit. To the rational and biological modalities, it adds the symbolic, the interpretive domain. One humanly integrated whole of three distinct dimensions is harmonized into a unique species without exception. We are unitary beings with our various human capacities depending on and interacting with one another.

This third feature—the interpretative—was recognized by the classical Greeks as the primordial home of language. From the mythological Hermes, inventor of language, they coined the term *hermeneia* (hermeneutics, interpretation). Aristotle's genius brought hermeneutical consciousness into focus as a constituent feature of the human species, and in the

Nicomachean Ethics he gave the interpretive art its richest meaning.[8] *Hermeneia* is not theoretical knowledge (*episteme*) nor is it practical skill (*techne*) because it concerns more than habit and utility (cf. Gadamer, 1965/1975, pp. 274-289). In making a moral decision, Aristotle argues, *hermeneia* discerns the appropriate action, in the right amount, and with proper timing. This is Aristotelian language confirming that we are moral beings with an orienting system beyond the senses yet one differing from logic.

Certainly, moral insight (*phronesis*) in Aristotle's ethics has a rational, cognitive element. Moral insight arises from "the ability to deliberate and consequently to believe through deliberation that something is or is not to be done" (Engberg-Pederson, 1983, p. 152). However, *phronesis* is not merely a static grasp of "true universal propositions," but is necessarily practical "in the sense of actually leading to action" (pp. 168-169). It presumes desire and will also. "Reasoned argument is not sufficient" to make us act nobly; it only makes us see in particular situations what acts "we already want to do" (p. 135). Rather than automatically applying a universal good lodged in the intellect, through moral insight humans discover "what should be done in situations in which this is not yet clear" (p. 238). The point of ethical theory is "action as opposed to mere knowledge," and therefore, *phronesis* presupposes a "desiderative state; it is necessarily motivational" (pp. 238-239; cf. Farrell, 1993, ch. 2).[9]

Language has the same human home as morality in the center of our being. Neither can be isolated in the *cogito*. In dialogic theory, communication rests not in *episteme* or the monads but in the interpretive capacity, the spirit. Discourse is born of conscience. A fulsome anthropology of organic wholeness moves language from its Enlightenment site in cognition to an interpretive axis in values and worldviews—or, as the center of our being is sometimes called—to the human spirit.

If the interpretive domain is lingual, and if language is the matrix of community, then human bonds are not constituted by reason or action but through finding common meaning in *hermeneia*. The commonplace, "we're with you in spirit," reflects the powerful truth that our species' oneness is born along the stream of consciousness. We resonate through our spirit cross-culturally to the moral imagination of others everywhere.

The sinews that hold the world together are moral—we are connected as a human whole, spirit-to-spirit. Contrary to what functionalism contends, our international web is not primarily political power or economic interdependence or information technology but a commitment of conscience that preconditions the ethos of these external apparatuses. Our mutual humanity is energized by moral obligations that activate our conscience toward the bondedness we share inescapably with others.

Such protonorms as reverence for life can only be recovered locally and inscribed culturally. Language situates them in history. Master norms are of a universal order conceptually speaking; they reflect our common condition as a species. Yet human beings enter them through the immediate reality of geography, ethnicity, and ideology. We distinguish between the universal and particular as with a windowpane, knowing there is a decisive break yet recognizing that the universal realm is only transparent in the local. "The mind itself, for all its reflexivity, does not penetrate into its own ontological ground. It never encounters anything but representations, and consequently it is the identity or similarity of those representations which makes understanding possible" (Henrici, 1983, p. 3). Buber's (1965) earthiness protects us from a naive and sterile universalism: "A legitimate philosophical anthropology must know that there is not merely a human species but also peoples, not only a human soul but also types and characters, not merely a human life but also stages in life" (p. 123).

A communication ethics situated in creatureliness entails a thicker view of moral judgments. Rather than privileging an individualistic, transcendental rationalism, moral commitments are inscribed in our worldviews through which we share a view of reality and establish human community. This ontological model is actually closer to the way the moral imagination operates in everyday life and refuses to separate moral agents from all that makes them unique.[10] Instead of constructing a purely rational foundation for morality, our mutual human existence across cultural, racial, and historical boundaries is the touchstone of ethics. The moral order is positioned fundamentally in the creaturely and corporeal rather than the conceptual. "In this way, ethics . . . is as old as creation. Being ethical is a primordial movement in the beckoning force of life itself" (Olthuis, in press, p. 141).

Basic Principles

The primal sacredness of life is a protonorm that binds humans into a common oneness. And in our systematic reflection on this primordial generality, we recognize that it entails such basic ethical principles as human dignity, truth, and nonviolence.

The universal reverence of life, in fact, presupposes the strongest possible definition of *human dignity* as

> the respect-worthiness imputed to humankind by reason of its privileged ontological status as creator, maintainer and destroyer of worlds. Each self shares in this essential dignity insofar as it partakes in world-building or world-destroying actions. Thus human dignity does not rest on intention, moral merit, or subjective definitions of self-interest. It rests on the fact that we are, in this fundamental way that is beyond our intention, human. . . . To assert dignity is to both acknowledge the factuality of human creative agency and to accept responsibility for its use. (Stanley, 1978, pp. 69-70)

From this perspective, one understands the ongoing vitality of the Universal Declaration of Human Rights issued by the United Nations General Assembly in 1948. As the Preamble states it, "Recognition of the inherent dignity and of the equal and inalienable rights of all members of the human family is the foundation of freedom, justice and peace in the world" (Universal Declaration, 1988, p. 1). Every child, woman, and man has sacred status, with no exceptions for religion, class, gender, age, or ethnicity. Humans are a unique species. This common sacredness of all human beings regardless of merit or achievement is the shared commitment out of which we begin to generate notions of a just society.

Truth-telling is another basic ethical principle that follows from the ontological grounding of ethics in the sacredness of life. Language is the primary means of social formation and, therefore, human existence is impossible without an overriding commitment to truth.

> Imagine a society, no matter how ideal in other respects, where word and gesture could never be counted on. Questions asked, answers given, information exchanged—all would be worthless. Were all statements randomly truthful or deceptive, action and choice would be undermined from the outset. There must be a minimal degree of trust in communication for language and action to be more than stabs in the dark. This is why some level of truthfulness has always been seen as essential to human society. . . . Even the devils themselves, as Samuel Johnson said, do not lie to one another, since the society of Hell could not subsist without truth any more than others. (Bok, 1979, pp. 19-20)

In Bok's (1979, cf. p. 19) terms, deception is as blatant, destructive, and morally outrageous as physical assault. In an intellectual trajectory connecting to Aristotle, the positive worth of truth-telling has been generally accepted at face value, with deception an enemy of the human order: "Falsehood is in itself mean and culpable, and truth noble and full of praise" (Aristotle, 1942, bk. 4, ch. 7). Though often only a rhetorical flourish and reduced in meaning, media codes of ethics typically appeal to truth as the cornerstone of social communication; thus, they reflect in their own way its intrinsic value. As a primary agent of the symbolic theater in which we live, the public media have no choice but to honor this norm as obligatory to their mission and rationale. The result is a richer epistemology than minimalist notions of accurate representation and objectivist ways of knowing. Truth-telling is axiological rather than a problem of cognition per se and integrated into human consciousness and social formation.

Nonviolence—a commitment to living together peacefully—is likewise an example of a nonnegotiable imperative rooted in the sacredness of life. In fact, Mahatma Gandhi and Martin Luther King, Jr., developed this principle beyond a political strategy into a public philosophy. According to Philippe Nemo, in Emmanuel Levinas, interaction between the self and the Other makes peace normative. "The first word of the Other's face is 'Thou shalt not kill.' It is an order. There is a commandment in the appearance of the face, as if a master spoke to me" (Levinas, 1985, p. 89). In the face-to-face encounter, the infinite is revealed. "The Other's presence is one of height and majesty; it involves an obligation . . . to which I owe allegiance and my assistance" (Chase, 1994, p. 8).

Darrell Fasching's comparative study of religions identifies hospitality to strangers as a common commitment, "giving birth to a cross-cultural ethic of non-violent civil disobedience . . . through movements of liberation which seek to protect the dignity of those who were treated as strangers" (Fasching, 1995, p. 15; cf. 1992, 1993). The public's general revulsion against physical abuse in intimate settings, and our consternation over brutal crimes and savage wars, are glimmers of hope reflecting this principle's validity. Out of nonviolence, we articulate ethical theories about not harming the innocent as an obligation that is cosmic and irrespective of our roles or contracts.

If we could establish master norms, such as justice, truth, and nonmaleficence, we would have a frame of reference for critiquing media conventions and codes of ethics. It would ensure that the issues addressed in our pedagogy and theorizing would be stitched into the common morality. Instead of seeking consensus about prescriptive maxims, master norms of this sort would favor intersubjectivity models and theoretical paradigms that are gender inclusive and culturally diverse. Rather than debilitating relativism, we would have a more vigorous response to the classic paradox—that is, one cannot insist on philosophical relativism without rising above it, and once outside it you have given it up.

Normative ethics grounded in a universal protonorm is a complex architecture. And to shape our communication theory and media practice more effectively by basic principles—themselves universal by virtue of their inscription in an underlying protonorm—more experiments are needed that come to grips with our moral obligation in global terms. Some glimmers of that consciousness are emerging over the environment; abusing one's share of the world's resources has now taken on moral resonance. But statecraft, demands for health care, educational strategies, military weapons, modes of transportation—all should be brought to judgment before the ultimate test. Do they sustain life, enhance it long term, contribute to human well-being as a whole? The challenge for the mass media is not just political insight in news and aesthetic power in entertainment but moral discernment.

This is discourse that irrigates public debate, refusing simply to focus on politics or entertainment per se but connecting the issues to universal norms, speaking not only to our minds but vivifying the spirit, grafting the deeper questions underneath the story onto our human oneness. In the process of invigorating our moral imagination, they enable readers and viewers to resonate with other human beings who also struggle in their conscience with human values of a similar sort.

Conclusion

Without first principles, "moral reasoning falls into an infinite regression which ends in nothing" and all ethical discourse becomes meaningless (Johnstone, 1993, p. 4). If moral claims are "unstable and indeterminate," the "possibility of doing ethics at all" is jeopardized (pp. 1, 4). "If ethical theory is properly concerned not only with defining key concepts but also with determining the authentic grounds of moral standards, what can be done" if no such grounds exist (p. 4)? Therefore, rather than introduce a set of moral maxims but leaving their anchorage unattended, I have focused in this chapter on a protonorm inscribed in being.

Without such a primordial norm and the ethical principles derived from it, how can we argue that bombing a federal building in Oklahoma City is wrong, that the wanton slaughter of Rwandese in a refugee camp is morally outrageous, that killing journalists in El Salvador is despicable, that ransacking the earth's ecosystem is evil? On what grounds are terrorists condemned for trying to achieve political ends by assassinations? How can we despise Hitler or praise the protectors of Anne Frank? Without a commitment to norms that are beyond one's own self-interest, moral claims are merely emotional preferences.

In normative universals, one finds an alternative to radical approaches that lack transformative power. Critical theorists, for example, call for oppositional readings of the dominant ideology, for emancipation from the webs of power that define concrete historical practice. Granted, one should advocate struggles for social justice. But without a philosophically rigorous normative center, there is no rationale for them other than the arbitrary choice of self-appointed elites. Without norms that are more-than-contingent, emancipatory intentions are threatened fundamentally. Revolutions born of revenge are self-destructive. Successful revolts are normalized by conciliation and peace; machine-gunning a tyrant destroys the revenger's legitimacy (cf. Christians, Ferré, & Fackler, 1993, p. 177). Without a protonorm on behalf of human solidarity, history is but a contest of arbitrary power.

Over the last decade, the social ethics of Agnes Heller, Charles Taylor, and Edith Wyschogrod, and the feminist ethics of Nel Noddings, Carol Gilligan, and Seyla Benhabib have made a major impact on ethical theory. Their achievements are of crucial importance for defining the issues in communication ethics as well. Social and feminist ethics make a radical break with the mainstream morality of individual rights. Their communitarian commitment fits hand in glove with an interactive philosophy of communication, whereas atomistic ethics is at odds with it. Truth is understood as authenticity in a social context, and its validity is freed from the correspondence tradition. Confidentiality and promise keeping are no longer encumbered with Enlightenment privatism. Noddings's (1984) *Caring* makes the I-Thou encounter normative. Edith Wyschogrod's (1990)

Saints and Postmodernism serves as a counterpoint to benign politics, working as she does on human struggles under conditions of oppression.

However, for all their apparent achievements in the particular, on what grounds do we endorse contemporary work in social and feminist ethics except as they presuppose and apply universal solidarity? Without their contributions to human dignity, truth-telling, or nonviolence, why should we not insist on maintaining the rationalist canon instead? Why should any post-enlightenment turn be considered an intellectual advance, rather than endorsing a cynical will of the stronger or a nihilism in which no right or wrong is conceivable?

In asking whether universal truths are possible, I have centered on the irrevocable status of respecting human life. If one understands the nature of history, language, and our dialogical personhood as cultural beings, human sacredness is inescapable. And as we come to live inside universal human solidarity, we recognize that a basic list of ethical principles is entailed by it—social justice, truth-telling, nonmaleficence, and possibly others.[11]

To postmodernists and other detractors, universalist positions have discredited themselves because over history they have seemed to breed totalitarianism. "Once any group or individual lays claim to knowledge of universal, transcendental truth, then dissenters must be either converted or controlled. This is the genesis of the Inquisition, of the Gulag, and of any ideological oppression" (Johnstone, 1993, p. 6). Universalism is said to threaten diversity, whereas relativism liberates us to reject all oppressive claims to truth.

In light of this objection, it must be reiterated that the protonorm of human sacredness is not a foundational *a priori*. This universal, in fact, belongs to a different category, philosophically speaking, than that of objectivist absolutes. Adherence to presuppositions is

> a matter of commitment, not epistemic certainty. We initiate any inquiry or action with . . . presuppositions because we must do so, not because they have been demonstrated. One's commitments are always open to question, and thus are liable to be modified or replaced. But one cannot proceed in any enterprise without taking something as given. (Johnstone, 1993, p. 7)

Cartesian rationalism and Kant's formalism presumed noncontingent starting points. Universal human solidarity does not. Nor does it flow from

Platonism, that is, the finite participating in the infinite and receiving its essence from it. Without a protonorm of universal scope, ethical theory and politics are trapped in the distributive fallacy—one ideological bloc presuming to speak for the whole.

Universal humanness seeks to liberate on behalf of the Other. Its dialogic, participatory axis is at odds with the deductivist monologues of one-way tyranny. In Paulo Freire's terms, this protonorm radically reinvents power—power in principle no longer adversarial, competitive, and interventionist but instead a sovereignty of relation and mutuality. Power in this perspective is an empowering reciprocity between subjects, a relationship not of "distance and domination, but rather of intimacy, vulnerability, and exchange" (Freire, 1968/1970, p. 69)—power akin to Alcoholics Anonymous where surrender to the community enables members to gain control. Its measure, in Freire's terms, is solidarity, the reciprocal enhancement of community. It presumes a populist theory of democratic participation.

A commitment to universals does not eliminate all differences in what we think and believe. Normative ethics grounded ontologically is pluralistic. The only question is whether our values affirm the human good or not. As our philosophies of life and beliefs are lobbied within the public sphere, we have a responsibility to make public the course we favor and to demonstrate in what manner it advances our common citizenship. The issue is whether our values help to build a civic philosophy and thereby demonstrate a transformative intent. This is worldview pluralism, which allows us to hold our beliefs in good faith and debate them openly rather than be constrained by a superficial consensus. The standard of judgment is not economic or political success but whether our worldviews and community formations contribute in the long run to truth-telling, human dignity, and nonmaleficence. Ethical principles grounded in being do not obstruct cultures and inhibit their development. On the contrary, they liberate us for strategic action and provide a direction for social change.

Czech president Václav Havel has understood more clearly than most of us that this present historic juncture requires a new vision cosmic in scope. We are rightly preoccupied, he says, "with finding the key to ensure the survival of a civilization that is global and at the same time clearly multicultural" (Havel, 1994, p. 614; cf. 1989). We fret over the possibility of "generally respected mechanisms of peaceful coexistence" and wonder "on what set of principles they are to be established." Many believe that this central political task at the end of the century "can be accomplished through technical means. . . . But such efforts are doomed to failure if they do not grow out of something deeper, out of generally held values" (Havel, 1994, p. 614). In Havel's terms, appeals at international forums for human rights and freedom are meaningless if they do not derive from respect for "the miracle of Being, the miracle of the universe, the miracle of nature, the miracle of our own existence" (p. 615). The ethics of being contributes to Havel's project. Through human solidarity rooted in a universal reverence for life, we respect ourselves and genuinely value the participation of others in a volatile age where "everything is possible and almost nothing is certain" (p. 614).

Notes

1. An earlier version of this chapter was presented as a plenary address at the convention of the International Association of Mass Communication Research in Portoroz, Slovenia, on June 29, 1995 (cf. Christians, 1995). The support of the Pew Evangelical Scholars Program is gratefully acknowledged.

2. Counter examples of rigorous and formal universal theories are Gerwith (1978) and Donagan (1977).

3. Cf. Jacques Ellul (1989, pt. 2, 1980) for a similar description of the technical artifice. In fact, Ellul could well be cited here; he integrates the mass media spectacle more satisfactorily into his philosophy of technology as a whole. Whereas Stanley Arnowitz and Henry A. Giroux (1991) generally provide a constructive treatment of Baudrillard, I agree with their reluctant conclusion following Douglas Kellner: "Baudrillard's society of simulations . . . translates less into a provocative analysis of the changing contours and features of the age than it does into a nihilism that undermines its own radical intent" (p. 66).

4. Robert Holmes (1993, ch. 2) summarizes the issues surrounding ethical relativism in terms of both cultural diversity and metaethics.

5. For a review of the important literature since Max Scheler's (1928/1962) *Man's Place in Nature* in 1928, see Schacht (1990). A classic essay is Ricoeur (1960). Michel Foucault (1973) indirectly recognizes the implications of focusing the issues in human terms by considering the contemporary era "the end of man" (p. 385, cf. ch. 10). For Foucault, "the idea of 'man' as an interpretive conceptual invention" is no longer viable (Schacht, 1990, p. 158).

6. David Wong (1984) argues that metaethics needs to account for recent developments in the philosophy of language. He is correct that the ethical theorists who have dominated the North Atlantic in the 20th century (G. E. Moore, C. L. Stevenson, R. M. Hare, for example) have presupposed an analytic-synthetic approach to language that has been largely discredited (pp. 1-9). Wong concentrates on three issues in the philosophy of language where the changes are most apparent: the nature of moral truth statements (ch. 2), theories of reference (ch. 5), and translation theory (ch. 8).

The dialogic philosophy of communication described in this section illustrates this revolution in the philosophy of language. Dialogic theory is interpretive, symbolic, contextual, and interactionist, in contrast to the traditional paradigm, which is verificationist, sentential, and formal. Whereas the purpose of this chapter is not to engage the detailed arguments introduced by Wong, it supports and contributes to the basic thesis that the most difficult questions of metaethics require a struggle over the philosophy of language. This section demonstrates that a radically human philosophy of communication (rather than a theory modeled off machine systems or mathematical formulas), one that is radically opposed to monologic and transmission theories, can enable us to take Hans Jonas's first-level approximation about responsibility for life and develop it into a complex protonorm.

For an introduction to some of the theoretical issues regarding a dialogic approach to language and mind, see Wold (1993). Gadamer's (1965/1975) work is particularly helpful. As Bernstein (1986) summarizes it, "Gadamer's entire project of philosophical hermeneutics can be read as an attempt to recover . . . the quintessence of our being [as] dialogical" (p. 65).

7. This irreducible anthropological phenomenon cannot be decomposed into simpler elements without destroying it. There are not three components, sender-message-receiver, to be dismembered for scientific analysis nor even separated and then reconnected dialectically.

For an answer to postmodern critics who insist on a more radical alternative than Buber's I-Thouness, see Kepnes (1991, ch. 6). Kepnes argues that Buber's interactional self stands between modernity's autonomous self and poststructuralism's decentered self, trapped by neither and filling up the space left by both. In other words, posthumanism's fragmented self challenges Enlightenment individualism, but Buber's social ontology contradicts both. Buber joins the contemporary critique of atomistic selfhood and offers an alternative model. For Buber's mutuality in a broad intellectual context, see Christians et al. (1993, ch. 3).

8. Aristotle found *hermeneia* worthy of a major treatise by that title, *On Interpretation,* and he outlined a formal theory in his *Rhetoric.*

9. My summary situating Aristotle's ethics in his anthropology is rudimentary, of course. D. S. Hutchinson (1986) is undoubtedly correct that an adequate study of Aristotle's moral philosophy must go beyond his *Nicomachean Ethics* and *Eudemian Ethics* and even further than philosophical anthropology, to encompass metaphysics and psychology as well.

10. This model benefits from recent philosophical efforts to develop a rationality that is closer to the actual process of making moral decisions: for example, Polanyi (1966), Toulmin (1972), White (1981), and Putnam (1975).

11. A primordial commitment to the sacredness of life and a general pretheoretical understanding of these three basic principles do not result in shared ethical theory or even require it. Human dignity, for example, is defended and articulated differently in terms of Judeo-Christian theism ("everyone is made in the image of God and therefore has equal status"), humanism, communalism, or contractarian rights theory. We can generally agree about the meaning of nonviolence (on the level of the Golden Rule, for example) but disagree in our theorizing over capital punishment, warfare, and euthanasia (Adams, 1993, p. 95). From the perspective of ontological ethics, our different justifications for our moral beliefs and our various theoretical disputes are inevitable given the character of formal language; however, humans live in several symbolic universes at the same time, and protonorms and the norms entailed by them can receive recognizable moral agreement (pp. 102-107).

References

Adams, Robert Merrihew. (1993). Religious ethics in a pluralistic society. In Gene Outka & John P. Reeder, Jr. (Eds.), *Prospects for a common morality* (pp. 93-113). Princeton, NJ: Princeton University Press.

Aristotle. (1942). *Nicomachean ethics* (Trans., W. D. Ross). London: Oxford University Press.

Aristotle. (1952). *Eudemian ethics* (Trans., H. Rackham). London: William Heinemann.

Arnowitz, Stanley, & Giroux, Henry A. (1991). *Postmodern education: Politics, culture, and social criticism.* Minneapolis: University of Minnesota Press.

Baudrillard, Jean. (1983). *Simulations* (Trans., P. Foss, P. Patton, & P. Beitchman). New York: Semiotext(e).

Benhabib, Seyla. (1992). *Situating the self: Gender, community and postmodernism in contemporary ethics.* Cambridge, UK: Polity.

Bernstein, Richard J. (1986). *Philosophical profiles: Essays in a pragmatic mode.* Philadelphia: University of Pennsylvania Press.

Bok, Sissela. (1979). *Lying: Moral choice in public and private life.* New York: Vintage Random House.

Buber, Martin. (1965). *Between man and man* (Trans., Ronald G. Smith). New York: Macmillan.

Buber, Martin. (1970). *I and Thou* [*Ich und Du*] (Trans., Walter Kaufmann). New York: Scribner.

Cassirer, Ernst. (1951). *The philosophy of the Enlightenment.* Princeton, NJ: Princeton University Press.

Chase, Kenneth R. (1994, May). *Rethinking rhetoric in the face of the Other.* Paper presented at the Third National Communication Ethics Conference, Gull Lake, Michigan.

Christians, Clifford G. (1995). The problem of universals in communication ethics. *Javnost [The Public], 2*(2), 59-69.

Christians, Clifford G., Ferré, John P., & Fackler, P. Mark. (1993). *Good news: Social ethics and the press.* New York: Oxford University Press.

Derrida, Jacques. (1984). Deconstruction and the Other. In R. Kearney (Ed.), *Dialogues with contemporary continental thinkers: The phenomenological heritage.* Manchester, UK: Manchester University Press.

Donagan, Alan. (1977). *Theory of morality.* Chicago: University of Chicago Press.

Ellul, Jacques. (1980). *The technological system* (Trans., J. Neugroschel). New York: Continuum.

Ellul, Jacques. (1989). *What I believe* (Trans., G. W. Bromiley). London: Marshall Morgan & Scott.

Engberg-Pedersen, Troels. (1983). *Aristotle's theory of moral insight.* Oxford, UK: Clarendon.

Farley, Margaret A. (1993). Feminism and universal morality. In Gene Outka & John P. Reeder, Jr. (Eds.), *Prospects for a common morality.* Princeton, NJ: Princeton University Press.

Farrell, Thomas B. (1993). *Norms of rhetorical culture.* New Haven, CT: Yale University Press.

Fasching, Darrell. (1992). *Narrative theology after Auschwitz: From alienation to ethics.* Minneapolis, MN: Fortress.

Fasching, Darrell. (1993). *The ethical challenge of Auschwitz and Hiroshima.* Albany: State University of New York Press.

Fasching, Darrell. (1995, January). Response to Peter Haas. *The Ellul Forum, 14,* 15.

Foucault, Michel. (1973). *The order of things.* New York: Vintage.

Freire, Paulo. (1970). *Pedagogy of the oppressed* (Trans., Myra B. Ramos). New York: Continuum. (Original work published 1968)

Freire, Paulo. (1973). *Education for critical consciousness.* New York: Continuum. (Original work published 1969)

Gadamer, Hans-Georg. (1975). *Truth and method [Wahrheit und Methode]* (Trans., G. Barden & J. Cumming). New York: Seabury. (Original work published 1965)

Gerwith, Alan. (1978). *Reason and morality.* Chicago: University of Chicago Press.

Havel, Václav. (1989). *Living in truth* (Ed., Jan Vladislav). London: Faber & Faber.

Havel, Václav. (1994, August 1). Post-modernism: The search for universal laws. *Vital Speeches of the Day, 60*(20), 613-615.

Henrici, Peter. (1983, March). Towards an anthropological philosophy of communication. *Communication Resource, 1,* 1-4.

Holmes, Robert L. (1993). Ethical relativism. In his *Basic moral philosophy* (pp. 19-42). Belmont, CA: Wadsworth.

Hume, David. (1739). *Treatise of human nature.* London: J. Noon.

Hume, David. (1963). *Enquiries concerning the human understanding and concerning the principles of morals.* Oxford, UK: Clarendon. (Original work published 1748 and 1751)

Hutchinson, D.S. (1986). *The virtues of Aristotle.* London: Routledge & Kegan Paul.

Johnstone, Christopher L. (1993, November). *Ontological vision as ground for communication ethics: A response to the challenge of postmodernism.* Paper presented at convention of the Speech Communication Association, Miami, Florida.

Jonas, Hans. (1984). *The imperative of responsibility [Macht oder Ohnmacht der Subjektivität? Das Lieb-Seele Problem im Vorfeld des Prinzips Verantwortung].* Chicago: University of Chicago Press.

Kepnes, Steven. (1991). *Buber's hermeneutic philosophy and narrative theology.* Bloomington: Indiana University Press.

Levinas, Emmanuel. (1979). *Totality and infinity.* The Hague, Netherlands: Martinus Nijhoff.

Levinas, Emmanuel. (1981). *Otherwise than being or essence.* The Hague, Netherlands: Martinus Nijhoff.

Levinas, Emmanuel. (1985). *Ethics and infinity: Conversations with Philippe Nemo* (Trans., R. A. Cohen). Pittsburgh, PA: Duquesne University Press.

Lotz, J. B. (1963, Winter). Person and Ontology [Person und Ontologie]. *Philosophy Today, 7,* 279-297. (Reprinted from *Scholastik, 38*(3), 335-360)

Noddings, Nel. (1984). *Caring: A feminine approach to ethics and moral education.* Berkeley: University of California Press.

Olthuis, James H. (in press). Face-to-face: Ethical asymmetry or the symmetry of mutuality? In James H. Olthuis (Ed.), *Knowing Other-wise* (pp. 134-164). New York: Fordham University Press.

Outka, Gene, & Reeder, John P., Jr. (1993). *Prospects for a common morality.* Princeton, NJ: Princeton University Press.

Paul, Ellen F., Miller, Fred D., & Paul, Jeffrey. (Eds.). (1994). *Cultural pluralism and moral knowledge.* Cambridge, UK: Cambridge University Press.

Peukert, Helmut. (1981). Universal solidarity as the goal of communication. *Media Development, 28*(4), 10-12.

Polanyi, Michael. (1966). *The tacit dimension.* Garden City, NY: Doubleday.

Putnam, Hilary. (1975). *Philosophical papers: Vol. 2. Mind, language and reality.* Cambridge, UK: Cambridge University Press.

Ricoeur, Paul. (1960). The antinomy of human reality and the problem of philosophical anthropology (Trans., D. O'Connor). *Il Pensiero, 5,* 273-290.

Schacht, Richard. (1990, Fall). Philosophical anthropology: What, why and how. *Philosophy and Phenomenological Research, 50,* 155-176.

Scheler, Max F. (1962). *Man's place in nature* (Trans., Hans Meyerhoff). New York: Noonday. (Original work published 1928)

Schlick, Moritz. (1949). Is there a factual *a priori?* In H. Feigl & W. Sellers (Eds.), *Readings in philosophical analysis* (pp. 277-285). New York: Appleton-Century Crofts.

Schlick, Moritz. (1992). The future of philosophy. In Richard M. Rorty (Ed.), *The linguistic turn: Essays in philosophical method* (pp. 43-53). Chicago: University of Chicago Press.

Stanley, Manfred. (1978). *The technological conscience: Survival and dignity in an age of expertise.* Chicago: University of Chicago Press.

Stout, Jeffrey. (1993). On having a morality in common. In Gene Outka & John P. Reeder, Jr. (Eds.), *Prospects for a common morality* (pp. 215-232). Princeton, NJ: Princeton University Press.

Theunissen, Michael. (1984). *The Other: Studies in the social ontology of Husserl, Heidegger, Sartre, and Buber* (Trans., C. Macann). Cambridge, MA: MIT Press.

Toulmin, Stephen. (1972). *Human understanding.* Oxford, UK: Oxford University Press.

Universal Declaration of Human Rights. (1988). *Human rights: A compilation of international instruments* (pp. 1-7). Geneva: Centre for Human Rights.

Verene, Donald P. (1976). Vico's science of imagination: Universals and the philosophy of symbolic forms. In G. Tagliacozzo & D. P. Verene (Eds.), *Giambattista Vico's science of humanity* (pp. 285-317). Baltimore, MD: Johns Hopkins University Press.

Vico, Giambattista. (1948). *The new science of G. Vico* (Trans., T. G. Bergin & M. H. Fisch). Ithaca, NY: Cornell University Press.

Welch, Sharon. (1985). *Communities of resistance and solidarity: A feminist theology of liberation.* Maryknoll, NY: Orbis.

White, Morton G. (1981). *What is and what ought to be done.* New York: Oxford University Press.

Wittgenstein, Ludwig. (1953). *Philosophical investigations.* Oxford, UK: Basil Blackwell.

Wittgenstein, Ludwig. (1956). *Remarks on the foundation of mathematics.* Oxford, UK: Basil Blackwell.

Wold, Astri Heen. (Ed.). (1993). *The dialogical alternative: Towards a theory of language and mind.* Oslo: Scandinavian University Press.

Wong, David B. (1984). *Moral relativity.* Berkeley: University of California Press.

Wyschogrod, Edith. (1990). *Saints and postmodernism.* Chicago: University of Chicago Press.

CHAPTER 2

The Moral Dimension of Communicating

ANTONIO PASQUALI

Today, more than any other time, it is common to accumulate and manipulate concepts and terms. Notions that have been arduously debated and improved throughout the centuries by human reasoning are bounced back by the omnipresent network of big communicators in pitifully reduced, sifted, sweetened versions—emasculated, if not caricaturesque. Such appropriations of words affect the language of human science particularly, legitimizing the logic of dominion, social engineering, and manipulation. What do terms such as neighbor, morality, code of ethics, justice, or respect mean to a manager today? Amplified by the media, how deep have certain terminological deformations cut? What chance does human thought have to restore pristine senses and to counter today's distilling filter?

Recovering Terms

As expected, some residue of those terminological hyper-simplifications cling even to scientific thought. Therefore, all philosophical practice today should be on guard. Care is especially needed when philosophy deals with its own expression, in its pragmatic or communicative phase. This introduction lists some of those measures that must be taken and indicates the major terms that need to be recaptured. It clears the way for considering the protonorms of a morals of communication that is still undeveloped.

Warnings and Limitations

The moral dimension of communicating should be studied, of course, from a multicultural perspective, one that is multimoral and multisituational. Otherwise, the result may be immoral due to false reasoning and the ethnocentric fallacy. Without such a broad perspective, we would assume that the moral codes of Western society are the only depositories of authentic morality. More than three decades after this hypothesis was first articulated by P. Taylor (1963), it is evident that the globalization of market and mind is pressing us to adopt Western plutocracy as our only moral code. This is a strong reason to remind ourselves of the existence of diversity.

However, two matters need to be clarified: a) The word multicultural should take on not just a topographical sense, so to speak, but one that is equally interdisciplinary and interdoctrinal; and b) the confusion and disarticulations of eclecticism must be avoided in the process. The *dividi et distrahi [divide and disperse] necessary to delve into the different aspects of the problem must, however, be considered as a simple methodological resource of a subsequent and inevitable colligi ad unum* [gather together into one]. Multicultural diversity, in fact, is not a conservative concept, opposed to the notions of world and open plurality.

Criticizing compulsive globalization does not mean rejecting the interconnection among the different forms of mutual respect. That would introduce a *contradictio in adjecto* [contradiction in itself] to the very concept of communicating. Identities would, therefore, turn into a fetish, which can be preserved only in the state of noncommunication. Multiculturalism should also avoid a patchworklike final product, and it should not conclude in a lament that the world's cultural diversities are being contaminated by unipolar communication. Notions of diversity and pluralism and those of dialogue and noncompulsive transculturation must all be saved.

What is at stake here is obviously important. Postmodernist and globalizing discourse insist that the growing communication facilities will finally turn all cultural identities and diversities into anachronisms, ontologically isolationist and incommensurable. The terms "identity" and "communication" have a *mors tua vita mea* [your death is my life] antithetical relationship between them in this lineal, and not dialectical, vision of history bereft of everything multicultural.

Timeliness

As soon as the East-West crisis ended, the North-South structural conjuncture regained its dramatic potential, now without alibis. It is the greatest problem of our time; no morality that really belongs to its own age can escape it. We will have to live with this problem side-by-side, between tensions of lesser or greater intensity, because it gives final meaning to the other challenges of today (demographic, ecological, economic, technological, governance, and so forth). With the end of the East-West conflict, the barriers also disappeared that had stalled for decades one of the ultimate moral obligations of humankind—that is, defining the teleology of a more equitable human relationship, forging one world. But the notion of solidarity and the generous postwar ideal of the "human family" endure with their heads down. In the last 30 years, the gap between rich and poor has multiplied fivefold worldwide: Tokyo has more telephones than the entire African continent (South Africa excluded); the ratio between the largest density of telephone lines in the World (Monaco) and the smallest (Chad) is now 1,245 to 1; between the world's most efficient mail (Switzerland) and the most inefficient (Mozambique), 5,515 to 1.

The South, as a gift, constantly receives more and more access facilities for messages from the North; but the South's possibilities for participation as producers and broadcasters are progressively being cut down. Beyond the ataraxic speeches of the powerful, ethically honest discourse must continue to denounce, and vigorously refute, all the *raisons d'état* [reasons of state] by which this situation is defined as irreversible.

With its feet on the ground—and aiming to recover its lost credibility—contemporary ethics must absolutely shoulder responsibility for this major world problem. Far from falling into misery, the affected people of the South—together with all people of good will in the entire world—should continue to elaborate a new morality and new, feasible communication models that can be applied universally. Other great revolutions that have changed the face of the earth have also originated in remote provinces of some empire.

Correct Usage

The vocabulary with which reason refers to praxis today is pitifully instrumentalized and confused. When searching for the protonorms of a new communications morality, semantic exactness is one of the preconditions. Several terms need to be assessed and agreed on to move forward intellectually.

Deontology is a narrow and coherent ensemble of self-regulatory duties relevant to a specific profession or activity and generally devoid of *foro exteriore* sanctions, that is, external legal sanctions, but not those of the conscience (*in foro interiore*). Many specific deontologies are a mix of clever precepts for the self-esteem of professionals and for appropriate behavior in their work, including respect for those who benefit from their activity (which would represent their Hippocratic side). In many other cases, deontological codes, wrongly called codes of ethics, implicitly pursue freedom on behalf of professional groups, corporations, employer associations, trade unions, and guilds. These codes replace society's watchdog function with internal self-surveillance rules. The political body and its legal institutions are prevented from judging a segment of the social body. These codes implicitly address a claim to the Leviathan state: Do not interfere in our activities; we prefer to set our own rules. We do not accept sanctions imposed by others who do not understand our profession or by those who may have contrary pursuits.

Thus, certain codes of ethics are examples of the most perverse use of ethics, because they aim at preventing some aspects of professional conduct from social and political surveillance. Karl Popper (1994) is correct: "There should be no political power free of control in a democracy. . . . Television has turned into a colossal political power, potentially the most important of all. Democracy cannot exist if it does not put television under control" (pp. 35-36). The history of social communication—in Latin America, for example, the only region of the world devoid of any genuine experience of radio and television public service—contains whole libraries of codes of ethics that their authors have never followed. Instead, they were perfect alibis to continue working in a legal vacuum outside the public's authority.

This poses a major question, among many others. Would it be reasonable to believe that a new communications morality could be entrusted only to deontologies (employers' and employees' scrutinies)? Or would something else besides self-regulatory duties be necessary to improve certain situations? Who guarantees that future deontologies will be more Hippocratic than the preceding ones? The immoral and distorted way in which many deontologies function brings up once again the perennial question in the 10th book of Plato's *Politeia*: For justice to reign in the Republic, do we have to wait for every single person to become just? And would the sum of such deontologies be the just society? Or would it be preferable to assist the coming of a just society with laws and sanctions against the unjust? Must societies wait with infinite patience (and with boundless respect for the freedom of those who do not respect our freedom) for television magnates of the world to convince themselves—through a new and respected set of principles—of the harmful effects of certain programs? Do not the worldwide users have any right at all to demand better communications?

These are problems, obviously related to the freedom of communication, that pose difficult practical questions for the moralist (in the good sense of the word). Should we continue preaching to producers, broadcasters, and experts to obtain from them better communications? Or should we join with legislators and honest politicians who are capable of establishing strong, more consensual, democratic rules for communicators to abide by?

Morals are historical, generic, extensive, coherent ensembles of norms that constantly evolve but can be systematized. They provide axiological-practical criteria for every type of action among groups of people united by shared principles and beliefs. Contrary to deontologies—that is, voluntary expressions of submission to specific norms—morals always and necessarily exist. Consciously or not, in a written form or not, they are necessitated by a practical vision of the world, as reflected in the Cartesian sentence *la morale ne souffre point de délai* [morality will brook no delay]. Morals that differ in origin and time coexist or clash, confronting each other over meaningful principles. A collection of popular proverbs is a variegated mix of moral protonorms, not always necessarily filled with wisdom, and on occasion strongly contradictory. However, morals are rational and have an axiological hierarchy and must be able to be expressed and synthesized philosophically. These criteria help us, for instance, to determine whether the 298 brief texts attributed to Democritus constitute a rosary of disconnected dicta or if they are fragments of a coherent moral system.

The life span of a moral system depends on its capacity to provide norms of behavior, even in situations that have not existed before. When those situations transcend the capacity of a moral framework, its credibility and effectiveness subside. Such is the case with all the laic and confessional moralities surviving today; they are being left behind, if not forgotten, by unrelenting technical and scientific progress. When norms of behavior are not provided and when the correct moral response before so many new problems is not given, the human conscience paradoxically starts to secrete amoral interpretations. This results in prototypes of even more profound demoralization processes. Technological and pan-economic stupor obviously helps to increase this tendency, further legitimating the amoral vision of the world. Morality has no other alternative than to regain its lost credibility and usefulness by returning in a fresh way to the great timeless principles of the major ethical systems. From which of those systems could it likely determine the ontological features of human communication and deduct a morals for communicating?[1] Thus, in summary, given the purpose of this chapter, it is more accurate to refer to a "morality of communicating" than to an ethics.

The term *protonorm* is multisignificant with several intended meanings.[2] But two definitions best correspond to the aims of this chapter: (a) An aggregate of frequently applied practical norms that a group considers exemplary, emblematic, introductory, fundamental, or recurring, capable of being structured. In this sense, protonorms serve as the prolegomenon of a moral system. And (b) the protonorms of a morality of communication refer to "meontic" norms, that is, the purely "not yet" or "should be." They could be desired norms that have not yet been implemented and that are considered therapeutic when applied to axiologically negative realities.

This introduction can be summarized as follows: Pursue a multicultural perspective cautiously. With a collection of exemplary and meontic protonorms, satisfy certain deontological requirements for the purpose of obtaining a new morality of communications.

The Need for a New
Morality of Intersubjectivity

Technological and scientific developments in communications have caused more social, political, cultural, legal, and moral problems than they ever intended to solve. The conceptual core of a communication theory that paradoxically confines and desocializes seems today largely abandoned. In the meantime, however, the truth it expressed has been supported by a great deal of scientific literature. The politicians of the West are now showing serious concern for recent and partially successful attempts to transfer some of their power to communication *parvenus* [professional upstarts].

Perhaps the reminder is unnecessary, but many cultural analysts continue to be greatly disturbed by the "veil of Penelope" that has been woven for decades in many parts of the world between cultural-educational efforts on the one hand and trash TV on the other. The heads of the major regulatory bodies have not stopped warning us about an ever-increasing technological sophistication that makes the latest rules rapidly obsolete. A situation of urgency has emerged in which the protection of consumers and free competition have become increasingly difficult. Attempts to moralize communication that is downright immoral or simply to remind communicators of their obligations and responsibilities have caused such an uproar among editors and broadcasters that it has never been possible to move beyond the strictly declarative phase. Great communicators often refuse to talk about communication (those who do it freely will be regarded suspiciously). In general, they follow religiously the unwritten law of contemporary capitalism, limiting themselves to the defense of the principle of liberty. This is an exhilarating and porous principle that has sex appeal. In the process, they leave to the poor the abstract and no-income-earning notion of "equality and fraternity."

However, Cartesian rationalism gives way to optimism. The human spirit is constituted in such a way that it can withstand the worst metaphysical, political, legal, and cultural vacuums. But, it cannot stop secreting—not even for an instant—an axiological conception of the world, which classifies the behavioral universe in a *bonus-malus* [good and bad] way. As moral beings *malgré soi* [despite themselves], even the most distracted media users understand in their own ways the important relationship between communications and morals (two ways of being-with-the-other). Deep down, they find themselves seeking a minimum reorganization of communications so that their culture may be improved, and they wish for better policies and regulations in social communication.

For its capacity to disrupt preexisting moral canons, progress in communications is comparable only to progress in nuclear physics and genetic biology. To cope with these developments, a new morality of intersubjectivity has become the prime need of our time.

Morality is our neighbor; it means to coexist with others and show respect for them as part of one's life. It is *eukoinoonia* [good living together]. Morality is, therefore, the term used to give an anthropological dimension to one of the supreme categories of understanding—relation. But communication is also a way of declining relationships. It is, in fact, the relational category closest to Kant's "community"—that is, mutual action between people, or total reciprocity.

For thousands of years, human relationships have essentially been grounded in nonmediated communication, using natural communication channels. The artificial aspect of practically all trends in communications today has substantially shifted from its human axis. As a result, there are three principal side effects: (a) a growing apartheid between interlocutors; (b) an easy introduction of noise into messages; and (c) the curbing of all direct and immediate responses, preventing lineal messages from developing into dialogue. Ergo, the need to emphasize the anthropological dimension of relationships; ergo, morality. Communicating (a situation halfway between the fusion of communion and the coercion of causality) is perhaps relationship's state of grace, the fundamental achievement of a moral nexus. But progress and money have come to slowly deprive that rightful human power—discrediting it by instilling an amoral *raison d'état* [reason of state] and subjecting it to a rationale within power and markets. However, even the most perverse or manipulative forms practiced in communication today have a good side. They remind morality of its essential interpersonal dimension and of communication's ontological place as a privileged form of being-with-others.

The Status of Communicating

The evolution of morals—including the ethical systems that have sprung up from them—reveals a conceptually problematic stamp that is characteristic of its great moments: the morals or ethics of virtue, the conflicts between reason and passion, Kantian deontology, jusnaturalism (natural law), utilitarianism, and so forth. We live in a communications era still devoid of a morality of communicating. Several conceptual confrontations over the historical materialization of freedom and justice—which in other times involved the great debates over human nature, the origin of righteousness, and even free navigation—today have the casuistry of information systems, telecommunications, or social communications as their own privileged scenario. But in today's diatribes, we should acknowledge that the *grandeur* of other historical times does not seem to exist. Our Montagues and Capulets, devoid of their Francisco Vitoria or Hugo de Groot, send their managers and public relations officers to fight in the international arena. During the great world debate regarding communications in the 1970s and 1980s, no first-rate philosopher was known to have come up with illuminating ideas. So far, we do not seem to be up to the standards of the periods that gained jusnaturalism, a new shipping right, and the abolition of the death penalty and slavery. Perhaps the powers that have to be transcended and transformed are greater today, whereas thought is weakening.

Our own age is characterized by an extreme subdivision of labor and great distances among virtues or states of perfection. One notable difference between this and the preceding periods is that the philosopher and the scientist are no longer the same person, as they had been from Pythagoras to Descartes, Galileo, Pascal, or Leibniz. Triumphant and vulgarized, science allows philosophy to continue reflecting morally about the world and the problem of ends (which are scientifically irrelevant today), whereas it imposes a mechanical rationality of achievement and progress, completely lacking in a teleological dimension.

Most governmental powers today initiate moralist discourses; but they are inspired by positivistic and scientistic amorality when they make their grand political, economic, social, or ecological decisions. Knowledge tends to be identified with self-interest. More sophisticated social programs are invented each time and passed on as the macroreforms of a new order, whose success increasingly depends on there always being poor people.

The main thesis of this chapter is that we are living in an era whose unpostponable need is a new morals of intersubjectivity. This entails a new understanding of communication, capable of returning credibility and usefulness to moral cosmo-visions and of discrediting the sizable hierarchies imposed by plutocracy. Nearly all the old rules of the game are being questioned overtly. Everywhere, and for apparently dissimilar reasons, social contracts of a radically new kind are being demanded, even with weapons.

Moreover, our era is a heap of contradictions, some of which are induced and are instrumental. The age of indifference lives side by side with social unrest; certain developments that have changed the face of the world have been bloodless, whereas local conflicts have left thousands dead. Great *rites de passage* to globalization and cosmopolitanism are taking place, and separatism of all kinds is being revived. A great amount of noncharitable help—channeled by multilateral diplomacy that was perfected in the postwar period—coexists with the most aggravating egotism, terrible corruption, and widespread moral slackness.[3] Poverty is growing immeasurably; it is getting out of control and is increasingly obvious, but we have muzzled it. Progress, of course, has multiplied the opportunities to be with others, but the quality of relating is abysmal today. Experts say that the impassiveness of television viewing goes hand in hand with the declining commitment to intersubjectivity, which shrinks like Balzac's "sharkskin," or *peau de chagrin*.

Authority and Power

One of the most important objectives of a new morals of intersubjectivity will consist of giving back to everybody the ability to express themselves and to communicate in a concrete and innovating fashion—though sometimes vicariously. This will originate a virtuous circle: A liberated communication will in turn engender the highest quality of intersubjectivity. Today, the capacity for participatory expression has been confiscated right under democracy's nose by economic and political powers.

Nearly 30 years ago, Umberto Eco (1967) wrote, "Not long ago it was possible to control the political power of a country by simply controlling the army and the police. Today, a country belongs to those who control the media" (p. 181). Since then, the North, the privileged sender, has strengthened its communications kingdom, raising the global disequilibrium and increasingly exercising international controls. Certain mergers of communications companies have led to the most important transactions in recent economic history, increasing the concentration of production, storage, transmittal, and message reception capacities. Veiled behind a purely numerical plurality of broadcasting channels—or glossed over by deregulation that created ephemeral pluralistic situations—the number of great communicators and broadcasters has shrunk in the last decades; in contrast, the number of mute receptors has increased.

In 1994, in the country of Umberto Eco and for the first time in history, a multimillionaire tycoon and communications magnate managed to become prime minister, thanks to a successful marketing campaign triggered by his own media. Once in office, he continued conveniently stripping the radio and television public services that competed with his commercial network. Historians of economics and civilization will have to explain how and where the global power coalesced after the end of the Cold War; how it gradually deprived traditional institutions of their niches (family, churches, traditional opinion leaders, political parties, representative governments, and so forth) and how it was shifted to the industrial military complexes, to banking and stock markets, or to the communications conglomerates. Although the outcome could not be foretold, the Frankfurt School had emphatically insisted half a century ago that the concept of authority would be one of the most important interpretative categories of our time.

This can be demonstrated by the tight causative relationship between the quality of public opinion and the quality of the corresponding democracy and how the weakness or iniquity of the first will be reflected, invariably, in the latter. Mass media today are the most important shapers of public opinion; they are the greatest mediators. But the plus value of communications associated with technological progress has altered the traditional apparatus of the agora. It has been a blinding process, indeed. A foolish commentator blabbing out stupidities to an audience of 200,000 people can have a 200,000 times stronger effect on public opinion than a wise man talking with his or her next door neighbor. Progress it has been but without equal opportunities. All sorts of communicators in all parts of the world have committed the social felony of misusing power in communications. In fact, important political-military decisions, changing the course of some countries, have been made because television subtly favored them one way or the other.

In this evolving scenario, staying with the grass roots and the facts is the best thing to do. The growing technological development of communications has no doubt caused a double phenomenon: (a) For some socioeconomic strata, a great cost reduction and satisfactory democratization of personal communications have occurred, notably those means of communication that do not have an immediate social impact, such as mail, telegraph, cable and wireless telephones, facsimile, electronic mail, and so forth.[4] And (b) Antidemocratic concentrations of the big mass media are reducing user participation to the minimum. These concentrations have taken advantage of the costly technical and industrial complexity of the mass media, reinforced by 50 years of ideological and military strategy—from Goebbels to the Cold War.

The mass media have constituted a center line of sociopolitical power due to the control of ownership and their dominance of the patterns of actual usage (varying, of course, within certain margins). The mass media's threat to the future of democracy is no longer hypothetical, and they are a major obstacle to the development of less manipulated and free human relations.

Attributes of a New Morals of Intersubjectivity

There are several major features of a new morality of intersubjectivity that can be identified. As the needs and challenges of these various aspects become clear, the complexity of this ethical project is obvious.

The Relation as Its Supreme Category

One of the most revealing characteristics of a nascent morality of intersubjectivity will no doubt be schematizing on an anthropological scale the supreme categories of relation. No praxis philosophy has totally satisfied this demand so far, and therefore, it has been incapable of rehabilitating and dignifying the communications function.

A systematic metaphysics of social relations does not yet exist. In fact, it seems inconceivable, immersed as we are in the social logos. Kant's great model of relation unfailingly comes up, although he did not apply it in an anthropological way. In his idealism, Kant was interested in determining the relation of the "I" to pure, practical reason or the imperative. But his categorical system of relation continues to be highly inspiring and can be transferred (Pasquali, 1974) to the communication plane as inherence (communion), causality (information aimed at effects), and community (reciprocal or dialogic communication). In a world in which practically all intergroup and intersubjective dimensions of life are in an escalating crisis, a more exact reduction of relation to the anthropological plane is needed today. Traditional human sciences are in fact less and less capable of providing the axiological orientation that would allow us to overcome any of those crises.

Real Intersubjectivity

We must rethink the world, no longer in the traditional way as "the whole of all phenomena," but as "the whole of all human beings." This is a way of retrieving the postwar concept of the "human family," which was soon substituted by "globalization," a mercantile term. This commitment, in fact, implies that we remake the entire theme of intersubjective relationships from subject to subject and not from subject to object, or to reason, to law, to mediation, to being, and so forth.

In classical morality, and even in the great religions (Confucianism and Christianity, for example), we find intuitive glimpses—not much more than that—which make the flourishing of the moral dimension of human beings unachievable in the abyss of solipsism. Whether our moral reference is competitive or complementary, the human species is the irrevocable goal of virtuous behavior. Even in the belief of being finally judged by a supernatural tribunal or of not being judged at all (the myth of the ring of Giges), the absolute "absence of the other" obstructs the exercise of reaching a moral dimension. In an ethics such as Plato's, where the maximum virtue is justice, there is no room for the moral Robinson Crusoes. Modern French philosophy has recognized, perhaps more than any other, the determining character of the "presence of the other" and the impossibility of reaching the status of a moral person in the absence of another moral person (even if that other moral person ends up being our "hell," to use Sartre's term).

In a new morality centered on the intersubjective relation, the Kantian themes of respect and paritetic reciprocity—devoid of their reference to the law—will be wholly transferred to the relation between subjects as touchstones of an ethically just relationship. Once the great new principles have been established of just dealing, of the social contract between parties, and of mutual respect, the human being will be asked to submit criteria of good and evil to judge them. These criteria will apply not only to the tribunal of internal jurisdiction but also to negotiating the new principles *coram populo* [before the people] in open communication and within the tribal spirit of solidarity.

Illusory? Perhaps not. What other solutions are suggested by the irreversible crises in all concepts of authority, the current problems of governability, and the mismatch between morality and right? Crises such as these drive us to a universal aspiration for another kind of moral clarity, for the reopening of an authentic dialogue without the shrewdness of mediators or the exclusion of interlocutors.

New Social Contracts

The idea and practice of the social contract needs to be restated in depth, though the foreseeable characteristics are unclear. That need is seen explicitly not only in theoretical conclusions and moral postulates but also in historical facts of recent years. This spontaneous tendency comes embedded in a universal purpose. It is contrary to the compulsive globalization of political and economic models that restructure institutional life and reduce the scope and meaning of the *res publica* [the public realm]. This tendency corresponds to the already widespread will to increase participation.

Social communication—no matter how important its role has become to society—is governed by an appalling sort of unwritten social contract. Vast mute majorities have ceded their potential use of the mass media to a reduced cast of broadcasters, demanding practically nothing in exchange. They have not even insisted that media practitioners be true spokespeople of their opinions and aspirations. For this somewhat obscure reason, social communication is one of today's most intersubjective relational activities that most urgently needs new social contracts to redefine roles and to guarantee mutual balance, rights, obligations, and responsibilities. The employing sector should be allowed to continue voicing its well-known right to exercise free speech. But it must not be forgotten that the same freedom to which they are entitled has to be guaranteed to all as well; therefore, we must all think and act with that purpose in mind. The basic principles of a new social contract for communications will be no different than the ones contained in Article 19 of the *Universal Declaration of Human Rights* (1988, p. 107). They are likewise included in the *International Covenant on Civil and Political Rights* (1988), though the section where everybody is guaranteed equal rights to make their messages known by whatever medium is not followed worldwide.

From this perspective, the presence of monopolies, of oligopolies, and of private or sectarian interests in social communications (key instruments of intersubjective relationships) will become increasingly unacceptable. The yearning for pluralism will demand other rules of the game—a new social contract. All senders or transmitters will potentially be the speakers for their audiences. Users or perceivers will be granted the right to look into and coparticipate in the decisions that affect their communications environment. A genuine decentralization of communication power, without patronage, will slowly substitute the present concentrations and grossly unilateral flows of information. Without shared decision-making power, communication is an artificial intersubjectivity, even if a sophisticated remote control is put into one's hand.

Expanding Spatial and Temporal Frontiers

This expansion of intersubjectivity must be done in a way unknown to all preceding periods of history.

Space, used here metaphorically, refers to an open dialogue concerning all morality, respecting the cosmo-vision of each. This task obviously reaches the roots of cultural identities and differences, which are the prototypes of the human behavior Vico (1725/1801) described for the first time. Subsequently, social psychoanalysis, cultural anthropology, and ethnography have confirmed the existence of nearly identical behavioral models, myths, and beliefs in many cultures. The idea of developing something like a moral anthropology of humanity—strengthened by the modern human sciences—is particularly interesting.

Regarding the temporal expansion of moral frontiers, the task looks even more interesting and beneficial to humanity's practical progress. Slowly, but progressively in spite of appearances, tolerance and empathy have started to expand, not only to an unknown, distant, and foreign "other" in geographical and cultural space but also to a nonexistent "other." For the first time in history, humanity is developing a new sensitivity toward demographic and ecological concerns and has started to discover a new kind of philanthropy toward an "other" that is yet to be: generations to come, projected into the future, toward whom, perhaps, a new moral outlook is being developed. Although acknowledging the existence of this new frontier, we suddenly realize how narrow are all the ethical systems that philosophy has developed so far; they limit anchorage to contemporaneity and to the principle of reality imposed by the present, without perusing the kingdom of possibility. Our altruism, for example, which is embodied in the sheer dimension of the present, loses much of its shine when compared to the love for future others who will not even know about us.

Strategies to Liberate Interlocution

It is important not to forget the short history of communications media, their sometimes military origins, and the aggressive and commercial behavior that estranged them from social interests and from an equal distribution of power. From that awareness, it becomes obvious that one of the fundamental protonorms of the new morals of intersubjectivity concerns interlocution. This refers to freedom of speech, discourse, and dialogue—but that freedom must be preceded by a worldwide effort to reduce to a minimum the use of the monological and propagandistic forms of communication that dominate now.

Genuine freedom of communication transcends (a) the so-called "alternative media"—a phenomenon of local usefulness but one that has never reached critical mass to become a macroalternative of importance. Nor is it related to (b) the ever-increasing number of receiving channels through satellite, cable, and digital technology, which is expanding the empire of the big communicators. Nor does it have anything to do with (c) making every citizen become a transmitter, the chaotic utopia of Enzensberger (1974).

The kind of liberation referred to here will go through concrete processes, such as

structuring and granting users' representation;

guaranteeing participatory local production of messages by a wide number of independent producers;

having the users of certain communication services participate as responsible contributors;

placing user representatives on the board of directors and in the program management of all public radio and television services;

creating consumer protection organizations for communication services; and

universally applying the right to reply.

Welcoming more direct interlocution will not just be an exclusive process for the mass media, because contemporary civilization has tried to desocialize people in many other spheres of life. Education has much to contribute to the project of interlocution. Urban planners will have to redo the city square and the urban network to reactivate social communications. Cultural agents will have to look for ways to compensate the growing solitude produced by *l'informatique* and *la robotique*. The ethics of "I" will be replaced by the ethics of "us." Communications will be, finally, the central category of the new morality, within an improved environment of coexistence and respect for our alter ego.

Most of the conceptual work and strategic means remain to be done before the participatory goals can be reached. But in the new strategy, at least the following two steps might be considered essential: (a) Take away the problems from academic and government circles and give them to the users and (b) align the legal powers to clearly understand the complexity of communication problems. Regarding communication relations or contracts, a dialogue between the law and philosophy of praxis is of utmost importance. The most recent history of mass communications has been partly written by the same authors who wrote the judicial decisions concerning communications in the high courts of justice.

More Distributive Justice

As we have seen, each historical period has applied its own conceptions of ethics (philosophical-systematic)—and of freedom, perfection, happiness, justice, and so forth—to a preferred moral or sociopolitical problem. Philosophy can ascertain that one of the most relevant problems of this period is communications; some of the biggest debates on freedom and justice in the 1970s and 1980s have taken place in this field.

Invariably, contemporary debates have all been won first by the political and then by the commercial sector. For future reference, therefore, it is important to point out that these confrontations have been characterized by double-talk: a tantalizing version for the "great public" and another version with an ideological orientation that is less perceptible. In the tantalizing version, some of the great Western powers adamantly and successfully defended the theory and praxis of a free information flow, indicating that freedom, and freedom of commerce, are totally identifiable. The opposing group, basically consisting of developing countries, underlined the noncommercial characteristics of information. They prompted the United Nation's notion of the special responsibilities incumbent on communicators, and the political-cultural need for a more balanced distribution of information and news.

Behind its tantalizing aspects, the controversy revealed, for one thing, a significant incompatibility between North and South over the minimum criterion of distributive justice to social communication. Second, a contrast emerged between the Judeo-Christian and Protestant-capitalistic ethical concepts. The philosophical tendency of the Northern hemisphere—where the strongest communicators are concentrated—holds an antinomic relation between justice and freedom. In this perspective, the free flow of information is a kind of freedom so strongly required that it must be fought for even if it causes injustice in the surroundings. Communicators in the South maintain that this antinomy should be broken up into a more balanced distribution of communication power; if liberty creates injustice rather than more freedom, they argue, it cannot be true freedom and altruistic justice.

However, in the best of circumstances, this discourse has been considered naive by the North, which understood it as a request to give away part of its wealth, and its ideological and commercial power, to a lost cause. Therefore, discussions about communications have been and continue to be a result of the clash between two ethical conceptions. Reaching an agreement between the present conceptions of justice and freedom is a deep and universal process that will take time, in and out of the area of communications. But, can there be any doubt? There will be no peace in the codes of moral communications until an acceptable minimum of distributive justice can be included.

Summary and Conclusion

Is it really viable to develop a new morality of intersubjectivity starting from the communicative relation as the key concept? In a world now globally dominated by political and economical intolerance, how can we guarantee a transformative capacity for this new practical reason and its protonorms without which a morality cannot be moral? Do we have enough doctrinal reference points to continue advancing in the proper direction?

The first two questions should not take a Tertullian act of faith to provide a positive answer. Several specific historical situations on the previous pages have indicated the constant warfare that moral principles, democracy, culture, education, and common sense fight against the worst cases of communication misuse. These situations reflect also a strong desire to change the present situation.

The third question may be given a more explicitly encouraging answer. During the past decades, at least two attempts have been made to set the basis for a new anthropocentric morality, based on a relationship with others, able to ensure the Kantian "reciprocal action between agent and patient," including, of course, the act of communications.

The pinnacle of the first attempt undoubtedly corresponds to the Critical Philosophy of Society, or the Frankfurt School. Unfortunately, the dominant trends have ignored it, even before its complex discourses about negative thinking, social control, authority, communications, or cultural industries could be assimilated enough to employ them usefully. The Frankfurt School is waiting to be reread, even if for the mere joy of feeling once again the enveloping breath of the last great philosophy marked with moral obsession.

The second attempt that has reinforced the new morality of intersubjectivity comes from the philosophy of language. Its most significant current for our reflections is that which complied with the structures of the communications discipline, first defined by Charles Morris (1938). It has always been believed that there is a causal relationship between language and sociability. Democritus expressed it by claiming that the hominoid became a social and political being through the invention of speech. Centuries later, an interlocutor in Galileo's 1632 *Dialogues* pays highest homage to the "eminent thoughts of the person who imagined being able to communicate his deepest thoughts to another person, even when separated by the widest distance of time and place, through the intervention of some twenty small characters" (Galileo, 1970, p. 130).

The line of thought represented by Charles Pierce, G. E. Mead, C. Morris, L. Wittgenstein, K. O. Apel, and L. Kohlberg has led to Jürgen Habermas, in books whose titles are a complete program: *Theory of Communicative Action* (1984) and even more explicitly *Moral Consciousness and Communicative Action* (1990). Morris had distinguished the three essential aspects of semiotics as semantics, syntactics, and pragmatics, defining the latter as the science of the relationship between signs to their users. The pragmatic dimension—that is, the communicating and socializing element of discourse—moves into first place with the family of thinkers identified here. According to Mead and Wittgenstein, language and reason are co-original. Reason only advances by means of establishing communicable expressions, and language is the sole true and concrete manifestation of reason. In turning itself into a communicative or pragmatic act with those who share a code, language becomes the basis, form, and substance of intersubjectivity or socialization, its *ratio essendi* and *cognoscendi,* its reason for being and knowing. Also from the point of view of linguistics, it has been possible to show that true socialization is generated only in communication, the pragmatic momentum of expression.

Because of this, every society can be ultimately defined as a structure modeled by the main trends of its communication networks. The following principle of social philosophy is axiomatic: Two incommunicative beings, unaware of each other, cannot even constitute the smallest cell or social nucleus. Our two previous conclusions—(a) that no morality can be exercised in the absence of other moral subjects and (b) that no communicative act can be carried out in the absence of an interlocutor—meet and combine perfectly in this founding exercise of a new moral philosophy of intersubjectivity.

But the philosophy of language has taken one more step, which also agrees with the line of thought indicated here. From the semiologic pragmatic evidence that communication is the founding act of everything social or anthropologically relational, and that any communicative trauma will *eo ipso* [by itself] be a social trauma, springs the other evidence that it is proper to establish a morality of discussion or discourse at a time of power abuse in communications. Habermas (1990) explicitly calls communications the pragmatic phase of language, and undertakes the task of founding a critique of communicative reason. The unjust appropriation of a speech is denounced as usurpation and social domination, a communication pathology requiring social therapy. As with his predecessors, Habermas finds that reason is only found in the formal intelligibility generated by mutual understanding between interlocutors. Therefore, in a definition that is at first reductive but that on a second reading reveals its depth, Habermas (1990) defines dialogue as nothing less than taking decisions together: "I call communicative those interactions in which the interlocutors agree to coordinate in good faith their plans of action" (p. 79). This implies that all the rest is to be considered *ersatz* of communication and of solidarity, in other words, forms of indoctrination, false reciprocity, promotion, persuasion, or conditioning.

Through their approximations to relation as a form of coexistence and as a pragmatics of language, social, philosophical, and linguistic thinking join in attempting to define communicative actions. They are no longer the imperfect terrestrial imitations of the Augustinian communion of the saints but the epiphany of human morality and rationality, recognition of the alter ego in the other, the spark of sociality. The relational universe (linguistically and morally speaking) is now conceived as inherent in the communicative function. From this verification, we can claim that the foundations of a new morality of intersubjectivity centered on relation, and more particularly on communication, are partly laid.

Habermas asserts that the moral essence of human beings in their fullness will only be realized when an ethical reason for discourse or dialogue is established and the evidence of communicative pragmatics is analyzed. This moral essence would be indefinable in a monologic situation. Thus, as heir to the Frankfurt School, Habermas states that philosophy has only one ethical road to travel: in its negative phase, the demolition of authoritarian discourse that refuses to accept mutual decisions; in its positive phase, the search among communicative actions for a norm of universal validity. As with Kohlberg, he calls this latter phase postconventional, one that will have to be founded on the triad of reversibility, universality, and reciprocity.

We can now confidently say that communicative science, sociology and other human sciences, moral philosophy, and the philosophy of language have accumulated so many conceptual and empirical resources, have elaborated so many normative propositions on points in common, that undertaking the project of a morality of communication seems viable today.

Notes

1. To avoid confusion, it is best to keep the term *ethics* as connoting the metaphysical and epistemological systematization of real morality; in other words, the philosophy of morals. Kant's definition of ethics as the metaphysics of morals is clear and still impeccable. Ethics is the attempt by purely philosophical reason to clarify the everlasting, universal, and supreme principles that imbue all concrete and historical moralities, to define the ultimate categories of praxis, and to answer the question of why people are moral beings. The term *ethics* connotes, therefore, a systematic branch of pure philosophical speculation and no concrete morals. Ethics

exists, strictly speaking, within true philosophical systems, consistent with the metaphysical and epistemological points of view. Therefore, to be correct, one can only refer to the ethics of Aristotle, of Kant, and of Utilitarianism, or to this or other ethical principles considered by a given philosophy as pertaining to the supreme categories of praxis.

2. In addition to the two definitions employed in this paper, protonorm could be taken to mean: (a) practical norms in their pure, asystematic, prereflective, and extemporaneous state, with proven application and (b) a practical set of norms discovered in its nascent or experimental state, as a group's response to new social situations.

3. A North American survey institute recently indicated that 60% of the university students of economics would accept spending up to 3 years in jail if they could get hold of a large sum of money (Forecasting International, 1994).

4. In its early days, a transatlantic cable message cost 10 gold francs per word.

References

Eco, Umberto. (1967). *La strategia de la ilusión*. Barcelona: Ed. Lumen.

Enzensberger, Hans Magnus. (1974). *Palaver: Politische Überlegungen*. Frankfurt: Suhrkamp Verlag.

Forecasting International. (1994). *America's future: 74 trends*. Bethesda, MD: World Future Society.

Galilei, Galileo. (1970). *Dialogo Sopra i due Massimi Sistemi del Mondo*. Turin: Einaudi.

Habermas, Jürgen. (1984/1987). *Theory of communicative action* (2 vols.). Boston: Beacon.

Habermas, Jürgen. (1990). *Moral consciousness and communicative action*. Cambridge, MA: MIT Press.

International covenant on civil and political rights. In *Human rights: A compilation of international instruments* (pp. 18-42). Geneva: Centre for Human Rights.

Morris, Charles. (1938) *Foundation of the theory of signs*. Chicago: University of Chicago Press.

Pasquali, Antonio. (1974). *Comprender la Comunicación*. Caracas: Monte Avila.

Popper, Karl. (1994). *La Télévision: Un Danger pour la Démocratie*. Paris: Anatolia.

Taylor, Paul W. (1963). The ethnocentric fallacy. *The Monist, 47*(4), 563-584.

Universal Declaration of Human Rights. (1988). *Human rights: A compilation of international instruments* (pp. 1-7). Geneva: Centre for Human Rights.

Vico, G. B. (1801). *Principi di una Scienza Nuova*. Firenze, Sansoni, 1971. (Original work published 1725, 1730-1744)

CHAPTER 3

Discourse Ethics and Its Relevance for Communication and Media Ethics

EDMUND ARENS

In contemporary German-language philosophy, the communicative or discourse ethics advanced by Karl-Otto Apel and Jürgen Habermas is the theoretical approach that enjoys the widest critical attention. The discourse ethics of these two Frankfurt philosophers understands itself decidedly as a communication ethics. As such, it is of the greatest relevance for inquiring into the fundamental principles of communication ethics and protonorms of communication. Admittedly, discourse ethics has not yet come to grips explicitly with questions of media ethics. Neither Apel nor Habermas takes into account the textuality of communication and thus cannot do justice to the communications media. This is a limitation of both their approaches—a deficit that has not been removed nor even recognized to date.

Nevertheless, by claiming to unearth the universal structures of communication and to reflect on their basic ethical orientations, discourse ethics approaches communication ethics in a way that offers a basis for further elaboration. By pointing to ethical universals, discourse ethics also provides a philosophical resource for grounding media ethics.

To demonstrate its fundamental significance, I shall first sketch the two approaches to discourse ethics. Second, I shall introduce Habermas's conception of discourse ethics in greater detail. And third, the implications of discourse ethics for communication ethics and the consequences for media ethics will be addressed.

Approaches to Discourse Ethics

Discourse ethics stands in the tradition of the European, specifically German, Enlightenment, situating itself with particular reference to Immanuel Kant. Its goal is to clarify from a reflexive or reconstructive perspective the normative foundations of human action, communication, and interaction.

Within discourse ethics, two different approaches can be distinguished: Karl-Otto Apel's and that of Jürgen Habermas. Apel develops his version within the framework of his transcendental pragmatics, which he understands as a transformation of Kantian transcendental philosophy. Apel pursues the goal of translating Kant's critique of knowledge into a philosophy of the conditions for linguistically mediated understanding. In this enterprise, Apel has succeeded in combining the philosophy of language, epistemology, and ethics.

A first elaboration can be found in his work *Transformation of Philosophy* (Apel, 1973, 1980b).[1] He begins with the community of communication presupposed in every act of speaking and acting as the condition of their possibility. From that starting point, he reflects on the foundations of human knowing and acting. He shows in the "*a priori* of the community of communication"[2] that a rational grounding of ethics is possible in the age of science. In the last few years, his work has concentrated on a discourse ethics that investigates the presuppositions and procedures of rational argumentation. Apel elaborates the foundations of the process of reaching an understanding by means of argumentation. He develops his conception of discourse ethics in part by following the same route as Jürgen Habermas and in part by clearly distancing himself from him.[3] Apel's work published under the title *Diskurs und Verantwortung* [Discourse and Responsibility] (1988) serves to ground and develop his approach. In addition, that book defends discourse ethics against other positions and explicates it with regard to problems of application.

Apel's approach, which aims at providing a grounding for discourse ethics by means of an ultimate philosophical foundation, is conceived on two levels. Part A of the foundation argues by means of transcendental pragmatics. Part B concerns the problems associated with the historically focused application of the principles and norms of discourse ethics. On the basis of parts A and B, discourse ethics can then be fruitfully applied to politics, law, and science, for instance, or to media ethics (see Apel & Kettner, 1992). Apel's comprehensive goal is the rational grounding of an intersubjectively valid, universal macroethics of humanity, which he conceives as an ethics of responsibility in solidarity.[4]

According to Apel, the abstract part A delivers the ultimate philosophical grounding of ethics. To do so, it uses the foundational ethical norm demonstrated by means of strict reflection, that performative self-contradiction is to be avoided. According to this foundational ethical norm, everyone who enters into argumentation has necessarily recognized normative conditions. Apel takes argumentative discourse to be the ideal agent for grounding and justifying all norms. From this perspective, he shows that every person engaged in argumentation presupposes an ideal community of communication with all human beings as equal partners. The actual community of communication points to this ideal community and counterfactually anticipates it. To that extent, the ideal community of communication represents the regulative idea of moral progress. In Apel's words, the "foundational norm of the generalized reciprocity of all validity claims"—always recognized by everyone who engages in argumentation—is at the same time the "metanorm of the formation of consensus about norms . . . under the conditions of discourse of an ideal community of communication" (Apel, 1988, p. 99). That foundational norm likewise has the character of a regulative idea.

For Apel, universalization is the foundational principle of discourse ethics. This principle is attained and given an ultimate philosophical foundation by recourse to that which cannot be disputed without performative self-contradiction. Although universalization is a formal procedural principle for practical discourse, it is not in Apel's view devoid of content. It points rather to the achievement of universal understanding as a possible result.

Universalization is directed toward the consensual and communicative grounding of norms and provides the ideal criterion for judging them. But in contemporary historical situations, human beings cannot orient themselves to ideal norms alone. They must also vouch for their own systems of self-preservation and gauge the degree of risk that they can responsibly assume. For universalization to become a principle of realistic action in such situations, an ethics of responsibility requires in Apel's (1988) view a supplementary principle:

> In resolving real-world conflicts, the principle of universalization should be applied to the extent that it can be done without making irresponsible demands.
>
> Where the conditions of its application are not (yet) given, effort must be made toward removing the barriers to its application. (p. 14)

This work is to be a long-term strategy that is oriented teleologically. Its goal is the historical and in particular institutional realization of discourse under the conditions of a postconventional morality, where its realization can only be approximated.

In a volume dedicated to Apel "with thanks for having instructed me for three decades," Habermas (1983, p. 6) rejects both Apel's claim to an ultimate philosophical foundation and Apel's two-level conception of discourse ethics. Habermas sees in those two aspects of Apel's program a fundamentalistic element inherited from the philosophy of consciousness. This element separates philosophy from the sciences and gives it a superior position over them. For Habermas, the king's highway of transcendental reflection is no longer accessible to philosophy. Instead of taking that road, Habermas situates his approach within a reconstructive theory of communicative action. Within this framework, he works out his discourse ethics by means of a universal or formal pragmatics.[5] He thereby anchors discourse ethics in a broad research program structured along interdisciplinary lines.

In this project, Habermas further develops the early Frankfurt School's basic concern for a critical theory of contemporary society that combines social-scientific research and philosophical reflection (see Benhabib, 1986; Held, 1980; Ingram, 1990; Roderick, 1986). Admittedly, he gives only secondary attention to a theory of the mass media, which was important for the older Critical Theory.[6] To be sure, his hooking up with the Frankfurt School in a specific way and continuing it in a specific respect does not occur without profound corrections. Chief among them is a shift away from an orientation toward the philosophy of mind to one conceived within the philosophy of language.

Habermas's conception of discourse ethics is thus woven into a widely cast theoretical net. Taking his orientation from the reconstructive sciences, he seeks from one angle after another to elaborate a comprehensive theory of communicative action. A universal or formal pragmatics is the systematic core of that theory. He understands such a pragmatics as reconstructing the universal conditions for reaching an understanding (see Arens, 1994, pp. 90ff.).

One of the ways Habermas develops these foundations is through a critical analysis of the major social-theoretical conceptions of the 19th and 20th centuries—from Marx by way of Durkheim, Max Weber, and George Herbert Mead to Adorno and Horkheimer. He locates his discourse ethics in the context of his comprehensive theoretical undertakings, which include a whole series of specific trajections. In many respects, his early investigation of *The Structural Transformation of the Public Sphere* (1989)[7] has been continued right into his theory of discourse. Another area of his continual reflection is on a theory of the subject. His constitution of the subject in terms of intersubjectivity contains a theory of the subject's unfolding cognitive competence, linguistic competence, and interactive competence. Attention should also be paid to Habermas's theory of intersubjectivity and of society, developed on the basis of a communicative theory of action. In addition, he used the theory of action to reconstruct historical materialism as a theory of social evolution and for his theory of modernity. In the latter, argued against the thinkers of postmodernism, Habermas sees modernity as an uncompleted project. Furthermore, Habermas's location of philosophy in the age of postmetaphysical thought is of importance here. In particular, one theory is central to all his work, namely, his notion of a comprehensive rationality that, over against instrumentalist reductions, includes the communicative dimension that is constitutive of rationality. Last, his theory of law and of democracy, developed on the basis of his theory of discourse, should be mentioned.[8]

The Habermasian version of discourse ethics is to be located with this broad framework. The following section presents its basic features—with occasional sidelong glances at Apel's version.

Habermas's Discourse Ethics

Because discourse ethics stands in the Kantian tradition, it is characterized by four features proper to every Kantian ethics. It has a deontological, cognitivistic, formalistic, and a universalistic character (see Habermas, 1991, p. 11).

First, discourse ethics is deontological insofar as it concerns the oughtness of norms that specify right or just action. The validity of these norms is in turn "to be justified in the light of principles worthy of being recognized" (Habermas, 1991, p. 11). Second, discourse ethics is cognitivistic insofar as it conceives of normative rightness as a validity claim analogous to truth, that is, as something that can be rationally grounded. Third, discourse ethics is formalistic in not distinguishing any specific normative contents. Instead, like Kant's categorical imperative, it constitutes a formal criterion to justify norms of action. In discourse ethics, the process of moral argumentation assumes the place of the categorical imperative. Fourth, discourse ethics is universalistic in maintaining that universalization is applicable not just to one specific culture or epoch, is comprehensible not just for some cultural or historical settings, but also has universal validity. According to this principle, "only those norms may claim validity which could find approval by all those affected by them, were all affected parties to be participants in a practical discourse" (Habermas, 1991, p. 12).

Apel concentrates on argumentative discourse and on the one universal validity claim regarding the truth of statements. Habermas is interested in a reconstruction of *all* dimensions of the communicative process for reaching an understanding. In analyzing the constituents and basic orientations of the use of language for reaching an understanding, he discerns four such dimensions (cf. Habermas, 1979, pp. 1-68, 1984a, pp. 441-472, 1984c, pp. 367-452). He sees in them the operation of four universal validity claims that are simultaneously raised in every communicative act, with one of these claims being thematized in any particular case.

According to Habermas, a speech act is understood when listeners know the conditions of its acceptability. Listeners take a position in relation to these conditions with "yes" or "no." Insofar as what is offered in the speech act is accepted, hearers thereby assume a specific obligation for their further action. A speaker raises these claims in communicative action to come to an understanding with a listener. For these, Habermas reconstructs the validity claims of the *truth* of the statement, the *rightness* of the intended interpersonal relationship, and the *truthfulness* of that which is expressed. A fourth validity claim is that of *understandability*. This claim, however, is not raised in the action itself but is presupposed for the action to take place at all. In communicative action, a speaker must choose an understandable expression "in order to come to an understanding with a hearer about something and thereby to make himself understandable" (Habermas, 1984c, p. 307).

If communicative action aims at achieving agreement on all three levels—truth, rightness, truthfulness—speech acts must be accepted on precisely these three levels. According to Habermas, such an agreement is rationally motivated insofar as it is open to criticism. When it is criticized, it must and can be restored by providing grounds.

> With his "yes" the hearer grounds an agreement with regard, on the one hand, to the contents of the utterance and, on the other hand, to the guarantees immanent in the speech act and to the obligations relevant to the consequences of the interaction. (Habermas, 1984b, p. 596)

With a speech act, speakers pledge to redeem, if necessary, the validity claims that have been raised. Speakers achieve this redemption by providing grounds for their claims to truth and rightness and by demonstrating through consistent behavior that their claims to truthfulness are justified.

This implies at the same time that each of the three validity claims can be disputed. When they are disputed, the continuation of action for reaching an understanding depends on restoring the agreement broken by the act of disputing the validity claims. This restoration occurs by means of redeeming the validity claims. The fact that each of the three validity claims can be disputed and redeemed shows that the agreement presupposed in communicative action is rationally motivated, that is, it can be examined, grounded, and renewed. Validity claims are open to criticism; as such, they are both in need of and capable of being grounded. To that extent, they embody a form of rationality that Habermas sums up in the concept of *communicative rationality*. To understand the concept of communicative rationality and the discourse ethics implied by it, it is of central importance to analyze the procedure by which disputed validity claims can be grounded. Generally speaking, this happens by means of argumentation. Habermas (1984c) characterizes argumentation as a type of speech "in which participants thematize contested validity claims and attempt to vindicate or criticize them through arguments" (p. 18). He differentiates discourse and critique as two types of argumentation. Discourse must approximately satisfy the conditions of an ideal speech situation. In Habermas's view, we can speak of *discourse* only "when the meaning of the problematic validity claim conceptually forces participants to suppose that a rationally motivated agreement could in principle be achieved . . . if only the argumentation could be conducted openly enough and continued long enough" (p. 42).

Critique does not require this supposition. Nor must the conditions of a speech situation—free of external and internal coercion—be regarded as fulfilled in critique.

Theoretical discourse is the form of argumentation in which disputed truth claims are thematized and grounded.[9] By contrast, practical discourse is concerned with the disputed status of norms of action. Practical discourse is carried out with the goal of achieving a consensus that will resolve the dispute about their normative rightness, thereby argumentatively justifying the norms in question. The truthfulness of expressive utterances is likewise amenable to argumentative examination, although not to discursive examination. Such argumentative examination occurs according to the model of therapeutic critique, which is concerned with clearing up instances of systematic self-deception. In the realm of evaluative utterances, there is a similarly nondiscursive process of argumentation and examination, namely, aesthetic critique. Last, the validity claim of understandability or wellformedness in explicative discourse is amenable to rational examination; it occurs when the goal is removing disturbances to communication.[10]

Of particular interest for discourse ethics is that practical discourse is concerned with justifying the rightness of norms. Karl Otto Apel (1988) makes clear that discourse ethics is "not a special ethics for argumentative discourses, but rather an ethics of the responsibility, shared in solidarity by all who can engage in argumentation, for all problems of the lifeworld that are amenable to discursive treatment" (p. 116). Discourse ethics is not merely an ethics for conducting discourses. Rather, from the structure of discursive argumentation, it ascertains principles of communicatively reaching an understanding—principles that any and all norms of action must satisfy.

The central question here is how to secure a consensus attained by argumentation. According to Habermas, consensus concerning disputed norms is guaranteed and intersubjectively secured by means of the formal conditions of discourse, which must satisfy "to a sufficient degree of approximation" (Habermas, 1984c, p. 71) those of an ideal speech situation.[11] This must be understood as communication in which there is no limitation of participants and themes and no burden of action or coercion. The participants can change the form of discourse and they have free movement between action and discourse. They all potentially "have the same chance to put forward interpretations, assertions, recommendations, explanations and justifications, and to problematize, ground or refute their claim to validity, so that no prior opinion has a lasting exemption from thematization and critique" (Habermas, 1984d, p. 177).

Picking up on Habermas's theory of discourse, Robert Alexy has put forward rules of practical discourse. Habermas in turn has brought these rules into his reflections on grounding a discourse ethics (cf. Alexy, 1978, 1986; Habermas, 1990a, pp. 87-92). Along with the basic rules on the logical-semantic level, the procedural rules are of special importance.

> (3.1)   Every subject with the competence to speak and act is allowed to take part in a discourse.
> (3.2a) Everyone is allowed to question any assertion whatever.
> (3.2b) Everyone is allowed to introduce any assertion whatever into the discourse.
> (3.2c) Everyone is allowed to express his attitudes, desires, and needs.
> (3.3)   No speaker may be prevented, by internal or external coercion, from exercising his rights as laid down in (3.1) and (3.2). (Habermas, 1990a, p. 89)

The principle of universalization is decisive for practical discourse. It is supposed to secure the argumentative process of reaching an understanding concerning disputed norms of action and thereby to ground these norms in an intersubjectively obligatory manner. The principle of universalization is already contained in Kant's categorical imperative, according to which only those norms that serve as universal laws are accepted as valid. In Habermas's (1990a) view, the categorical imperative "can be understood as a principle that requires the universalizability of modes of action and maxims, or of the interests furthered by them (that is, those embodied in the norms of action)" (p. 63). In contrast to Kant, though, discourse ethics does not tie universalization to the reflection and imagination of isolated individual subjects who in each particular case seek to hypothetically assume for themselves the universal perspective. Instead, discourse ethics ties universalization to the real argumentation and the actual discourse of potentially all affected parties.

Starting from the assumption that valid norms must merit the recognition of all affected parties, universalization is supposed to guarantee that the interests of all are taken into account. Formulations of an interest common to all can count on universal approval and intersubjective recognition. In Habermas's words, the principle of universalization is supposed to "compel the universal exchange of roles that G. H. Mead called 'ideal role taking' or 'universal discourse.' " Thus, every valid norm has to fulfill the following condition. "All affected can accept the consequences and the side effects its general observance can be anticipated to have for the satisfaction of everyone's interests (and these consequences are preferred to those of known alternative possibilities for regulation)" (Habermas, 1990a, p. 65).

According to Habermas, this principle of universalization (U) is not to be confused with a moral principle that would already bring to expression the fundamental conception of discourse ethics. (U) merely designates a procedure for how a consensus concerning norms can arise and be intersubjectively secured. If everyone who enters into argumentation must make presuppositions that correspond to the rules of discourse (3.1-3.3 presented earlier) and if norms are justified only when they regulate the common interest of all affected parties,

> then everyone who seriously tries to discursively redeem normative claims to validity intuitively accepts procedural conditions that amount to implicitly acknowledging (U). . . . But once it has been shown that (U) can be grounded on the presuppositions of argumentation through a transcendental-pragmatic derivation, discourse ethics itself can be formulated in terms of the principle of discourse ethics (D), which stipulates: Only those norms can claim to be valid that meet (or could meet) with the approval of all affected in their capacity as participants in a practical discourse. (Habermas, 1990a, pp. 92-93)

In opposition to Apel, Habermas refuses to derive basic ethical norms immediately from the presuppositions of argumentation. He thus characterizes universalization as a formal-procedural principle and not as an ethical principle. By contrast, according to Apel (1988), universalization is

> *a priori* to be a principle, aimed at consensual-communicative implementation, of universalized reciprocity. To that extent the principle of universalization is

not devoid of content or open to arbitrary application, but points to the possible
result of a universally attained understanding. (p. 121)

The principle of universalization contains the "fundamental norm that all
communication partners have in principle equal rights" (Apel, 1988, p.
116). At the same time, it contains the obligation to share the responsibility
for the argumentative solution of morally relevant problems that emerge
in the lifeworld. In the sense that the solution is argumentative, it is in
principle capable of sustaining a consensus on the part of all possible
partners in the argumentation (p. 116).

In Habermas's earlier works he maintained that in discourse, a counter-
factual anticipation of an ideal speech situation or even of an ideal form of
life occurs. More recently, he has become significantly more skeptical.
Now, he presents only the formal and procedural character of discourse
ethics, which in his view does not make any statements of content. By
contrast, Apel understands his transcendental-pragmatic discourse ethics
as a reflection on, and an ultimate foundation for, the norms of an ideal
community of argumentation (see Apel, 1988, pp. 103-153, 179-216,
1980a, 1989; Fornet-Betancourt, 1990, 1992, 1993, 1994).

In *Justification and Application: Remarks on Discourse Ethics*, Habermas (1993b) makes an important differentiation in the concept of practical
reason. He distinguishes three ways of seeing or using it. Practical reason
can solve pragmatic questions—those determined by the goals and preferences of agents, ethical questions—which "take their orientation from the
telos of one's own life" (Habermas 1993b, p. 6), or moral questions—seen
from the perspective of universalizable norms of action. In Habermas's
view, the pragmatic, the ethical, and the moral uses of practical reason
supplement each other.

Paired with these uses of practical reason are pragmatic discourse, ethical-existential discourse, and moral-practical discourse. In pragmatic discourse, grounds are provided for technical and strategic recommendations.
Ethical-existential discourse is concerned with processes of individual or
collective self-understanding and ascertaining identity. Moral-practical
discourse—and only such discourse—serves the grounding of norms. In
differentiating the threefold use of practical reason, Habermas also empha-
sizes that the unity of practical reason can no longer be rooted, following
the Kantian model, in the unity of moral argumentation. The unity of practical reason can now be realized only in a network of those "public forms

of communication and practices in which the conditions of rational collective will formation have taken on concrete institutional form" (Habermas, 1993b, p. 17). Clarifying those practices and forms of communication is the responsibility of the philosophy of law.

For Habermas, Apel's fundamental-philosophical specification of discourse ethics is purchased at too high a price: It equates communicative and practical reason. In Habermas's opinion, Apel's privileging of a foundational discourse reveals an architectonic inheritance from the philosophy of consciousness. This inheritance grants philosophy priority over the particular sciences and sees philosophy as foundational in relation to them. Habermas holds that, because we possess no stronger equivalents for Kant's transcendental deduction than weak transcendental arguments, an ultimate foundation of ethics is neither possible nor necessary. From Habermas's perspective, Apel's two-level conception is wrong. It erroneously contrasts Part A as "an ethics of conviction indifferent to consequences" with Part B as "an ethics of responsibility oriented to consequences" (Habermas, 1993c, p. 86).[12] In particular, that conception establishes a false hierarchy of discourses. Habermas considers it more promising to explain the normative relations between morality, law, and politics in a step-by-step manner, by correlating discourses of grounding with those of application. In discourses of grounding, the role assigned to the principle of universalization corresponds in discourses of application to the principle of appropriateness. Discourses of application are in fact concerned with the contextual-concrete application of grounded and thus valid norms in specific situations under the circumstances particular to those situations. This brings to bear, according to Habermas (1993c), "the hermeneutical insight that the appropriate norm gains concrete significance in the light of the salient features of the situation, and the situation is described in turn in the light of the conditions specified in the norm" (pp. 37-38; cf. Forst, 1994; Günther, 1988).

Implications and Consequences

Discourse ethics is a procedural moral theory that as such does not itself ground any norms. Instead, it clarifies the procedures for universally grounding norms of action and of law. But the grounding can occur only in practical discourses, whose formal characteristics are ascertained by discourse ethics. Accordingly, Habermas (1990a) concludes that "basic norms of law and morality fall outside the jurisdiction of moral theory; they must be viewed as substantive principles to be justified in practical discourses" (p. 86). As moral theory, discourse ethics reflects on the presuppositions and procedures of the grounding of norms. It discerns just these presuppositions and procedures in practical discourse. Practical discourse in turn represents a reflected type of moral argumentation with the goal of reaching a consensual understanding about normative validity claims. This type of moral argumentation is characterized by specific fundamental and procedural rules. The contents of a practical discourse can be any disputed norm of action or of law with regard to which the participants in the discourse seek to reach an understanding.

Although no grounding of concrete norms of action can be expected from discourse ethics qua moral theory, this approach does contain normative implications that point not only to how such norms can be ascertained but also to the qualifications they must fulfill. These implications are initially formal procedural claims. But they also disclose ethical principles that one could characterize as ethical universals, even if discourse ethics does not employ this concept. On the basis of these universals, we can elucidate and unfold the implications for communication ethics and its consequences for media ethics.

In my opinion, the procedures of discourse ethics imply three ethical universals that need to be elaborated within media ethics. They can also be seen as claims that should be posed to mass media communication. These claims should in turn be used to examine and judge whether and to what extent mass media communication does justice to them. This presupposes, of course, that in principle, media communication could do justice to them and ought to satisfy them. At issue are three universals that are implied in the three universal validity claims of truth, truthfulness, and rightness, and thus the ethical principles of (a) orientation toward truth, (b) truthfulness, and (c) justice.

Orientation toward truth means an orientation toward reaching an understanding as the process of finding a consensus. This basic ethical orientation encompasses in turn three dimensions: first, "speaking the truth;" second, "being open to the truth claims of others;" and third, "aiming at shared, common truth." Accordingly, orientation toward truth means, first, that the participants in communication only make statements, advance assertions, and deliver judgments of whose truth they are convinced and for which they can adduce explanations, grounds, evidence, and so forth. Orientation toward truth implies, second, that the conversation partners are ready and able—at least in principle—to expose their assertions of truth to criticism from others and to mutual criticism. This includes the continual readiness to reexamine these claims or allow them to be reexamined and to revise them should they no longer prove tenable in view of continued criticism, opposing evidence, new knowledge, and so forth. Orientation toward truth entails, third, that the participants in communication mutually recognize each other as able to contradict one another and, although in potential contradiction, as also being in a communicative, cooperative search for a mutual understanding of the disputed claims.

The principle of orientation toward truth signifies for media ethics that it should investigate and judge mass media communication regarding its orientation toward truth in the threefold sense of "speaking the truth," "being open to the truth claims of others," and "aiming at shared, common truth." Here it would be necessary to ascertain more precisely (a) whether and to what extent those engaged in mass media communication speak the truth and show it in their images, sequences of images, and programs;[13] (b) whether and to what extent they adduce the explanations, grounds, evidence, and so forth available to them and provide the addressees with the information necessary to judge these claims; (c) whether and to what extent they articulate the truth claims in such a way that these can clearly be seen as claims that are placed over against other claims and are checked and solidified in mutual critique; and (d) whether and to what extent—when disputed questions are laid out and taken up—they at the same time have in view the possibility of reaching an understanding and prepare and disseminate potential points of agreement.

Truthfulness is complementary to the orientation toward truth. In the perspective of discourse ethics, truthfulness means that participants not only communicate to each other the contents that are asserted to be true, participants in communication also assume and communicate a posture toward themselves. This posture is truthful when they deceive neither themselves nor others about their own intentions, interests, and claims. Participants in communication are truthful when they give authentic expression to their drives and needs in relation to others. Participants in communication are truthful when they neither dissimulate nor conceal their

own person. They are truthful if they bring themselves into the communication process and "present" themselves, in an expressive posture toward
their own person, in relation to others. This "presentation" needs to be done
self-critically, with an eye to possible illusions and delusions.

For media ethics, the principle of truthfulness in discourse ethics implies
that in mass media communication, the person behind the information
needs to become visible. Truthfulness implies that persons engaged in mass
media communication give authentic expression—that is, expression free
of illusion and delusion—to their positions and that in doing so, they present their lifeworld and themselves [*sich selbst darstellen*] without performing self-promotion [*Selbstdarsteller*]. Such self-promotion would in
any case be merely the feigned, untruthful reduction of communication to
mere entertainment, which is not oriented toward truth, not capable of the
truth, and not truthful.[14]

The third ethical universal is justice. Karl-Otto Apel's discourse ethics
recognizes universalization as a "principle of justice and responsibility."
As such, it "takes into account from the very beginning the interests of all
affected parties" (Apel, 1988, pp. 280-281). Axel Honneth (1986) also discerns the "implicit concept of justice" within discourse ethics.[15]

Justice here encompasses two basic dimensions related to each other.
One dimension involves entering into just relationships, the other, standing
up for just relations. In my opinion, these aspects can be articulated in the
concepts of participation, emancipation, and advocacy. Participation
means that just relationships are realized only where all have the right and
the possibility to participate in discourse. The procedural rules of discourse
ethics insist that everyone who is capable of speaking and acting can participate, that anyone can introduce any question or concern, that anyone
can articulate his or her positions, wishes, and needs, and that nobody can
be prevented from using his or her right without coercion.

These procedural rules imply a concept of social justice that is directed
toward egalitarian freedom and mutual recognition as free and equal participants in communication and as members of society. Such a concept of
justice presents at the same time a regulative principle of democracy or of
a democratic civil society. The core of a democracy is formed by

a system of association that institutionalizes problem-solving discourses concerning questions of general interest. This institutionalization takes place

within the framework of structured spheres of public discourse. In their open and egalitarian forms of organization, these "discursive designs" mirror essential features of the art of communication around which they crystallize and to which they lend continuity and longevity. (Habermas, 1992, pp. 443-444; cf. Cohen & Arato, 1992; Rödel, Frankenberg, & Dubiel, 1989).

Justice in the sense of equal opportunity to participate in discourses requires, in addition, "an egalitarian possibility of access to those social pieces of information and those traditions of cultural formation that are necessary in order to be able to assert one's own convictions argumentatively in the circle of discussion participants" (Honneth, 1986, p. 191).

The principle of justice implies that nobody may be excluded from participation in the process of reaching an understanding. It also requires that none of those who are, in fact, not taken into account remain excluded and that work be done toward the goal of communicative and social relations in which such exclusion is no longer the case. Herein lies the emancipatory moment of discourse ethics. The principle of justice aims at the realization of egalitarian freedom and reciprocity in an "ideal community of communication" (Apel's phrase)—even if it can never be more than approximately attained—or in a society that is fundamentally democratized and just in its "process of forming political opinion and will" (Habermas, 1992, p. 361).

Last, along with the participatory and the emancipatory moments, advocacy belongs to the principle of justice.[16] One does not do justice to this conception if it is understood as an ethics that only takes into account those who are capable of rational action and that excludes those who are not rational. On the contrary, advocacy means that it is necessary to bring to bear the interests, claims, and needs of those who can no longer or not yet articulate them. Precisely for that reason, "solidarity of the rational with those who are not rational" is a "constitutive principle of . . . discourse ethics" (Kissling, 1990, p. 250). Justice that assumes the task of advocacy means criticizing and denouncing those communicative and social relations in which human beings have no voice, in which there is no word from them, in which they are not heard. At the same time, it means lending them one's own voice, becoming the temporary spokesperson for their interests, needs, and claims—with self-critical caution over against possible paternalism and the well-intentioned misuse of the voiceless. Justice that assumes the task of advocacy means proceeding against the exclusion of

themes and (groups of) persons from public discourse. It means demanding
the right of "communication for all" (see Hamelink, 1983; Lee, 1986), and
as an advocate, claiming that right with the goal of overcoming existing
excommunication and realizing more participatory forms of communication that are free of coercion, oriented toward truth, truthfulness, and justice
(see Lesch, 1992, 1994). Justice that assumes the task of advocacy means,
finally, not losing sight of the annihilated victims of injustice and violence
but instead bringing them to remembrance, recalling them in "anamnestic
solidarity" (see Arens, 1995; Peukert, 1984), and demanding justice for
them and for their unmet claims.

It goes without saying that such a principle of justice, oriented toward
participation, emancipation, and advocacy, must be made context-specific
and needs application. The implications and consequences for media ethics
are obvious. They can be designated by the same key words: participation,
emancipation, and advocacy.

The mass media obstruct and fragment the public sphere, pushing it toward depoliticization. The human lifeworld is increasingly colonized and
commercialized by gigantic communications systems. The potential of the
mass media is *eo ipso* ambiguous, both authoritarian and emancipatory. In
the face of all this, at issue is the interplay of, on the one hand, a critical
theory of the public sphere and, on the other hand, a discourse ethics that
is normatively and universally grounded, and situationally and contextu-
ally applied (see Calhoun, 1992; Habermas, 1987, pp. 301-403, 1989,
1992, pp. 435-467; Holderegger, 1992; Lichtenberg, 1990; Thompson,
1990, pp. 261ff.). The interplay of the two is concerned with investigating
mass media communication and judging (a) whether and to what extent it
aims at, supports, and enables participatory forms of communication; (b)
to what extent it contributes to guaranteeing equal opportunity for participation in discourses; (c) whether and to what extent it uncovers existing
relations of distorted, restricted, or obstructed public communication and
works toward overcoming them; and (d) whether and to what extent it
stands up as an emancipatory advocate for the right and possibility of all
to engage in communication.

The implications of discourse ethics for communication ethics and the
consequences for media ethics can be summarized in the following manner:
The ethics of mass media communication needs to be conceived in such a
way that it understands itself as discursive. That is, in its own discourses

of grounding and application, it ascertains the conditions, limitations, and possibilities of media communication. Not the least of the goals in doing so would be for media ethics in turn to initiate and stimulate mass media discourses and to reflect on their possibilities and limits with regard to participation, emancipation, and advocacy.

Notes

1. See Apel's *Selected Essays* (1994b and 1996); particularly helpful is the introduction to Apel's thought by E. Mendieta (pp. ix-xxi). Volume 2, *Ethics and the Theory of Rationality*, has appeared in 1996. On Apel, see also Arens (1994, pp. 78-89, 123-138, 141-145).

2. This is the subtitle of Volume 2 in the German edition, as well as the first part of the title of the final essay in both the German and the English editions.

3. For Apel's critical analysis of Habermas's approach, see especially Apel (1989, pp. 15-65).

4. Refer also to the debate that has occurred in the 1990s between Apel's discourse ethics and Latin American philosophy of liberation, particularly the position of Enrique Dussel. That debate is documented in four volumes (Fornet-Betancourt, 1990, 1992, 1993, 1994).

5. See Habermas (1990b, 1993a, 1984c, 1987); Ferry (1987). Rehg (1994) also offers an excellent overview of Habermas's conception.

6. See Habermas (1987, pp. 389-391). On the media theory of the Frankfurt School, cf. Jay (1973, Chs. 6-8) and Kausch (1988).

7. The revised German edition (Habermas, 1990c) has an instructive preface that is not included in the English translation (cf. Calhoun, 1992). In its core statements, this work has remained relevant right into his theory of discourse.

8. These latter two theories are complementary to Habermas's work on discourse ethics. They demonstrate how the emphasis on discourse ethics can be incorporated into, and explicated within, a political ethics (see Habermas, 1992).

9. On Habermas's discursive consensus theory of truth, see Habermas (1984d). Apel's transcendental-pragmatic concept of truth is sketched in Apel (1994a; cf. 1987).

10. With this position, Habermas corrects the view he advanced in "Theories of Truth" that only claims to truth and to rightness are discursive. Compare Habermas (1984d, p. 139) with Habermas (1984c, pp. 21-22).

11. See Habermas (1990a, p. 88). Still more cautious is Habermas (1992, p. 392); cf. the stronger formulations in Habermas (1984d, pp. 179ff).

12. In opposition, cf. Apel (1993) and Apel and Keltner (1992).

13. J. R. MacArthur's (1993) analysis of the reporting of the Gulf War confirms in a both paradigmatic and striking manner the urgency of the truth question for media ethics and media politics.

14. For a critique of the media's public discourse as entertainment, see Postman (1986). Different judgments of entertainment can be found in Tannenbaum (1980).

15. Forst's work (1994) goes further, both confirming discourse ethics's principle of justice and differentiating it by distinguishing four contexts of justice. Forst does so in response to

the communitarian critique of the "abstract" universalism of the principle of justice in discourse ethics.
16. Habermas underscored the advocate role of critical social theory as early as *Legitimation Crisis* (1975).

References

Alexy, Robert. (1978). Eine Theorie des Praktischen Diskurses. In Willy Oelmüller (Ed.), *Normenbegründung— Normendurchsetzung* (pp. 22-58). Paderborn, Germany: Schöningh.

Alexy, Robert. (1986). *Theorie der Grundrechte.* Frankfurt, Germany: Suhrkamp.

Apel, Karl-Otto. (1973). *Transformation der Philosophie* (Vol. 2). Frankfurt, Germany: Suhrkamp.

Apel, Karl-Otto. (1980a). The *a priori* of the communication community and the foundations of ethics: The problem of a rational foundation of ethics in the scientific age. In *Towards a transformation of philosophy* (Trans., G. Adley & D. Frisby; pp. 225-300) [The International Library of Phenomenology and Moral Sciences]. London: Routledge & Kegan Paul.

Apel, Karl-Otto. (1980b). *Towards a transformation of philosophy* (Trans., G. Adley & D. Frisby). The International Library of Phenomenology and Moral Sciences. London: Routledge & Kegan Paul.

Apel, Karl-Otto. (1987). Fallibilismus, Konsenstheorie der Wahrheit und Letztbegründung. In Forum für Philosophie Bad Homburg (Ed.), *Philosophie und Begründung* (pp. 116-211). Frankfurt, Germany: Suhrkamp.

Apel, Karl-Otto. (1988). *Diskurs und Verantwortung: Das Problem des Übergangs zur postkonventionellen Moral.* Frankfurt, Germany: Suhrkamp.

Apel, Karl-Otto. (1989). Normative Begründung der "Kritischen Theorie" durch Rekurs auf lebensweltliche Sittlichkeit? Ein transzendentalpragmatisch orientierter Versuch, mit Habermas gegen Habermas zu denken. In A. Honneth et al. (Eds.), *Zwischenbetrachtungen im Prozess der Aufklärung: Jürgen Habermas zum 60. Geburtstag* (pp. 15-65). Frankfurt, Germany: Suhrkamp.

Apel, Karl-Otto. (1993). Das Anliegen des angloamerikanischen "Kommunitarismus" in der Sicht der Diskursethik. In M. Brumlik & H. Brunkhorst (Eds.), *Gemeinschaft und Gerechtigkeit* (pp. 149-172). Frankfurt, Germany: Suhrkamp.

Apel, Karl-Otto. (1994a). C. S. Peirce and Post-Tarskian Truth. In E. Mendieta (Ed.), *Selected essays: Vol. 1. Towards a transcendental semiotics* (pp. 175-206). Atlantic Highlands, NJ: Humanities Press.

Apel, Karl-Otto. (1994b). *Selected essays: Vol. 1. Towards a transcendental semiotics* (E. Mendieta, Ed.). Atlantic Highlands, NJ: Humanities Press.

Apel, Karl-Otto. (1996). *Selected essays. Vol. 2: Ethics and the theory of rationality.* Atlantic Highlands, NJ: Humanities Press.

Apel, Karl-Otto, & Kettner, M. (Eds.). (1992). Diskursethik vor der Problematik von Recht und Politik: Können die Rationalitätsdifferenzen zwischen Moralität, Recht und Politik selbst noch durch die Diskursethik normativ-rational gerechtfertigt Werden? In K.-O. Apel & M. Kettner (Eds.), *Zur Anwendung der Diskursethik in Politik. Recht und Wissenschaft* (pp. 29-61). Frankfurt, Germany: Suhrkamp.

Arens, Edmund. (1994). *The logic of pragmatic thinking: From Peirce to Habermas* (Trans., D. Smith). Atlantic Highlands, NJ: Humanities Press.

Arens, Edmund. (1995). *Christopraxis: A theology of action* (Trans., J. Hoffmeyer). Minneapolis, MN: Fortress.

Benhabib, Seyla. (1986). *Critique, norm, and utopia: A study of the foundations of critical theory.* New York: Columbia University Press.

Calhoun, C. (Ed.). (1992). *Habermas and the public sphere* [Studies in Contemporary German Social Thought]. Cambridge, MA: MIT Press.

Cohen, J. L., & Arato, A. (1992). *Civil society and political theory* [Studies in Contemporary German Social Thought]. Cambridge, MA: MIT Press.

Ferry, J. M. (1987). *Habermas: L'Éthique de la Communication.* Paris: Presses Universitaires de France.

Fornet-Betancourt, R. (Ed.). (1990). *Ethik und Befreiung.* Aachen, Germany: Verlag der Augustinus Buchhandlung.

Fornet-Betancourt, R. (Ed.). (1992). *Diskursethik oder Befreiungsethik?* Aachen, Germany: Verlag de Augustinus Buchhundlung.

Fornet-Betancourt, R. (Ed.). (1993). *Die Diskursethik und ihre lateinamerikanische Kritik.* Aachen, Germany: Verlag der Augustinus Buchhandlung.

Fornet-Betancourt, R. (Ed.). (1994). *Konvergenz oder Divergenz? Eine Bilanz des Gesprächs zwischen Diskursethik und Befreiungsethik.* Aachen, Germany: Verlag der Augustinus Buchhandlung.

Forst, R. (1994). *Kontexte der Gerechtigkeit: Politische Philosophie jenseits von Liberalismus und Kommunitarismus.* Frankfurt, Germany: Suhrkamp.

Günther, K. (1988). *Der Sinn für Angemessenheit.* Frankfurt, Germany: Suhrkamp.

Habermas, Jürgen. (1975). *Legitimation crisis* (Trans., T. McCarthy). Boston: Beacon.

Habermas, Jürgen. (1979). What is universal pragmatics? In *Communication and the evolution of society* (pp. 1-68) (Trans., T. McCarthy). Boston: Beacon.

Habermas, Jürgen. (1983). *Moralbewusstsein und kommunikatives Handeln.* Frankfurt, Germany: Suhrkamp.

Habermas, Jürgen. (1984a). *Aspekte der Handlungsrationalität.* In *Vorstudien und Ergänzungen zur Theorie des kommunikativen Handelns* (pp. 441-472). Frankfurt, Germany: Suhrkamp.

Habermas, Jürgen. (1984b). Erläuterungen zum Begriff des kommunikativen Handelns. In *Vorstudien und Ergänzungen zur Theorie des kommunikativen Handelns* (pp. 571-606). Frankfurt, Germany: Suhrkamp.

Habermas, Jürgen. (1984c). *Theory of communicative action: Vol. 1. Reason and the rationalization of society* (Trans., T. McCarthy). Boston: Beacon.

Habermas, Jürgen. (1984d). Wahrheitstheorien. In *Vorstudien und Ergänzungen zur Theorie des kommunikativen Handelns* (pp. 127-183). Frankfurt, Germany: Suhrkamp.

Habermas, Jürgen. (1987). *Theory of communicative action: Vol. 2. Lifeworld and system: A critique of functionalist reason* (Trans., T. McCarthy). Boston: Beacon.

Habermas, Jürgen. (1989). *The structural transformation of the public sphere: An inquiry into a category of bourgeois society* (Trans., T. Burger & F. Lawrence) [Studies in Contemporary German Social Thought]. Cambridge, MA: MIT Press.

Habermas, Jürgen. (1990a). Discourse ethics: Notes on a program of philosophical justification. In *Moral consciousness and communicative action* (Trans., C. Lenhardt & S. Weber Nicholsen; pp. 43-115) [Studies in Contemporary German Social Thought]. Cambridge, MA: MIT Press.

Habermas, Jürgen. (1990b). *Moral consciousness and communicative action* (Trans., C. Lenhardt & S. Weber Nicholsen) [Studies in Contemporary German Social Thought]. Cambridge, MA: MIT Press.

Habermas, Jürgen. (1990c). *Strukturwandel der Öffentlichkeit: Untersuchungen zu einer Kategorie der bürgerlichen Gesellschaft* (Rev. ed.). Frankfurt, Germany: Suhrkamp.

Habermas, Jürgen. (1991). Treffen Hegels Einwände gegen Kant auch auf die Diskursethik zu? In *Erläuterungen zur Diskursethik* (pp. 9-30). Frankfurt, Germany: Suhrkamp.

Habermas, Jürgen. (1992). *Faktizität und Geltung: Beiträge zur Diskurstheorie des Rechts und des demokratischen Rechtsstaats.* Frankfurt, Germany: Suhrkamp.

Habermas, Jürgen. (1993a). *Justification and application: Remarks on discourse ethics* (Trans., C. Cronin) [Studies in Contemporary German Social Thought]. Cambridge, MA: MIT Press.

Habermas, Jürgen. (1993b). On the pragmatic, the ethical, and the moral employments of practical reason. In *Justification and application: remarks on discourse ethics* (Trans., C. Cronin; pp. 1-17) [Studies in Contemporary German Social Thought]. Cambridge, MA: MIT Press.

Habermas, Jürgen. (1993c). Remarks on discourse ethics. In *Justification and application: Remarks on discourse ethics* (Trans., C. Cronin; pp. 19-111) [Studies in Contemporary German Social Thought]. Cambridge, MA.: MIT Press.

Hamelink, Cees J. (1983). *Cultural autonomy in global communications: Planning national information policy.* New York: Longman.

Held, David. (1980). *Introduction to critical theory: Horkheimer to Habermas.* Berkeley: University of California Press.

Holderegger, A. (1992). Einführung: Ethik in der Mediengesellschaft. In A. Holderegger (Ed.), *Ethik der Medienkommunikation.* Friburg, Germany: Universitätsverlag.

Honneth, Axel. (1986). Diskursethik und implizites Gerechtigkeitskonzept. In W. Kuhlmann (Ed.), *Moralität und Sittlichkeit.* Frankfurt, Germany: Suhrkamp.

Ingram, D. (1990). *Critical theory and philosophy.* New York: Paragon House.

Jay, M. (1973). *The dialectical imagination: A history of the Frankfurt School and the Institute of Social Research 1923-1950.* Boston: Little, Brown.

Kausch, K. (1988). *Kulturindustrie und Populärkultur: Kritische Theorie der Massenmedien.* Frankfurt, Germany: Suhrkamp.

Kissling, C. (1990). Die Theorie des kommunikativen Handelns in Diskussion. *Freiburger Zeitschrift für Philosophie und Theologie, 37,* 233-52.

Lee, Philip. (Ed.). (1986). *Communication for all: The church and the new world information and communication order.* Maryknoll, NY: Orbis.

Lesch, W. (1992). Unparteilichkeit und Anwaltsfunktion: Anmerkungen zu einem Dauerkonflikt der theologischen Ethik. *Stimmen der Zeit, 210,* 257-270.

Lesch, W. (1994). Theologische Ethik als Handlungstheorie. In E. Arens (Ed.), *Gottesrede— Glaubenspraxis: Perspektiven theologischer Handlungstheorie* (pp. 89-109). Darmstadt, Germany: Wissenschaftliche Buchgesellschaft.

Lichtenberg, J. (1990). *Democracy and the mass media.* Cambridge, UK: Cambridge University Press.

MacArthur, J. R. (1993). *Second front: Censorship and propaganda in the Gulf War.* Berkeley: University of California Press.

Peukert, Helmut. (1984). *Science, action, and fundamental theology: Toward a theology of communicative action* (Trans., J. Bohman) [Studies in Contemporary German Social Thought]. Cambridge, MA: MIT Press.

Postman, Neil. (1986). *Amusing ourselves to death: Public discourse in the age of show business.* New York: Penguin.

Rehg, W. (1994). *Insight and solidarity: The discourse ethics of Jürgen Habermas.* Berkeley: University of California Press.

Rödel, U., Frankenberg, G., & Dubiel, H. (1989). *Die demokratische Frage.* Frankfurt, Germany: Suhrkamp.

Roderick, R. (1986). *Habermas and the foundations of critical theory.* New York: St. Martin's.

Tannenbaum, P. H. (Ed.). (1980). *The entertainment functions of television.* Hillsdale, NJ: Lawrence Erlbaum.

Thompson, J. B. (1990). *Ideology and modern culture.* Stanford, CA: Stanford University Press.

CHAPTER 4

Universal Values and Moral Development Theories

DENI ELLIOTT

V iewed from a wide angle, the world's communities and subcommuni-
ties appear to be an array of values, a colorful moral kaleidoscope. But
these dissimilarities among values, as striking as they are, mask the similarity behind the "colors"—the species-specific "crystals" that create dis-
cernible and consistent patterns amid the array of value-colors. The argument for universal values, like moral development theories, builds on the
notion of similarities among human behavior that stretch across space, culture, and time. Variations can be explained by adequate theory. As James Q.
Wilson (1993) explains,

> Two errors arise in attempting to understand the human condition. One is to
> assume that culture is everything, the other to assume that it is nothing. In the
> first case there would be no natural moral sense—if culture is everything, then
> nature is nothing. In the second, the moral sense would speak to us far more
> clearly than it does. A more reasonable assumption is that culture will make

some difference some of the time in the lives of most of us and a large difference much of the time in the lives of a few of us. (p. 6)

Wilson argues that both culture and nature are necessary for the individual expression of values. This chapter attempts to distill the universality of values from their culturally based expressions and show how theories of moral development rest on this assumption of universality. Together, universal values and moral development attempt to create a unified explanation for moral attitudes and behavior across cultures. But some of the objections to such a unified theory of values and development shall also be discussed. The chapter concludes with a philosophical reevaluation of how moral development theories presuppose universal values.

Universal Values

Valuing is a basic activity in conscious humans from the infant who kicks off her blankets or grimaces at the taste of strained squash to politicians or religious leaders condemning the entertainment industry for corrupting the values of youth.[1] But attempts at defining value are rarely adequate for general use. For example, a definition is offered by British philosopher Alan Montefiore (1988):

> Positive values [may] be taken to be whatever give positive meaning or point to any object, state of affairs, activity, or institution that people, consciously or unconsciously, explicitly or implicitly, individually or collectively, may treat as good, important, useful, interesting, obligatory, beautiful, and so forth, and that value itself [may] be taken as being whatever is the common or family characteristics of these. (Negative values, this reasoning might continue, could be treated in an appropriately mirror-image-like fashion.) (p. 13)

The problem with such definitions, as Montefiore points out, is not that they are wrong but that they are too broad to be useful. A discussion of values can best be advanced by stipulating the scope of the analysis.

Values, as examined here, are beliefs expressed in judgment statements rather than in fact statements. That is, statements about values are normative as distinguished from descriptive statements that express facts.

The scope is narrowed further by excluding statements of aesthetics and taste. "That is a good painting" and "that poet is lousy" are forms of aesthetic judgments that clearly express the speaker's valuing behavior but will not be included in this discussion. Nor will the valuing behavior of personal choice ("I like the look of redwood rather than cedar for house siding") or of etiquette ("She should know not to dress like that") be examined.

The scope of values that result in ethical or moral-normative judgments is the important issue here.[2] These are judgments that implicitly express an assumption about harm or benefit. If the judgment is that for Person A to perform Action X or to refrain from performing Action Y is wrong, immoral, unethical, or bad, the implicit assumption behind the judgment is that some person (perhaps A but usually some other person) will be caused or is likely to cause unjustified harm through A's action or nonaction.[3] Judgment statements can be positive as well as negative. If the judgment is that for Person A to perform Action X or to refrain from performing Action Y is right, moral, ethical, or good, the implicit assumption is that someone will benefit.

There is obviously a gray area between the judgment statements excluded in this study and those included. The statements of aesthetic judgment may have moral implications in that the painting may be judged "good" because it is considered to promote a good in society or not cause viewers pain or displeasure in the viewing; the poet may be judged "lousy" because he or she persuades people to break laws or violate accepted conventions through his or her provocative words. Redwood may be preferred by the speaker because redwood is an indigenous wood and the speaker holds an implicit belief that using anything but indigenous woods harms the environment and future generations. And the judgment concerning the woman's style of dressing may concern a social taboo rather than express a fashion faux pas. But it is only by articulating clear standards rooted in universal values that one can have a basis for determining when borderline cases such as these should be included. The rationale, then, for dividing ethical or moral judgment statements from fact statements is that judgment statements necessarily contain a speaker's implicit belief concerning harm or benefit.

Specieswide Moral Values

Whatever the experience or context in which they live, human beings share a particular kind of valuing "hardware." It would be odd if humans did not share what sociologist Handley Cantril (1965) calls "a genetically built-in design that sooner or later must be accommodated" (p. 315).

Based on a survey of representative samples of adult populations from Brazil, Cuba, the Dominican Republic, Egypt, India, Israel, Nigeria, Panama, the Philippines, Poland, the United States, West Germany, and Poland in the early 1960s, Cantril (1965) developed a list of 11 basic uniformities and similarities in human needs and desires:

1. Satisfaction of survival needs
2. Physical and psychological security
3. Sufficient order and certainty to allow for predictability
4. Pleasure: both physical and psychological excitement and enjoyment
5. Freedom to act on ideas and plans for improvement of self and context
6. Freedom to make choices
7. Freedom to act on choices
8. Personal identity and integrity; a sense of dignity
9. Feeling of worthwhileness
10. A system of beliefs to which they can commit themselves
11. Trust in the system on which they depend

This list, based on empirical study, is consistent with a conceptual list derived independently through logical analysis by philosopher Bernard Gert 20 years later. Gert (1988), in seeking to describe a moral system that provides a basis for normative judgments of right and wrong, defines an evil as "the object of an irrational desire." "This definition," Gert says, "provides us with a list of evils: death, pain, disability, loss of freedom and loss of pleasure. . . . No rational person insofar as he is rational desires any evil for himself without a reason" (p. 48).

That reason may be factually incorrect, like the mother who throws herself in front of a truck because she (mistakenly) believes that her child would otherwise be hit by it. The reason may be easy to understand, as in the case of the woman who chooses amputation over death from bone cancer. Or, rational people may disagree about the correctness of the reason, as, for example, in the disagreement over the need for physician-assisted suicide or active euthanasia.

A human analogy is required to bridge the chasm between self-interest and morality. The analogy is that other humans are like me in that no one desires for him or herself harm without reason. What is irrational to want for oneself is immoral to cause another. That is, if it is irrational to desire death, pain, disability, loss of freedom, or loss of pleasure unless one has a reason, then it is immoral to cause these evils to another person without reason.[4] It is immoral to do so because we recognize that it is irrational for the other person to desire these evils.

Labeling an action immoral does not deny that such actions happen; people do cause unjustified harm to one another.

> We do have a core self, not wholly the product of culture, that includes both a desire to advance our own interests and a capacity to judge in a disinterested way how those interests ought to be advanced. Our selfish desires and moral capacities are at war with one another, and often the former triumphs over the latter. However great this war may be and no matter how often we submerge our better instincts in favor of our baser ones, we are almost always able, in our calm and disinterested moments, to feel the tug of our better nature. In those moments we know the difference between being human and being inhuman. (Wilson, 1993, p. 11)

The descriptive reality that some people do bad things does not imply the lack of a universal morality. Few would agree that the moral rule "don't kill" is absolute. Yet few would disagree that "don't kill" is a moral rule that usually ought to be followed. It would be irrational for individuals (without mitigating reason) to desire that the rule "don't kill" not be followed in regard to how others treat them.

One can argue that specific cases of killing are justifiable and still hold that killing is generally wrong. One might argue that killing is wrong except in times of justified war with identifiable combatants; one might argue that it would be rational to wish for assistance in one's death in a time of terminal illness and intolerable pain. Thus, whether a specific act of killing is morally permissible would, indeed, depend on the specific circumstances. But by requiring an explanation for exceptions to be justified, those exceptions actually support the notion of a general law. The result is that one can be universalistic without being absolutist.

> Take murder: in all societies there is a rule that unjustifiable homicide is wrong and deserving of punishment. To justify an exception requires making reasonable arguments. My critics will rejoin that if only unjustifiable homicides are wrong, and if societies differ radically in what constitutes a justification, that is tantamount to saying that there is no rule against homicide. I grant the force of their argument, but I suggest in response that the need to make an argu-

ment—to offer a justification for the killing—is itself a sign that every society attaches some weight to human life. (Wilson, 1993, p. 17)

Nor is the existence of a law, rule, or convention necessary for one to act in a way that is consistent with a notion of universal moral values.

But the existence of a natural moral sense does not require the existence of universal moral rules. . . . Most important human universals do not take the form of rules at all and hence are not likely to be discovered by scholars searching for rules. Even the incest taboo, though a universal rule, scarcely needs to be a rule because incest is so rare. As Robin Fox has noted, what is cultural is the rule against incest; what is universal is the avoiding of incest. Much of the dispute over the existence of human universals has taken the form of a search for laws and stated practices. But what is most likely to be universal are those impulses that, because they are so common, scarcely need to be stated in the form of a rule, and so escape the notice of anyone scanning indexes to ethnographic studies. The impulse to avoid incest is one such. Another—and to me the most important—is the impulse to care for one's children. (Wilson, 1993, p. 18)

The impulse to care for one's children provides a world of examples of cultural expression that show the impulse to be universal. Yet, whatever the cultural variation, some behavior toward children—torture, for instance —is universally accepted as wrong.

Moral Development

Moral development theories rest on the notion that human beings develop morally in a way that is analogous with the ways humans develop physically, cognitively, and linguistically. Just as a baby must acquire reciprocal leg motion before he or she can walk, a person must develop a sense of caring for oneself before one can take others' needs into consideration. He or she must be able to understand how external authority interprets "good" and "bad" before one can independently evaluate the appropriateness of the external rules for oneself.

Although moral development theories differ in scope and context, each has four necessary components:

1. First, moral development theories contain a description and explanation for sequential progression. In language development, for example, children babble consonant-vowel combinations before they can intentionally produce words, and they must make a symbol-referent connection before producing meaningful sentences.

Sequential progression in moral development theories includes a move from focusing on self to focusing on others in addition to self. The progression is also from a heteronomous stance, in which right and wrong are defined externally, to an autonomous stance in which morally mature persons have internalized values and are able to use reflective judgment in determining whether or not to follow a moral rule or in explaining the meaning and relevance of the rule.

2. Universality is a second component. Moral development theories are dependent on the concept of universal values. If human beings develop morally in a way that is analogous to the way they develop in other aspects, the correctness of the theory is dependent on having it hold up cross-culturally. Development theories must also be culturally sensitive, however. Two infants may conform to a single developmental description of language acquisition, although one ends up speaking Japanese and the other Swahili.

The combination of universality and sequential progression explains why people cease developing as well as how they do develop. Development of any kind beyond a rudimentary level is dependent on the context in which the person is developing and on the capacities that are encouraged or discouraged.

Superb athletic performance requires attention toward developing physical ability beyond the rudimentary level. Moral excellence requires training and encouragement beyond a conventional level. It is consistent with development theories to find persons or groups within a society who lack the ability to communicate beyond the most rudimentary level, who fall far short of norms for physical fitness, or whose moral reasoning is at a preconventional level. A person may have the natural capacity for a level of development yet never attain that level. And he or she certainly will mature in an environment that favors one type of development over another.

3. The developmental stage limits a person's ability to understand more mature levels of development. Although a person will not be able to

understand or use higher levels of development than one has attained, he or she will understand, sometimes use, and often recognize the inadequacies of the less complex developmental levels. By analogy, a novice tennis player will not be able to understand or use the highly polished moves of the tennis professional. The pro, however, will understand the basic skills and, on occasion, will make a very basic mistake.

4. Moral development theories assume that humans grow to goodness naturally, just as they grow to physical and cognitive maturity. Wilson (1993) calls this the "moral sense" (p. 12). To say that people have a moral sense is not the same thing as saying that they are innately good. A moral sense must compete with other senses that are natural to humans—the desire to survive, acquire possessions, indulge in sex, or accumulate power—in short, with self-interest narrowly defined. How that struggle is resolved will differ depending on character, on circumstances, and the cultural and political tendencies of the day. But saying that a moral sense exists is the same thing as saying that humans, by their nature, are potentially good.

Wilson's notion here mirrors what I have earlier termed the human analogy. The moral sense is dependent on the realization that one being is like another in wishing to avoid harm. The moral sense is further dependent on an empathy that as I would not want this to happen to me, I do not wish it for others either.

Examples of Moral Development theory[5]

Kohlberg's Theory

Lawrence Kohlberg, a Harvard professor and psychologist until his death in January 1987, advanced the moral development theory of Jean Piaget. Piaget (1952), a developmental psychologist, recognized that children used a progressively more sophisticated manner of moral reasoning that complemented their intellectual and cognitive development. Kohlberg (1984) describes six stages of development within three societal levels.

The first level is termed preconventional. At this level, the actor believes that the rightness or wrongness of an action is determined by an authority figure who is able to give pleasure or punishment to the actor. We see this in the action of very small children all the time and by people of all ages when caught in life-threatening situations.

The first stage in this preconventional level is "fear of punishment." The actor believes that the "right" action is the one that avoids pain or punishment. The second stage of this level is "hope for reward." Now, the actor believes that the right action is the one that is likely to result in something good for the actor.

The second level is called conventional because it describes the level of morality on which most people operate most of the time. At this level, the actor has shifted his or her perception of a moral arbitrator from an authority figure to the community at large. In the first conventional stage (Stage 3), the actor determines what is right by looking for peer approval. The actor is seeking acceptance by others rather than attempting to avoid pain or achieve direct pleasure.[6] By Stage 4, the actor has respect for a system that is larger than any one authority figure. Loyalty to the system and adherence to its rules also replace the group as the basis for determining moral prohibition.

With appropriate experiences, actors can reach the postconventional level and operate on that basis at least some of the time. This is the move from heteronomy to autonomy. Actors at this level use reflective judgment to reason through to their own sense of what makes an action right. Whatever an individual, group, or society might say is right, the actor recognizes the individual's responsibility to reason through his or her own beliefs and actions. Again, this level is made up of two stages. The first stage (Stage 5) involves an understanding of social utility. What makes an action right is that it can be decided impartially, without specific loyalties, to bring about the greatest social benefit. The last of Kohlberg's stages, Stage 6, includes an understanding of the principles of justice. Now the actor uses these principles (fairness, equity) to determine moral permissibility and prohibition. The principles of justice are based on the perception that individual human beings have equal and inviolate worth.

Gilligan's Theory

Carol Gilligan (1982b), a protege of Kohlberg, argues that Kohlberg's scope of morality is incomplete. Kohlberg's developmental scale is based on a notion of rights and equity. Gilligan developed a complementary theory that illustrates the progression of a person's caregiving, which she contends is also part of the moral sphere. Gilligan (1982b) provides a developmental scheme that contains "the language of responsibilities that sustains connection" (p. 210).

Gilligan's developmental scheme is based on an analysis of women's development, which had been largely ignored in Kohlberg's theory. However, Gilligan does not argue for gender-based differences in moral development. Indeed, the integrated, morally mature person would exhibit both feminine and masculine structures. Gilligan (1982a) says,

> To understand how the tension between responsibilities and rights sustains the dialectic of human development is to see the integrity of two disparate modes of experience that are in the end connected. While an ethic of justice proceeds from the premise of equality—that everyone should be treated the same, an ethic of care rests on the premise of nonviolence—that no one should be hurt. In the representation of maturity, both perspectives converge in the realization that just as inequality adversely affects both parties in an unequal relationship, so too violence is destructive for everyone involved. (p. 174)

The developmental sequence, in Gilligan's (1978, pp. 65-80) theory, progresses from care of self to care of others to a final mature level of integrating the care for self with the care for others.

In an ethics of care, the actor at Level 1 is concerned with individual survival. One perceives oneself as powerless and a victim. One is unable to care for onself or for anyone else. The first transition in her moral growth is to a state of "responsibility." During this transition, the person for the first time tries on the feelings of others. One begins to think about others' needs in determining what is right and wrong but tends to blame others when one fails, instead of taking responsibility for one's own action.

At Level 2, the actor is still unable to care adequately for oneself but has learned that sacrificing oneself for others is the way to be judged "good." At the next transitional state, she or he begins to see that inserting oneself into moral decisions is not selfish but honest. She or he begins to realize that caretaking can include oneself. Last, at Level 3, the person no longer perceives a conflict between caring for oneself and caring for others. Nonviolence is perceived as the unifying principle, with the moral objective of minimizing pain and harm for everyone.

Problems for the Unified Theory

Values Versus Valuing Process

Whereas ethicists tend to identify universally held values, loosely described as a negative obligation to avoid actions that cause evils without justification, moral development theorists emphasize a valuing process. Value theory has traditionally been concerned more with process than outcome. Dewey, the American father of value theory, held "an interpretation of value in terms of active reflective choice that refashions or creates outcomes for human demands, desires, satisfactions, enjoyments. The central phenomenon is the valuational process" (Edel, 1988, p. 18).

Rather than seeing the means versus ends dichotomy as a conflict in interpretation, moral development theory, as illustrated by Kohlberg and Gilligan, provides an explanation of how the two converge. The morally mature person not only uses her or his own reflective judgment to reach decisions about what is right, according to Kohlberg's scheme, she or he also reasons rightly. Moral development in this way can be understood as analogous to mathematical development. A child understands a particular math concept when she or he can both reach the right answer and reason on her or his own why this is so. Appreciating each person (including oneself) as intrinsically deserving of respect and care both reflects an integration of Kohlberg's and Gilligan's morally mature person and the universal value of requiring justification if one is to cause evils.

Are Moral Development Theories Cross-Cultural?

Some researchers have argued that Kohlberg's theory fails to represent the notion of morality as expressed in other cultures. For example, Snarey and Keijo (1991) argue, "building on the classic work of Ferdinand Tönnies, we theorize that Kohlberg's model incompletely represents a communitarian or *Gemeinschaft* voice" (p. 396). The authors conclude that

> Future research needs to be maximally open to discovering different modes of moral reasoning, especially at the postconventional level. Such a constructive approach to future research will result in a more adequate and holistic understanding of the universality and variation in moral development. (p. 421)

This is an argument of incompleteness, not of flaws within the theory itself. Gilligan also argued incompleteness. The sphere of morality may be larger than any particular development theory has yet described.

What Counts as Moral Maturity?

Kohlberg has received a variety of criticisms, most often directed at his notion of a more sophisticated morality.[7] Because the Kantian-Rawlsian concept of reversibility-universality is not fully accepted as the pinnacle of moral maturity, the notion that one would necessarily develop in that way is suspect. Although moral development theory is consistent with descriptive data on universal values, intersubjective agreement is certainly not the equivalent of objective truth. In some respects, there is no answer to this problem; there is no way of "proving" the correctness of Kohlberg's Stage 6.

However, the lack of proof does not constitute a fatal flaw for a unified theory of universal values and moral development nor does it constitute a fatal flaw for the notion of moral development. The developmental explanation of language acquisition does, indeed, both explain and predict how one progresses to a certain level of language production and comprehension. Theories of language development do not adequately explain how and why one becomes a poet, a sports announcer, or a skilled litigator—three occupations that require language excellence. Theories of development do not adequately explain how these dramatically different forms can all be reflective of linguistic excellence.

In an analogous way, theories of moral development can be appreciated for providing structures to help us understand how it is that people progress to a point of understanding the basic universal value, "don't cause evils without justification." The theories can help us understand how and why it is that some people never reach a certain level. Only when compared with what we expect all people to achieve is it possible to appreciate true moral excellence in its variety of examples.

Conclusions

Moral development theories have their origin in observations of the growth processes of moral consciousness in individual children. The observed facts and progressions have then been subjected to philosophical reflections, from which theories emerged. The empirical roots of moral development theories are still visible and cause an obvious problem for their universal applicability. The original scientific observations were narrow; they did not sufficiently cover moral development in, say, African or Asian cultures.

The most pressing challenge for moral development theories today, however, is not their cross-cultural verifications but their grounding in philosophical anthropology. Significant new insights on how humans develop into moral beings can be gained from a vigorous rational analysis of common human nature. In this process, some clear contours of universal principles can be discovered behind and within the kaleidoscope of different cultural colors.

The social nature of the human being, namely the need for being-in-community, is the most fundamental philosophical premise from which to start. Moral reasoning and consciousness are not, primarily, about our individual selves but about judgments on actions, or intended actions, regarding others. The socialization of the moral being takes place in the individual's relationships with others. Families and peer groups are obviously of special importance in this process. The central issue of moral development, however, is not the well-being or self-fulfillment of the individual but how individuals become members of groups and communities with an acceptable and accepted moral ethos.

Most if not all cultures, and particularly non-Western cultures, have a rich depository of wisdom on what it means to become and be a member of a moral community. That moral heritage, often enshrined in wisdom literature, both written and oral, has over space and time been variously adapted and fashioned into moral guidelines with the intention of upholding desired moral standards in different communities. These multicultural expressions of moral wisdom and their moral norms—on the processes of becoming members of moral communities—could greatly enhance and challenge moral development theories advanced in North America and Europe.

This point can be illustrated by Gilligan's theory of an ethics of care. That no one shall intentionally be harmed without reason is the minimum requirement, resulting in negative precepts such as thou shalt not kill or steal. The richness of Gilligan's theory is on the positive side, namely, that part of being human is to care for each other. Ways of caring, and the priorities within, are expressed by myriad norms across cultures—from simple common courtesy and respect for others to the active commitment toward those whose lives are most vulnerable.

Following Gilligan's theory, Benhabib (1986) introduces the concept of the "concrete other" in contrast to the "generalized other." The concrete other

> requires us to view each and every rational being as an individual with a concrete history, identity, and effective-emotional constitution. In assuming this standpoint, we abstract from what constitutes our commonality and seek to understand the distinctiveness of the other. We seek to comprehend the needs of the other, their motivations, what they search for, and what they desire. Our relation to the other is governed by the norm of *complementarity* (rather than formal reciprocity). Each is entitled to expect and to assume from the other forms of behavior through which the other feels recognized and confirmed as a concrete individual being with specific needs, talents, and capacities. (p. 341)

The moral criteria guiding such interactions are, according to Benhabib (1986), "love, care, sympathy, and solidarity" (p. 341). This ethics of care not only confirms the other's general humanity but his or her human individuality.

The ontological center from which an ethics of care emanates is crucial for the theme of universal values. Gilligan's moral axiom is that person-hood must be respected and revered and that human life must be cared for and cultivated. The ideal moral community or society is a caring commu-nity, in which all life is respected and cared for within its concrete context.

Nothing then is more genuinely universal than the essential structure of human nature with its quest for the preservation and development of life, one's own and life in common. Both depend on, and are made possible by, developing patterns of caring relationships to other living beings. These patterns can be called ethical protonorms of communication or universal human values. Moral development theories steeped in philosophical an-thropology thus synthesize how humans become morally what they are ontologically. Or to put it more succinctly, how humans learn to conform to their being.

Wilson (1993, p. 7), as noted earlier, is right not to seek universality in moral norms but in the moral sense, that is, in the claims that humans everywhere make on each other as a matter of course—from the claim of "let me live," to the expectations of conviviality that are based on certain irreducible moral principles, such as caring for each other. The awareness of these specieswide moral claims are crucial when cultures lose their authentic and authoritative moral traditions. When societies are no longer clear about the type of moral order that should prevail, the moral development of children is jeopardized, and moral character formation is hampered. The history of civilizations is littered with cultural aberrations and periods of moral decline and decadence. The same holds true, of course, for individual families and peer groups that influence the process of moral development.

This raises the question about the genetically built-in moral "hardware" or moral compass, which, in general, appears to continue functioning regardless of the moral degradations in the cultural environment. It also raises the question of the collective search for a new, utopian, moral community to which history attests. There seems to be no other satisfactory explanation for these phenomena than the assumption that certain universal values pertain to the human condition as such. It is on this implicit assumption about human nature that moral development theories ultimately rest.

Notes

1. Valuing behavior appears in other sentient creatures but will not be discussed in this essay.

2. The terms *ethics* and *morals* are used synonymously here. Ethics derives from the Greek "ethos" and morals derives from the Latin "mores." Both are typically translated as "custom."

3. This is admittedly an anthropocentric view of ethics, one that places humans as the necessary condition for something being a victim. Although many theories include environment and animals as entities that can be harmed without human victimization, such beliefs are not universally expressed in ethical theories. However, a theory that does not include harm caused to humans is missing the necessary (if not sufficient) condition for something being an ethical theory. It is, therefore, the obvious starting point for building a notion of universal values.

4. *Reason* is obviously a philosophically loaded word and is meant here as a placeholder for some theory of justification. Specific theories of justification (which answer the question, "when is it morally permissible to violate a generally held moral rule?") will differ among cultures and even within a particular culture.

5. This description of theories appeared previously in Elliott (1991).

6. It is easy to understand that at the transition between Stage 2 and 3, the actor when asked might explain that he or she seeks the acceptance of others because that's what makes him or her feel good.

7. See, for example, Modgil and Modgil (1985).

References

Benhabib, Seyla. (1986). *Critique, norm and utopia: A study of the foundations of critical theory.* New York: Columbia University Press.

Cantril, Handley. (1965). *The pattern of human concerns.* New Brunswick, NJ: Rutgers University Press.

Edel, Abraham. (1988). *The concept of value and its travels.* In M. Murphey & I. Berg (Eds.), *Values and value theory in twentieth century America* (pp. 12-36). Philadelphia: Temple University Press.

Elliott, Deni. (1991, Autumn). Moral development theories and the teaching of ethics. *Journalism Educator, 46*(3), 18-24.

Gert, Bernard. (1988). *Morality: A new justification for the moral rules.* New York: Oxford University Press.

Gilligan, Carol. (1978). *In a different voice: Women's conception of self and morality.* In Harvard Educational Review (Ed.), *Stage theories of cognitive and moral development: Criticisms and applications* (pp. 52-89). Cambridge, MA: Harvard Educational Review.

Gilligan, Carol. (1982a). *In a different voice: Psychological theory and women's development.* Cambridge, MA: Harvard University Press.

Gilligan, Carol. (1982b). New maps of development: New visions of maturity. *American Journal of Orthopsychiatry, 52*(2), 199-212.

Kohlberg, Lawrence. (1981). *The philosophy of moral development.* San Francisco, CA: Harper & Row.

Kohlberg, Lawrence. (1984). *The psychology of moral development.* San Francisco, CA: Harper & Row.

Modgil, Sohan, & Modgil, Celia. (1985). *Lawrence Kohlberg: Consensus and controversy.* Philadelphia: Falmer.

Montefiore, Alan. (1988). Values. In B. Almond & B. Wilson (Eds.), *Values* (pp. 13-28). Atlantic Highlands, NJ: Humanities Press.

Piaget, Jean. (1952). *The origins of intelligence in children.* New York: International Universities Press.

Snarey, John, & Keijo, Kurt. (1991). *Handbook of moral behavior and development: Vol. 1. Theory* (pp. 395-425). Hillsdale, NJ: Lawrence Erlbaum.

Wilson, James Q. (1993). *The moral sense.* New York: Free Press.

PART II

Protonorms Across Cultures

CHAPTER 5

The Basic Norm of Truthfulness

Its Ethical Justification and Universality[1]

DIETMAR MIETH

Truthfulness is generally considered the basic norm of communication. Is this true? And what consensus exists about it? Or do we accept this norm only if there is no other, greater, and more important norm—such as love of neighbor, or the protection of life, or the assertion of one's own authentic selfhood? And what about another dimension of communication, namely, to bring into communications the flower of imagination, the creativity of fantasy, and the skill of clever lying when telling good stories? Why are we prepared in everyday life to invoke at one moment the norm of truthfulness and at the next moment the right to lie, depending on circumstances and contexts? I do not pretend to give answers to all these questions. But I hope to shed some light on our contradictory approaches to communication behavior.

The first part of this chapter justifies truthfulness as a protonorm. The second presents an explication of truthfulness in terms of ethical responsibility. The third part places truthfulness in the context of different ethical theories. The fourth section, presupposing the universality of negation, examines misdemeanors against the truth imperative. The final part designates fundamental duties that might arise regarding the basic norm of truthfulness.

Justifying Truthfulness as a Basic Norm

Let us suppose that truthfulness—the recognition of the obligatory nature of truth in our own practices—is interpreted differently in different cultures and among different ethical schools. However, in every instance where it is assumed that the basic norm of truthfulness does *not* apply categorically, this noncategorical validity is nevertheless regarded as an exception to the rule. In other words, we have a duty to justify this nonvalidity in individual instances. For example, if we say that in an Asian culture, something like "face-saving" represents a higher norm than the basic norm of truthfulness, then this would still amount to an attempt to justify the deviation from truthfulness. Even if the basic norm of truthfulness were to be set aside for the sake of love—for instance, at a sickbed or for the sake of a falsely understood loyalty to one's community (in the case of pious lies on the part of church leaders, for example)—the same thing would hold true.

Sometimes, truthfulness is set aside because of a particular style of communication in which, even if we lie, we are telling the truth because everyone knows perfectly well about the lie's existence. Konrad Adenauer is said to have once made a disrespectful remark about Mendès France, a Jew who at the time (1954) was Prime Minister of France. When Adenauer's statement was publicized, there was an official inquiry on the part of the French Embassy, and a member of the Chancellery was supposed to confirm whether Adenauer had indeed said it or not. The employee truthfully confirmed that the statement had been made and was at once dismissed from his post. He ought to have said that Adenauer would never have said such a thing; it went without saying that the French merely wanted a diplomatic *démenti* and not the truth. In a communication genre of this kind, there is no longer any naked truth but, let us say, a truth of contextual communication.

The important point, in my view, is that although these instances depart from the truth, each of them nonetheless represents an exception to a generally valid imperative. The imperative is recognized in advance—otherwise, there would be no need to justify such exceptions as special cases. Therefore, the first justification of truthfulness as a protonorm lies in the fact that those who relativize such a norm are indirectly recognizing it by offering reasons to justify their limitation of its categorical validity.

A second general justification of moral obligation is presented by Klaus Steigleder (1992) in his book on the "moral ought." For brevity's sake, I shall call this a justification based on the principle of recognition. In fact, it concerns the principle of constitutive consistency. Given the presuppositions accepted by those involved, it follows that to carry out their activities, they must respect mutual rights and privileges both for themselves and for the other actors. Accordingly, we may say that there is a basic respect owed to one another by people engaged together in activities. It then follows from this principle of respect that they also owe it to each other to describe the reality about which they communicate—or the relations by way of which they communicate with each other—in such a way that they can maintain these rights and duties reciprocally. Hence, the basic norm of truthfulness would be among the first norms deriving from this principle of recognition.

Kant (1990) provides a third justification. As one who supports the argument from convergence, my position is that one single approach to justification cannot in itself be compelling. There are always limits to plausibility. I therefore call to mind Kant's (1990) approach to justification on the basis of duties toward oneself:

> A lie is a violation of duty towards oneself more than towards others. It is wide of the mark to say that duties towards oneself rank lower; on the contrary they rank highest and are most important of all, for before ever explaining what duty to oneself is, we may already ask what more can be expected of a person if that person dishonors himself or herself? (p. 244)[2]

Here we have a picture of persons making themselves the means to an end. This is the end-in-oneself formula of the categorical imperative applied to individuals in their actions relating to themselves. This formula runs, "So act as to treat humanity, both in your own person and in another, always as an end, and never only as a means." The point of "in your own person" is that by making myself the means for deception, I take my own person out of the condition of being an "end in myself." Instead, it is given a role that endangers communication and thus destroys the regard for reason in every human being. In this moment, I have failed to respect my duty toward myself as a rational being who is an "end in myself." Kant does not think that the question of truthfulness comprises only the question of one's duty toward oneself, but he elaborated especially on this duty. Thus, this categorical duty toward oneself rests basically on all of us bearing humanity within us—*humanity* meaning a rational nature. In Kant's practical lectures on ethics, we also find reflections on how far possibilities or reasons exist for assigning priority to other norms where there is a conflict of duties. But he does not allow for other norms in his basic argumentation regarding deception (Kant, 1990).

A Hermeneutical Consideration

Other forms of justification could be added to these three.The type of justification I personally prefer is hermeneutical. It is based on a hermeneutic of the need for meaningfulness. The starting point here is the idea that morality is the reflected recognition of an anthropological need. In other words, in my moral consciousness and in moral actions, I try to translate anthropological presuppositions into the language of moral obligation. It is well known that it is problematic to reason from what is to that which ought to be. Nor ought one draw conclusions in a one-way deductive process. The important thing is translating empirical plausibilities into clear (moral) obligations. This happens only through structural correspondence and analogy, not through deductive logic.

Truth exists as a human need in two ways: First, in the sense that human beings do not wish to lose their relation to tangible reality. They have to live in that reality; they cannot live constantly in an abstract state removed from it. Although this sometimes happens, it is not the model for successful human life but is rather a form of degeneration. Second, human beings feel that communication between them is worthy of respect only if the criterion of truth is given its proper place. Otherwise, communication between human beings is felt to be disrespect. Thus, we can speak of truth as a threefold need of human beings: in relation to reality, to oneself, and to other people.

If we make Seev Gasiet's (1980) theory of necessity our starting point, we can situate this necessity for truth under the need for meaningfulness. He distinguishes between four categorical necessities: the need to survive, the need for social recognition, the need for personal relations, and the need for meaningfulness. The type of need I have so far outlined—the need for truth as a relation to oneself, as a relation in terms of communication, and as a relation to reality—is part of the need for meaningfulness. Truthfulness in this sense is simply the practical recognition of a state of meaningfulness in relations between human beings. Thus, truth becomes a good that is morally worth striving for and is therefore also a moral obligation.

In a hermeneutic of truth, we must heed the different forms in which theories of truth seek to understand it. These theories are well known: truth as an approximation to reality, as communication and consensus, as coherence and contextuality, and as narration. I cannot deal in detail with these different forms of truth. I merely set out the thesis that even here, a certain perspectivism or an argument from convergence is rewarding, because each of these theories has a different scope. Consequently, they are interconvertible in so far as they are not understood as exclusive alternatives. For example, it is important that a coherence theory of truth—which sees truth as a conclusively self-consistent system of thought—should also take into account truth's contextuality. Otherwise, we could end up in systems of truth-coherence that no longer have anything to do with the contexts of life. This can be illustrated from the moral doctrines of the Roman Catholic Church.

In addition, narration includes truth in the sphere of imagination. Narratives do not lie, because storytelling is not only about reality but equally about our imagination concerning reality. The real world of humankind is made up of both facts and fiction and essentially about dreams. The world of a child, for example, consists of the reality that surrounds children and the fantasy they construct about it. Narratives, therefore, include the truth contained in the sphere of imagination. In my view, it is important not to omit the imagination as a locus for the truth.

The hermeneutic of truth thus distinguishes between a variety of perspectives: faithfulness to reality, consensus, coherence, contextuality, and narration. If this richness of content in the hermeneutic of truth is accepted, we must recognize from the start that truth is more than a mere piece of information. Truth cannot be reduced to a hermeneutic of information. To draw a parallel by way of illustration, the hermeneutic of perception has a similar wealth of content. We can perceive something affectively (with our feelings), that is, feel it is genuine. We can perceive something cognitively, that is, recognize it as logically conclusive. And we can perceive something practically, that is, by actually doing it. These three elements—the affective, the cognitive, and the practical—are part of a performative understanding that enables the truth in its different hermeneutical facets to be incorporated into practical living, through the very fact of perceiving (*wahrnehmen*), or taking (*nehmen*) something to be true (*wahr*).

What I have described so far in terms of understanding—for, in fact, hermeneutics is quite simply understanding meaning—can be translated into the ethical plausibility of obligation. The ethical field reflects recognized anthropological needs in parallel language. Each instance of empirical plausibility can be observed in what is obligatory, and each clear indication of an obligation can be observed in empirical reality, as it were, on two parallel paths.

One can understand the model of recognizing truth as meaningfulness in the ethical sphere, first in the form of effort and second in the form of obligation. Here I draw on a distinction made by Hans Kramer (1992), where he distinguishes a form of the ethical that he calls *striving*—striving for success in life or for happiness—and a form of the ethical that is subject to the claims of obligation or of duty (more or less in the Kantian tradition). Both have a claim to empirical plausibilities on the parallel path of the ethical. If in the sphere of ethics I reflect on the basic norm of truthfulness using the paradigm of striving, then clearly approximation to reality is more important than, for instance, the standpoint of faithfulness to the truth in communication. The latter is much more strongly felt as an externally impinging obligation that exists in humanity's claims on an individual. However, striving for one's own good fortune and success takes account of truth to a much greater extent as an approximation to reality. The loss of reality would in fact cancel out my own effort for success and good fortune. Thus, in the field of morality, the ethic of effort and the ethic of obligation may each emphasize different components in the empirical plausibility of a hermeneutic of truth.

In summary, this attempt to approach truthfulness—veracity—through a hermeneutical justification of the basic moral norm is independent of a justification based on the principle of recognition and of one based on duty to oneself. But, on the other hand, it does not exclude these approaches, and it remains open to other approaches. It is thus an argument from convergence—not a categorical justification based on deductive thinking, but different approaches to justification in combination.

Moral Responsibility in
Deploying the Basic Norm

Truthfulness that is given a hermeneutical justification must be interpreted in terms of moral responsibility for actions in specific fields. In other words, such interpretation cannot be reduced to one basic attitude applying to all circumstances. What are the fundamental factors in interpreting the protonorm of truthfulness in terms of moral responsibility? Fundamentally, *truthfulness* means commitment to the truth on the part of the individual (intrapersonal), to the truth between individuals (interpersonal), and to the truth in relation to reality.

The multiple relationship of interpersonal responsibility that we may look at first is the responsibility of a subject (P1) to herself or himself and to another subject (P2), in relation to the content of information in which what is meant by truth cannot be reduced solely to the content of what is communicated. This four-figure relation has been summarized as follows by Dietrich Bonhoeffer (1977) in his reflections on how one can speak the truth: (a) by knowing where I stand (P1's situation also includes his or her intrapersonal truth), (b) by knowing to whom I am speaking (P2 as the person addressed), (c) by knowing what I am talking about (this will be developed later), and (d) by knowing what rules apply to this realization of the truth in terms of the criterion of responsibility.[3]

Together with these basic factors, others must be taken into account in terms of moral responsibility.

One additional factor concerns the area of applicability or validity in the immediate sphere of encounter between human beings. We know those with whom we speak or have relatively close relations. Then there is the question of applicability in the mesosphere (or middle area), that is, in group communication. Here we might think of groups such as the scientific community, that is, specialized scientific communication with its particular ethical demands. Last, there is the question of the remote sphere, the public sphere where anonymity prevails. Here another structure of mutual intercourse applies, which is determined to a greater extent by abstractness and is accompanied by legal structures and by institutions.

These three spheres of communication create differences in how we state the truth and in the type of claim truth makes. A discreet, personal truth pertains to the immediate sphere; a bold experimental statement belongs in the specialized field of scientific examination; in public law, a statement may be refused if it incriminates the persons making it or those close to them. But a statement may also be demanded in the public interest if it is a matter of getting at the truth. Arriving at the truth by means of evidence in court depends on the acceptance of that evidence so that in law, truth differs from empirical plausibility in a number of respects. Hence, the ranges and structures of communication play different parts in establishing the claim to truth in various cases.

Time is another important factor and is mostly overlooked in connection with morally responsible interpretation. For example, if someone has given an interview that is to appear the next day in the press, the journalist's task is to summarize it in such a way that the main points intended by the interviewee come across. But the journalist has only limited time to do this; that is, decisions must be taken that possibly involve a margin of uncertainty and doubt: What did the interviewee really mean? How is this to be communicated in terms of the public's interest in the subject matter and in what the interviewee said? The manner of quoting—what context was left out and what was included—represents decisions made in time. In other words, we cannot talk abstractly about the capacity for truth in practical questions nor can we talk about morally responsible interpretation without reference to time; these must be seen in relation to practical time scales. If we do not take time into account, we are limiting our interpretation of the truth-claim in terms of the complexities of moral responsibility.

A third additional factor is the degree or stage of moral consciousness. Piaget's and Kohlberg's theories on the degrees of moral consciousness distinguish in principle three fundamental stages: acting as we please and with reference to punishment, acting in accordance with law and order, and acting in accordance with autonomously selected maxims that we ourselves have laid down and accepted. Action cannot always be situated at the highest stage of ethical autonomy. We have an ethical task to make our own interpretation of moral responsibility in such a way that we try to elevate the question of the truth's moral character to the highest level of awareness. This is an element in the moral education of the personality. To use Dietrich Bonhoeffer's (1977) formulation of this personal relation, it has to do with the question of knowing where I stand.

And last, a fourth factor merits attention—the question of the addressee. As with the distinction between the immediate, intermediate, and remote spheres, we must distinguish between individual subjects, communities, publics, and institutions. For instance, dealing with institutions in the communication of truth poses the question of how someone fills in bureaucratic forms. Considerations come into play here that then certainly also have to be seen in terms of the time and space factor (considerations, incidentally, which would probably have no part to play in the immediate sphere). By way of example, note how one presents oneself in an application for employment.[4]

Truthfulness in Different Ethical Theories

Within the scope of this chapter, an adequate presentation of ethical theories cannot be given. But it is necessary to clarify the scope and universality of the basic norm of truthfulness, as found in the claims of ethical theories.

It is well known that Kant proposed transposing the basic norm of truthfulness into a deontological key. In his famous essay, *On the Supposed Right to Lie out of Love for Humanity* [*Über ein vermeintes Recht, aus Menschenliebe zu Lügen*), Kant (1986) argues against the justification of lying as an exception. He appeals to an obligatory quality in the truth even in circumstances in which the safety of a friend's life is put at risk. Kant advocated the fundamental validity of telling the truth, even if there is a conflict of duties: Tell the truth whether it is convenient or inconvenient, regardless of the consequences. We also find this explicit stance in scriptural statements: "Let your yea be yea and your nay nay."

The fact that a clear stance in the light of competing norms is sustained in a theory of deontology, as Jean-Claude Wolf (1988) shows, presupposes that the duty to tell the truth is conceived here as analogous to a contractual obligation. The idea that *pacta sunt servanda* [agreements are to be kept] affects duties both toward oneself and toward others. Jean-Claude Wolf objects that we may question whether contractual obligations apply to all circumstances and in every respect. Where there are competing norms, the issue is not the norm's validity but whether another norm applies and has precedence. In a clash of duties, the issue is whether another duty—for instance, the protection of life and love—is to be preferred over the duty to truth. If so, the latter continues to be valid but may no longer be the morally dominant norm in this instance.

Deontological theory, however, is well aware that situations exist in which the obligatory nature of truth has to be relativized. Using an example provided by Jean-Claude Wolf (1993), this can actually be demonstrated from Kant (1990) himself:

> In so far as I am compelled by violence used against me to make an admission, and illegitimate use is made of what I have said, and I cannot save myself by keeping silent, a lie is a defense. The misused statement I have been forced to make gives me the right to defend myself. (p. 244)

This is in line with the reflection that in this specific instance, which is likewise categorical, the dictum relating to self-defense applies.

We find similar considerations in other fields. Even strict deontological conceptions—such as the Roman Catholic moral theology of the universal Roman magisterium—really cannot answer the question whether norms other than those usually evoked apply in specific situations. The so-called "Bosnian pill" is a celebrated example. This refers to Cardinal Palazzini's suggestion in 1993 that if women are raped, they may take the pill in self-defense because self-defense against an unjustified attack supersedes all other norms. In this instance, the categorical version of a deontological norm manifestly means that the norm with primary relevance stands. Thus, much depends on the definition of the moral problem to decide what norms are relevant.

It goes without saying that teleologists—who look exclusively at the consequences of actions—have always kept sight of this. In the teleological approach, telling the truth can be modified by the consequences. From this perspective, everyone should ask what observing the duty to tell the truth means for those affected by it—for the individuals themselves, for other people, sometimes also for the institutions concerned. The right to be allowed to learn the truth—which the principle of recognition asserts—can be forfeited. The torturer has no right to expect the truth nor does the indiscreet person. The latter is an example occurring also in Kant, which Dietrich Bonhoeffer (1977) explains in the following way: A teacher asks a pupil during a morning lesson, "Did your father come home drunk again yesterday?" If, although that is what happened, the pupil answers "no," it is a defense against indiscretion. It is a statement referring not to the reality but to defense against indiscretion in a situation of dependence. Thus, the truth of the statement can only be ascertained by way of the context, though it is dangerous to substitute styles of communication for the correspondence of content to reality.

Such reflections introduce circumstances and consequences into the issue of the truth's obligatory nature. And we may wonder whether there really is a contradiction between teleologists and deontologists. This author would even be bold enough to say that—if we look closely at the matter—it turns out that for deontologists, the norm applies where it applies (as we have just seen). Moreover, teleologists make a judgment about which rules have priority given the circumstances, and such reflection cannot be omitted by deontologists, either.

Our reflections so far derive from universalist theories. We may regard the ethic of discourse in the theory of communication as a third universalist theory. Its basis is that in the criterion of a supposed *a priori* of the social group that is communicating, the capacity for truthfulness must be present as a prerequisite for, and expression of, consensus. This approach to truth-discourse in communication theory presupposes that truth is a condition for successful communication. It is parallel with the obligatoriness of truth—understood not in reified or fixed terms but as fair [or just] communication through which agreement can be reached, because it is morally correct and has a claim to truth. Here truth seems to be subordinate to, and derived from, communicative justice. Logically, the approach in terms of communication theory likewise has a universal scope even if one can imagine that modifications in its applicability are possible in certain communicative contexts.

There are ethical theories, however, that are not universalist and see themselves as covering another domain. The first of these theories might be called *perspectivism*. One might illustrate this theory from Nietzsche and his understanding of the obligatoriness of truth, using an example from Akiro Kurosawa's *Rashomon*. In the film sequence, four modes of understanding an event are described. The subject is the rape of a woman and the killing of her husband, a Samurai, by a robber. This robber, the woman, the Samurai, and a farmer who comes on the scene give four different descriptions of the course of events.[5]

According to the perspectivist view, the basic norm of truthfulness does not exist universally as such. Rather, there are only some approximations to reality or another, which may be assumed to show the limitations of

subjectivity and of communication and indeed also the objective limitations. As a result, every individual can perceive only a part of reality as
such. The film raises the question whether it is possible to uphold a total
relativity of truth. It does not push this kind of relativism to extremes,
however, but interprets the different approximations to truth in a way that
leaves the "true" reality open. In the final sequence of the film—where the
question is who will take care of an abandoned child—the criteria of truth
emerge clearly, that is, the promotion of life and humaneness. Such criteria
can provide legitimation for discovering who is being truthful.

These criteria recall an answer Thomas Mann (1977) gave in his essay
on Chekhov: On the one hand, only truth promotes life and on the other
hand, only what promotes life is true. The thesis that "only what promotes
life is true" leads to the question raised at the beginning of this section
when dealing with competing principles: Must not "truth" be ranked at
different levels? Is there not another basic principle that enjoys a higher
status, for example, life, freedom, or love? This question is posed in a new
way from the standpoint of perspectivism. The question is whether perspectivism actually is making a plea for partial norms or whether it is not
merely pleading for another universal standard in cases of conflicting
norms, namely, love.

Second, among the ethical theories that do not at first glance appear to
be universal, *communitarianism* must be mentioned. The idea behind this
concept is that people must recognize reality in terms of the socialization
that exists in their community. The rules under which communication takes
place determine the norm. This means that possible exceptions that must
be justified appear from this point of view to be cultural variants and not
exceptions—face-saving in regions of the Far East, loyalty to the community, the style of communication that alienates the substance of reality, and
so forth. The reflections initially presented on exceptions would then each
pertain to a particular pattern of socialization or to a specific community.
For example, politicians as a community do in fact communicate differently from typical citizens. The author has frequently experienced instances of this, and anyone who expresses surprise when it happens is considered naive.

These are somewhat trivial examples, but the communitarian approach
to the obligatory nature of truth contends that a community that has

emerged historically shapes the way in which the truth's obligatoriness is interpreted as binding. No one will wish to dispute this. Communitarianism may possibly be more faithful to reality than are universal theories precisely when actual morals and actual social behavior are being described. But on the other hand, even among communitarians, it will have to be conceded that the very description of these differences as special—and indeed the stress is on their partial nature (*Partialität*)—does not escape the question about universality. This can most appropriately be called the partial approach to universality, for we cannot isolate partial and universal from each other but can think of them only as binary codes: Those who think of one must of necessity include a definition of the other.

Last, there is a third theory, which, of course, is not to be regarded as excluding others. This can be called *model ethics*. This ethical theory concerns above all the obligation to be truthful as an expressive act. Specifically in connection with the duty toward oneself that Kant had highlighted, the basic norm of truthfulness is presented as consistency within oneself. It may be that in some circumstances, this consistency is so important that certain consequences are accepted that would possibly pose problems in a straightforward weighing up of moral goods. This is true, for instance, in the case of martyrs—to use an example that occurs repeatedly in history. An expressive act of this kind not only ratifies the consistency of a person's own life but also tries to show symbolically, by way of negating a negative, that normal communication has already been corrupted regarding the obligatoriness of truth or truthfulness. Specifically in the context of a form of communication where the truth can be told in the guise of a lie, the role of an expressive action is to set a direct negative against this.[6]

This look at ethical theories and at the scope of their reflections has tried to show that even where the range is seen to be relatively small—in perspectivism, communitarianism, expressive acts (model ethics)—the tendency toward the universal is basically not abandoned. One sees here a confirmation of the initial thesis that the limitations of the scope of universal validity actually demonstrate the superiority of that validity. The reason is that the limitation is always described in terms of a specific partial applicability, for otherwise we would have to argue for the universality of the partial. The impossibility of that kind of logic is the strongest argument for the universal validity of general ethical principles, such as truthfulness.

Sins Against the Truth Imperative

By examining partial perspectives for their range of validity, the tendency to universality has been asserted so far in an argument from convergence. It should be recognized that this tendency can more readily be expressed negatively than positively. Thus, the basic norm of truthfulness can be more effectively maintained if it can be shown in extremes where it would be completely invalidated or where its existence would be endangered. This negative is easier to express than is a comprehensive positive statement of the basic norm of truthfulness. Five examples of this universality *ex negativo* can be adduced.

The first sin against the obligatory nature of truth is its concealment when there are legitimate claims to learn it. This negative rule or prohibition is a formal one. One can debate about legitimate claims as to their content. But where these claims to learn the truth are recognized, there would be a universal, definite norm to the effect that no concealment of truth must take place on this occasion. For example, if I believe that only especially competent people have a right to receive all the information about a particular problem, then I have narrowed the scope of the legitimate claim. But I must then give a reason for restricting it, and generally, that will become very difficult under the criterion of universalization. Not even face-saving would, as a possible exception, say that such a claim does not exist here.

A second example is falsification where knowledge of the facts exists. Falsification here is not the same as concealment or silence. It represents not a passive but an active attitude, an offensive stance. Knowledge of what is correct in communication is transformed into what is incorrect. This occurs, for example, in propaganda activities from totalitarian states or in the rigging of elections and the like. As we all know, something of this kind also takes place in media culture.

And third, there is the assertion of facts in spite of ignorance or only partial knowledge of them. Asserting a truth is a form of communication in which empirically verifiable truths can be expected. In a mode of communication that involves storytelling, that kind of truth is not what we expect to find; hence, the emphasis here is on the communication of empirical truth. In this communication of truth, persons imparting news or information have a duty to assert nothing that has not been verified to the best of their knowledge and belief. This also has to be examined in noncognitive or nonverbal forms of communication because deceptive tactics can also be nonverbal. Nothing must be stated in the mode of certainty that we cannot affirm with certainty. In journalism ethics, this can be a very crucial point, and yet sins against this injunction occur under the constant pressure to provide information at high speed.

A fourth illustration is that of unreasonable expectations when someone adopts a defensive position. In communicating the truth, there is also a right to see the personal, intimate, private sphere as claiming discretion. This kind of reflection is found in Kant (1990); and Bonhoeffer's (1977) example of the child who wards off a teacher's inquiry is, in fact, chosen precisely from this sphere. In communicating the truth, it would be morally wrong to expect information and assert rights when these clash with other legitimate claims that are ranked higher by those involved. But this is to concede in advance that in a conflict between the basic principles of what is right in human terms, the question as to the supremacy of the obligatory nature of truth always has to be looked at afresh, case by case. Otherwise, this duty would be set on a higher plane than the much more general criterion of human dignity.

Fifth, there is exaggeration in communicating the truth. In narrative structures, overdramatizations are in fact possible, and even correct, but they are readily allowed because of the particular narrative as such. For instance, exaggeration in a satire is part and parcel of the mode in which satires are presented. But where the truth is being communicated—that is to say, where people are actively involved in a process of communication by recognizing each other as human beings who can expect the truth—exaggeration and overdramatization are acts of deception.

This section has tried to show that negative universality is built on low-key assertions, which means that they do not hold independently of the circumstances. They are rather rules of thumb that claim validity generally, because the validity of a duty that is recognized as relevant for a particular sphere does not exclude a possible conflict of that duty with other duties.

Duties Toward the Truth Imperative

Fundamental duties, as suggested so far, are neither exclusive nor are they to be understood as exceptionless assertions. Rather, fundamental duties are the general results based on the earlier reflections. There are five, and they can be summarized as follows:

1. The process of approximation to reality must be intensified. This corresponds to the character of plausibility in the theory of truth that tries to apprehend the truth as an approximation to reality.

2. Communicative competence should be promoted, that is, the capacity to perceive reality as a discursive form in which individuals, as participants in communication, can develop specific claims.

3. There is a fundamental duty to establish a balance between coherence and contextuality. This is particularly striking in an example from church life. The abstract coherence theory of truth dominates exclusively in an ethical system governed by a magisterium; this excludes any contextual elements, for example, relative to the norm of the indissoluble nature of marriage. As the author sees it, the balance between coherence and contextuality seems to be something that the life-promoting nature of truth demands.

4. A fourth fundamental duty is advancing the autonomy of moral consciousness among the individuals involved. Theoretical reflection on the stages or degrees of cognitive moral advancement is well known as a basis for understanding this process.

5. The convergence of all fundamental duties is also obvious. When discussing the universality of the truth obligation, it must always be done in convergence with the self-determination of individuals and their dignity, in convergence with solidarity with the weak and marginalized, and moreover, in convergence with justice (the same things must be dealt with in the same way and those that differ must be dealt with in line with their differences). The principle of convergence between our fundamental duties presupposes in fact that the basic norm of truthfulness is never advocated in isolation. It must always be seen from the perspective of bringing it into harmony with other fundamental duties. This does not in any way attenuate the duty to the truth. In the context of reality, the norms that make the duty to the truth coherent from the outset—the principle of recognition, legitimate discourse, life-promoting love—can claim priority only because they help to justify the duty to truth, just as the norm of truth plays a part in justifying them or at least in prohibiting contradiction.

Love, it should be noted, presupposes truth. Love is not truthful if it is instrumental, that is, merely makes use of another person. True love accords full recognition to the person, and his or her story, the past, the present, and the future. Thus every genuine relationship of love contains an inner kind of truthfulness.

Truthfulness vindicates the principle of recognition because respect must be based on truth. There cannot be authentic truthfulness that is outside the context of other ethical principles or basic norms. The universality of the basic norm of truthfulness is guaranteed by its capacity to integrate other duties and norms. And when these norms in turn are integrating truthfulness, they become part of a contextuality that is so rich that those norms can be applied to the complexities of everyday life and every kind of communication.

Notes

1. This chapter was translated from the German by the Language Service of the World Council of Churches.

2. Jean-Claude Wolf (1993) has reexamined Kant's position on this matter. Wolf is the source of the quotation from Kant (1990, p. 244) on the lie as "self-defense" where violence is used to compel an admission.

3. In the initial reflections on justification *ex negativo*, it became apparent that it is manifestly impossible to use one categorical dictum to cover all spheres of activity and all possible human action or to decide about their moral justification on that basis.

4. This has been a very fragmentary attempt to delineate individual factors that play a crucial part in a morally responsible interpretation of truthfulness. Here its purpose is merely illustrative, in the context of fundamental considerations.

5. The problem of perspectives was turned into a marvelous film and was later repeated in an American film version from Hollywood, apparently because it is such an impressive illustration of the theory in question.

6. *Politik wider die Lüge [Politics Against Lies]* is the title of a book by Herwig Büchele (1982), which presents reflections of this kind.

References

Arendt, Hannah. (1967). *Wahrheit und Lüge in der Politik*. Munich-Zürich: Piper Verlag.

Augustinus, Aurelius. (1953). *Die Lüge und Gegen die Lüge* (Ed., Paul Keseling). Würzburg: Augustinius Verlag.

Bien, Günther. (1900). Lüge. In *Historisches Wörterbuch der Philosophie* (Vol. 5, pp. 533-544). Basel: Schwabe Verlag.

Bok, Sissela. (1986). *Lügen: Vom täglichen Zwang zur Unaufrichtigkeit*. Hamburg: Rowohlt Verlag.

Bonhoeffer, Dietrich. (1977). *Ethics* (E. Bethge, Ed., 10th ed.). Munich: Kaiser Verlag.

Büchele, Herwig. (1982). *Politik wider die Lüge: Zur Ethik der Öffentlichkeit*. Vienna: Europa Verlag.

Craemar, Otto. (1933). *Die Christliche Wahrhaftigkeitsforderung und die Frage ihrer Begründung und Begrenzung*. Dresden: Ungelenk Verlag.

Eggensberger, Thomas, & Engel, Ulrich. (Eds.). (1995). *Recherche zwischen Hochscholastik und Postmoderne* (Vol. 9). Mainz: Walterberger Studien, Philosophische Reihe, Grünewald Verlag.

Falkenberg, Gabriel. (1982). *Lügen: Grundzüge einer Theorie sprachlicher Täuschung.* Tübingen: Niemeyer Verlag.

Gasiet, Seev. (1980). *Eine Theorie der Bedürfnisse.* Frankfurt: Campus Verlag.

Geisman, Georg, & Oberer, Hariulf. (Eds.). (1986). *Kant und das Recht der Lüge.* Würzburg: Verlag Königshausen and Neumann.

Kant, Immanuel. (1968). *Die Metaphysik der Sitten* (Karl Vorländer, Ed.). Hamburg: Meiner Verlag.

Kant, Immanuel. (1986). *Über ein vermeintes Recht: Aus Menschenliebe zu Lügen.* Würzburg: Verlag Königshausen & Neumann.

Kant, Immanuel. (1990). *Eine Vorlesung über Ethik* (Gerd Gerhardt, Ed.). Frankfurt: Fischer-Taschenbuch-Verlag.

Kramer, Hans. (1992). *Integrative Ethik.* Frankfurt: Suhrkamp Verlag.

Mann, Thomas. (1977). *Versuch über Tschechov: Ausgewählte Essays.* Frankfurt: S. Fischer Verlag.

Mieth, Dietmar. (1984). Wahrhaftigkeit-Aufrichtigkeit-Glaubwürdigkeit: Die Idee einer ethischen Kultur der Politik. In *Die neuen Tugenden* (pp. 154-169). Düsseldorf: Patmos Verlag.

Mieth, Dietmar. (1989). Warum das Lügen so Schön Ist: Eine Anleitung zu den feineren Formen der Unmoral. *Orientierung* (Zurich), *53*, 73-75.

Müller, Gregor. (1962). *Die Wahrhaftigkeitspflicht und die Problematik der Lüge.* Freiburg-Basel-Vienna: Herder Verlag.

Steigleder, Klaus. (1992). *Die Begründung moralishen Sollens: Ethik in den Wissenschaften* (Vol.5). Tübingen: Attempto Verlag.

Über die Lüge. (1984, December). *Zeitschrift für Literatur, 23*(8) [Special issue].

Wolf, Jean-Claude. (1988). Kant und Schopenhauer über die Lüge. *Zeitschrift für Didaktik der Philosophie, 10*, 69-80.

Wolf, Jean-Claude. (1993). *Wahrheit und Lüge.* Unpublished manuscript.

CHAPTER 6

The Arab-Islamic Heritage in Communication Ethics

MUHAMMAD I. AYISH
HAYDAR BADAWI SADIG

An urgent concern in the global debate over a new world information and communication order during the 1970s and early 1980s centered on incompatible perceptions of communication ethics in Western and Third World nations. Although several attempts had been made toward establishing professional universal codes of ethics in mass communication (MacBride, 1980, p. 243), academic and political discussions of the issue seemed to underscore increasingly irreconcilable attitudes.

With the demise of East-West politics (which for decades had shaped international debates over media issues, including communication ethics) and with new problems confronting modern societies, the quest for answers to important questions of ethical communication has taken on a greater urgency than ever. In the postmodern era of the approaching 21st century, moral universalism—which had failed to account adequately for important human problems in different spheres, including communication—has given way to moral relativism, whereby culturally based ethical orientations are given greater weight. As Benhabib and Dallamayr (1990) note:

> Moral theory is limited, on the one hand, by the macro-institutions of a polity, politics, administration, and the market, within the limits of which choices concerning justice are made. On the other hand, moral theory is limited by culture, its repertory of interpretations of the good life, personality, and socialization patterns. (p. 364)

This chapter discusses basic moral principles of normatively governed behavior that have prevailed in Arab-Islamic history and that have a bearing on communication. These norms are important for understanding the dynamics of communication in the Arab-Islamic heritage and for gaining insight into the modern ethical and legal context in which Arab mass communications operate. It enables us to see more clearly how the particular and universal are interconnected.

Dimensions of Arab-Islamic Morality

Mowlana (1989, pp. 139-140) notes that the ethical thinking practices pertaining to communication in Islamic societies (including Arab societies) are currently based on both religious and secular ethics. Discussions of the issue within the normative religious dimension have taken place within Islamic jurisprudence (*fiqh*) and have been based on ethical views enunciated in the Qur'an and the Sunnah (traditions of the Prophet Muhammad, 568 or 570 to 632 A.D.). They have also drawn on broader philosophical and theological debates pertaining to Arab-Islamic thinking on norms of morality (Jaafar, 1978, p. 352). These Islamic orientations have taken faith in God (*iman*) as a point of departure for understanding ethics.

Discussions of normative secular ethics in Arab history have drawn on works of literature and wisdom that either dominated pre-Islamic Arabia or were introduced as a result of Arab contact with foreign cultures. Jaafar (1978) notes that a good number of virtuous pre-Islamic (*jahilyya*) behavioral patterns, having been imbued with "an Islamic spirit," were accommodated into the new way of life in Arabia, whereas others were either rectified or totally prohibited (p. 343). Those patterns originally centered on the concept of honor as the ultimate source and object of virtue.

Honor-Centered Morality

Pre-Islamic (*jahilyya*) Arabs based their behavior on an unwritten code of law that drew on the dichotomous notions of honor (*sharaf*) and shame (*aib* or *arr*). For centuries, this polarity had delineated the boundaries of the relatively simple Arab moral system. Morality was embedded in practices maximizing honor, whereas shame characterized any behavioral patterns that brought dishonor. Subhi (1969, p. 15) observes that many moral norms that had dominated in the pre-Islamic era were part of the Arab tribal system that was maintained over generations through sanctions. Although the Arab code of morality was never put into writing, its emphasis on physical courage in battle, generosity, hospitality, consanguinity, gallantry, manliness, and preference for the oppressed was widely noted. The attainment of these "virtues" or moral ideals was likely to confer honor on a person, reinforcing the inner ego and gaining public esteem.

That very code, on the other hand, tolerated infanticide, the suppression of women, slavery, revenge, and sensuous acts such as alcoholic consumption and adultery. Qaradawi (n.d.) notes that "the Arabs of the pre-Islamic era led a life of utter confusion relating to the criteria for permitting or prohibiting things and actions" (p. 12). In this male-dominated and class-structured society, ethics drew largely on a deep sense of personal and tribal honor that manifested itself in highly individualistic and outwardly oriented utilitarian norms.

Faith-Centered Morality

With the advent of Islam in the 7th century, the customary outwardly oriented Arabian code of honor was replaced by the inwardly oriented concept of belief (*iman*) in Allah as the cornerstone of Islamic ethics, namely belief in the oneness (*tawhid*) of Allah who alone is worthy of worship, and in Mohammad as the messenger of God, bearing witness to God's message. The notions of honor (*sharaf*) and shame (*aib*) gave way to the Islamic concepts of the permissible (*halal*) and the prohibited (*haram*). As an anchoring point for all Islamic virtues, the concept of belief also serves as a threshold for crossing into the jurisdiction of a comprehensive Islamic law (*sharia'*) that directly relates to the theoretical and practical aspects of morality. Individuals can flourish as moral beings in Islam only within the context of belief in God. Without belief, all acts are vain, a "mere mirage in the waste" (XVIII:105).[1] This ethical system is broad enough to tackle general issues confronting the Islamic community (*umma*) and specific enough to take care of the slightest manifestations of human behavior.

Whereas faith (*iman*) defines man's personal relation to God, the realization of such a relation is termed *ihsan*. According to one of the Prophet's statements, *ihsan* means "you should worship Allah as if you are seeing Him, for He sees you though you do not see Him."[2] This is regarded as the basis of true devotion. It implies that a human being is completely in tune with the divine will. Consequently, humans begin to like what is liked by God and to abhor what is disapproved by Him (Ahmad, 1976, p. 24).

Although the concept of *iman* (faith) denotes an inwardly oriented ethic that stresses the purity of the inner self, the outwardly and action-oriented manifestations of Islamic morality are no less significant. Although *iman* and the devotional rituals are vital for the individual's initiation into Islamic morality, it is not by itself sufficient to qualify for true Muslimhood. This is evident from this Qur'anic verse:

> It is not righteousness to turn your face towards East and West; but it is righteousness to believe in God and the Last Day, and the Angels, and the Book, and the Messengers; to spend of your substance out of love for Him, for your kin, for orphans, for the needy, for the wayfarer, for those who ask, and for the ransom of slaves; to be steadfast in prayer; and practice regular charity; to fulfill the contracts which you have made; and to be firm and patient in pain (or suffering) and adversity, and throughout all periods of panic; such are the people of truth, the God-fearing. (II: 177)

Consistency between attitudes and behavior is a central component of the Islamic ethical system. An action may not acquire moral legitimacy in Islam unless there is an underlying good intention (*niyya*) related to its ultimate goals. *Niyya* is the consciousness of doing things for the sake of God (Radwan, 1993, p. 9). According to the Prophet, "God does not look at your images or money, but at your hearts and acts."[3] In another statement, the Prophet said, "God would not accept any speech unless substantiated by action and would not accept any act unless it is based on intention."[4]

Winning the pleasure of God in this life and on the Day of Judgment have become the highest reward and thus the most outstanding goal of human life in the Islamic ethical system. People are empowered to achieve servility to God through a complex—yet humanly possible—system of morality that spells out what is virtuous (*halal*) and what is evil (*haram*).

As derived from the Qur'an and the Sunnah, the Islamic ethical system draws on what is called *tawhid,* a doctrine of ethical monotheism in which God is viewed as a single being who is also the embodiment of moral virtues in their absolute form. This system seeks to elevate human beings to a divine status through conformity to a wide range of virtues that were manifested in the personality of the Prophet of Islam who is described in the Qur'an as "the exemplar of virtues" (LXVIII: 4) and a "perfect model" (XXXIII: 21).

Basic Arab-Islamic Moral Norms

When Arabs embraced Islam, they did not relinquish good customary ethical values and practices but placed them into a framework of belief in the one God. Secular and Islamic Arab sources of morality began operating interactively in handling the affairs of the Arab-Islamic community (*umma*). Courage, gallantry, generosity, and respect for parents continued to serve as the basis for ethical practices (although it is impossible to ascertain whether they were motivated by a quest for personal honor or out of obedience to God). In the Islamic ethical system, God's knowledge of the inner self (*niyya*) is an important reason for individuals to steer their actions to winning God's pleasure rather than to gaining worldly interests. But human beings are not prohibited from enjoying the worldly benefits as long as their actions are religiously motivated. Thus, though one may speak of two different dimensions of Arab-Islamic morality, it is impossible to view its ethical components independently.

Arab-Islamic morality was discussed in virtue-centered ethical philosophy and theology. Arab-Islamic philosophers defined the concepts of virtue (*fadila*) and vice (*rathila*) and how they contribute to developing good character. Some of these ethicists, such as Miskawayh (d. 1030) and Ibn Hazm (d. 1046), were influenced by Greek moral philosophy. Many theologians of that time were concerned with moral questions from a rational point of view. Others such as Al Ghazali (d. 1111) based their arguments on explicit religious texts such as the Qur'an and the Sunnah. What follows is a discussion of basic Arab-Islamic moral principles and how they bear on communication in Arab society.

View of Human Nature

According to Islamic teachings, God has created humans to affirm their servitude to Him through an all-encompassing relationship of worship called *ibadah*: "I have only created *Jinns* and man, that they may serve me" (LI: 56). As God's vicegerents on earth, humans are entrusted with the task of establishing goodness and combating evil in line with divine commandments as revealed to successive prophets and messengers, the last of whom was Mohammad of Arabia. Radwan (1993, p. 88) notes that Islam takes human nature seriously, without extending our capabilities, responsibilities, and duties beyond what is humanly possible. Islam does not view human nature as intrinsically evil or corrupt: "We have indeed created man in the best of molds" (XCV: 4). Human beings innately know about good and evil. What matters most is the free use of senses, reason, and intellectual potentialities.

Human life is highly revered in Islam. Aggression against human life is the second greatest sin in the sight of Allah, second only to His denial (*kufr*):

> If any one slew a person—unless it be for murder or for spreading mischief in the land—it would be as if he slew the whole people. And if any one saved a life, it would be as if he saved the life of the whole people. (V: 35)

The significance of a human life was first manifested in the prohibition of infanticide (*waad*), which had dominated pre-Islamic Arabia for fear of possibly incurring shame over female children or poverty associated with many children in general. The dream of the Prophet Abraham that he was slaughtering his son Ishmael to fulfill a divine vision, as reported in the Qur'an, and God's prevention of that act by sending a sacrificial sheep is also indicative of the value of human life in Islam.

Inasmuch as Muslims respect the principle of life, they also accept the principle of death. When the Prophet of Islam died, some of his followers developed doubts about his mission. That caused the would-be first *Khalifa* (successor) Abu Bakr to deliver a speech in which he affirmed that those who were worshipping Mohammad should know that Mohammad had died, and those who worship God should know that God is living and never dies. Muslims believe that we die when our preallocated life period (*ajal*) expires.

Whereas the concept of dignity in secular Arab morality is individualistic, in Islam it is derived from the sacredness of human nature. Naqvi (1981, p. 45) notes that according to the Islamic ethical system, human beings occupy a central place in the universe. Humans are not just one element in the vast expanse of God's creation but are the raison d'être for all that exists. Humans are required to realize their theomorphic potentialities.

The Islamic doctrine of doing good and abstaining from evil provides the means by which God-conferred human potential is to be realized. Doing good means finding the pleasure of God from which emanates happiness, harmony, and creativity. Any discrepancy between the inner and outer dimensions would amount to hypocrisy (*nifag*), a sin in Islam deserving harsh punishment.

The realization of the divine mission of doing good and avoiding evil would not be possible unless the God-given powers, including communication, are fully used. God has conferred on humans the gift of reason and sensory capacities in order to use them to the maximum in line with Divine commandments. According to Islamic teachings, our intellectual and sensory potential will witness against us if we fail to use them in ways other than establishing good and eliminating evil. Constraints and taboos on creative communicative potentialities in the service of the divinely revealed moral good deserve punishment.

It thus becomes clear that communication in Islam is both a fundamental right and a duty, as explained by Waddy (1982):

a) The right to know and to be educated is also a duty to search for and acquire knowledge, and to place it at the service of the Muslim community. The Prophet said "seeking knowledge is compulsory for every Muslim man and woman."

b) The right to express an opinion involves the duty to speak out. If individuals believe something is not right, they have no right to remain silent about it. The Prophet said: "He who remains silent about truth is a dumb devil." This principle is congruent with the concept of commanding good and forbidding evil. In matters of public concern, individual interests are subordinated to those of the general public to safeguard the highly-cherished ideals of the community.

c) The right of political opposition and of honest criticism of authorities is also a duty. The first Muslim Caliph Abu Bakr, in his inaugural speech said: "If I do wrong, correct me." The second Caliph Omar asked, "What will you do if I do wrong?" One of those present stood up and said: "By God, Omar! We will put you right with the edge of our swords." Omar replied: "If you don't do so, you'll lose God's blessings, and if I don't accept your correction, I will lose God's blessing." (p. 39)

Responsible Freedom

Islam views responsibility and freedom at individual and collective levels as indivisible. Freedom without responsibility leads to transgressions of others' rights. In the absence of freedom, however, it is impossible to exercise responsibility. Both concepts operate in an interactive fashion within the Islamic ethical system.

Freedom in Islam is both a philosophical and social concept. In a philosophical sense, individual freedom in Islam denotes the capacity to choose. Ahmad (1976, p. 23) observes that because we are free to choose, we are accountable to Allah. Once God has shown the way, the responsibility for going astray is wholly ours and we will have to suffer for our wayward behavior (Naqvi, 1981, p. 55):

> Now truth hath reached you from your Lord! Those who receive guidance, do so for the good of their own souls; those who stray, do so to their own loss, and I am not (set) over you to arrange your affairs. (X: 108)

Like freedom, responsibility has individual and collective manifestations. Although humans are responsible for their individual actions within the Islamic moral system, they are also entrusted with duties and commitments to the community. Islamic commandments of support for the poor and the needy, sacrifice for upholding the interests of the Islamic community, and establishing good and righteousness reflect a great deal of commitment and responsibility on the part of the individual. The Prophet says,

> Everyone of you is a keeper or a shepherd and will be questioned about the well-being of his fold. So, the Head of the State will be questioned about the well-being of the people of the State. Every man is a shepherd to his family and will be answerable about every member of it. Every woman is a shepherd to the family of her husband and will be accountable for every member of it. And every servant is a shepherd to his master and will be questioned about the property of his master.[5]

In case of conflict between individual and collective interests, priority is given to the community. The Prophet was quoted as saying:

A group of people were sailing in a ship and one of them was tampering with the floor of the vessel, trying to drill holes. Would they let him do his work so that he and they would drown and perish or would they take action against him so that he and they would survive?[6]

The Prophet was quoted as saying, "Support your brother if he is an oppressor or an oppressed."[7] When the Prophet was asked by his scribes how they would support brothers who are oppressors, he said they would do that by talking them into rescinding their injustice.

Ethical Principles of Communication

Responsible freedom suggests that all communication should be conducive to fostering goodness and combating evil. It is the responsibility of both the individual and the community to work within the confines of this principle. The Qur'an cites several situations in which communication loses its legal and moral legitimacy when it is not done ethically.

The most fundamental ethical principle of Islamic communication is truthfulness. Telling lies is as evil as worshipping idols, which is the worst offense Muslims can commit. The Qur'an says, "Shun the abomination of idols, and shun the word that is false" (XXII: 30). The Sunnah quotes the Prophet as saying, "He who deceives us is not of us."[8] Genuine truthfulness, however, is an inner quality of mind that can best be described as integrity and authenticity. "O ye believers! Why say ye that which ye do not?" the Qur'an asks, and replies, "Grievously odious is it in the sight of God that ye say that which ye do not" (LXI: 2-3).

Islam holds people responsible not only for what they say but also for what they think and contemplate. Thinking or suspecting evil of others violates truthfulness. The Prophet said, "Avoid suspicion, for raising suspicion is the most lying form of speech."[9] Similarly frowned on is gossiping or the passing on of information that is likely to sow dissension among people or sour relationships. "And do not obey any despicable man, ready with oaths, a slanderer, going about with calumnies" (LXVIII: 10-11).

Truthfulness is more than truth telling. Not only the teller but also the recipient of messages is obliged to seek the truth. Information that is sketchy or incomplete needs to be researched further and verified. "O ye who believe! If a wicked person comes to you with any news, ascertain the truth, lest ye harm people unwittingly" (XLIX: 6).

A second ethical principle of Arab-Islamic communication is respect for others or the social recognition of another's human dignity, regardless of that person's physical, social, and idiosyncratic traits.

> Let not some men among you laugh at others. It may be that the (latter) are better than the (former). Nor let some women laugh at others. It may be that the (latter) are better than the (former). Nor defame nor be sarcastic to each other, nor call each other by offensive nicknames. (XLIX: 11)

Respect for others includes the right to privacy. For example, Muslims are not allowed to enter each other's homes without permission. "If someone peeps into the house of a people without their permission, it becomes allowable to them to gouge out his eyes," says the Prophet.[10] Nor may Muslims try to extract secret information or keep a secret watch on the movements of others, even if they are involved in acts that they may not approve.

Calumny is another sin that violates human dignity. "And do not . . . speak ill of each other behind their backs. Would any of you like to eat the flesh of his dead brother? Nay, ye would abhor it" (XLIX: 12). When an absent person is accused, the listener is obliged to defend the accused, because the listener is to act as defender of those accused in their absence. "If anyone defends his brother who is slandered in his absence it will be (his) due from Allah to set him free from the Fire (of hell)," says the Prophet.[11] Respect for others and the quest for justice thus coalesce here. Persons who have been wronged have a right to complain about the wrongdoing to secure justice (see Qaradawi, n.d., p. 318). "God loves not public avowal of evil words, save he who has been wronged; for God hears and knows all things" (IV: 147).

The strongest endorsement of the principle of human dignity is every person's right to honor and a good reputation, which is one of the pillars of Arab-Islamic communication ethics. This is one of the rare features that both the religious and secular Arab traditions have in common. A person's worthiness must be socially expressed and accorded. The infinite worth of every human being, regardless of age or sex or status or personal achievement, has to be recognized socially by an attitude of reference and esteem. The opposite of honoring a person is defamation, that is, depriving people of their good name in the community. Qaradawi (n.d., p. 322) notes that Islam safeguards the sanctity of a person's honor against backbiting, even when what is said is true. The Prophet said: "If anyone says something about a person which is not true in order to defame him, Allah will confine him in the fire of Hell until it extinguishes his utterances."[12]

The principle of honor is most severely tested in the case of the weak and vulnerable, particularly when their sexual morality is at stake. The vilest kind of attack on personal honor is that of accusing a virtuous woman of immorality. Such an accusation not only ruins her reputation and that of her family, destroying her future, but also broadcasts scandals within the Muslim community. This is why the Prophet listed it among the most heinous sins and the Qur'an threatened its perpetrators with dire punishments (XXIV: 13, 14, 19).

Third, communication in Arab-Islamic ethics should be gracious. It must be marked by kindness of heart and wisdom of mind. "Invite (all) to the way of thy Lord with wisdom and beautiful preaching; and argue with them in ways that are best and most gracious" (XVI: 125). Muslim believers were described in the Qur'an as responding to the shouts of ignorant disbelievers with the word "peace:" . . . the servants of (God), most gracious are those who walk on the earth in humility, and when the ignorant address them, they say peace" (XXV: 63). It is no wonder that the phrase of salutation in Islam is *salamu alaykum,* meaning peace be upon you.

Justice as Social Equilibrium

Being committed to goodness and righteousness is not enough. Justice must guide all human actions relating to others. Justice denotes a balance of forces in the universe resulting in equilibrium and harmony: "It is not permitted to the sun to catch up the moon, nor can the night outstrip the day. Each (just) swims along in (its own) orbit (according to the Law)" (XXXVI: 40). Justice is God's supreme attribute; its denial constitutes a denial of God himself. It follows that at the everyday level, the quality of equilibrium that characterizes all God's creation must be reflected in our individual lives. Within ourselves, there is a world of errant desires and ideas that must be contained and held together in correct proportions to produce a just human being: "Make not unlawful the good things which God hath made lawful for you. But commit no excess, for God loveth not those given to excess" (V: 90).

Some Arab Muslim theologians, such as Al Hassan Al Basri, have equated justice with piety and righteousness (moral good). They have made a distinction between ethical and political justice, holding humans responsible for the former but not for the latter (Khadduri, 1984, p. 107). Al Hassan Al Basri maintained that the revelation is clear on matters of political justice: "Obey God, and obey the Apostle, and those charged with authority among you" (IV: 59). Because political justice is an expression of the will of the sovereign, final decisions on all questions of political justice must be made by the Caliph, in his capacity as God's vicegerent on earth.

Al Razi (d. 924), an Islamic philosopher heavily influenced by Greek thinkers, noted that

> the supreme end for which we were created and towards which we have been led is . . . the acquisition of knowledge and the practice of justice: these two occupations are our sole deliverance out of the present world into the world wherein is neither death nor pain. (Khadduri, 1984, p. 106)

According to another Islamic philosopher and theologian, Al-Ghazali (d. 1111), the standard of ethical justice may be summed up in three virtues: wisdom—the quality of mind by which humans make choices; courage—the quality of indignation or moral courage, neither rash nor cowardly, but a state between the two; and justice—which is not just one virtue but the whole of the virtues, consisting of balance (equilibrium) and of moderation in the conduct of personal and public affairs (Khadduri, 1984, pp. 120-121). For Nasir al din Tusi (d. 1274), an Arab-Islamic philosopher, the theory of ethical justice is based on two fundamental concepts: equivalence and oneness. "Among the virtues, none is more perfect than justice, for the true middle point is justice, all else being peripheral to its reference thereof" (Khadduri, 1984, p. 122). The Islamic concept of justice includes its origin from a divine source, and its identification with divine qualities. The subjects of divine justice are those who believe in the One and just God. All others, the rest of humankind, are to be treated as objects of that justice. And the standard of justice, whether determined by reason or revelation, indicates the paths of right and wrong so that all, according to their own light, would pursue the right thing and reject the wrong to achieve the good in this world and salvation in the next (see Khadduri, 1984, pp. 192-193).

The Arab-Islamic concept of justice suggests that communication, like action, is subject to the distribution of good and bad, rewards and penalties. Harboring ill suspicions, spying on others, leveling false charges against innocent women, backbiting, and lying, are also seen as symptoms of an excessive abuse of the equilibrium in interpersonal and social relations in the community. Not only does the Islamic justice system seek to rectify those imbalances, it also generates temporal and religious rewards for those who adhere to its principles:

Equality. "O mankind! We created you from a single (pair) of a male and a female, and made you into nations and tribes, that ye may know each other (not that you may despise each other). Verily the most honored of you in the sight of God is (he who is) the most righteous of you" (XLIX: 13).

Honesty. "O ye believers! Fear God and (always) say a word directed to the right: that He may make your conduct whole and sound and forgive you your sins" (XXXIII: 70-71).

Humility. "Nor walk on the earth with insolence: for thou canst not rend the earth asunder, nor reach the mountains in height" (XVII: 37).

Trust. "God doth command you to render back your trusts to those to whom they are due; and when ye judge between man and man that ye judge with justice. Verily how excellent is the teaching which He giveth to you!" (IV: 58).

Forgiveness. "The recompense for an injury is an injury equal thereto (in degree), but if a person forgives and makes reconciliation, his reward is due from God" (XLII: 40).

Mercy

In Islam, mercy is a central attribute of God who is referred to as *Rahim* or the Merciful. "If they accuse thee of falsehood, say: Your Lord is full of all-embracing mercy" (VI: 147); "And were it not for the grace and mercy of God on you, not one of you would ever have been pure" (XXIV: 21);

"We sent thee not, but as a mercy for all creatures" (XXI: 107); and "To whom belongeth all that is in the heavens and on earth? Say, to God: He hath inscribed for himself (the rule of) mercy" (VI: 12). In the Sunnah, or traditions of the Prophet, mercy is also emphasized as a basic component of true Muslimhood. The Prophet says, "Give mercy to others and forgive them, so you will be given mercy and forgiven by God."[13] The Prophet reports the story of a woman who would go to hell for incarcerating a cat and starving it to death, whereas a man who met a thirsty dog in the desert, fetched for it water from a well, would go to Paradise (Qaradawi, n.d., p. 122).

In Arab-Islamic morality, mercy is organically intertwined with compassion and forgiveness. Mercy is shown not merely because the recipient deserves it but because a person is full of compassion, extending it to others, and because a person bears no grudges against others. This suggests that mercy, as an Arab-Islamic ethical norm, is practiced as a gift, as a matter of grace, based simply on the compassion, kindness, charity, or benevolence of the giver. To willingly forgive an offender from a position of strength is a highly valued attitude in Arab-Islamic traditions. For example, the Islamic *qasas* (law of equality) allows the victim to inflict the same degree of harm on a transgressor, but forgiveness is preferable.

> O ye who believe! The law of equality is prescribed to you. In cases of murder: the free for the free, the slave for the slave, the woman for the woman. But if any remission is made by the brother of the slain, then grant any reasonable demand, and compensate him with handsome gratitude. This is a concession and mercy from your Lord. After this whoever exceeds the limits shall be in grave penalty. (II: 178)

Offenders, however, who do admit their guilt and do show repentance, may qualify for mercy. God is forgiving (*gafour*) and accepts repentance (*tawwab*) from offenders. He asks believers to be merciful to others, especially orphans, female relatives (who are described as *rahem,* a word derived from *rahma,* which means mercy), and parents at old age:

> Thy Lord hath decreed that ye worship none but Him, and that ye be kind to parents. Whether one or both of them attain old age in thy life, say not to them a word of contempt, nor repel them. But address them in terms of honor. And out of kindness, lower to them, the wing of humility, and say: my Lord, bestow on them thy mercy even as they cherished me in childhood. (XVII: 23-24)

Although the notion of mercy in Islam may seem to contravene some aspects of the concept of justice, it should be noted that mercy as voluntarily conferred on an offender is an integral part of justice. The granting of mercy as a matter of benevolence involves no encroachment on the victim's rights. The provision of mercy is compensated by a sense of self-satisfaction, social prestige, material benefits (if human life was involved), and most important, by God's reward in the Day of Judgment. Yet, in the context of the Islamic concept of *hudoud* or punishment, which reflects aspects of retributive justice, the case for punishment is based on what the offender did and not on expected consequences. In the following six cases, mercy may not be applicable, even if the victims rescind their social and legal rights:

Hiraba. This describes a situation in which a group of trouble makers start to destabilize the community by inciting acts of violence and inflicting human losses and material damage in defiance of religious, legal, and ethical norms. They are to be killed or their hands and legs cut off or exiled:

> The punishment of those who wage war against God and His Apostle, and strive with might and main for mischief through the land is: execution, or crucifixion, or the cutting of hands and feet from opposite sides or exile from the land. (V: 36)

Ridda [converting from Islam to atheism or to another religion]. The Prophet was quoted as saying that the killing of Muslims is forbidden except in three cases, one of which is conversion from Islam to another religion or giving up Islam for atheism.

Theft. "As to the thief, male or female, cut off his or her hands: a punishment by way of example, from God, for their crime" (V: 41).

Consuming alcohol. "Intoxication and gambling . . . and (divination by) arrows are an abomination, Satan's handiwork" (V: 93). Alcohol consumers receive 40 lashes.

Adultery. "The woman and the man, guilty of adultery or fornication, flog each of them with a hundred lashes; let no compassion move you in their case" (XXIV: 2).

Evil charges. "And those who launch a charge against chaste women, and produce not four witnesses (to support their allegations), flog them with eighty lashes and reject their evidence everafter" (XXIV: 4).

The value of mercy suggests that communication can be instrumental for merciful behavior. Gracious communication expressing kindness becomes a central feature of Arab-Islamic social interactions. The word *mercy* is invoked in the most common Arab-Islamic salutation (*al Salam Alaykkum wa Rahma Tullah Wa Barakatu* [May Peace and the Mercy of God be on You]). The addressee would respond using the same statement. When the Prophet's preaching of the Islamic message was confronted with verbal and physical abuses from his own people, he was always asking for God's pardon and guidance for them. Mercy in Islam transforms communication into a truly humane process of symbolic interaction. Although human beings are always liable to make mistakes, mercy becomes vital for making up the damage. Communication is not only an instrument for expressing forgiveness and compassion but becomes an act of mercy in itself. Given the influential oral nature of Arab-Islamic communication, good words are often perceived as strong sources of comfort and security.

Implications for Modern Arab Communications

The contemporary Arab media are strongly influenced by a traditional Arab-Islamic ethical frame of reference that encourages communicators' involvement rather than detachment in the communication process. A growing mode of communication, rooted in secular grounds, insists on objectivity as an ethical communication norm. But traditional mainstream communication is embedded in Islamic discourse, whereas the secular mode is influenced by Western ethical norms. However, these modes cannot be clearly separated. These two discourses intertwine and exchange discursive patterns in ways that defy clear-cut demarcations. Nonetheless, they remind us of the distinctions drawn in Western communication between the communicator as "gatekeeper" and the communicator as "counselor" (Hulteng, 1981).

The modern secular scheme in Arab communication corresponds to the gatekeeping approach where emotional involvement is discouraged. The religious and nationalist Arab-Islamic schemes of communication correspond to the counselling approach where communicators are encouraged to be involved in social change by taking pro-Arab-Islamic positions on the events and issues they cover, albeit without tainting the facts. This approach still seems to control the formulation of media ethics and ethical codes; it outstrips the secular approach in fundamental ways in decision making and critical/cultural studies.

The Arab-Islamic influence on contemporary public communication coalesces around three points: honor, responsibility, and defense of Islam.

Honor is central in ethical discourse. The two major communication charters (codes of ethics) in the Arab-Islamic World—one issued by the Islamic States Association and the other by the Arab League—both emphasize the centrality of honor in modern Arab-Islamic media ethics. The title of the media code of ethics of the Islamic States Association is *Mithaq Al-Sharaf Al-Ilaami Al-Islami* (Charter of Honor of Islamic Media). Modern Arab-Islamic ethical discourses borrow heavily from secular Arab discourse, which equates honor with ethics. The media code of ethics of the Arab League is entitled *Mithaq Al-sharaf Al-Ilaami Al-Arabi* (Charter of Honor of Arab Media). The charter implies that correct media practices should enhance the collective honor of Arab-Islamic ideals. It is important to note that collective honor replaces pre-Islamic secular individualistic honor. It is also interesting that the word for honor (*sharaf*) used in the Arab League media charter is substantive, whereas it is only discursive and figurative in the case of the Islamic media charter.

Responsibility is both a communal and an individual duty. It was noted earlier that moral responsibility applies primarily to individuals. However, communal responsibility is given priority if individual and collective modes are in conflict. Article 2 of the Islamic media charter says,

> All media practitioners will work toward uniting the world of Muslims. They will call for the embodiment of Islamic mindhood and brotherhood, and forgiveness in solving their own problems. They should be committed to fighting colonialism, atheism, and aggression in all forms . . . in all alertness to confront all ideas and currents in conflict with Islam. (Islamic Countries Association, 1980)

A Muslim communicator is expected to work toward building up and strengthening the Islamic community with a clear thrust of Islamic communal values and ideals. Therefore, a communicator is not only asked to implement Islamic ideals but also to fight ideas and currents in conflict with Islam, driven by a sense of Islamic duty and responsibility toward the Islamic community and its principles. The Arab media charter recognizes this responsibility in both individual and communal terms. Article 3 of the charter reads as follows:

> Arab mass media bear a responsibility towards the Arab person. They are committed to providing the truth, aiming at solving Arab causes, working towards perfecting Arab personality and developing it intellectually, culturally, socially, and politically. [They bear the responsibility] to educate the youth to respect human rights; to instill pride in their national identity; and to develop a sense of duty towards their community, state, and Arab nation as a whole. (Arab League, 1978)

These examples illustrate that Arab communicators cannot function within the framework of Western codes of ethics that conceive of responsibility and fairness in terms of individual detachment and noninvolvement in the communication process. An Arab-Muslim communicator is responsible at the individual level to observe Islamic principles of honesty and truthfulness but equally responsible for observing and building up communal values. Journalists in such an ethical context are not just conduits but social change agents as well.

Defending Islam. All legal and ethical media codes in the Arab world refer to Islam and Arab culture in terms that would leave no doubt as to the overwhelming importance of their value systems for media practitioners. The TV charter of the Arab Gulf Cooperation Council (GCC, 1993), for example, expects television in the Gulf region to maintain "the moral and social values of conduct originating from the Islamic faith which are the cornerstone of the spiritual, educational, and cultural basis of this (Gulf) region" (Boyd, 1993, P. 97). Furthermore, it maintains that foreign programs should not include any offense to the religious (Islamic), social, or cultural values of the viewers or any insult to their national or human feelings or any embarrassment to the political authorities of the Gulf states. "One of the targets this Charter seeks to achieve is to maintain the local cultural characteristics as these are considered among the major attributes of the Arab culture" (Boyd, 1993, p. 97).

The Press and Publications Law of the United Arab Emirates states that "the law shall prohibit the publication of any material containing an offense against Islam and the political system of the country." According to Article 71, "it is not permitted to publish any offense against Arabs or any distortion of their civilization and heritage" (UAE Ministry of Information, 1980, p. 23). Similar references are found in Saudi and Jordanian press laws. Article 7 of the Saudi Press Law clearly prohibits "printing, publication, and circulation of any material that conflicts with a legislative source, debases the sanctity of Islam and its encompassing *Sharia* (law), or offends public decency" (GCC General Secretariat, 1993). The Jordanian Press and Publications Law forbids the publication of articles defaming religion (Islam) and offending public morality (Armouti, 1982, pp. 21-22). Article 18 of the new law excludes those who were convicted of a "crime or misdemeanor involving honor or public morals" from ownership of newspapers and magazines (Jordan Ministry of Information, 1993).

Islam is not only central in the day-to-day cultural life of Arabs but defines the ethical and legal boundaries of the institutions that preserve and recreate culture—the communications media. A conference of information ministers of 52 Islamic states and observers from 20 Islamic and international organizations stressed in 1995 that more powerful Islamic media were needed to enable Muslims to address the world in a direct manner, to defend themselves and to explain their just causes. This should be done, among other things, by improving the efficiency of the Islamic News Agency and by setting up an Islamic television network to be called "Islamvision" ("Islamic Information Ministers," 1995, p. 5).

Conclusions

This chapter has sought to explain the basic components and features of the Arab-Islamic ethical system, as derived from secular and religious traditions, and show their impact on communication ethics. In a general sense, Arab-Islamic morality has placed a good deal of emphasis on speech, making it equivalent to action in terms of rewards and penalties. The main implication of this view is that communication plays a role in individual development and in community progress, and no barriers should obstruct the realization of these goals. This flows from the fact that communication is important for realizing the ultimate goal of affirming service to God within the divine scheme of creation. To abstain from communicating to further the good and the righteous cause is considered immoral.

Although the individual is granted full freedom of communication within the concept of establishing good and combating evil, it is regarded as immoral to get involved in communication that contravenes belief in God or that impinges on the rights of others or the community at large. Explicit references in the Qur'an and the Sunnah to specific communication situations that might violate the Islamic ethical system set the limits of good and bad communication and underscore the ethical importance of communication in general.

Islamic morality is not based on the consequences of actions nor on self-interest. It is based instead on something higher than the mundane events of the imperfect human and natural world, that is, on the revealed Message of Allah, the All-Good God who has communicated to human beings what they should do and not do in a moral sense. To be moral, then, human beings must follow what is permissible (*halal*) and avoid what is prohibited (*haram*) without concerning themselves with consequences, self-interests, or anything else.

Arab-Islamic communication ethics is thus radically based on religious authority and on a religion that constitutes a whole way of life, excluding nothing. Therefore, the act of communication, as has been shown, has specific spiritual-religious dimensions. However, within them are certain focal points that suggest universal human values. Three such elements can be readily identified.

First, the value of honor: For most readers of this chapter, honor must be an old-fashioned term that has almost disappeared from current ethical discourse. Characteristically, perhaps, the deprivation of honor plays a major part in media ethics, usually in testing the limits of how far the media can go and still avoid court cases against slander and defamation. Honor as a positive concept, however, acknowledges a person's dignity and shows respect for social-cultural institutions and communal practices. Honor also implies the right to reputation, which is socially recognized and conferred in communications. It is part of the respectworthiness of every human being and social groups such as family and community. Holding a person in high repute is a fundamental ethical norm. And in case of proven ill repute, forgiveness is another.

Second, the quality of mercy: In Islam, every call to prayer begins with an invocation of God who is *Rahman Al-Rahim,* whose nature is to be merciful and compassionate, and who commands humans to be likewise.

Few of God's attributes play such a central role in the lives of Muslims as that of mercy. Mercy is another term that has almost disappeared from the ethical vocabulary of modern Western culture. Yet, it denotes a fundamental human attitude that should govern human interaction and communication. Mercy recognizes the ontological nature of human beings. They are weak and frail; they do not always measure up to expectations; they disappoint themselves as well as others; they often need help to get out of an impasse. Humans have to be treated in human ways, and such paths are marked by feelings. Communication consists of more than merely bits, bytes, and digits. A sense of mercy and compassion is elementary for individuals and society, for being in community and for being co-responsible for the created order. Endowed with mercy, communication is an intensely humanizing activity.

Third, justice through communication: In the theological framework of Islamic ethics, the notion of justice is even more important than that of mercy. Justice, we have seen, is the supreme attribute of God and the epitome of human virtues. Justice is not primarily concerned with the distribution of goods and services in society but with the positive forces that build up and maintain harmony and equilibrium in the community (*umma*). One of these social forces is communication. Speaking, discussion, and the media ought to convey knowledge and wisdom, piety and respect, and thus undergird and activate the community of believers. Justice is a communal value, yet it engages every individual to bring about justice. This is the ultimate aim of many of the specific norms of communication ethics as described in this chapter. Communication thus assumes a universal, even a cosmic, dimension—an equilibrium and harmony comprising God, human beings, and the created order.

Notes

1. The translation of the Qur'an used in this chapter is *The Meaning of the Glorious Qur'an* (Trans., Abdullah Yusuf Ali), Vols. 1-2. Cairo: Darl Al-Kitab AlMasri, n.d. The Roman figures refer to books (chapters), the Arabic figures to verses.

Statements attributed to the Prophet (*hadisths*) are documented by a number of Islamic scholars who are considered authoritative sources on those statements. These scholars are Al Bukhari, Ahmad, Tabarani, Muslim, and Al Tirmithi. Their documented *hadiths* or Prophets' statements are compiled in books called *sahihs* or *musnads,* which trace the origins of those statements to multiple sources.

2. Reported by Al Bukhari.
3. Reported by Al Bukhari.
4. Reported by Muslim.
5. Reported by Muslim.
6. Reported by Muslim.
7. Reported by Al Bukhari.
8. Reported by Muslim.
9. Reported by Al Bukhari and others.
10. Reported by Al Bukhari and Muslim.
11. Reported by Ahmad.
12. Reported by Al Tabarani.
13. Reported by Al Tirmithi.

References

Ahmad, Khurshid. (1976). *Islam: Its meaning and message.* London: Islamic Foundation.

Arab League. (1978). *Charter of Arab media.* Cairo: Arab League Press.

Armouti, M. (1982). *Communication development and society.* Irbid, Jordan: Yarmouk University Press.

Benhabib, Seyla, & Dallamayr, Fred. (1990). *The communicative ethics controversy.* Cambridge, MA: MIT Press.

Boyd, Douglas. (1993). *Broadcasting in the Arab world: A survey of radio and television in the Middle East.* Philadelphia: Temple University Press.

GCC General Secretariat. (1993). *Press and publications laws and regulations in the states of the Arab Gulf Cooperation Council.* Riyadh, Saudi Arabia: Author.

Hulteng, John. (1981). *Playing it straight: A practical discussion of the ethical principles of the American Society of Newspaper Editors.* Old Saybrook, CT: Globe Pequot.

Islamic Countries Association. (1980). *Charter of Islamic media.* Mecca, Saudi Arabia: Author.

Islamic information ministers stress media role. (1995, May 25). *Gulf News,* p. 5.

Jaafar, Mohammad. (1978). *Philosophical and ethical studies.* Cairo: Dar Al Uloum Bookshop.

Jordan Ministry of Information. (1993). *Jordan press and publications law.* Amman, Jordan: Author.

Khadduri, Majid. (1984). *The Islamic conception of justice.* Baltimore, MD: John Hopkins University Press.

MacBride, Sean et al. (1980). *Many voices, one world: Report by the International Commission for the Study of Communication Problems.* Paris: UNESCO Press.

Mowlana, Hamid. (1989). Communication ethics and the islamic tradition. In Thomas Cooper et al. (Eds.), *Communication ethics and global change* (pp. 137-147). New York: Longman.

Naqvi, Syed Nawab. (1981). *Ethics and economics: An Islamic synthesis.* Leister, UK: Islamic Foundation.

Qaradawi, Yusuf. (n.d.). *The lawful and the prohibited in Islam* (Trans., Kemal El-Helbawy, M. Moinuddin Siddiqui, & Syed Shukry). Indianapolis, IN: American Trust.

Radwan, Zeinab. (1993). *Islam in the heart of contemporary times.* Dubai, United Arab Emirates: Dar Al Qir'a Li' Jamee'.

Subhi, Ahmad M. (1969). *Ethical philosophy in Islamic thought.* Cairo: Dar Al Maaraef.
UAE Ministry of Information. (1980). *UAE press and publication law.* Abu Dhabi: Author.
Waddy, Chris. (1982). *The Muslim mind.* London: Longman.

CHAPTER 7

Ethics and the Discourse on Ethics in Post-Colonial India

ANANTHA SUDHAKER BABBILI

My language is aphoristic; it lacks precision. It is, therefore, open to several interpretations. (Lord Krishna's conversation with Dharmadev, *The Collected Works of Mahatma Gandhi*, Government of India, 1958, p. 485)

If we define ethics as involving intention, will, freedom, the relation of one individual to another, we are imposing a western concept on India. Admittedly, Hinduism has little or no ethics in this sense. But if ethics involves a set of standard behavior based on duty, social custom, religious faith in *karma*, then Hinduism puts a high premium on moral conduct. Hinduism has no concern for others as others, as individuals deserving separate treatment, but it does have concern for others as members of the group or as part of Universal Reality. (Father Raymond Panikkar as quoted in Lacy, 1965, p. 27)

This chapter deals with Indian ethics in its cultural context and with the intellectual challenge that the discourse on ethics in a post-Colonial situation offers. It begins with the latter to arrive at the former. In doing so, the chapter explores the perplexing morass of ethical reasoning that dictates

Indian daily life. The discursive analysis hopes to sketch a normative vision and describe an encompassing theory of discourse on ethics.

The intent here is to introduce students of ethics to the ethical schemata of India. And this task is not easy. The journey into Indian ethics is essentially an excursion into the contestable terrain of conflicting cultural narratives—native and those imposed from the outside. Thus, any narrative on Indian ethics must first wrestle with the difficulty of dealing with ethics in its post-colonial condition.[1] It must provide a description in the context of contemporary India's geography, society, culture, and politics. Also, to imagine the particular location of ethics, one must understand the history of the culture and society. The philosophical basis for the specific principles governing Indian life can then be discussed meaningfully from an indigenous "ethical systems" perspective.

The study of Indian ethics calls for eschewing the traditional dualisms that exist in Western thought. The typical dichotomies of subject-object, fact-value, individual-society, material-spiritual, good-evil, and so forth are inconsequential for understanding Indian society and ethics. The Western need to understand is basically puzzling to Indians. One seeks the experience of the Self [*Atman*] to find one's *dharma* [duty and righteousness]—not to explain away but to accept, not to articulate but to experience. Telling a story is as important as speaking the truth, but most often, it is telling the story that indicates profound insight not preaching truth as one sees it.

In India, everything important is told in paradoxes. Oliver (1971) writes that subtlety is the hallmark of the Indian mind. The rhetorical milieu includes the manner of talk, how people address each other on what topics, styles of conversation, nonverbal cues, and intended effects between senders and receivers. Nothing is as it first appears. What is said must be understood in terms of what has been left unsaid. "Opposites are coordinates; contradictions are illusionary. The world is a dramatic portrayal of God playing hide and seek with Himself—trying to reassemble all the divergent parts into their original unity" (pp. 15-16). Death is life; continuity is change.

The potent force of such Indian ethical paradoxes and conduct can be seen in Mahatma Gandhi's twin battle (Gandhi, 1948; Misra & Gangal, 1981) against British colonial rule in India based on *dharma* and *ahimsa* [nonviolence]—destined to permanently change the colonizer as well as the colonized (Nandy, 1983). Gandhi's ability to translate social ethics and

ethical ideals into political action laid the foundations for achieving social
justice for millions for the first time in world history through nonviolence.
With a clever use of nonverbal methods evoking the cultural ethics laden
in the texts and epics of nationhood, he struck a chord of unity among its
diverse people and effectively disarmed a colonial military machine.

Geography and the Cultural Ethos

Understanding the land—the geography of modern India and its geologi-
cal formulations—is critical to comprehending Indian ethics.[2] Major battles between good and evil have been fought in mythology that carry insight
into ethics. The *Mahabharatha* and *Ramayana* point to wars and warriors,
virtuous and treacherous gods, benevolent and punishing gods, and to goddesses and androgynous gods. They describe gods who provoked warfare,
gods who switched sides, gods that are human, partly human, partly non-
human, partly from the rest of the animal kingdom, half-god, half-human,
half-animal, perfect, and imperfect gods. Three million of them—each reflecting virtues and antivirtues—reside in one of the oldest civilizations
that extends from the Indus River to the Himalaya mountains, from the
genesis of the sacred rivers Brahmaputra and Ganga to the Vindhya mountains, and from central plains to the lush greenery of Kanyakumari at the
tip of south India. The sage then shows, following different ways of enu-
merating them, how each of these views could make sense (Davis as cited
in Lopez, 1995, p. 3). The narratives that have sprung from this land domi-
ciled between the Indus and Ganges rivers are indeed peculiar to India and
Indians, though their imprint can be seen in the Greek and Roman, Chinese
and European civilizations (Halbfass, 1988).

Contemporary studies of Indian ethics cannot be understood without
coming to terms with its post-independent (after 1947) political, cultural,
social, and religious fragments. Located in southern Asia between the Arabian Sea, Bay of Bengal, and Indian Ocean, between Bangladesh and Pakistan (both creations from the former "India" of the colonial era), India
experienced Islamic colonialism for nearly three centuries until the arrival
of the British in the 1600s. Ethnically, 72% of the nearly 950 million Indians are Indo-Aryans and 25% are Dravidians of the south. Indians, however, never really identify themselves along ethnic lines as Aryan or
Dravidian. India harbors many religions, including the Hindu majority

(80%), Muslim (14%), Christian (2.4%), Sikh (2%), Buddhist (0.7%), Jains (0.5%), and other faiths. Religious plurality—including Zoroastrianism with origins in Persia and in Judaism—is a historical reality, although the fundamentalist backlash from the Hindu Right against two colonialisms—Christian and Islamic—is presently a feature of Indian politics. Linguistically, India has had a burst of creative languages over the past 5,000 years. There are 18 major languages with their own unique alphabet and script, which formed the basis of statehoods; yet there are 25 languages spoken by 1 million or more Indians and more than 1,100 dialects—some with written scripts and others strictly oral. Literacy rates in 1991 were estimated as 63.86% for males and 39.42% for females. Agriculture and village-cottage industries take the lion's share of the labor force. Politically, the colonial imprint can be seen on India's political structure (federal republic) and on its legal system (based on English common law), although compromises with Islamic law to appease the Muslim minority are often allowed.

India is the world's largest and most populous democracy, with 950 million people. Governance of India is virtually unimaginable with such a multitude of classes, castes, subcastes, religions, regionalisms, linguistic divisions, and a population nearing 1 billion. Yet suffrage is extended universally to citizens 18 years and older, and they have exhibited in India's post-independent history a vibrant propensity for democratic institutions and a disdain for dictatorships. The Indian constitution embraces a social activism that encourages equality for caste and religion. Reservations in employment and in higher education akin to affirmative action in the United States have been in place since 1947, and accommodations to the lower castes have gradually increased—much to the chagrin of the upper castes. However, as governmental measures to eradicate caste discrimination take root, discrimination based on economic status has begun to emerge as even more important than the traditional caste distinctions. The gap between the rich and poor is wide and gets wider every year.

Communication in a culturally diverse environment is a given in India. The Indian model of communication can be called at best a "mixed system," with a blend of written and oral traditions. Print media include 30,000 newspapers with a combined circulation of 60 million. Government ownership of newspapers is disallowed. Daily newspapers 3,000 strong—although relying heavily on government-approved newsprint—provide the most vocal criticism of political and social institutions. The broadcasting

system, however, is under the government's control, ensuring public interest with a balance of regional, linguistic, and religious representations on
radio and television. Radio, with its appeal for nonliterate audiences
reaches about 94% of India, and television has a nearly 84% reach, the
latter confined to India's middle class. India boasts the world's largest film
industry with about 900 full-length feature films produced every year.
Bombay, India's Hollywood, produces the largest number of films in the
Hindi language, spoken by about 30% of Indians. Films are seen by 100
million people every week in 13,000 cinema halls. Often, the largest build-
ings in small villages are the temple and the cinema hall. Although most
films ape Western story-telling, violence, and escapism, many do construct
narratives of caste injustice, marriages based on love (as opposed to forced
or arranged marriages), the triumph of the lower and poorer castes of people over the upper caste and the arrogant elite, the triumph of the gentler
and the androgynous over the powerful and hypermasculine (Nandy, 1995).
Films and government-sponsored television productions aim to propagate
religious tolerance, national unity, and environmental protection. Radio
shows promote development programs and cultural cohesion. The broadcast media deal with subject matter that relates to tradition and the family
as a unit. Films, in particular, critically examine the cultural consequences
of Westernization even as they follow the cinematic logic established by
the West. Cable TV and imported programming are on the rise.

When partitioned from British India, Pakistan chose to become an Islamic Republic, whereas India made secularism an inherent part of its plurality (Sen, 1993) by choosing a secular constitution for its Hindus and
Muslims. Although diversity and tolerance within Hinduism did not come
with Western secularism, they have become a political necessity. It was a
moral and ethical choice that neutralized temporarily sectarian nationalism, ultra-right Hindu fundamentalism, and militant obscurantism until India gained the strength to stand on its own feet in the wake of independence
from the British.

Ethics and Religion in India

India's social ethics cannot be understood without locating them in a
broad definition of religion. The caution here is that Hinduism must be
understood in pre-colonial terms to extract the nation's ethical underpin-

nings. Hinduism is a collection of a broad group of south Asian religions. It has been challenged by other religions that came to exist in the region—Buddhism, Islam, and Christianity—but it remains the most prevalent. Hinduism is one of the world's oldest continuously recorded religions, dating from 4500 to 1200 B.C.E. A text was already edited and put into final shape by about 1200 B.C.E. (Davis, cited in Lopez, 1995, p. 3). Both terms, Hinduism and India, were framed by outsiders—the former an invention of this century by the British and the latter the coinage by the Greeks and Persians referring to a geographical location rather than a collection of beliefs and peoples (Lopez, 1995; Sen, 1993). The word "Hindu" was coined by the Arab colonizers referring to people who lived near the Sindhu river. It was later incorporated into the Indian lexicon by Indians eager to construct for themselves a counterpart to the seemingly monolithic Christianity of the colonizers (Lopez, 1995, p. 6).

Because ethics is derived from Hinduism as a whole, it is pertinent to discuss the term *Hinduism*. It remains useful for describing and categorizing the various schools of thought and practice that have sprung up within a shared Indian society and have employed a common religious vocabulary. However, applying this single term to a wide array of Indian religious phenomena across a historical continuity raises some obvious questions (Lopez, 1995, p. 6).

What is the center of Hinduism? And who determines this center, if any? Scholars and Indians have largely adopted two contrasting views on this matter that have a bearing on ethics—one centralist and the other pluralist. Centralists identify a pan-Indian hegemonic, orthodox tradition transmitted primarily through the Sanskrit language, chiefly by the Brahmanic upper caste. Davis contends that the tradition centers around a Vedic lineage of texts that includes the Vedas themselves but also the *Mimamsa, Dharmasastra,* and *Vedanta* corpuses (Lopez, 1995).[3] Vernacular challenges to Sanskrit questioning the caste order and rejecting the authority of the Vedas may periodically show up as a rebellion against the center, but the orthodox, through the adept use of inclusion and repressive tolerance, have managed to prevail in authority. The pluralists envision a decentered profusion of ideas and practices all tolerated and incorporated under Hinduism (Lopez, 1995).

The textual history of Hinduism and of Indian religions begins in 4000 B.C.E. and since then has encouraged its own versions of dissent, lively religious interaction, and criticism through satire and polemic. Various contending religious narratives have vied to each present a view of divinity, human society, human purposes, and social ethics as more compelling than the others. As quoted in Lopez (1995), Davis writes,

> One finds such all-encompassing visions presented in many Hindu texts or group of texts at different periods of history: the Vedas, the Epics, the puranic theologies of Vishnu and Siva, the medieval texts of the bhakti movements, and the formulations of synthetic Hinduism by modern reformers. (p. 7)

The theoretical exegesis of Indian ethics flows from such a synthesis of Indian thought. To speak of Hinduism as a "religion" in India is not to say much of anything at all theoretically or analytically. Hinduism defies a Western category of religions, encompassing actually "a diversity of gods, texts, and social practice, and a variety of ontologies and epistomologies. Without an organized church, it is innocent of orthodoxy, heterodoxy and heresy" (quoted by Larson, 1995, p. 279). Religion—a fundamental anthropological notion on analogy with culture, language, and society—goes beyond the theoretical categories of European history of religions, theology, and Western social science (pp. 280-281). Uniquely, "India has been instructive in exhibiting forms of religion in which determinate cognitive formulation regarding ultimate truth is neither essential or possible" (p. 281).

The anthologies that hold the treasures of Indian thought, Indian morality, and human virtue are the *Rg Veda* (the Vedic period of Indian history stretches roughly from 2500 to 500 B.C.E.), the collection of hymns that form the bedrock of the Hindu tradition; the *Upanishads* (700 to 300 B.C.E.), the story of creation and classic discourses that form the foundation for Hindu religious and philosophical speculation; the *Bhagavad Gita* (400 B.C.E. to 400 A.D.), the basic text of religious and philosophical synthesis and the basic scripture of Hindu devotionalism; the *Mahabharatha* (400 B.C.E. to 400 A.D.), the political history of humankind with contending moralities and nondualistic thought; and the *Ramayana* (200 B.C.E.), the second of the great epics that exemplifies the fundamental values and tensions in the classical tradition.

No one text represents a complete statement of Buddhism, but the *Dhammapada* comes closest to the basic discourse, which teaches that the greatest sin is ignorance or thoughtlessness and that the holy life begins with, and is founded on, moral earnestness and the spirit of inquiry and self-examination. Indian ethical extrapolations can also be found in the fables of *Panchatantra*, which uses classic Indian humor to spell out five doctrines of conduct or modes of action, namely, confidence or firmness of mind, creation of prosperity or affluence, earnest endeavor, friendship, and knowledge. *Panchatantra* reveals the ancient Indian affinity toward non-human beings and the sanctity of nature by evoking the imagery of animals when discussing the doctrines of conduct—especially for children. The basic authority for India's legal and moral philosophy today seems to be the *Code of Manu*, a text written between 600 and 300 A.D. that contains a mythological rationalization for the caste system and family ethics (Doniger & Smith, 1991). Thus, the ethics of India stems from those basic Hindu religious texts that are often considered cultural and philosophical texts.

Hindu philosophy teaches that the metaphysical ideal is higher than the ethical ideal (Brown, 1970; Crawford 1974, p. 229); nevertheless, both are synthetically related. Those who have achieved the mystical state of *moksa* [liberation] do not consciously follow the ethical path but neither can they deviate from it. The path of an enlightened person is paved with virtue (Crawford, 1974, p. 230). Love and compassion to all creatures are the spontaneous products of wisdom. This thought, for example, is relevant to an ecologically conscious world. Ecology presupposes ethics. To attain a right relationship with nature, modern human beings must assume vital obligations for the web of life in which their own life is wonderfully woven. Material investments do not recover and preserve nature. The obligation to life forms is a matter of conscience—an individual's ecological conscience. The ecological conscience views the human being as a spectator and participant in nature.

> This means, if we are going to be scientific in our approach, we cannot speak of man and nature, but of man in nature. The first view is anthropocentric; the second is biocentric. The first view has characterized Western man's approach to nature; the second has been more characteristic of the Hindu perspective. (Crawford, 1995, p. 177)

The outlook on life underlying the *summum bonum* of Hindu ethics is fundamentally cosmic. The essential self is not only identified with the group or society or nation or even with the whole human race, but it is inclusive of these and much more. The nature of the self in Hinduism includes all lesser forms of existence, and therefore, it also has an ecological conscience. Crawford (1974) cites this passage from the *Upanishads*: "The essential self or the vital essence of man is the same as that in a gnat, the same as that in an elephant, the same as that in these three worlds, indeed the same as that in the whole universe" (p. 232).

The Nature of Ethics and Continuity in India

Hindus call their religion *Sanatana Dharma*, which literally means "Eternal Law." The term does not imply that the ethical ideals connected with religion are eternal in the sense of being fixed, static, and unchanging. To the contrary, Hindu ethics,

> like the river Ganges, has been in a state of ceaseless flow during the ages, constantly changing its course and currents relative to the hard, intervening realities of Indian history. Under the rubric of eternal law, universal law, Hindu ethics combines continuity with dynamic diversity. (Crawford, 1974, p. i)

Hinduism does not have a science of morals fashioned after some Aristotelian or Thomistic model (p. xiv). However, it does have a moral philosophy that postulates a *summum bonum* and specifies the proper means to achieve it. This highest ideal is the state of *moksha* or liberation where one finds self-fulfillment and deepest bliss. *Moksha* serves as the ultimate standard of right conduct; it measures the value of an act by the extent to which it either helps or hinders the attainment of freedom. Actions most distinctly oriented to *moksha* are those characterized by truth, non-violence, sacrifice, and renunciation (p. xiv).

In the ancient texts, the earliest Indian scribe, Sage Narada, was charged with the responsibility of mediating messages between the mighty deities and their earthly subjects. Narada was given the basic objective of establishing *lokakalyan* [universal peace and prosperity]. In his role, he depicts himself as the master oral communicator who sought liaison between the rulers and the ruled and as one who kept an empathetic discourse between the people and the various kingdoms of the gods. It is essential to notice the fact that sages, when narrating each other's intentions and motives in the interest of maintaining peace and tranquility, would deliberately slant the truth. Even when the clever role of Narada was to be found out, he would still be revered for his intent to keep peace between people over truth-telling. Similarly, the two great epics *Mahabharatha* and *Ramayana* are wrought with such paradoxes in human action. The former text includes *Bhagavad Gita*—the conversation between Lord Krishna the chariot driver and Arjuna the ultimate warrior on one's *dharma* and ethics of being. *Bhagavad Gita* is the famous philosophical dialogue that lays the foundation for Indian ethical conduct in the present life. Nondualisms and contradictions prevail in which the choice between good and evil is never clear-cut.

Indian ethics appear most often as subtle manifestations of human conduct in the narratives of prominent cultural and religious texts, traditions, and customs. These narratives carry diverse interpretations, multiple and authoritative translations into other Indian languages, dialects and semantics within oral traditions (Richman, 1991), vernacular expression and ahistorical arrangements. In addition, Buddhist doctrines espoused in *Dhammapada* shed light on problems of human existence, goals of Buddhism (King, 1946), Buddhist ethics, the problem of evil, and ethics for laypersons. The dominant Hindu ethics revolve around the issue of moral obligation. Indian texts point to minute details of Indian life that expound on the ethics of environmental protection, universal morality, and the ideal of human perfection, knowledge as virtue, the parallelism of thought and action, and intersections of theory and practice.

The original texts of Hinduism reflect throughout a continuity of ethical discourse in the midst of paradoxes and contradictions (Govinda Das, 1947; Herman, 1991). The Vedic period produced the oldest known book in human civilization, the *Rg Veda*, which contains no evidence of caste, child marriage, prohibition of widow remarriage, or other such antisocial practices. "Women wore the sacred thread of Brahminism, participated in metaphysical discourse, and enjoyed a moral and intellectual status never achieved since then" (Lacy, 1965, p. 14). Ethics during the Vedic period espoused obedience to divine law. "*Rta*, the law or order of the world, provides the standard of morality. . . . Virtue is conformity to the cosmic law" (Gandhi, 1948; quoted by Lacy, 1965). *Rta* contains discourses on love and fear, kindness and benevolence, order and duty. Out of *rta* comes the central ethical concept of *dharma* in subsequent moral philosophy. During the Vedic age, life was viewed in an affirmative sense rather than according to the later ideal of renunciation. Only later did the ideal of high ethnicity become withdrawal rather than service, spiritual achievement not abasement (Lacy, 1965, p. 15).

Upanishads essentially nullify ethics as commonly defined. Under the *Upanishads,* a person's highest spiritual aim is to blend the individual soul (*Atman*) with the Universal-Ultimate Reality, the *Brahman* (not to be confused with the upper-caste Hindu Brahmin) creating *Brahman-Atman*, a supramoral soul. Because the spiritual goal possesses no moral characteristics, the process of salvation includes no moral challenge. The *Upanishads* contain various instructions: to speak the truth, respect gods and ancestors, honor parents and guests, and control desires. Another reason for the nullification of ethics in the *Upanishads* is the denial of the material world because the only reality is represented in the *Brahman-Atman's* impersonal and supramoral Soul. The physical universe and human existence are *maya* [illusion] and *lila* [play]. In such a society, one may have prescribed duties, but any free, spontaneous, creative relationship to other beings becomes imaginary and meaningless. The attainment of *nirvana*, a Hindu-Buddhist term for the extinction of desire and attachment, is a transcendence of all relativity and relationships. A devout Hindu or Buddhist would find supreme union with the *Brahman* as the ultimate, positive, and ecstatic experience (Lacy, 1965, p. 16). But, clearly, in the arena of human ethics and in a traditional epistemological view, this concept of salvation offers neither guidance nor incentive.

Another reason for the de-emphasis of ethics in the *Upanishads* is the emphasis on two doctrines crucial to all subsequent Hinduism: *karma* and *samsara*. Ethically speaking, the law of *karma* simply recognizes that a person reaps what a person sows—if not in this life, then in a life to come. According to *samsara,* all those who die without achieving *nirvana* will reappear in another and yet another birth, either higher or lower in the orders of creation and social scale (Herman, 1991). Many Indians and some Westerners today, without justifying caste discriminations in any sense, uphold the doctrine of *karma* on various grounds. Metaphysically speaking, it provides a consistent theory of evil and suffering.

> No theistic system, including Christianity, has been able to reconcile the goodness and omnipotence of God with a world of pain and sin. . . . The Hindu

advocate of *karma* may be quite right that such a belief provides a powerful incentive for personal ethics. . . . At best, therefore, these basic Hindu beliefs inspire a self-centered morality (and social ethics), whose sole criterion for ethical behavior is the merit being stored up by *karma*. (Lacy, 1965, p. 17)

By the time the *Code of Manu* (Doniger & Smith, 1991) makes an appearance in the continuum of Indian philosophical thought, it is obvious that neither lawmakers nor philosophers of ancient India sought to construct a systematic ethical theory. Morality consisted of obedience to the divine law, expressed less in legal commandments than in social custom and religious sanction. Not unlike *Rg Veda*, the *Code of Manu* offers a mythological rationalization of ethical behavior through the caste system: that the Brahmins must be priests wielding verbal authority, the Kshatriyas must be the warriors to defend the *raj*, the Vaisyas craftsmen, traders and farmers are to be used for manual skills, the Shudras servants for performing menial tasks, and India's outcasts (the *harijans*) are the untouchables. Many enlightened Hindus have discarded all justifications of the caste system, and the brutal exploitation of caste stands universally condemned. Although many Indians, including Mahatma Gandhi and Rabindranath Tagore, believed in the *varna-dharma* (caste obligations) for different reasons, Gandhi particularly became an active crusader against caste with the profound belief that caste was alien to Hinduism having found no support in the *Vedas* (Crawford, 1974, p. 220).

Every social, economic, and cultural justification of the caste system was purchased at a great price—the loss of freedom and the sacrifice of social progress. Freedom was lost because the individual was required to submit totally to the system; social progress was sacrificed because the principle of heredity was the sole determinant of a person's role in life (Crawford, 1974, p. 219). The doctrine of *karma* could explain one's present position in relation to the past and even provide incentive to perform good deeds with a view to meriting a higher caste in the future existence, but too often this doctrine was only a moral rationalization of social inequities (p. 219).

However, the inherent quality of Hinduism—the many voices of dissent against the hierarchial order of caste—has always been vibrant. It should not be assumed that the Hindu embarrassment over the caste system developed only from contact with Western ideals of liberty, equality, and fraternity. "Actually there has always been a counter movement, questioning and

controverting the rigidity and inviolability of the principle of heredity"
(Crawford, 1974, p. 219). Regardless of the assigned caste, one reaches
the stage of the *Brahman* if one observes "truth, charity, fortitude, good
conduct, gentleness, austerity, and compassion," says Yudhisthira in *Mahabharatha*. The actual attainment of the Ultimate Soul—the *Atman*,
the *Brahman*—is contingent on one's ability to denounce social status
and caste affiliation and embrace nothingness. Unlike earlier texts, the
Code of Manu codified family ethics and a lower status for women. Pre-
puberty marriage, polygamy, divorce, voluntary *sati* [widow cremation],
and bans against widow remarriage—all found acceptance in this book of
Hindu law.

The epic *Mahabharatha* anchors the major problem of Hindu social ethics. This text represents the sublime pinnacle of morality even as it describes an impersonal superdeity who deprives his followers of the involvement essential to genuine ethical choice. Compassion, forgiveness,
devotion, life without love or desire or goodness are cast in genuinely prob-
lematical terms. Because Hinduism encompasses a wide variety of beliefs
and interpretations with no official orthodoxy or hierarchy, the philosophy
of India that is captured in this epic demands no logical consistency or
precision. Completely contradictory conclusions may be drawn by equally
competent scholars and devotees; any objective appraisal leads to the gen-
eralizations of ethical theory and to observations of moral practice (Lacy,
1965, p. 14).

The centripetal ethical arguments of *Mahabharata* find their home in the
Bhagavad Gita, the song of the celestial Lord. Millions of Hindus turn to
it for daily inspiration and guidance; many can recite the entire text. The
central theme of *Gita* is this: Perform your duty with detachment. The most
dominant school of Hindu philosophy has emphasized detachment—the
freedom from emotional involvement and from concern for consequences.
The other school gaining influence in modern India today puts stress on
action and on courageously making decisions. The result is the classic collision between "world-and-life negation" and "world-and-life affirmation"
in Indian ethics (Lacy, 1965, p. 20). Consequently, Hinduism does not deny
dilemmas. The epics and other cultural texts are not just works of antiquity
but embody the social sinews that connect past with present and make the
epics timeless treasuries of true dilemmas.

Dharma, Ahimsa, and Ethical Values

Although the earlier texts based morality on law and ritual, *Gita* gives new weight to the personal conscience. Though the union with the Supreme Soul is based on spiritual terms, it calls for benevolence toward others. "Morality, which is eternal . . . consists of universal friendliness (and) is fraught with beneficence to all creatures" (*Santiparva* 262:5; quoted by Lacy, 1965, p. 20). True detachment is problematic when one considers this passage from *Gita*:

> Neither with eye, nor with mind, nor with voice should one injure another. . . . He indeed is exalted in heaven who looks on all other beings with an eye of affection, who comforts them in affliction, gives them (food) and speaks kindly to them becoming one (with them) in their grief and joy. (Lacy, 1965, p. 20)

It is in the *Bhagavad Gita* that the inner tension of Hindu ethics pulls at one's soul. What is unmistakably clear is the final message of the *Gita*: "Perform thou right action (regulated, prescribed duty) for action is superior to inaction. . . . Therefore, without attachment, constantly perform action which is duty, for by performing action without attachment, (a person) verily reacheth the supreme" (III: 8, 19; quoted by Lacy, 1965, p. 21). Both action and escape may lead to salvation, but the former is the nobler choice. One of the lessons of *Gita* is that all persons should do their own duty, fulfill their own *karma,* and accept their lot in life. "Better one's own duty, though destitute of merit, than the duty [*dharma*] of another, well discharged" (III, 35; cf. XVII, 47; quoted by Lacy, 1965, p. 22). It is better to be a good slave than an immoral master. Here a moral standard is implied, though it is no more than a fulfillment of duty.

Equality is also emphasized in the *Gita*. Some scholars contend that if this basic element of Hindu ethics can be examined apart from the caste system, or even within the framework of a single caste or community, it would have many advantages (Creel, 1977; Lacy, 1965, pp. 22-23). Lord Krishna insists in his discourse with Arjuna that detachment leads to the virtues of impartiality, fairness, and justice—at least within the group. The equality of *dharma* (meaning here that each has his or her ordained duty) to many Hindus represents an excuse for noninvolvement and a lack of concern for others. One of the Hindu arguments in defense of *karma* is that it puts ethical responsibility where it belongs, on persons themselves leaving them dependent neither on other people nor on the whim of God. Such a view, admittedly and without apology, leaves no room for vicarious suffering by the innocent nor for atonement by an incarnate deity (Lacy, 1965, pp. 20-25).

The major element of Hindu ethics developed in the *Gita* is the concept of *dharma*. Whereas in ancient Vedic times, *dharma* meant the whole body of truth, the cosmic law, Buddhism narrowed it to a particular set of teachings, to the creed and the doctrines. Hinduism, on the other hand, gradually expanded the idea until *dharma* came to mean the all-inclusive focus of ethics. *Dharma*, in the text *Gita*, can be translated as duty, righteousness, customs, traditions, law, nature, justice, virtue, merit, and morality (Khan, 1965; Noble, 1915).

The unattached individual lives the life of virtue. *Dharma* or virtue has three forms: virtues of the body—charity, helping the needy, social service; virtues of speech—truthfulness, benevolence, gentleness; and virtues of the mind—kindness, unworldliness, and piety. *Gita*, India's sermon on the mount several centuries before Christ, makes *dharma* the pillar of all virtues.

> *Dharma* is the cosmic process, the Kantian moral law, the Quaker Inner Light, the Communist dialectic. It is the Decalogue, the Mosaic Covenant, and the "righteousness" of prophecy. For the Hindu it is what he does and why he does it. (Lacy, 1965, p. 23)

Lord Krishna, towards the end of *Gita*, spells out the attributes of the righteous person:

> Fearlessness, cleanness of life, steadfastness in the Yoga of wisdom, alms-giving, self-restraint and sacrifice and study of the Scriptures, austerity and straightforwardness, harmlessness, truth, absence of wrath, renunciation, peacefulness, absence of crookedness, compassion to living beings, uncovetousness, mildness, absence of fickleness, vigor, forgiveness, fortitude, purity, absence of envy and pride—these are his who is born with the divine properties. (XVI: 1-3)

The final phrase tosses responsibility to one's *karma*, denying the freedom essential for moral action. However, the significance of *Gita* for Hindu ethics lies in the dialogue Indians have with Lord Krishna, finding a God concerned with human problems, human temptations, and human values. Lacy (1965, p. 24) maintains that the faith Krishna offers and rewards is more tolerant and more universalistic. Therein lies Hinduism's chief claim to superiority. Whatever the weakness of nonattachment, duty, and eclecticism in formulating ethics, the freedom and open-mindedness of Hinduism provide a strong appeal.

The true nature of moral character espoused by the *Gita* depends on the faithful performance of duty without regard to consequences: "Thy business is with action only, never with its fruits; so let not the fruit of action be thy motive, nor be thou to inaction attached" (II: 47; Lacy, 1965, p. 25). One follows without question the universal law of *dharma* and the particular law of *karma*.[4] Whereas Hinduism draws a sharp distinction between the spiritual and material, the eternal and temporal, these dimensions of existence are polarized but correlated within the concept of *dharma*. *Dharma*, writes R. N. Dandekar, is a "unique joint product of the speculative and practical wisdom of the Hindus" (quoted by Crawford, 1974, p. 202). *Dharma* describes many modes of conduct, including speak the truth, do not be negligent of truth; do not be negligent of virtue; do not be negligent of welfare, of prosperity, of study and teaching, of duties to the gods and to the fathers; live as one to whom a mother is a god and to whom a father is a god and to whom a teacher is a god; those things that are irreproachable should be practiced and no others; only good deeds should be revered, not others; one should give with faith; one should give with plenty, with modesty, with fear, and with sympathy (Crawford, 1974, pp. 211-212).

What are the universal duties of human beings? One sacrifices because of debt to the community, because one is culturally and experientially indebted to humanity and must, therefore, serve the universal good. The 10 laws of Manu also operate on those premises of virtuous conduct in *dharma*: steadfastness, forgiveness, application, nonappropriation, cleanliness, repression of the sensuous appetites, wisdom, learning, veracity, and restraint of anger. Also, although speaking truth is customarily good, if telling the truth will result in the death of an innocent, it is prudentially expedient to tell lies. In such cases, the end justifies the means. Here, one can see that Hindu ethics is not absolutist and unbending but is reflective and contextual in its approach to ethical problems. However, to safeguard this situationalism from degenerating into privatism, the *dharma sastras* make it clear that exceptions are only to be made for the sake of others, not for one's own private advantage (Crawford, 1974, p. 223).

Dharma must be understood in relation to other values in society (Radhakrishnan, 1989). The traditional categories of *kama, artha, moksa,* and *dharma* are used to express an inclusive recognition of temporal values of which *moksa* is on the highest of the hierarchy. *Kama* refers to artistic or emotional or sensual experience or a combination of them; *artha* refers to economic and material interests; *dharma* comprises duties in the world or the requirements of the social order; and *moksa* is supreme freedom or realization or highest intuitive knowledge of reality.[5] When *dharma* is interpreted as the capstone of earthly value, the major contrast is between the transcendental realm of *moksa* and the empirical, limited, and relative realm of *dharma, kama,* and *artha*. The great Indian philosopher Sri Aurobindo spoke of the Indian social system as an attempt to achieve the harmony of the complex factors of these values, in which *dharma* is the guiding principle of the social order founded on an innate law of individuals and of societies. *Dharma* stands as a contrast to *moksa's* spiritual freedom (Creel, 1977, pp. 45-57).[6]

Dharma represents the moral order of the universe that ensures the victory of righteousness over evil, so that even a weak person can hope to defeat the strong through righteousness (Jhingran, 1989, p. 167). The naive belief that *dharma* [righteousness] or *satya* [truth] always wins in the end so characterizes the Indian ethos that the Indian government has accepted the phrase, *satyameva jayate* [truth alone triumphs], as the motif on the national emblem. *Dharma,* in all its ethical tentacles, embraces both virtue and duty. Certain moral terms like non-violence, truthfulness, and forgiveness denote both virtues and duties.

A human being of *dharma* demonstrates ethical behavior in several ways: kindness towards all, forbearance, nonhostility, cleanliness, quietude, doing good acts, freedom from avarice, and freedom from covetousness. Unless accompanied by the practice of these universal virtues, fulfillment of religious duties is considered useless. Throughout Sanskrit literature, there are many more listings of moral virtues, including purity, charity, mercy, self-restraint, control of the senses, patience, absence of pride and anger, intelligence, modesty, spiritual knowledge, helping the distressed, serving the elderly, speaking truth [*satya*], agreeableness of speech, indifference to material well-being, and piety.

Gita teaches fearlessness, purity of heart, nonviolence, truth, serenity, absence of enmity, compassion for creatures, and absence of hatred, whereas *Mahabharatha* enumerates forgiveness, patience, nonviolence, equality towards all creatures, truthfulness, simplicity, magnanimity, nongreed, compassion, and speaking gently and pleasantly. According to the scriptures, if *dharma* is conceived in terms of nonviolence and compassion, it presents a universal morality in that, "those who follow the principle of universal love and are adorned with mercy towards all living creatures are called godly" (Jhingran, 1989, pp. 173-179).

Paradoxically, truth is perhaps the most important cardinal virtue of Hindu *dharma*. It is unanimously recognized and cherished in all the traditions of Hinduism. Truth is the highest *dharma* and the source of all other virtues. Manu's law says being guided by truth in one's action is the greatest virtue, whereas acting in disregard to it is the greatest sin (Jhingran, 1989, p. 170). To be truthful means never to indulge in any kind of lies or slanderous and malicious talk and to adhere to the highest measure of rectitude in one's conduct. It also means knowing the metaphysical nature of reality (*satya*) and acting in harmony with it. However, as noted earlier, Hindu texts also make allowances for untruthful representations to protect the innocent. As Krishna argues, promise-keeping and truth-telling cannot be unconditional obligations when they conflict with the avoidance of grossly unjust and criminal acts such as patricide or fratricide (Jhingran, 1989).

The cardinal virtue of Hinduism that equals *dharma* in importance is *ahimsa* [nonviolence]. Nonviolence along with truth in *dharma* forms the basis of the entire superstructure of Hindu religio-culture. The ethical principle of nonviolence introduced into Hinduism through the direct influence of Buddhism and Jainism, eventually came to be accepted as the guiding principle of life. *Ahimsa* is the all-encompassing ideal both in its concept and scope. The contemporary example in Indian history is Mahatma Gandhi, who used *ahmisa* as a potent weapon in India's independence movement against the British Empire. Gandhi literally interpreted the term as never hurting another in any way and harboring positive feelings of friendship and goodwill toward all—including one's own enemies. The ideal of *ahimsa* means that a human being must never hurt others physically or mentally or cause fear in them or in any creature. Absolute harmlessness and friendliness toward all beings are expected in *ahimsa*. The *Mahabharatha* contends that a human being who causes no harm to others through body, mind, and speech, and who never thinks ill of others, reaches the stage of supreme *Brahman* (Jhingran, 1989, p. 191).

The real worth of *ahimsa* lies in its exceptionally broad application— expanding from individuals, their group, community, nation, world, nature and all living things therein, and eventually to the cosmos. All living beings from gods and humans to the smallest creatures are *jivas*. (The term *jiva* is used for the individual soul basically referring to one who has life breath.) *Ahimsa* is applicable to all and in all circumstances of life. Nowhere in the history of human thought have the animal kingdom and the plant kingdom been treated as deserving equal consideration and kindness as human be- ings as in the concept of nonviolence. Millions of Indians reject meat eating on the sole consideration that animals who are killed for meat have the same *jiva* as humans. Animals cannot be killed, beaten, or treated cruelly.

Closely associated with *ahimsa*, then, is the virtue of compassion or universal kindness to all beings. The puritan Jain concept of *ahimsa* allows taking the life of a plant if and only it helps in the survival of another living being. Vegetarians who rely on plants do so with extreme apology and for frugal subsistence. Kindness, compassion, and nonviolence are to be nur- tured and practiced by all in day-to-day life. Other branches of Hinduism affirm that kindness toward others or magnanimity toward other living creatures motivates great souls to work for the good of suffering human beings. Jhingran admits that it is always difficult to say what exactly Hin- duism means by doing good to others (*paropakara*). "It definitely includes magnanimity and philanthropic works, as digging wells, planting trees, etc., though perhaps active physical service is not included" (Jhingran, 1989, pp. 190-191). Prominent Hindu philosophers come down squarely on each end of the spectrum of compassion. Some contend that a human being must not merely provide physical service but ought to help fellow humans obtain freedom from transmigratory existence. Others emphasize the need to provide for the physical needs of the masses before offering them spiritual guidance. Universal love and compassion are integral to the concept of *ahimsa*. Truth is an end to which *ahimsa* is the means.

Ethics in Contemporary India

India's hybrid discourse of modernity and of progress involves a search for a new beginning. All the ethical ideals discussed here—*dharma* and *ahimsa*, in particular—have to be recast in terms of a modern and post-colonial India. This task is essentially an urban phenomenon, though the outcome will have a drastic impact on India's rural life.

Modern India now confronts the compelling challenges paramount to the survival of her civilization: the secular as religion, the community as a citizen, caste politics and economic inequality, Hindu-Muslim discord, regionalism, linguistic divisions and the burden of English, social harmony and welfare, status of women, unity and plurality, individuals and the social order, cultural integration, protection of environment and wildlife, population control and family planning, abortion and the dilemmas of life and death, and the challenges brought forth by Western dominance in culture, education, urban values, and ways of thinking. India's success in confronting these challenges depends on her ability to harness the resources of her philosophy and ethical ideals to bring them to bear on her native solutions.

The public rhetoric of the government and the constitution of India is built on the concept of a secular state in a country that is overwhelmingly Hindu. India is indeed a secular state, but it is also much more than that (Larson, 1995, p. 284). It combines a Gandhian-Nehruvian model of a Neo-Hindu civilization-state. Its Gandhian nationalist ideology has a Nehruvian variant in terms of socialism, with nonalignment existing alongside the liberal democratic traditions of the Indian National Congress. The reformist impulses of Hindu religious movements have a quasi-protestant veneer of individualism and the privatization of religious belief. India's multilayered cultural heritage of the Indic, the Indo-Brahmanical, and Indo-Anglian, however, reflects the conventional mind-set of India's high-caste ruling elite. It is a breathtaking exercise in the "solution of synthesis" (p. 285) and what John F. Kennedy called an "experiment in democracy." Gerald Larson (1995) writes,

> It is also useful to see the Neo-Hindu "secular state" . . . as a Gandhian-Nehruvian Indic civil religion that exists alongside the many other religious traditions in modern India, a civil religion mainly of high caste, English-educated and English-speaking elites in government, the modern industrialized economy, the professions, communications and the academy. (p. 285)

India's hybrid discourse of modernity includes the pervasive use of the terms "secular" and "secular state," whereas some Indian leaders refer to India as a "nation of Hindu chauvinism," "upper caste Hindu *raj*," and so forth. The Kashmiri Muslims see it as a repressive, totalitarian Hindu regime that rules by the barrel of the gun (p. 285).

Given the contentious environment between dominant religions ranging from Hinduism to Islam, from Jainism to Sikhism, and all faiths that lie in between, the secularist ideology borrowed from the West and later codified in the constitution of India raises a nebulous specter of Hinduism's ability to embrace tolerance. However, post-colonial critics such as Nandy (as quoted by Larson, 1995) are skeptical about secularism:

> To build a more tolerant society we shall have to defy the imperialism of categories of our times which allows the concept of secularism . . . to hegemonize the idea of tolerance, so that any one who is not secular becomes definitionally intolerant. (p. 290)

The notion that tolerance came to India through Western secularism is what Nandy appropriately resists. The prevailing models of dissent, diversity, and tolerance in early and modern Hinduism continue to elude the post-colonial, urban, English-educated Indian. To build a tolerant India, one has to retrieve modern-day *dharma* from the cultural narrative of authentic and tolerant India rather than depend on the disarming and yet alien ideologies associated with Western secularism.

> It would be a mistake to trace the . . . religious formulation of the "secular state" solely to the Western and largely Protestant notions of secularization, individualism and the privatization of religious belief, although it certainly is the case that these Protestant notions appear to be dominant in modern Indian discourse. (Larson, 1995, p. 291)

As Larson notes, India's communities within communities within communities represent fundamental and major features of social reality in terms of the traditional or premodern caste system with its religio-hierarchical ranking based on ritual purity. These multiple layers of communities are the fundamental structure of modern, secular India with its caste, tribes, backward classes, caste associations, sectarian movements, extended families with carefully arranged marriages, and any number of other minority communities based on language, religion, or regional culture. For India, it has become the ultimate challenge to make relevant the concept of *dharma* to retrieve unity and harmony within India's 4,599 or more distinct communities in the midst of hundreds of languages and dialects. In this cultural milieu, the notion of community becomes central to the understanding of what India has been and continues to be. Political scientists have coined the term "community-ship" to parallel the notion of "citizenship" as one way of capturing this dimension of India's hybrid discourse of modernity. In modern India, the claims of community-ship are at least as strong and maybe much stronger than the claims of citizenship. This notion of community-ship takes the place of communalism, nationalism, secularism, sectarianism, and other inaccurate and divisive notions in Indian society (Larson, 1995).

Two major social explosions in the early 1990s occurred in the area of caste politics and Hindu-Muslim relations. The first was associated with the government-initiated Mandal Commission, which studied the status of lower-caste Indians and proposed higher quotas for their employment and educational access and privileges. When the commission released its report late in 1990, members of different castes pitted against each other in a manner that was never before seen in India's history. The backlash in the guise of student protests and upper-caste reaction resulted in urban violence and self-immolations. The government's quest to balance tradition with equality and fairness in the face of injustice exemplifies how India is confronting the challenges posed by caste politics and modernity. Questions of entitlement, the search for alternative political and cultural traditions, human rights and economic rights for lower caste and untouchable populations, the classification and politics of community in today's India are all best seen in the contemporary formation of narratives on caste. The fact remains, however, that the lower-caste people—particularly in the villages—live under a hegemony of the Brahmanic and other upper castes and subcastes that is oppressive and often cruelly inhumane.

The second incident was associated with the holy city of Ayodhya that pitted Hindus and Muslims against each other over the control of a sacred site (cf. Breckenridge & van der Veer, 1994, pp. 314-315).[7] In a dramatic entry into the arena of conflict, Hindus wanted to demolish a mosque supposedly built on the site of the birthplace of Lord Rama. Fundamentalist religious groups and political parties turned this confrontation into a national settling-of-scores between Hindus and Muslims. India witnessed perhaps its most serious Hindu-Muslim rioting since the partition of 1947. The number of dead ran into thousands across the country and the mosque was demolished by Hindu militants to "recapture injured Hindu pride" (Hardgrave & Kochanek, 1993, p. 182). The Muslims in India, although a minority of less than 15%, number more than 100 million—making India the fourth most populous Muslim nation in the world, after Indonesia, Bangladesh, and Pakistan. India's Muslims, however, are heterogeneous.

> They are not only culturally varied (distinguished, for example, by language and custom among the Urdu-speaking Muslims of North India and Andhra Pradesh, the Malayalee-speaking Mappillas of Kerala, and the Tamil-speaking Labbais of Tamil Nadu), they are also divided on religion and politics. They range from Islamic fundamentalists to secular Communists. (Hardgrave & Kochanek, 1993, p. 183)

Many Indian Muslims today feel threatened and look to the government as their protector. They have traditionally supported the Indian Congress Party for its commitment to secular ideology. Although the vast majority of Muslims remain depressed in rural areas, there is a rising urban middle class, many of whom have ties to the economic pipeline in the Middle East. India's ethical balance has consistently strived to accommodate Islam's Shariat law and India's uniform civil code—a dual legal system that accommodates Muslim injunctions of faith. This does not always come without acrimony. Urban communal riots are regular and constant because most rural Muslims are too weak to offer resistance or pose a threat. Hindu chauvinism and the militant Islamic factions are fortunately considered as extremes in politically moderate India as a whole, but the continued Hindu hegemony will pose problems for Indian morality in the coming decades (Hardgrave & Kochanek, 1993, pp. 175-205). Even though the constitution of India has abolished untouchability and discrimination on the grounds of religion, race, caste, sex, or birthplace, tension between religions will remain a challenge to the formation of a permanent reconciliatory ethics in Indian society.

Regional cultures and linguistic groups have also asserted their right to dominance in post-independent India. The divisions between the North and the South, between the Hindi-speaking northerners and the southerners who speak Tamil, Kannada, Malayalum, and Telugu have become pronounced. The South with its longer traditions in art, music, dance, drama, and literature perceives the North as politically dominant and culturally bullish. Similar situations exist between Northeast and West. Regional conflicts and politics based on language are common and pose a constant threat to India's unity and harmony.

English that forms the "link language" extends its hegemony and control over other languages, and yet it is the *lingua franca* that has continued to serve the nation in the post-independent era. Critics have argued that colonialism manifests its power and entangles the colonized people "in webs of cohesion and domination; the most insidious—because not often perceived as a tool of conquest—is the superimposition of the colonial language over the languages of the subject people" (Niranjana, Sudhir, & Dhareshwar, 1993, p. 334). Conquest of the language was a necessary adjunct of economic and political conquest (Suleri, 1992). Nonetheless, the demands for regional autonomy are tied to questions of dominance among Indian languages.

The concept of *dharma* and *ahimsa*, which provides the rationale for Indian ethics, specifically promotes unity of existence, the oneness of all, social harmony, social welfare, and plurality. The struggle for social harmony, the growth of the women's movement for equal status in India, and cultural-social integration have gathered increased momentum during the last two decades. *Dharma* with its established kinship among fellow human beings runs into its toughest contemporary test in these areas of social upheaval. Noted Indian philosopher Radhakrishnan, as quoted by Creel (1977), says that it is *dharma* that must be evoked to keep society together and to nurture "national solidarity, cultural and social integration, equality of women" (p. 86). The women's struggle[8] involves increased political participation, access to higher education, liberation from social practices that have historically been oppressive—that is, the dowry system, nonmarriage of the widow, the rare but alarming practice of *sati* (self-immolation of the widow),[9] and a revolt against the oppressive ideology of the masculine at the societal level (Niranjana et al., 1993).

It is interesting and instructive to juxtapose the advocacy of social integration with that of individual ethics. The individual and the social order remain suspended in an enigmatic relationship in India. Individuals determine *dharma* in the process of reaching *moksa* [liberation]. Gandhi stressed discipline, self-control, and individual purity as the necessary foundations of social righteousness. Social justice is deemed a spontaneous reflection of justice in individual life, and the moral discipline of individuals is considered the key to social reconstruction. If individual perfection is emphasized, social welfare will follow automatically (as cited by Creel, 1977, p. 101). The closest Hindu ethical tenet associated with individual discipline is the idea of *sva-dharma* [service to humanity], which is reflected in Gandhi's view of *swadeshi* [respect for the indigenous]. Gandhi wished to preserve the ancient village structure with its reciprocal patterns of duty and inward-looking solutions to native problems. Gandhi defended this position with the argument that only traditional villages will resist Western materialism and permit a modest social development that leaves people time to pursue spiritual growth. The other reason for his position was an innate law that arranges people in the social order determining their stations and roles. *Swaraj* [home rule] and *swadeshi* [preference for things native] became hallmarks in Gandhi's struggle for independence; modern India strives to anchor these terms in *dharma* and *ahimsa* as the country comes to terms with her hybrid discourse of modernity.

Typical of *Gita*'s moral dilemmas tugging at the heart and mind is the modern Indian's quest for tranquility in the midst of chaos. As Crawford (1974) notes,

> Hindu ethics is a moral system which acknowledges genuine moral dilemmas. We encounter a dilemma when values to which we are equally committed are brought into conflict, so that the honoring of one value necessitates the violation of the other. The Hindu position is to be distinguished both from the religious fundamentalist, who views dilemmas in the light of revelation, and the secular rationalist, who views them as problems to be solved by the use of reason. For the one, the problem is the need for better faith; for the other, it is the need for superior knowledge. In either case, there are no genuine dilemmas. (p. 6)

What, then, is the applicability of *ahimsa* to India and to the Indians? Perhaps the question ought to be: What is the relevance of *ahimsa* to the world at large (Tahtinen, 1976; Walli, 1974)? The dilemmas of life and death are continuous. The view that life in the womb is not tissue of the mother's body but a separate life bearing the essential marks of humanity before the time of conception is *ahimsa*. "In the Indian view, perhaps the greatest hiatus in Western religions is the failure to explain birth" (Oliver, 1971). *Ahimsa* is also present in the rules of hospitality; gentleness; care for the young and aged; kindness to the land, birds, insects, animals, and the child in the womb. One can locate the concept of *ahimsa* (and *dharma*) in India's politics of population control and family planning. How India will reconcile a burgeoning population with voluntary family planning strategies remains to be seen. India will reach the 1 billion mark in population by the year 2000. Hindu philosophy equates death with life and life with death. Life exists before one is conceived and life exists even after cremation. *Samsara*, the eternal cycle of life, is a metaphysical reality until one reaches *moksa* through one's doing of *dharma* to perfection. The contemporary Indian struggles to find a compromise in the paradoxes that are offered in today's world.

One of the most pertinent principles of early Hindu ethics concerns the sanctity of the natural environment. Hindu philosophy is a rich repository of ideas, attitudes, ethics, and values that can furnish the necessary principles for a proper management of the physical environment (Crawford, 1995, p. 169). Indian environmental thinking dates back to the earliest of the pre-Aryan religions and cultures around 4500 to 3000 B.C.E. Rituals that emphasized the figurines of mother goddesses and representations of other gods were accompanied by animals and plants. A great deal of the imagery of poetry and religion reveal to the human imagination a nature that seemed living and animate. Lord Krishna rides on a cow, Lord Brahma's main transportation is the gentle bull, Goddess Lakshmi sits on a lotus flower, Lord Ganesha is half god and half elephant. Lord Vishnu is protected by a cobra that is coiled around his neck. The universe itself at the time of creation was supported by a serpent that eventually became the pillar on which life itself rested. Hindus have reflected long and hard on the relationship God has with humans and the physical nature of the world. The principles of unity, of interconnectedness, of interdependence, and of restraint are reflected not only in evolving governmental policies in India but more so in village life.

The struggle to bring economic development into rural India is the latest battle between the Western model of technology-driven social progress and Gandhi's *swadeshi* principle empowering villagers to attain self-sufficiency through cottage industries. The next two decades will determine what direction India will pursue. The speculative wisdom of India is essentially intuitive and cosmic. It purports the view of a deep ecology that places people *in* nature, as opposed to a shallow ecology that is anthropocentric and that ascribes to Homo sapiens a position of dominance and superiority *over* nature (Crawford, 1995, p. 177). Issues in biodiversity are related to Hinduism's nondiscriminatory embrace of all life forms, including the lowliest plants and insects. It is interesting that Hindu ethics is sensitive to the moral and practical difficulties of its post-colonial condition. The destruction caused by poverty and population, the struggle to feed their burgeoning numbers have not diminished the people's worship of nature—more so in the nonurban Indian milieu. The flexibility of Indian ethics makes accommodation and relevance possible to contemporary situations. For example, the concept of *dharma* is essentially a dynamic notion open to processes of change as different situations arise. The general idea behind Hinduism's environmental ethics is that the individual *Atman* is one with the universal *Brahman*. This *Brahman* force is manifest uniformly in the divinity of human, animal, and plant life on earth. All these entities live an apparently independent existence, but they all emanate from *Brahman*—oneness in all, which transcends the natural divisions between people and people and between humankind and nature. "Its ecumenism is existential and environmental. It sees humanity in nature and nature in humanity" (Crawford, 1995, p. 200).

India's opposition to the signing of the Comprehensive Test Ban Treaty (CTBT) to ban nuclear testing is based on India's global consciousness in which all humans are viewed as members of a single family; that solidarity is seen as extending beyond human welfare to include all creation. India's sole condition to signing the CTBT is that every nuclear weapon must be destroyed before the CTBT must go into effect. India's view on this treaty is a rare display of a developing country standing up to the global powers. The conquest of nature is unreal and peoples' sense of separateness is the product of ignorance. Referring to Hinduism's environmental ethics, Crawford (1995) writes,

> This calls for self-knowledge. Humans cannot act ethically toward nature as long as they are ignorant of themselves. Lacking a sense of universal identity, people cannot identify with the trees and the mountains, nor can we feel empathy for the beasts of the field. Nature is perceived as mechanical because people have become mechanical. Nature is perceived as empty because we have become empty. We manipulate nature because we manipulate ourselves. The loss of our relation to nature is the corollary of the loss of our own lives. (pp. 168-202)

Conclusion

This chapter has attempted to glean a vast array of cultural sources and interpretations in India to highlight her ethical orientation in the context of her post-colonial condition. Ethics in India is beset by the challenges of continuity and change both in its ethical ideals and normative orientation.

On this journey, readers may discover for themselves what traits of the ancient philosophical and religious traditions of India can invigorate an ethics of communication and contribute to the universal ethical project so badly needed for the 21st century. Perhaps the most practical insight from this tradition is its emphasis on virtue ethics. The moral person is indispensable. People who are truthful, forthright, gentle, and compassionate are able to perform their duties —also as communicators— without analytical recourse to ethical codes or so-called standards. This point can be of great significance for media professionals having to make complicated decisions against immediate deadlines. There are no shortcuts in ethics. Being is prior to acting, and nothing can substitute for the ongoing struggle of becoming moral persons.

Morality, however, is not acquired in isolation. Moral practice usually, if not always, relates to others. The curious meshing of individual and social ethics derives from the notion of relatedness. If individuals are truthful to others, acting justly toward them, charitable and helpful to them, they will be able to attain (as it were) self-fulfillment and freedom (*moksha*). The principle of relatedness is even more evident in the radical demand of universal kindness to all beings, better known as nonviolence.

The basis of this relatedness is a cosmic order, embracing both the local and global. Only its awareness and contemplation can ultimately make humans genuinely human and, thus, moral beings. As Crawford (1995, p. 202) points out, the basic message of Hindu ethics in the ancient idea of *Rta* is that harmony is already here. We do not have to create it, only discover it.

Notes

1. Any normative discourse on Indian ethics must necessarily take into consideration the hermeneutic situation of the 20th century, the Orientalist constructions (Said, 1978, 1993) in

Western epistemologies, and the problem of authenticity (Halbfass, 1988, 1991). For three centuries, the construction of non-Western ethics, particularly those of India, was mainly the project of the Anglo-Saxon curiosity. With its bias rooted in the Euro-Enlightenment, the Anglo-Saxon project initiated and appropriated the discourse on philosophy and ethics. Halbfass (1988) and Nandy (1983) contend that a degree of intellectual honesty in the East-West conversation and the balance between the colonized and the colonizer must be restored for an authentic understanding of the ethics of "the Other." Most discourses were founded on the European understanding of Indian ethics, which later became the staple of higher education and pedagogy of the Indian elite. The latter, although claiming their Indianness with authority, legitimated European thought as more authentic and "objective." Consequently, any discourse on non-Western ethos begins as a response to that which has been already erected. However, it is beyond the scope of this chapter to demonstrate the difficulties in scholarship relating to ethics when one attempts to look for native sources of ethics, its rhetorical composition, its terms, its categories, its meanings, and its dogma—in the midst of the 20th-century hermeneutics of suspicion.

This dilemma gives the reader a sense of the challenge facing colonial scholarship. It must at the same time not romanticize one's civilization and attempt to restore a native hermeneutics in the quest for authenticity. Rhetorical continuity, evaluation of communicative acts, the undecidability of truth, the nonfoundational aspects of ethics, the multiplicity of meanings, the multitude of discourses within one tradition, such competing narratives as strong versus the meek and dominant versus the subservient, the lack of acceptable grounds for ethical values, the categories of ethics, and the understanding of Self—all present the self-aware Indian a genuine problematic in conversing with a non-Indian about ethics. Colonial societies were not simply colonized politically and economically; more important, they were colonized culturally and intellectually. One needs to be mindful of the intellectual colonialism (Oommen, 1995) in which the present-day discourses between societies take place. This is particularly critical for the understanding of the ethics of India.

2. In this chapter, I have used Hindu-India interchangeably. I have chosen to use the word Hindu *faute de mieux* for India. Hindu is any native-born inhabitant of India, whatever his or her ancestry or faith. But in this article, such "Hindus" as Mohammedans and Parsis have been excluded (see Hopkins, 1924).

3. I have avoided the diacritical signs, the *visargas*, thus minimizing the use of Sanskrit words.

4. This type of determinism explains not only the lack of missionary outreach in Hinduism (because a faith is bestowed on us at birth) but also the resistance to religious conversion or cultural change (Lacy, 1965, p. 25). It also explains why even the *Gita* has not inspired many Hindus to creative social and ethical reforms.

5. Because these values are prevalent in all of the epics and *sastras,* any attempt to simplify or venture into deductivist analysis will prove to be difficult due to the sheer ambiguity of the concepts.

6. Questions of *dharma* and the regulations of social life were not the province of the Indian philosopher. As Rangaswami Aiyangar (as quoted by Creel, 1977) says, "Writers on philosophy . . . take for granted a life lived according to the dictates of *dharma*, and do not, therefore, expatiate on them. Ethics do not accordingly form a separate branch of Indian philosophy" (p. 21).

7. The Hindu-Muslim communal strife in the city of Ayodhya is a classic study of political rhetoric and public action in post-colonial India. Soon after India gained freedom from Britain in 1947, the ultra-right Hindus rekindled an old controversy over the site of the Islamic mosque, Babri Masjid. They contested the same site as the Ramjanmabhoomi—the birthplace of Lord

Rama. The secular interventions from the government and courts temporarily restrained the attempt of Hindu fundamentalist political parties' to take over the sacred site. Neither the Muslims nor the Hindus could legitimately claim the site as their own for four decades. In February 1986, the district court decision to unlock the doors of the Babri Masjid assuring unhindered access for Hindu worship ignited the communal tension once again. It was destined to explode 6 years later. In 1992, the climax came in the wake of the call by the Hindu-revivalist organization, Vishwa Hindu Parishad, "to liberate Lord Rama from the Muslim jail." On December 6, the Hindu mob demolished and razed the mosque to the ground stunning predominantly moderate Hindu India. The national news media agonized over the onslaught of secularism in India.

    8. For Indian feminism and the women's movement for social and economic equality, see Niranjana et al. (1993), Kishwar and Ruth (1984), and Jeffrey (1979).

    9. *Sati*, the idea of compulsory suicide on the funeral pyre of one's husband, has been an ancient rite, though not widespread, in northern India. Strangely, the texts of earlier Hinduism do not carry references to this practice. In modern India over the past 50 years, sporadic cases of *sati* have been confined mainly to one state in northern India and, within that state, to one region (Nandy, 1995, p. 34). The British construction of Indian history emphasized such generalizations of *sati* as a widespread practice to justify its own oppression of the heathens. The *Rg Veda, Ramayana,* and *Mahabharatha* and other Hindu scriptures, on the contrary, carry directives to honor and respect widows, who were allowed to marry anyone without restrictions.

References

Breckenridge, Carol A., & van der Veer, Peter. (1994). *Orientalism and the postcolonial predicament.* Delphi: Oxford University Press.

Brown, W. Norman. (1970). *Man in universe: Some continuities in Indian thought.* Berkeley: University of California Press.

Coward, Harold G., Lipner, Julius J., & Young, Katherine K. (1989). *Hindu ethics.* Albany: State University of New York Press.

Crawford, S. Cromwell. (1974). *The evolution of Hindu ethical ideals.* Calcutta: Firma K. L. Mukhopadhyay.

Crawford, S. Cromwell. (1995). *Dilemmas of life and death: Hindu ethics in a North American context.* Albany: State University of New York Press.

Creel, Austin B. (1977). *Dharma in Hindu ethics.* Columbia, MO: South Asia Books.

Doniger, Wendy, & Smith, Brian K. (Eds.). (1991). *Laws of Manu.* New Delhi: Penguin.

Gandhi, Mohandas C. (1948). *The story of my experiments with truth.* New York: Public Affairs Press.

Government of India. (1958). *The collected works of Mahatma Gandhi* (Vol. 53, Appendix III). Delhi: Ministry of Information and Broadcasting, Publications Division.

Govinda Das, Buba. (1947). *Hindu ethics: Principles of Hindu religio-social regeneration.* Madras: G. A. Natesan.

Halbfass, Wilhelm. (1988). *India and Europe: An essay in understanding.* Albany: State University of New York Press.

Halbfass, Wilhelm. (1991). *Tradition and reflection: Explorations in Indian thought.* Albany: State University of New York Press.

Hardgrave, Robert, Jr., & Kochanek, Stanley A. (1993). *India government and politics in a developing nation.* Orlando, FL: Harcourt Brace Jovanovich.

Herman, A. L. (1991). *A brief introduction to Hinduism: Religion, philosophy and ways of liberation.* Boulder, CO: Westview.

Hopkins, E. Washburn. (1924). *Ethics of India.* New Haven, CT: Yale University Press.

Jeffrey, Patricia. (1979). *Indian women in Prudah.* London: Zed.

Jhingran, Saral. (1989). *Aspects of Hindu morality.* Delhi: Motilal Banasidass.

Khan, Benjamin. (1965). *The concept of dharma in Valmiki Ramayana.* New Delhi: Munshi Ram Manohar Lal.

King, Winston L. (1946). *Buddhism and Christianity: Some bridges of understanding.* Philadelphia, PA: Westminster.

Krishna, Daya. (1991). *Indian philosophy: A counter perspective.* New York: Oxford University Press.

Kishwar, Madhu, & Ruth, Vanita. (1984). *In search of answers: Indian women's voices from Manushi.* London: Zed.

Lacy, Creighton. (1965). *The conscience of India.* San Francisco, CA: Holt, Rinehart & Winston.

Larson, Gerald J. (1995). *India's agony over religion.* Albany: State University of New York Press.

Larson, Gerald, & Deutsch, Eliot. (Eds.). (1988). *Interpreting across boundaries: New essays in comparative philosophy.* Princeton, NJ: Princeton University Press.

Lopez, Donald S. (Ed.). (1995). *Religion of India in practice.* Princeton, NJ: Princeton University Press.

Misra, K. P., & Gangal, S. C. (1981). *Gandhi and the contemporary world.* Delhi: Chanakya.

Nandy, Ashis. (1983). *The intimate enemy: Loss and recovery of self under colonialism.* New York: Oxford University Press.

Nandy, Ashis. (1995). *The savage Freud and other essays.* New York: Oxford University Press.

Niranjana, Tejaswini, Sudhir, P., & Dhareshwar, Vivek. (1993). *Interrogating modernity: Culture and colonialism in India.* Calcutta: Seagull.

Noble, Margaret E. (1915). *Religion and dharma.* London: Longmans, Green and Co.

Oliver, Robert Tarbell. (1971). *Communication and culture in ancient India and China.* Syracuse, NY: Syracuse University Press.

Oommen, T. K. (1995). *Alien concepts and South Asian reality.* New Delhi: Sage.

Radhakrishnan, S. (1989). *Indian philosophy.* New York: Oxford University Press.

Richman, Paula. (1991). *Many Ramayanas: The diversity of a narrative tradition in South Asia.* Oxford, UK: Oxford University Press.

Said, Edward W. (1978). *Orientalism.* New York: Vintage.

Said, Edward W. (1993). *Culture and imperialism.* New York: Knopf.

Sen, Amartiya. (1993, April 8). The threats to secular India. *New York Times Book Review,* pp. 26-32.

Suleri, Sara. (1982). *The rhetoric of English India.* Chicago: University of Chicago Press.

Tahtinen, Unto. (1976). *Ahimsa: Non-violence in Indian tradition.* London: Rider.

Walli, Koshelya. (1974). *The conception of ahimsa in Indian thought.* Varanasi, India: Bharata Manisha.

CHAPTER 8

Communication Ethics in a Latin American Context

GABRIEL JAIME PEREZ

There are several important issues regarding the foundations of communication ethics within the Latin American social and cultural context. The purpose of this chapter is to identify principles of social ethics that rise above the oversimplifications that characterize traditional morality. Such a civic ethics cannot be content with a conformist adaptation to present reality by merely describing or reproducing it. And among the many challenges in undertaking this project, we face a crisis of moral values.

I mean crisis and not inversion. In an inversion mentality, moral values were central in the past, but now things have been reversed. We are facing a moral breakdown. It is a pessimistic conception of history going in reverse. Everything is presented in a defeatist fashion, in terms of decadence.

To consider communication ethics properly, it is necessary to overcome this way of thinking. Instead of the concept of inversion, today's problems must be faced in terms of a crisis with its more positive connotations. *Crisis* and *criticism* have the same etymological roots, and every crisis can help

159

us move forward. Crises force us to ask ourselves about new, imaginative possibilities in the present and in the future. Thus, we should face the current crisis in moral values by going beyond a nostalgic recovery of traditional values. We ought to move to the creative and dynamic stage of surpassing the two extremes—absolutizing tradition on the one hand and absolutizing a form of criticism on the other which denies all past values and wrongly assumes that it is possible to start from nothing (Ricoeur, 1986, pp. 19-35).

In this fashion, the particular concern of this chapter is whether we can effectively confront today's moral crisis by examining ethical values. It attempts a restatement of communication ethics by critically investigating three basic principles that make up the fundamental contents of ethics: truth, freedom, and justice. My purpose is to understand these protonorms within the concrete social and cultural context of Latin American communication.

Truth, Freedom, Justice

The concept of *truth* is usually examined from two extreme positions, dogmatism and relativism. In dogmatism, truth is considered someone's possession, forgetting that truth cannot be possessed but must be constantly sought. Relativism is the opposite extreme. From this perspective, it is not possible to affirm anything about anything in universal terms; it thereby leads to skepticism. Debates over truth usually oscillate between these two poles. To correctly understand the truth as a basic value in communication, these extremes must be overcome. Truth must instead serve as the goal of a continuous search in constructive confrontation. In dialogue and reciprocal investigation, meaning is found and constructed from multiple points of view in concrete cultural contexts.

Freedom as a value acquires its ethical connotation to the extent that it is directed toward the search for truth and the achievement of justice. With respect to freedom, two opposite positions must also be faced, namely, the poles of determinism and voluntarism. In terms of the former, we are determined by multiple physical, social psychological, or cultural factors. These circumstances lead to submission, the denial of freedom, and total pessimism. The other pole, voluntarism, understands freedom as the unlimited practice of power. Escaping these polarities, our challenge is to unlock the ethical value of freedom in communication. In this field, freedom of expression has to be understood in the sense of autonomy, as a right of individuals, groups, or communities, though situated in the context of intersubjective relationships.

Another fundamental axiological category is *justice.* The concept of justice in its ethical sense is correlated to the legal perspective but must not be equated with it. Justice entails participation as the basic requirement for communication processes. With this in mind, justice questions the relation between communication, democracy, and human rights. Justice understands them not from the exclusive criterion of merit, that is, giving individuals what each deserves. Rather, justice focuses on the basic needs of both individuals and social groups, giving individuals and social groups what they require to satisfy their needs as human beings. Therefore, an ethics of communication necessarily has to end in the politics of communication—local, national, continental, and global. Ethical responsibility in social communication requires a political commitment to transform society toward more participatory structures, in agreement with the basic human needs of individuals, groups, communities, and cultures.

Cultural Identity

Is it possible to elaborate on these basic values in the light of cultural ethos and cultural identity? When facing the crisis in values, we have to examine not only the content of the fundamental ethical values but also the wider cultural context. For example, when the validity of the concept "Latin Americans" is questioned, our ethical reasoning must consider the concrete historical situation, at the same time searching the contents of the underlying axiological proposition. This is particularly true of the narrative mediations that have been developing the sense of a Latin American ethos and its specifications in each region and country. It ought to be clear that identity does not mean cultural uniformity but refers to the whole plurality of cultures that make up the continent from Mexico to Patagonia. Communication ethics must recognize the plurality of ethical and cultural identities, which are diverse across the continent, even within each nation. In that sense, what does "we Latin Americans" mean, and what challenges does this imply in terms of social ethics? Although everyone is equal in dignity, differences in personality and culture must be respected. Therefore, no one can be assimilated or assimilate others; social equality in terms of justice is not the same as uniformity (Dussel, 1979, pp. 79-108).

We can approach the topic of collective identities by defining culture as "the web of symbolic relations and exchanges from which social identities are permanently built and rebuilt" (Martín-Barbero, 1991, p. 153). In this definition, cultural ethos can be integrated into the framework outlined by the Latin American philosopher, Juan Carlos Scannone. The cultural ethos in which our identity takes shape is "the particular way of ethically living and inhabiting the world which characterizes a historic community" (Scannone, 1984, p. 33). Scannone includes not only "economical, social, and political structures, but also the *ethical-sapiencial nucleus* of lived principles and values which guide a culture." And this nucleus gives special emphasis to "a *free ethical answer* (though structurally conditioned), which a community in its history gives to the absolute ethical imperative of 'good' by questioning it through values, realities and historical events" (p. 33). According to Scannone, in Latin America there are seven different historical projects of value mediation that have contributed to the configuration of its own cultural ethos: colonialism, modernization, subversion, dialectic processes, resistance, populism, and liberation. He understands liberation as the creation of spaces for coexistence "at the microsocial level (family, neighborhood, community parties, sports, trade unions and other spontaneous organizations) as well as at the macrohistorical levels" (p. 45). Thus, the Latin American cultural ethos, in its plurality and diversity, is characterized by a political ethos in which genuine spaces are sought for establishing participatory democracy.

In this ethos, the idea of cultural identities emerges with a Latin American orientation. In terms of plurality and diversity, the concept of cultural identity is a basic subject in a communication ethics that recognizes the present crisis of values. This crisis must be faced with concrete proposals for communicative action, but the struggle must occur on the conceptual level as well.

In the present world situation, the phantom of what is mistakenly called "neo-liberalism" is directly at odds with cultural identity. This neo-liberal ideology—paradoxically presented as the final elimination of all ideologies—camouflages itself behind a democratic model. It is expressed largely in economic terms and presented as the ideal that every nation must seek. In this context, the privatization of the mass media reinforces media power but in certain cases can weaken genuine public opinion and expression (Mejía Quintana & Tickner, 1992, pp. 15-18). In fact, as an ideology, neo-liberalism invalidates any position that questions its objectives and methods. Consequently, Latin America must battle philosophically. It needs to engage the neo-liberal perspective with an epistemology, philosophical anthropology, aesthetics, and ethics that correspond to its own sociocultural reality. Working on cultural identity in terms of protonorms helps to establish the ethical discourse within present conditions of Latin America's own search for democracy.

Within this framework, we can understand the relationship between cultural identities and axiological categories: truth, freedom, justice.

First, cultural identities, in their plurality, are an indispensable referent of the criterion of truthfulness. The concept of truthfulness as an ethical principle—corresponding to the notion of truth as opposed to lies, not only to mistakes—involves in its referential content an acknowledgment of cultural identities.

The UNESCO Declaration of 1978 (as quoted in Traber & Nordenstreng, 1992) establishes this fact:

> The mass media, by disseminating information on the aims, aspirations, culture and needs of all peoples, to make nationals of a country sensitive to the needs and desires of others (are) to ensure the respect of the rights and dignity of all nations, all peoples and all individuals. (p. 43)

The International Principles of Professional Ethics adopted by the Fourth Consultative Meeting of the International and Regional Organizations of Working Journalists, held in Prague and Paris in 1983, recognizes as a supreme duty the respect for the "distinctive character, value and dignity of each culture" (p. 73).

These codes of ethics represent basic principles that are very far from being accomplished in the field of public information, opinion, and expression, both on the intranational and international levels. Violations happen not only in print and audiovisual news but also in dramatized fiction, in advertising, and in other forms of message production by the mass media. Silencing critics, data distortion, lack of research, stereotyping social realities, and the partiality for certain points of view that are typical of a metropolitan ethnocentric culture—together, they perpetuate forms of colonialism that misrepresent the truth of Latin American cultural identities.

Second, the autonomy of cultural groups and communities, motivated by tolerance for their diversity, is also an indispensable referent for free expression and opinion. Article 19 of the Universal Declaration of Human Rights (1988) establishes that, "Everyone has the right to freedom of opinion and expression: This includes freedom to hold opinions without interference and to seek, receive and impart information and ideas through any media and regardless of frontiers" (p. 4). The Latin American Code of Professional Ethics (Federación Latino-Americana de Periodistas [FELAP], 1984) explicates freedom of expression as a right not only of individuals but also of social collectivities. The first duty of the journalist is "to encourage, consolidate and defend the freedom of expression and the right of information, understood as the right of communities to inform and be informed (FELAP, 1984, p. 38). Combining these two emphases, the Declaration of International Principles of Professional Ethics (1983), signed by international and regional journalists' organizations, recognizes as one of its first principles that "communities and individuals have the right . . . to express themselves freely through the various media of culture and communication" (Traber & Nordenstreng, 1992, p. 72).

What does this mean in relation to cultural identities? My proposal is that freedom of expression, as an axiological principle of social communication, supposes and demands the autonomy of both individuals and cultural groups and communities. It acknowledges that they must determine their own way of life and their own social and political organization and development. This concept of autonomy includes both creative and recreational abilities (activities that engage their imagination, enjoyment, and entertainment), as expressed in different ways of thinking, holding different opinions, and in different artistic and religious expressions.

The third axiological proposition constitutes the nucleus of a communication ethics that overcomes the reductionism of traditional professional morality. Individualistic ethics and those of the professional associations often limit the concept of ethics to deontology. In this view, receivers are clients, consumers who must be treated well. This implies that their demands can be increased and their responses will cohere with the messages offered by the professional class.

This conception contradicts Kant's second formulation of the categorical imperative: "Act in such a way as to treat humanity always as an end and not merely as a means." Antonio Pasquali (1979) has referred to this Kantian imperative as "the essence of the ethical problem of communication, which includes the possibility of the receiver's participation" (p. 138). In this context, participation must not be understood merely as receiving some sort of partial benefits in terms of so-called distributive justice. In its more complete sense, it means to take an active part in decisions concerning policies, processes, and contents of communication that affect one's own existence and development, both at the individual and collective or community level, and in the public and private spheres.

In this manner, the question of participation is specifically located in the context of justice. Paul Ricoeur (1990) defines ethics as "the search for a good life with and for the other, within institutions of justice" [*visée de la vie bonne, avec et pour autrui, dans des institutions justes*] (p. 202). The community dimension also means that ethics cannot remain at the interpersonal level but demands the creation of institutions that assure the fulfillment of justice. This requires that justice is not reduced to equal opportunities but that it is understood as active participation in public discourse about anything that affects people as persons and as members of cultural communities. Therefore, communication ethics, in its integral sense as social ethics, should explicitly accomplish the goals of Article 28 of The Universal Declaration of Human Rights (1948): "Everyone is entitled to a social and international order in which the rights and freedoms set forth in this Declaration can be fully realized" (p. 6). In the present social and political reality of the world and specifically in Latin America, communication ethics must continue to be a place for developing concrete possibilities for processes of democratization both on the national and international levels.

Communication Leading to Peace

If these protonorms help to establish a richer sense of cultural identity, what bearing might identity and the fundamental human values have for peace? The Latin American sociopolitical environment, in which violence prevails in multiple expressions, requires that the ethics of social communication concern itself with the quest for peace.

First, it must be clear that violence cannot be restricted to particular social or political demonstrations. Violence has been common to Latin

America since the beginning of its history in which natives, European whites, and later Blacks from Africa were present. Latin American social relations started with attacks on each other. The cultural cross-breeding that characterizes Latin America has resulted from the violence of an invasion that some Latin American philosophers consider an act of rape in every sense of the term. It is important to keep in mind that the current manifestations of violence have their structural origin in primal violence.

When seeking social communication that promotes peace, we have to consider the reality of the historical situation. But communication for the overcoming of violence does not mean to ignore conflicts by recourse to *irenismus* (a superficial peace imposed by force). Sometimes, we equate violence with social conflict, though the two are different concepts. They may coincide; there can be violent social conflicts, but not all social conflicts imply violence. Here, violence must be understood as unfair destructive aggression against individuals, groups, communities, cultures, and natural resources.

Given a commitment to truthfulness, the point is not to ignore, avoid, or conceal conflicts. Instead, the task is to look in the public arena for the structural causes of all kinds of violence, at the same time recognizing the existence of what Helder Cámara (1970) calls a "spiral of violence." In Cámara's terms, there is first a kind of violence that is institutional. It deals with unjust structures that generate everyday violence in the ecological, economic, sexual, educational, political, and religious arenas. From the second circle, subversive violence emerges as rebellion, as social and political insurrection, with all its manifestations. These, too, are the result of structural injustice, but frequently they have also turned into new forms of delinquency because they have become a modus vivendi for some people. A third circle of the spiral is repressive violence by private and governmental powers within the scope of the exercise of their "authority." This violence takes the form of militarist operations by paramilitary organizations or self-defense groups.

The unjust established order with its primary manifestation of violence is primary not just in the chronological sense but also because it forms the background of the current reality. It coincides with the lack of open participation that the principle of free expression demands. The lack of participation is reinforced by the mass media when they fail as agents of truth by following conventions such as sensationalism and spectacle.

Instead of encouraging thoughtful reflection and critique, media sensationalism deliberately stimulates the primary instincts, reinforcing them toward violence in verbal and visual language. By resorting to the ultimate criterion of impact ("this is what people like"), a superficial and conformist attitude is promoted among consumers of message merchandise. The relation between sensationalism and conformism must be stressed. The constant profusion of messages that incite instead of question lead us to become accustomed to the portrayed reality, paralyzing our capacity for taking action against violence. It makes us accept violence as a matter of course; it even encourages many people, especially children and teenagers, to reproduce violence as the only means for surviving and succeeding in life.

Second, "reality" is seen by the mass media primarily as a spectacle. It is not portrayed as the arena for transformative action, in which people search for fair and fraternal living conditions. The public, turned into a spectator, increasingly ignores the obligation of participation in the historical struggle for justice. In addition, the spectacular has turned many mass media professionals into marionettes of terrorists who seek to accomplish their goals by creating and manipulating the facts. How many times have we not witnessed reports in which, subtly and even bare-facedly, delinquents, drug dealers, and criminals are presented as heroes, as stars of everyday entertainment? This does not only happen in news or documentaries but also in sports when irrational nationalism is encouraged or in fiction programs that give prominence to violent characters—whether as "good guys" or "bad guys" (in the framework of a Manichaean mentality)—and present them as charming and attractive. How many mercenary heroes who are shown as "fighters against crime" and "just avengers" are justifying, implicitly or explicitly, the creation and rise of terrorist and paramilitary groups? In this empire created by fear, people start to think that it is preferable to be safe under the protection of the strongest instead of enjoying individual and social freedom.

Communications without multilevel truth and justice do not promote freedom but the ideology of success, of money, of immediate results. According to this mediated ideology, when people are facing a problem, they need only look for immediate relief to escape from it. They need not wonder about the causes of problems and the ways to challenge them. To what extent does the echo generated by the irresponsible handling of information

and advertising lead us to the easy solution of magical success achieved by
means of power or money, confusing order with the status quo brought
about by chains, and confusing peace with the silence of those who have
disappeared or died?

Conclusion

An integrated ethics of social communication does not impose a morality
of norms nor a deontology of instructions. Professional ethics cannot be
restricted to norms, instructions, or codes. This does not imply that codes
or case analyses are not necessary. They are useful as long as we avoid
falling into casuistry. The proper approach must be an ethical foundation
that generates basic questions from a global perspective and places them
in the concrete social and cultural contexts where communication processes take place.

In recent years, a special emphasis in communication studies has been
placed on the close relationship between communication and culture. Several Latin American scholars have identified an important difference between a standardized and homogenized mass culture and the popular cultures that manifest the production of meaning from subordinate and
dispossessed groups or sectors by their own uses of the mass media (González, 1983; Schmucler, 1983; Schmucler & Pasquali, 1987). This illustrates the need for taking into account the search for alternative media and
alternative uses of the media that facilitate the transformation of communication by the active participation of popular cultures in social processes.

Such a transformation is not easy because there are multiple factors that
hinder committed action. Moreover, it requires effort on everybody's part.
Nevertheless, we must start little by little, by nurturing a critical, autonomous, responsible awareness. Insofar as everybody contributes, according
to individual concrete possibilities, truly humane and humanizing communications can be established: communication for truth, freedom, and justice; communication that respects cultural identity; and communication for
peace.

References

Cámara, Helder. (1970). *Espiral de Violencia.*. Barcelona: Herder.

Dussel, Enrique. (1979). *Filosofia de la Liberación Latinoamericana*. Bogota: Nueva América.

Federacion Latino-Americana de Periodistas (FELAP). (1984). Latin American code of journalistic ethics (2nd Congress, Caracas, Venezuela, July, 1979). In Pofirio Barroso (Ed.), *Códigos Deontológicos de los Medios de Comunicación* (pp. 37-39). Madrid: Ed. Paulinas.

González, Jorge Alejandro. (1983, August). Cultura(s) Popular(es) Hoy. *Comunicacion y Cultura, 10* (UAM-Mexico), 7-30.

Martín-Barbero, Jesús. (1991). Etica y cultura. In *Colombia, Una Casa Para Todos: Debate Etico* (pp. 151-157). Santafe de Bogota: Antropos.

Mejía Quintana, Oscar, & Tickner, Arlene. (1992). *Cultura y Democracia en América Latina: Elementos para Una Reinterpretación Cultura y la Historia Latinoamericanas*. Bogota: M & T Editores/Tercer Mundo.

Pasquali, Antonio. (1980). *Comprender la Comunicación*. Caracas: Monte Avila.

Ricoeur, Paul. (1986). *Ethics and culture*. Paris: Seuil.

Ricoeur, Paul. (1990). *Soi Même Comme un Autre*. Paris: Seuil.

Scannone, Juan Carlos. (1984, April-June). La Mediscián Histórica de los Valores: Aporte Desde la Perspective y la Experiencia Latinoamericanas. *Cuadernos de Filosofia Latino-Americana, 19,* 32-48.

Schmucler, Héctor. (1983, August). Interrogantes Sobre lo Popular. *Comunicación y Cultura, 10 (UAM-Mexico) 3-5.*

Schmucler, Héctor, & Pasquali, Antonio. (1987). Comunicación y Cultura. In Rafael Roncogliolo (Ed.), *Comunicación y Desarrollo* (pp. 169-186). Lima: Instituto para América Latina.

Traber, Michael, & Nordenstreng, Kaarle. (1992). *Few voices, many worlds*. London: World Association of Christian Communication.

Universal Declaration of Human Rights. (1948). *Human rights: A compilation of international instruments*. Geneva: Centre for Human Rights.

CHAPTER 9

Communalistic Societies

Community and Self-Respect as African Values

ANDREW AZUKAEGO MOEMEKA

*In an age and society which decry increasing noise
pollution, hype, deceptive advertising infotainment,
oversexed and violent media messages, slick and superficial
conversation, and hollow communication in general, can
we learn about communication ethics from earlier quieter,
possibly wiser ancestors.*

—Cooper (1994, p. 328)

In the modern industrialized world, ethics is seen as a "cloud" of what ought to be done. Systems of moral principles hang up in the sky for everyone to observe but not necessarily for drawing long-lasting positive inspiration. In the individualistic environment of modern societies, actually adhering to the standards boldly written in the clouds has become a mark of weakness or of living outside the realm of reality. Not only is most ethical behavior, at best, based on the definition of the situation, but it is fast becoming a matter of merely personal choice. The age-old moral advice that relates means positively to ends has been turned around. We no longer insist that means should justify ends but rather that ends must justify means. It no longer matters how one's goals are achieved; all that counts is reaching them.

In communalistic societies (Moemeka, 1994), communication is a matter of human interrelationships. It is engaged in principally to confirm, solidify, and promote communal social order and secondarily, to maintain or improve interpersonal relationships. Therefore, effectiveness is an extremely important first step. But the greatest emphasis is placed on the way expected goals would affect current and future relationships. This is why, in communalistic societies, ethics is not a distant and loosely followed guideline for behavior. It is, instead, synonymous with communication rules, that is, tacit understandings about appropriate ways to interact with others in given roles and situations. These conventions are constrained through normative, practical, or logical force (or some combination of these) sanctioned by a cultural ethos. Hence, ethics in these societies is not a question of personal choice but a matter of social and cultural demands. Individuals do not just say or do whatever they want; words and actions are based solely on what is considered appropriate within the social system. The overriding principle is not the individual's comfort but society's welfare.

Ethical demands in communalistic societies are very closely tied to both verbal and nonverbal communication rules that are designed to ensure communal social order; ethics, therefore, plays a major role in determining who says what to whom, when, under which conditions, and for what purposes. Both content and context of communication are normatively determined. The appropriate level at which exchanging ideas should occur and the appropriate atmosphere for specific types of interaction are based on the ways they might affect the social order as a result of their possible impact on established interpersonal relationships.

In Africa, as in all communalistic societies, ethical demands and communication rules are given the status of primary social values with religious implications. There is no distinction in these societies between the sacred and the secular, between the religious and the nonreligious, between the spiritual and the material areas of life (Mbiti, 1969, p. 2). A crime in law is a moral vice and a religious sin; a duty is a moral obligation and a religious imperative (Moemeka, 1984, p. 45). When people violate the rules, not only do the living punish them socially (and sometimes legally), but also the spirits of the dead are believed to frown at or even punish them. This socioreligious union has imbued moral values in communalistic societies with a commanding influence on people's lives. From the Igbo of Nigeria (Moemeka, 1989) to the Shona of Zimbabwe (Gelfand, 1973), and from the Ashanti of Ghana (Moemeka, 1989) to the Shuswap of Southwest Canada (Cooper, 1994), the primary role of communication ethics is sustaining social order.

Communication in the more authentic communalism of rural Africa is carried out almost entirely through the interpersonal mode in dyads, small groups (for example, family meetings), and large groups (for example, village meetings). The marketplace, the village school, social forums, and funeral occasions also serve as very important channels for messages and exchange of information (Moemeka, 1981, pp. 45-46). Ballads, storytelling, and praise-songs are used to relive the exploits and experiences of past and present generations; thus they help to educate and guide the younger generation. How to communicate, what to communicate with whom and in what manner are all culturally regulated. For example, vertical communication follows the hierarchical sociopolitical ranks within the community. What individuals say is as important as who they are. Sociopolitical status within the community implies certain cultural limitations about what to say, to whom, how, and when to say it. Culturally, the degree of free expression for the individual is constrained by age and position.

African culture also imposes constraints on verbal and nonverbal interpersonal communication. Whereas elders have the right to communicate verbally and openly, young children and youths are generally expected to communicate mostly nonverbally with their elders. When they do use words, they should do it quietly and in private. This seemingly discriminatory cultural practice is intended to drive home the need for the young to listen and learn. Because the young have limited experience, they are required to watch and listen and act according to what is judged to be best for them in the context of the community's welfare. This is kept alive in different communities by relevant adages, such as that from the Wolof of Senegal: "The child looks everywhere and very often sees nothing, but the elderly person, while sitting down sees everything." The Aniocha of Nigeria extend this belief by conceding that although some children may see something, no matter how hazy, they have no cultural right to announce publicly what they have seen. They must tell it to the elders because "the child may own a cock, but it must crow in the compound of the elder."

Communication ethics that is expressed in cultural values and attitudes is informed by a number of philosophical principles that provide the rationale for the unique communication pattern in communalistic cultures (Moemeka, 1984). These fundamental principles, which Jahn (1961) has called "the philosophical foundations of African culture" (p. 26), are basic to the understanding of all aspects of the culture. They include (a) Supremacy of the Community, (b) Value of the Individual, (c) Sanctity of Authority (Leadership), (d) Respect for Old Age, and (e) Religion as a Way of Life.

Deriving from each of these fundamental principles are myriad overarching normative values to guide different aspects of people's communicative behavior and guard against infringement on the community's communication rules. Some of these underlying values, such as honesty, selflessness, and truth, are common to more than two principles; others such as charity, obedience, and valor are related to specific principles. But whether they are inclusive or exclusive, their impact on the individual's communication behavior and subsequently on the community's communication climate are far-reaching and socioculturally pervasive. For example, the principles of the Supremacy of the Community, the Sanctity of Authority, and Religion as a Way of Life underscore the necessity for recognizing that individuals are not all-powerful and self-sustaining citizens whose communication acts are guided only by assuming creative coordination (Cushman, 1989, p. 90). Communication content and patterns are not decided by interacting individuals solely on the basis of what is good for them. Instead, the philosophical principles implicitly but firmly demand the overarching ethical values of humility and respect. These, in turn, recognize a higher authority to which one should defer and because of whom the individual should acknowledge the necessity for appropriate communication behavior.

The principles of the Value of the Individual, Respect for Old Age, and Religion as a Way of Life underscore the need to respect human life and individuals as persons and the need for truth, honesty, and charity (love of, and service to, one another). The ultimate goal of these overarching human values is to give unswerving credence to the supremacy of the community. They also underscore the all-important cultural need for members of the community not to do (nonverbal communication) or say (verbal communication) anything that could put them in disrepute. Instead, they are to always strive for and maintain self-respect by not damaging the community's reputation and creating a negative image of its people. To understand how these demands affect the individual and the community in specific and practical terms, each of the five fundamental principles needs to be examined in their relationship to communication ethics.

The Supremacy of the Community

The most fundamental difference between individualistic and communalistic cultures is their completely opposite views regarding the individual's status vis-à-vis the community (society). In the former, individuals are supreme and first in importance and the community is second. Anything not directly serving the individual's interest is regarded with suspicion. In the latter, the community is given pride of place as a supreme power over its individual members. Individuals exist first to serve the community and second to benefit themselves through such communal service. The guiding dictum is "I am because We are." The value of such a communalistic principle lies in the unity that it sustains, the selfless service it generates, and the valor (honor) that it inspires.

The community's welfare takes precedence over the individual's. But individual needs and aspirations are not ignored; rather, they are seen as extensions of community needs and aspirations. The rationale is the cultural belief (proven over centuries) that communal welfare immediately or eventually benefits all members of the community. This unspoken belief that "the whole is greater than the sum of its parts" helps keep alive the ties that bind individuals to the community. Subtly but firmly, it strengthens the feeling of oneness among people, underscoring the bonds of common purpose and of a common destiny.

When people are bonded with one another in the name of their community, they are usually willing to make tangible and intangible sacrifices for one another. This finds expression in direct and indirect contributions to the community: what individuals have done for themselves that has a salutary effect on the community, what they have done for their neighbors in the name of a common destiny, and what they have done to directly improve the community's sociocultural and economic life. Manual labor from members in rural communities and financial and educational services from those living in urban settings are common demands. But whatever the service requested, community members from whom it is demanded are required to accept the responsibility as a binding duty. Following the adage that "the head of the elephant is as heavy on the elephant as the head of the ant is on the ant," services are demanded from all, everybody according to their strength and situation. In this way, no one is left out or overstressed, and all are seen as expressing, in practical terms, their appreciation of the community. No wonder communalistic societies are able to demand and count on the sacrifices of their members. It is not uncommon for urgent personal matters to be set aside if they conflict with community needs, for individual grievances to be played down (some, in fact, ignored) if they contradict the community's interest, and to forbid individuals from saying what is not in the community's best interest though very important to them personally.

It must be noted, though, that most of what is presented as problems or needs or aspirations of the community are, in fact, issues that at least some community members consider personal. For example, constructing a feeder road—seen as a purely community-related welfare issue—is actually a need very close to the heart of farmers (for transporting their products) and traders (for exchanging goods). And the practice of making a communal demand for sacrifices of time, money, and energy to provide for the widow and children of a deceased member turns a personal problem into a communitywide duty. For each of these tasks, every qualified member of the community, that is, all adult males and unmarried adult females—except those excused for acceptable reasons—are required to contribute. Sometimes, especially among the Igbo of Nigeria and for services of a strictly manual nature, the help of boys is demanded. They fetch drinking water, prepare and keep clean the spot for relaxation, and do any other thing adults need to not be diverted from their work.

Communication among members about the community always revolves around what individuals have done or can do (or both) for the community and not vice versa. Meetings, conversations, and discussions that surround the unique position of the community as a supreme authority concern the frequency, quality, and value of each individual's contribution and how such contributions have influenced the community's social order. The greater the contribution, the more individuals are seen as upholding the community's good name.

Making positive contributions to the community earns one respect and the blessings of the elderly and of community leaders. But for those who could make positive contributions but fail to do so, the "reward" is harsh treatment—mental, financial, and physical punishment. Distant community members (sons and daughters who live and work in the city) who fall into this category of defaulters may be prevented from returning to the community. And able-bodied members who cannot make financial contributions are required to pay with manual work or other services of a physical nature. The tacit implication here is that no one, except those chronically ill and the disabled as well as those officially excused, can refuse to participate in community service without facing sanctions.

Not only do defaulters suffer, but their close relatives are also subjected to humiliation. Parents are castigated if their children consistently renege on community service. Sarcastic remarks are made before friends and relatives about those family members who fail to meet this demand, and wives are sneered at if their husbands default on their cultural debt to the community. The principle of the community's supremacy demands selfless service to it and self-enhancing activities on its behalf. Being in the community means being with the community.

The cost of not only being physically present but being actively participative is so physically and emotionally high that members of the community jealously guard its good name and image. They would do anything for the community for which they have sacrificed so much and around which their whole life revolves. Especially before strangers, one's community is the best that ever existed. No evidence to the contrary is ever strong enough to dispel the claim that the community is supreme over its individual members and superior to other communities.

For all intents and purposes, every community member is expected to present the community in a good light in all places and at all times. Whereas one may criticize different members, one is traditionally bound to treat the community as sacrosanct. Individuals live and individuals die; but the community endures.

The Value of the Individual

The encroachment of Western values has diluted African tradition in urban settings. But in areas that are still authentically communalistic, the sanctity of life is an absolute value. For example, suicide and murder are seen as abominations, and they are visited with serious legal and social punishments. However, legal decisions and social actions against such abominations or any other antisocial behaviors are not taken haphazardly. Each case is considered on its own merit, and decisions and actions are based on the principle of impartiality to stress and sustain the values of justice and fairness. All (both the living and the dead) are considered useful members of the community until proven guilty. The body of a person found guilty of suicide is "carelessly buried" far out in the forest to ostracize that person's spirit. The convicted murderer is usually banished from the community forever. In the past, some communities required that murderers self-destruct, that is, kill themselves. Relatives become targets of direct and indirect scorn, sarcastic remarks, and public and private repulsion, even long after the offenders had been duly punished.

High value is placed on life because communities see people as the highest form of wealth. In most communities, people's wealth is measured by the quantity and quality of their children. In like manner, the community's wealth is measured, first and foremost, by the quantity and quality of its individuals (who are, in effect, children of the community). The community holds them as very important and treats them with respect and dignity. Individuals are useful not only to the community as an entity but also to other individual members. Therefore, the individual's value finds expression not only in community service but also through honesty and trust in interpersonal and group relationships and charity.

Communalistic communities enjoin members to serve as (a) looking glasses to other members, that is, as instruments that help members "see how others see them" and (b) as useful companions that help other members live as comfortably as commensurate with the community. A person without food is fed by a neighbor; widows depend on the generosity of the community; farmers who suddenly fall sick midway in the farming season have their farm work completed by the community; children who misbehave know that they will be punished, not just at home by their parents, but on the spot, by the first adult to find out what they did (Moemeka, 1989, p. 4). Communal acts have had such an indelible influence that their praises are sung daily in adages and proverbs. The Fante of Ghana express their communal ethos with the adage, "The poor kinsman does not lack a resting place;" and the Zulu of South Africa say, "Hands wash each other to keep the fingers clean."

The worth of individuals also involves aiding the community by being fair, truthful, honest, and trustworthy with one's neighbors. If members of a community do not trust one another, a false sense of social order is created at best; at worst, disorder sets in. Both of these possible outcomes have a negative impact on the community. The Igbo nation in Nigeria warns against such a disservice with the adage, "Two members of the same family should not need a lamp to eat from the same plate even in the darkest corner." To assure appropriate social order in any community, its members must live clean lives. They must be able to depend on and trust one another. This is true for any society—communalistic, collectivistic, or individual-istic. There are differences, however, in the way each society reacts to individual actions that threaten or disrupt the social order. Antisocial be-haviors, such as dishonesty, cheating, stealing, false accusations, and lying, are serious social crimes in truly communalistic communities. Punishment for committing such crimes is not only physical in nature but also emo-tional. When there is doubt as to a statement's truth or when it is reported that someone has been falsely accused, the community or the kindred (de-pending on the weight of the statement or accusation) summons a meeting to resolve the issue. Among the Igbo of Nigeria, such meetings to determine the veracity of the statements or actions under dispute are usually held late in the evening when farmers, market women, and itinerant traders have all safely returned home. Generally, these truth-determining, dispute-resolving meetings begin with the culturally sanctioned conviction that "Telling the truth does not consume a long wick." The ethical implication is that those who lie not only create an environment of mistrust but, more importantly, waste the community's time, energy, and material resources. Therefore, they must be made to pay dearly for their acts of falsehood.

Deserving special mention is the unique type of punishment against false accusation and lying seen by some Igbo communities as very painful active deceptions. Among the Aniocha, these antisocial acts are particularly ab-horrent. This group of Igbo communities views lying as forcefully but de-ceptively shifting the balance of power among community members. De-ceivers are seen as having stolen power from the deceived. "The person deceived is reduced in stature, symbolically nullified, while the impostor is temporarily powerful" (A. Klein as quoted in Henry, 1989, p. 459). In Aniocha communities, actions are taken to reverse such shifts in the bal-ance of power through deception. Those found guilty of falsely accusing others or of lying are made to walk the streets, using a gong to announce their presence, and publicly recanting the false statements they made, as well as apologizing both to the community and to those falsely accused.

Even long after those convicted have been punished officially, they are subjected to emotional punishment—name-calling, sarcastic remarks, repulsive treatment, and suspicion. They are denied the right to be trusted by the community. Once convicted, forever guilty! Nor is that all. Their crimes also rub off on members of their immediate families, their friends, and acquaintances. This is why parents keep a close eye on their children, and friends watch over one another.

The Sanctity of Authority (Leadership)

All societies accord to their leaders the authority to lead, but the form of and the extent to which authority is exercised differs from one society to another. In general, communalistic societies in Africa have two culturally recognized levels of leadership—formal and nonformal. The formal is composed of (a) the officially appointed or selected leader of the community and all subordinate sociocultural and political leaders that govern with him and to whom they are responsible and (b) parents and guardians who are responsible for those under their care. The nonformal level of leadership is predicated on one of the major characteristics of communalism, that is, the fluid type of leadership structure that derives from the philosophy of gerontocracy or leadership by elders.

Whereas formal community leadership positions are almost exclusively reserved for men in most West African communities, they are open to women in East and Central African communities, especially in Zambia and Tanzania. In Nigeria, among the Edo and the Aniocha, women also play very important leadership roles. Though they may not be appointed to community leadership as such, they have the exclusive right to the leadership of the women in the community. The leader of the women—referred to as the Queen of the community—is a highly placed member of the community's government, commanding as much respect as the community leader.

The community leader in communalistic societies is the first citizen. Once appointed or selected, the leader is bestowed with the honor and prestige befitting that position and is treated with utmost respect and dignity. In many communities, the leader is both the temporal and spiritual head and therefore is seen as representing divine authority. For example, among the Yoruba of Nigeria, the leader is "the King, the Commander and the Wielder of Authority, next only to the Almighty" (Okediji, 1970,

p. 205). This eulogizing maxim agrees with the proverb among the Ashanti of Ghana that says of the leader that "after the elephant there is no other animal."

The high honor and respect reserved for the community leader, however, must be deserved. Leaders are expected to be above reproach. Communities require of them no less than what their status demands. They must live exemplary lives; otherwise, they not only lose their leadership position but also fall into disrepute. The demands of the community's supremacy are in force even for the leader. They lead, but are not above, the community. As an Aniocha moonlight song warns, "If the mouth that speaks does not have the cooperation of the rest of the body, it would lose its power of speech."

Next in authority to the community leader are parents and guardians who, in fact, occupy the first leadership role in the lives of individuals. They have the primary responsibility for bringing up their children. Communalistic societies recognize their unlimited right of supervision and control. Parents and guardians, too, are required to lead not only by what they say but more important by what they do. Any dereliction of their parental duties makes them unworthy of the dignity of parenthood and thus guilty of disservice to the community. Both these negative outcomes always result in social sanctions.

Just as parents are required to dutifully perform their roles as parents so are children expected to carry out their own duties as children. They are required to respect and obey their parents according to the demands of the culture and to personally and fully take care of them in old age. Children who disobey, quarrel with, or disregard their parents are looked on with disdain and contempt; those who verbally or physically abuse them are charged with parental assault by the community and severely punished. Neglect of aged parents is culturally repugnant and socially despicable. It is treated as a violation of the sanctity of parenthood and a disservice to the community. Though not officially punished at the community level, such neglect incurs verbal and nonverbal condemnation. At the close family level, however, the story is different. Family members cajole, admonish, and warn recalcitrant children of the consequences of not providing for their aged parents. If such children continue to ignore these warnings, some other family members take over the task of caring for the elderly parents. But the children face the wrath of these family members on the death of the neglected parent. During the burial ceremonies, the defaulting children are subjected to humiliation and heavy fines for their insolence to parent-hood.

One of the major characteristics of communalism is gerontocracy—a fluid leadership structure in which everyone is involved, except the very young. This is the nonformal level of leadership that is buttressed by the African adage: "It takes a village (community) to raise a child." It empha-sizes the fact that the responsibility for ensuring the existence and mainte-nance of social order lies with everyone old enough to contribute. Those who find themselves in situations in which they are the oldest persons around are expected to assume the leadership position in that situation and to dutifully represent the community. Those over whom these individuals exercise this normative on-the-spot leadership are also expected to recog-nize and respect their authority. But to earn this respect, these "impromptu" leaders must be seen as fair, honest, and culturally committed. If such lead-ers have not been of good behavior in the community before this time or are perceived as partial or arrogant or self-serving, their leadership will be challenged. So, even in this fluid on-the-spot leadership structure, leading by example is extremely important.

Respect for Old Age

The traditional respect for the aged required of all is closely related to the sanctity of authority on the nonformal level. Therefore, much of what has already been said under nonformal leadership also applies, directly or indirectly, to this fundamental principle of Respect for Old Age.

In communalistic Africa, old age is honorable and old men and women are treated with dignity. The elderly are seen as the true repositories of wisdom and knowledge and, therefore, as assets of great value to the com-munity. The longer they live (until senility sets in), the wider their cultural and social span of authority becomes within the community and the more the community expects of them. The future of the community, though not placed in the hands of the aged, is intricately linked with the type and quality of advice they give. Such advice is hardly ever set aside or ignored. As the Fante of Ghana say, "The word of the elder is more powerful than thunder."

Traditionally, living to a ripe age is believed to be a providential reward for a life well spent, meticulously observing and respecting the norms and mores of the community—justice, fair play, integrity, honesty, respect, and charity. Therefore, the aged are good examples for the youth to emulate. This elder-youth sociocultural relationship is so important that there are many adages and proverbs that communalistic societies use to call attention to it (Moemeka, 1996). The Igbo of Nigeria, for example, warn that "Children who demand to be their own masters (to be left alone to do what they want) sleep in the cold." Self-gratification on the part of the young, irrespective of repercussions on others and on society, leads to dire consequences later in life. And the Igbo reinforce this adage with another that points out that, "What the young cannot see even if they climbed the tallest of palm trees, the elderly can see clearly without even standing up." The exalted position bestowed on old age in communalistic societies requires a high degree of service and exemplary behavior from the aged. Old age alone without appropriate ability for guidance and without a reservoir of goodwill deriving from appropriate social behavior does not earn honor and respect. To be seen as useful to the community, and to earn the prestige reserved for them, the elderly are required not only to guide the community by advising community leaders but also to educate, admonish, and guide the inexperienced and the young. Just as the communalistic culture demands that the younger generation must respect, listen to, and learn from the elders, so it demands from the elders appropriate action to provide conducive learning experiences for the younger generation. To guard against any dereliction of duty with regard to this sociocultural expectation, the Igbo of Nigeria constantly remind themselves that, "To foresee danger and not to forewarn is the bane of elders; to be forewarned and not to listen is the bane of youth" (Moemeka, 1996).

Religion as a Way of Life

Religion is an all-important part of the social order of communalistic societies—religion meaning any organized way of worship through which a people express and manifest their spiritual relationship to the Almighty. Religion pervades life in communalistic Africa. It gives force to the fundamental principles discussed earlier, and it is the ultimate justification for whatever is culturally acceptable. Religion is used for safeguarding social order and protecting social norms, communication rules, and ethical standards (Moemeka, 1994). "Wherever the African is, there is his religion; he carries it to the fields where he is sowing seeds or harvesting new crops; he takes it with him to the beer party or to attend a funeral ceremony" (Mbiti, 1969, p. 2).

To communalistic Africans, religion is not just a gloss on actions and behavior but an inseparable part of the rationale for anything done or not done. As a result, there is no formal distinction between sacred acts and secular behavior or between the spiritual and the material areas of life. Communalism demands that people's lives reflect a solid blend of the secular and the religious. Thus, people's behavior is guided not only by social and cultural rules and regulations but more important, by religious expectations and imperatives.

Religious norms also influence what and how individuals speak and live. In fact, religion helps create the conducive atmosphere in which meeting the demands of the fundamental principles of communalistic social order is assured. The religious symbols representing the ancestors or gods through whom most communalistic societies seek favors from the Almighty are physically near, and their presence is felt everywhere—in the home, in the village square, in the marketplace, along the footpaths, and in the streets. This symbolic proximity strongly implies the actual presence of ancestors or gods whose perceived watchful eyes help to ensure that communication rules and regulations are obeyed and that norms, mores, and moral obligations are observed. Thus, the task of maintaining social order is made much easier than it would be without the impact of religion.

"It's People Who Make People Become People"

The five fundamental principles or philosophical foundations and their underlying ethical values discussed earlier underscore traditional African culture and reflect in general the basis of the type of social order that obtains in strictly communalistic societies (see Moemeka, 1996). Each of these principles communicates its own values and thus helps to guide individual and communal interactions according to established communication rules. For example, the principle of the Value of the Individual demands that members of the community have considerate hearts, show positive concern for the underprivileged, abhor selfishness, love one another, respect life, and be committed to community service. All these reflect the wise saying of the Aniocha of Nigeria: "It's people who make people become people";

or, as the Japanese strongly believe, "One becomes a human being only in relation to another person" (Gudykunst & Antonio, 1993, p. 27; Yoshikawa, 1988, p. 143). The ethical injunction of charity toward others does not apply only to members of one's own community. It is required to be extended to strangers. "Those who refuse to give drinking water to a thirsty stranger," says an adage, "do not deserve to be called human beings." The implication is that the value of one's own community is acknowledged by helping others and treating them as fellow humans like members of one's own community. "The practice of hospitality," says Idowu (1962, p. 159), "is essential among the Yoruba and kindness involving generosity is accounted a great virtue." This is part of what imbues the individual with self-respect.

In a communalistic environment, communication is not just an everpresent act constitutive of every other act; it is the bedrock and sustaining power of social relationships and social order. Hence, individuals are wont to be on guard about the content of what they say verbally and nonverbally; but more importantly, they are concerned about the ways the context of what they say might affect existing or future relationships. To refuse to answer the community's call for public service, to speak openly before authorities without first being addressed by them, to deride the genuine efforts of an underprivileged person, to make careless remarks about another person or about the community, to show disrespect to the elderly, or to disregard religious injunction would all affect existing relationships and have a negative impact on possible future relationships.

Alongside the fundamental or overarching communication rules and ethical principles discussed earlier are hundreds of more practical, down-to-earth ethical demands and rights that serve as institutionalized safety valves. To laugh when it is inappropriate to do so (for example, during a religious ceremony), to show off how much you have to eat when many around you are hungry, or to give to the community less than you can afford when others are giving their utmost are some of the examples of nonverbal communication that implicitly go against many of the communication values of communalistic societies. An example of an institutionalized safety valve with regard to verbal communication is the unspoken leeway allowed boys and girls of dating age to converse in private in spite of the communication rule that forbids such private conversations. Parents and guardians tend to turn "deaf ears and blind eyes" when boys and girls of dating age are talking together privately, provided such a *tête-à-tête* does not last too long and is not held in very secluded areas.

Most of the values of Respect for Old Age are related to the values of the Sanctity of Authority, both of which reflect a unique pattern of interaction within communalistic societies. The two fundamental principles and their interaction values would seem to create what most Western communication specialists describe as the dominance-submission environment but what communalists see as an appropriate environment in which "water seeks its own level" for the benefit of all. This not only reduces conflict situations but also brings into focus the normative injunction for reciprocal sensitivity toward one another.

The demands of these fundamental principles are not one-sided. Just as the culture gives those in authority the right to the respect and obedience of those over whom they exercise authority, so it gives so-called subordinates the right to be treated with dignity and respect. But both respect and obedience on the one hand, and respect and dignity on the other, must be earned. Parents and elders must say what is appropriate at the right time; show good examples in speech and in deeds; perform their responsibility of educating, guiding, and protecting the young; and in general, uphold the community's ethical standards of behavior. The younger generation, on their part, must be willing to listen to and learn from their parents and the elderly, respect the elderly by, for example, giving up seats, helping to carry heavy loads, listening to their advice, and, in general, showing good behavior both at home and outside the home. For the sake of social order, to each is given the appropriate communication right, and from each is demanded the appropriate communication duty. A happy balance between the two creates a communication environment in which ethical values are seen to strengthen the supremacy of the community and positively promote self-respect for individuals and, therefore, ensure a conducive social order in the community.

The collective impact of the five fundamental principles strengthens the bonds that sustain communalistic societies. These bonds, which find expression in unique ways of avoiding interpersonal strife, disharmony, and social disorder, are the shared symbols, rituals, values, and beliefs of the members of the community; and it is in these that the meaning of communality is contained. Chief among these bonds are the ethics of communication (of interpersonal interaction) and the culturally prescribed communication rules (which are inextricably linked with the people's ethics of communication). They are strengthened and positively revitalized when those to whom the people look for guidance and leadership are perceived as transparently honest in their interactions and communicate according to the demands of the community's culture.

Communalistic Values Under Siege

The communication ethics of communalistic societies has been criticized for two main reasons. First, it is held that because of the wide range of ethical demands, communalistic societies operate a closed and autocratic system of communication. This, it is argued, tends to stifle free speech and opinions, especially for women and the young. Second, the demand for complete obedience to authority and the community is said to stifle individual initiative and tends to create a culture of dependence. To what extent these restrictions have been validated is a matter of opinion. But granted that they are in fact true, they would seem to constitute a small price to pay for a social order that celebrates being-with-the-community as central to human life.

The communication ethics of what we have called "authentic communalistic societies" of Africa has long been eroded and is now being challenged by (mainly young) Africans in the name of personal freedom. They tend to claim freedom as a personal right rather than recognize it as a communal right from which each person derives his or her rights to act or interact—but only in such a way as not to selfishly disregard the rights of others. These modern youths claim the right to say and do whatever makes them feel good, whether or not such acts fall in line with established norms or adversely affect others. However, there still are communities in the rural areas of Africa where individuals willingly and proudly submit to the supremacy of the community, where actions and omissions have both sociocultural and religious connotations, where obedience to authority, self-respect, love of and respect for others, and service to the community are seen as mandatory for social order. In these areas, freedom to act individually takes into account the ways such action would affect others. In these relatively unadulterated communalistic communities, freedom is exercised only when one recognizes how one's own rights in search of self-satisfaction can affect other people's exercise of their own rights.

In the modern world, however, communalism has lost much of its strength to the encroaching and diluting powers of two types of social order—individualism and collectivism. Individualism denotes a social order in which the individual takes precedence over the community. In collectivism, individuals are primarily considered part of the "masses" rather than members of a community. Collective rights are upheld, but the ultimate goal is safeguarding the individual's freedom. When a people (especially their youths) borrow from another culture, they usually borrow the outward signs of the culture rather than its soul. Even though both individualism and collectivism uphold freedom, they also demand that freedom be exercised responsibly and with self-respect to give positive effect to its exercise. But what modern Africans seem to have borrowed is freedom only and not freedom as a foundation of responsibility and self-respect.

> Today, the division between those standing firm in favor of the communalistic demands of ethics and those who oppose most of such demands is very clear. They use very contradictory communication codes, communicate on different arenas of the social environment, and have opposing views on what should constitute the "good" and for whom. (Moemeka, 1996)

The conflict between the traditional and the modern is most pronounced in the activities of the modern media of mass communication. The mass media, universally acknowledged as the watchdogs of the government (in the interest of the nation), have virtually become in Africa the watchdog for the government (in the interest of remaining in office). Almost completely owned by the government, African mass media institutions (especially the broadcast institutions) regard the adage that "he who pays the piper, dictates the tune" as a categorical imperative. Hence, in general, African media personnel operate on the basis of what Pratt (1994) has called the "ethical philosophy of African governments" (p. 54), which he identified as a mix between antinomianism and situationism and which Merrill (1975) has criticized as "non-ethics" or "anti-ethics" (p. 10). News and information decisions are rationalized, based on what the government has judged to be appropriate in the context of the situation. More often than not, such decisions reflect what is good and fitting for the government in power and not necessarily for the nation.

African governments operate under two basic assumptions. First, they see themselves as the constituted authority and therefore covered by the cultural principle—Sanctity of Authority. Second, because they seem to see themselves as the nation rather than as representatives of the nation, they also claim cultural protection under the Supremacy of the Community principle. But they call on these two fundamental principles only insofar as conferred rights are concerned; they pay little or no attention to the expected responsibilities. Nor do they apply in their day-to-day activities the principles of Respect for Old Age, Religion as a Way of Life, or even the Value of the Individual. Shamelessly, the contents of modern media conspicuously reflect these conditions. For example, in news coverage, the prominence of the source almost always takes precedence over the consequence of the event. Balance, fairness, and truthfulness are treated as relative criteria, at best, for news selection and presentation as well as for information dissemination; at worst, they are treated as antigovernment journalistic requirements.

Denis McQuail (1983, p. 94) has developed a theory that explains the practice of the mass media in developing societies (which, until recently, were completely communalistic). Called development media theory, it states, among other things, that in such societies, the media are required to join the government in the task of nation building but that in this collaborative venture, the government is presumed to have the right to sanction the media in the interest of the nation. Media personnel therefore have little or no room to maneuver. By tradition, they are expected to respect constituted authority and to work for the good of the community (the nation). But by modern standards of African democracy, it is not up to the media to determine what is good for the nation. That task is exclusively reserved for the government-of-the-day. In broadcast institutions, media personnel have no opportunity whatsoever to question the government's dictates. Those who raise their voices do so only in private, and they are usually ridiculed by their colleagues who believe that there is nothing wrong in dancing to the tune dictated by the government. In the print media, many voices have been raised against the self-protecting ethics of the government. But almost all those who have raised such voices have found themselves either in police custody or in prison. The struggle, however, continues.

This amounts to what Okigbo (1994, p. 75) has described as the ethics of indecency. Not only have truth, objectivity, and factual background information been virtually replaced by the exigencies of contextual appropriateness in favor of the powers-that-be but also the satisfaction of morbid desires is being glorified, whereas service to others and to the community, continence, temperance, self-control, and respect for others are at best ignored; at worst, they are derided. The consequences have been all-encompassing—affecting not only the mass media but also interpersonal interactions. In most urban areas in Africa, words and actions that are taboo in authentic communalistic societies are frequently used without any remorse or sanction. Intimate sexual relationships between boys and girls (roundly condemned in rural communities) are now not just tolerated but expected among city youths. Service to the community, which used to be a task of joy, is now perceived as an imposition by many city dwellers. Religion and religious principles as practiced under communalism are scorned, and respect for elders is seen as anachronistic.

Conclusion

The ultimate driving force behind these modern but disturbing patterns of behavior is personal freedom, that is, the right to do and say whatever one wishes, irrespective of who is hurt or happy. The consequences of such a morbid desire for freedom—armed robbery, greed, drugs, teenage pregnancy, deceit and falsehood, bribery and corruption, to mention but a few—are exacerbated by the poor economic conditions under which most city youths live. These social ills are even encroaching on rural communalistic communities, because interaction between the urban and the rural areas is constant. Just as "bad money drives out the good" in economics, so antisocial actions drive out the prosocial behavior in sociocultural relations.

Herein lies the importance of Cooper's (1994) statement quoted at the beginning of this chapter. If a communication environment based on personal freedom and the collective rights of modern representative governance has created, or is contributing to, myriad cultural, socioeconomic, and political problems, can we find solace in communication ethics as practiced in authentic communalistic communities? Is it possible in today's world to apply the demands of communalistic communication ethics in its entirety? Or can we attempt to create a hybrid ethics that could eliminate the weaknesses of the old and the new but maximize their strengths? These questions are not only important for the future of Africa but are of relevance for communication everywhere else, or indeed, for what is now called our global cultural environment. We may legitimately ask in the field of communication ethics: What contributions can communalistic societies make toward informing and upholding universal human values in today's new communication environment?

Many African media practitioners, now working in cities, grew up in a communalist environment. Many would remember the values bequeathed to them, and some practice communal norms when staying with rural relatives. Others wish—with some nostalgia—that these values would contribute to the ethical stance of modern mass communication. Hence, Moemeka and Kasoma (1994, p. 41) have called on African journalists to practice the moral virtues that made African communalistic societies tick: courage, bravery, fortitude, respect, endurance, hospitality, generosity, magnanimity, truthfulness, kindness, and hard work. All these are elements of the five fundamental principles that serve as the sociocultural foundation of a healthy social order under communalism. Okigbo (1994) calls for a closer and more positive identification of journalists with their people. Journalists "must be perpetual students of their society; they get energized by the society that nurtures their journalistic ambition to educate, entertain and, above all, contribute to the overall development of the community" (p. 87). Similarly, a group of journalists from East and Central Africa resolved to make their traditional cultural values more relevant for their work.

> We are happy and proud to discover in the African traditional way of life great insistence on the values of communal solidarity. These values can be observed in many of our customs; the extended family, the sense of hospitality, communal rites, symbolic rituals and drama which strengthen community relations, and systems of verbal communication which help to create a consensus. There also existed in the past a great emphasis on constant communication within the "total community"—living with the dead through prayers, offerings and rites, as well as the living among themselves. We realize that these values are a precious treasure that need to be preserved and adapted to the more complicated conditions today. All efforts must be made so that the modern means of social communications will help to perpetuate and enhance them. (Makunike, 1973, p. 41)

Regardless of whether African journalists operationalize the inherited moral principles in their work, African media audiences are likely to negotiate meanings of media messages in terms of their communalist ethical norms. Okigbo (1995) argues that African societies are

> in the twilight zone between full urbanization and traditional status. In such communities or societies the full effects of modern media are being moderated

by the enduring traditional practices and beliefs (social norms) which serve to give character and assign roles to communication. The majority of Africans have to make sense of modern communication in the context of their societies' values, traditions and norms. Any conflict between the new and the old is usually settled in favor of the latter. Therefore, no comprehensive knowledge of contemporary African communication can be gained without a perspicuous understanding of how the social values and norms relate to information exchange and management. (p. 5)

Behind this assertion is an ethical core value that can be exemplified by what the Lozi of Zambia call *likute,* "which variously means respect, appropriateness or good taste" (Kasoma, 1994, p. 28). *Likute* is the main moral principle by which people's actions are judged and by which they have self-respect.

A self-respecting journalist would not compromise his or her dignity by doing things which are morally wrong. Journalists who do not have *likute* are not honorable, and consequently cannot be entrusted with the task of contributing to improve their society. (p. 32)

Contributing to improving society, as we have seen, is the most fundamental principle of communalistic ethics. It explains the African media's overriding concern to be in the service of nation building and socioeconomic development. Even capitalist newspaper proprietors in Africa (of whom there are many) would dare not call their newspapers an industry for profit but would stress their contributions toward national cohesion and economic development.

National cohesion and integration may be seen as a postcolonial expression of the supreme value of unity and consensus in communalistic societies. Social and political disintegration is Africa's ultimate nightmare; consensus and unity are its panacea. In a policy statement, journalists from East and Central Africa identified commitment to unity as one of the main goals of the media.

Newspapers and periodicals in Africa must be especially committed to fostering unity . . . unity of the nation and common brotherhood and unity of our continent and all mankind. We will expose and condemn any disruptive forces which attempt to destroy unity. Our task is the reconciliation between men and groups of men to promote peace and unity. (Makunike, 1973, p. 38)

The concern for national cohesion and unity has, however, a harmonic counterpoint: the ethical norm of solidarity with the sick and elderly. As individuals and as a group, these people demand special attention and receive a specific call for action in communalistic ethics. Hence, Kasoma (1994, p. 34) has pointed out that another virtue African journalists could well adopt from their own heritage is the special love and care for the sick, aged, and handicapped. Reporting on such people should be done with empathy to arouse public support for them rather than using their situation for information and entertainment. Genuine Africans do not only want to know that individuals are sick; they are more interested in knowing what is being done to help them recover or alleviate their suffering.

These examples, which could be extended, demonstrate that the communication ethics of African communalistic societies—even under current postcolonial conditions—is not just a romantic musing from the past. It continues to nurture and, above all, to inspire media workers in modern mass communication. In spite of Africa's dire economic conditions, and in spite of the ruthless political exploitation of some of its leaders, there is an abiding current of ideas and ideals that upholds the African protonorm *par excellence*: respect for human dignity.

Human dignity is accorded in truth-telling, without which human interactions could not function in harmony. Human dignity is expressed in the essential being in and being for the community; human beings who are not anchored in a community tend to be adrift. And human dignity, above all, is recognized in the special care and love given to children, the sick, the poor, the elderly, and the physically or mentally handicapped. Material gains and advantages matter little in African communalistic societies. What makes Africans rich are human relationships. African culture is essentially a culture of human relationships, and therefore, a culture of affective communication, with high ethical norms and demands.

References

Cooper, Thomas W. (1994, December). Communion and communication: Learning from the Shuswap. *Critical Studies in Mass Communication, 11*(4), 327-345.

Cushman, Donald P. (1989). Interpersonal communication within a rules theoretic position. In S. S. King (Ed.), *Human communication as a field of study: Selected contemporary views* (pp. 88-94). Albany: State University of New York Press.

Gelfand, Michael. (1973). *The genuine Shona: Survival values of an African culture.* Gweru, Zimbabwe: Mambo Press.

Gudykunst, William B., & Antonio, P. S. (1993). Approaches to the study of communication in Japan and the United States. In W. B.Gudykunst (Ed.), *Communication in Japan and the United States* (pp. 18-48). Albany: State University of New York Press.

Henry, Stuart. Deception. In *International encyclopedia of communication* (pp. 459-462). New York: Oxford University Press.

Idowu, Bolaji E. (1962). *Olodumare—God in Yoruba belief.* London: Longmans.

Jahn, Janheinz. (1961). *Muntu: An outline of neo-African culture.* London: Faber & Faber.

Kasoma, Francis P. (1994). *Journalism ethics in Africa.* Nairobi, Kenya: African Council for Communication Education.

Makunike, E. C. (Ed.). (1973). *Christian press in Africa: Voice of human concern.* Lusaka, Zambia: Multimedia.

Mbiti, John S. (1969). *African religions and philosophy.* London: Heineman.

McQuail, Denis. (1983). *Mass communication theory: An introduction.* Beverly Hills, CA: Sage.

Merrill, John C. (1975). Ethics and journalism. In J. C. Merrill & R. Barney (Eds.), *Ethics and the press: Readings in mass media morality* (pp. 8-17). New York: Hastings.

Moemeka, Andrew A. (1981). *Local radio: Community education for development.* Zaria, Nigeria: Ahmadu Bello University Press.

Moemeka, Andrew A. (1984). Socio-cultural environment of communication in traditional/rural Nigeria: An ethnographic exploration. In *Communicatio Socialis Yearbook, 3* (pp. 41-56). Indore, India: Satprakashan Sanchar Kendra.

Moemeka, Andrew A. (1989). Communication and African culture: A sociological analysis. In S. K. T. Boafo (Ed.), *Communication and culture: African perspectives* (pp. 1-10). Nairobi, Kenya: WACC-African Region.

Moemeka, Andrew A. (1993). *Development (social change) communication: Building understanding and creating participation.* New York: McGraw-Hill.

Moemeka, Andrew A. (1994, April 29-May 1). *Socio-cultural dimensions of leadership in Africa.* Paper presented at the Global Majority Retreat, Rocky Hills, Connecticut.

Moemeka, Andrew A. (1996). Interpersonal communication in communalistic societies. In W. B. Gudykunst, S. Ting-Toomey, & T. Nishida (Eds.), *Communication in personal relationships across cultures* (pp. 197-216). Thousand Oaks, CA: Sage.

Moemeka, Andrew A., & Kasoma, Francis P. (1994). Journalism ethics in Africa: An aversion to deontology? In Francis P. Kasoma (Ed.), *Journalism ethics in Africa* (pp. 38-50). Nairobi, Kenya: African Council for Communication Education.

Okediji, Ola. (1970). *Sociology of the Yoruba.* Ibadan, Nigeria: University Press.

Okigbo, Charles. (1994). Towards a theory of indecency in news reporting. In Francis P. Kasoma (Ed.), *Journalism ethics in Africa* (pp. 71-87). Nairobi, Kenya: African Council for Communication Education.

Okigbo, Charles. (1995). *Communication in Africa: Toward a normative theory.* Unpublished Manuscript.

Pratt, Cornelius B. (1994). Journalism ethics and the new communication technology in Africa. In Francis P. Kasoma (Ed.), *Journalism ethics in Africa,* (pp. 51-69). Nairobi, Kenya: African Council for Communication Education.

Yoshikawa, Muneo J. (1988). Cross-cultural adaptation and perceptual development. In Y. Y. Kim & W. B. Gudykunst (Eds.), *Cross-cultural adaptation: Current approaches* (pp. 140-148). Newbury Park, CA: Sage.

CHAPTER 10

Emergent Values From American Indian Discourse

CYNTHIA-LOU COLEMAN

Uncle Joe lifts a sepia-tinted photograph from the living room wall and brings it to the table where we're drinking coffee. Two chiseled faces peer through the framed glass. The faces seem identical—they are blood relatives, close in age, but one face bears a black ribbon of hair on a shaved scalp. A wreath of talons circles a strong neck and, like little ladders, silver earrings climb both ears. The other image looks Indian too, but the dark hair is grown collar-length, and the shirt and coat look like a white rancher's. The framed photograph of Osage grandparents juxtaposes traditional and modern styles of living and thinking and being.

Like Uncle Joe's photograph, an image may tell us what constitutes Indian identity. But such images—portrayed in movies, television, and books—produce only a partial reality and can be poor interpreters of what it means to be a Native American.

To understand identity, we must examine Indian values, for values undergird ways of knowing. Yet there is a danger in describing Native Americans simplistically by a set of commonalties. Indians, after all, are heterogeneous. We are defined by blood quantum, hair and eye color, grandparents, geographic location, job title, tribal government, reservation, religion, and so on. Moreover, Indian culture has assuredly changed, with the greatest acceleration occurring in the last few hundred years.

This chapter relies on Indian scholars and story-tellers to explain identity and from their wisdom, extracts values. Three central tenets emerge from the literature. Each is interrelated and reveals an underlying set of core values that are central to American Indian thought, behavior, and world-view. These tenets include sense of identity, sense of place, and sense of connectedness. Although the three tenets are neither inclusive nor exhaustive, they provide a focal point for the discussion. Following is a description of these tenets and an explanation of how each is relevant in understanding ethics.

Sense of Identity

Indian writers frequently address the question of identity. Their discourse raises issues of what qualities constitute Indian-ness, which has been defined in many different—and at times—oppositional ways. As one contemporary Native American lamented,

> I search for something to validate myself as an Indian. I can make general statements about Indians such as: they are sharing and giving people, they lack materialism and live close to nature. But these apply only to Indians of the past who have lived close to the old culture. The true Indians are all but gone. (Nabokov, 1978/1991, p. 412)

I suspect that by "true Indians" and "old culture," the speaker means Native Americans before the encroachment of settlers and traders. However, by describing "true Indians" we run the risk of stereotyping them. Scholar D'Arcy McNickle (1973/1979) notes that by quantifying and aggregating characteristics, we separate quality and substance, ending up with a distillation that lacks meaning. "When the problem is dealt with quantitatively by cataloguing the known traits of a culture, the result is an abstraction describing nothing human" (p. 10). Moreover, few researchers have worked in depth with the hundreds of different Indian tribes and nations in an attempt to qualify characteristics that constitute tenets, values, or identity. Indeed, Vine Deloria, Jr. (1969) writes that "everyone" already knows that an Indian is "a food-gathering, berry-picking, semi-nomadic, fire-worshipping, high-plains-and-mountain-dwelling, horse-riding, canoe-toting, bead-using, pottery-making, ribbon-covered, wickiup-sheltered people" (pp. 81-82).

Although Deloria's tongue-in-cheek narration relies on stereotypical images, Indian-ness has hardly remained static. An illustration of how the image of Indians shifted dramatically occurs in proportion to the increased value attached to resources (land and water, for example) in colonized North America. Several historians observe that in initial encounters with natives, they are described as noble. Following Columbus's voyage to the New World, "the message was that there existed a people who did not live under the oppressive order that Europe lived under: the human being who lives this order of nature grows into a 'noble man,' a pure human being" (Mohawk, 1992, p. 440). But the noble being of the Americas would later be depicted as a bloodthirsty savage when settlers expanded westward, demanding further occupation of Indian territory (Berkhofer, 1978). The revised image paved the way for the justification of genocide:

> As long as whites were dependent on them [Indians], this image was tempered by a romantic image of the Indians as "noble red man." Gradually this gave way to an image of the Indian as blood thirsty savage, a menace to the white civilization. This new image not only reflected the increasingly violent relationship between whites and Indians, but also set the ideological stage for wars of extermination that would eliminate the Indian "menace." (Steinberg, 1989, p. 15)

Thus, Indian images shifted within a context, changing against the backdrop of a competing culture. Some argue strenuously that one cannot define Indian-ness without recognizing the "dominant" cultural context. Krupat (1993) writes, for example, that identity is grounded within such a context:

> Identity—and where one speaks from—location—means social location, or social identity, and locations and identities are plural, complex, and con-

structed. Identities are not, as in the essentialized native/non-native opposition, unitary, simple and fixed or given in advance. (p. 87)

And Indians cannot determine their culture, Krupat adds, "in a manner entirely independent of the culture of Euro-Americans, of the U.S. government, the state bureaucracies, and the omnipresent 'media' " (p. 84). A central question is raised: How can we distinguish so-called native culture from nonnative culture, particularly if we accept Krupat's and McNickle's views that culture is ever changing?

Deloria (1979) suggests that scholars should examine intersections where cultures conflict. Deloria points out that individualism (as opposed to communitarianism) is perhaps the most salient value to emerge from Euro-American ideology and is oppositional to native ideology. For Deloria, individualism is not so much an actual state of being as it is a construct reflecting false consciousness, and the grafting of external values—specifically Christian values—onto a native framework moves individuals "toward highly specific systems of obedience and disobedience and away from community" (Warrior, 1995, p. 76). Warrior and Deloria contend that Christian doctrine imposed on native societies presents an external system of values and one based on individualism.

Surely the value of individualism is one that unfolds within a social context. Constructionists such as George Herbert Mead (1962) argue that identity is operationalized within the family and community setting. It makes sense, then, that Euro-American culture would reinforce individualism, whereas native communities would reinforce communitarianism. And although many tribes have embraced Christianity (which Deloria says promotes individualism), some writers maintain that conversion hardly means a rejection of native values. Holm (1992) contends that "American Indians have a long history of altering ('syncretizing') alien cultural impositions in ways which serve their own sense of cultural identity and continuity" (p. 358). Holm uses the example of Cherokee Baptists who incorporate traditional (native) ways into Christian rituals, calling the process "nativization." Similarly, Clifford (1988) suggests that marginal groups cut a swath through modernity. He eschews viewing the world as "populated by endangered authenticities," instead viewing native cultures as negotiating their futures amid a complex social reality (p. 5). The resiliency to adapt to an ever-changing environment is characteristic of Indian people, despite continued attempts to ossify them in stasis.

The concept of culture, too, has shifted over time. In the mid-1900s, culture referred to a single evolutionary process with an emphasis on individuality. But the paradigm shifted to a more macrosocial conception of culture and began to be used in the plural, thus broadening its definition and marking a shift from an emphasis on the individual to the group (Clifford, 1988, p. 93). Culture, therefore, had been reconceptualized as dynamic and interactive.

When this conception is extended to Indian culture, we must recognize the inextricable relationship between Indian and non-Indian ("dominant") culture. This does not mean, though, that one culture simply envelopes another wholesale, as suggested by the view that the dominant society "neatly eclipse[s] every aspect of contemporary native reality, from land rights to issues of religious freedom" (Rose, 1992, p. 404). I disagree. Such thinking reduces native people to benign passivity and relinquishes values to the dominant culture. Indians reject being labeled as "relics," although many think of themselves as survivors—survivors of diseases such as alcohol and diabetes; survivors of a great Diaspora; survivors of communities scarred by uranium mining and toxic wastes; and survivors of external governments that displaced families wholesale and reconfigured tribal relationships. As a result, some external values have been adopted, some rejected, but American Indian ideals have been unquestionably entwined with Euro-American ethics, resulting in a sort of amalgam of reconstructed values.

Communities, central to tribal life, formed the foundation for values attached to freedom and kinship. Tribal life established the context for identity and social relationships, but colonization ripped apart traditional Indian families and communities. The word "tribe" as used here refers to Indian communities that are distinct from Euro-American communities. It is within the context of tribe that Indian identity emerges, which is why some writers note that extirpation of tribes resulted in a loss of identity. For example, Larson (1991-1992) notes that the general allotment act of 1887 and the Burke Act of 1906 "began the fragmentation of individual Indian identity that remains one of the more important issues to be addressed among Indian people and the systems with which they interact" (p. 57). Such legislation split tribes and redistributed land from communities to individuals. By placing ownership of property in the hands of individual tribal members, lands were carved up into discrete pieces and tribal life changed forever (Coleman, 1994). Federal actions corralled Indians on reservations and broke down their social structures and opened their land, water, timber, and mineral resources to exploitation by non-Indians (Abourezk, 1977). The result was the decimation of tribal lands (Berkhofer, 1978; Deloria, 1974; Svensson, 1973). Colonization brought pressure to "abandon the tribal notion of identity in favor of individuality, a divide and conquer strategy" (Larson, 1991-1992, p. 57).

As a result of tribal upheaval, Native Americans struggled over reconstructing identity and definitions of self—for these were grounded in the tribe. As tribes became restructured, so too did notions of individual identity. The individual within the community has been at the heart of much literature, says Larson (1991-1992), who calls the process of negotiating identity "cultural bridging." The method entails bridging Indian and Euro-American cultures in an attempt to "take Indian culture forward and Euro-American culture back" (p. 60). This is beautifully illustrated in McNickle's (1936/1993) novel, *The Surrounded,* where characters negotiate their identities. Archilde's mother, Catharine, confronts a host of externally applied values that reside uncomfortably with her tribally based values. She recognizes the conflict through her marriage to a non-Indian and through her childhood Christian teachings, and she continually tries to bridge these different worldviews:

> She learned also, after her marriage, that a white man does not care to have his relatives or his wife's relatives come to live with him. He will slam his door in their faces. That was contrary to the old way, because it was only right that if you could go and live with your relatives any time you got tired of your place, they in turn could come to you. A white man wanted his house to himself and you were not welcome there unless he asked you to come. . . . She was an old woman now, and it seemed that the older she got the further she went on the trail leading backward. (pp. 172-173)

In *The Surrounded,* Catharine continually confronts oppositional values over community, family, kinship, religion, and identity.

The struggle to forge a new American Indian identity is continuing against formidable odds. This search is based on the conviction that Native America, like all other nations, has a right to belong. It includes the right to adhere to and cultivate values that are in tune with both history and the future. This quest for social identity is one of the most deeply felt needs at this juncture of American Indian history.

Sense of Place

Whereas tribe may be considered a component of place, so too is land. "The central value of Indian life," Deloria (1974, p. 258) says, "is land." Land is understood—not in the sense of parcels, tracts, deeds, and fences—but rather through constructing land as place, home, hearth, and center. From this sense of place, meaning is derived and articulated. For the Lakota, religion and lands are "inextricable from identity" (Holm, 1992, p. 359).

Place as value. Land as value. Home as value. Each concept is inseparable from community. Family, tribe, and nation have not been held externally but incorporated into daily existence. An individual is not defined as being apart from community but physically and spiritually linked to people and place. As such, land is central to the tribe, and commodification of land has resulted in a clash over values.

> The Indians wanted control of their lands, as they wanted control over other areas of their social and economic interests, but they were not prepared to abandon traditional values and transform their land holdings into taxable and merchantable pieces of impersonal real estate. They saw no inconsistency in wanting control and at the same time maintaining the inalienability of the lands protected by treaty guarantees. (McNickle, 1973/1979, pp. 148-149)

Similarly, in writing about the Indian intellectual tradition, Warrior (1995, p. 85) finds that "land and community are necessary starting points for the process of coming to a deep perception of the conflicts and challenges that face American Indian people and communities." Warrior's thesis is that, to understand tradition, students of native cultures must first comprehend the deep interrelationships of land, community, and religion. This means linking a sense of place with spiritual well-being.

> Land is so intrinsic to Native Americans as to be considered their Mother. It is not just a romantic notion, but a cultural centerpiece providing spiritual sustenance as well as subsistence. . . . For Native America, this connection

often determines the values of the human landscape. (Larson, 1991-1992, pp. 61-62)

Sense of place is critical for John Joseph Mathews (1934/1988), an Osage writer. In *Sundown,* the character Watching Eagle notes that the values carried by the white man fit poorly onto native values. Watching Eagle says,

> White man came out of ground across that sea. His thoughts are good across that sea. His houses are beautiful across that sea, I believe. He came out of earth across that sea, and his songs are beautiful there. But he did not come out of earth here. His houses are ugly here because they did not come out of this earth, and his songs and those things which he thinks, those things which he talks, are ugly here, too. They did not come out of earth here. (p. 274)

Thus, for Mathews, aesthetics are tied to place and context ("his houses are ugly here because they did not come out of earth here").

Home for Native Americans is not just the family. Home is a geographic location that is circumscribed by a community's land. American Indians are creatures of the soil—the source of all nourishment and thus the source of life. In addition, home is hearth, where food is prepared and shared, where stories are told and retold, and where communal bonds are recreated in a celebration of life. But both community and family life are rooted in a concrete locality, and this sense of place is part of the grounding of life.

Sense of Connectedness

Interconnectedness of people to their communities, their past and future, and their land is a theme that permeates American Indian literature. "Balance" speaks to the relationships of individuals within communities and the relationships of all elements that constitute life. Balance ties values with behavior and religion with worldview. Indian writers often speak of a balance that exists between the natural world and native peoples. The balance can be upset, however, by external forces, such as the imposition of governmental structures. In writing about the environment in crisis, Winona LaDuke (1993) explains that the Ojibway people hold two central tenets as values—cyclical thinking and reciprocal relations. She writes that

Ojibway values represent "a continuous inhabitation of place, an intimate understanding of the relationship between humans and the ecosystem, and the need to maintain balance" (pp. 100-101). Her view is that industrialization cleaves people from their environments in an "insatiable quest for resources" (p. 100).

The conflict over resources reveals an underlying clash of values as Native American tribes wage battles in the courts and in the press over appropriate use of the earth (Coleman, 1995). This is the basis of the environmental struggle among the Ojibway of Northern Wisconsin, who bitterly opposed the siting of a copper mine on their territories in the early 1990s. Appropriate land use became a common thread in the conflict of values over the use of resources. According to one city councilman, who praised the mine: "The resources are here . . . they are of no value unless they are processed" (Rutlin, 1991, p. 1A). The Ojibway would argue, however, that the value of the copper cannot be separated from the earth itself. One tribal leader countered that, "We look at the environment as a whole, as something that we must abide with and live in and be a part of; and the non-Indian people in our view tend to look at the environment as something to be conquered and to modify and change to fit their own needs" (Treaty Rights, 1990, pp. 14-15).

In a similar vein, the values of environment, self, and community were addressed decades ago by Mathews, who, according to Warrior (1995), refused to separate life-forms from one another:

> The difference between the Osage way of living with the land and that of the invading Euro-Americans was a difference not so much between primitive people and advanced people but between people who channeled their ornamentation urge toward balance with nature and those who, disastrously, considered the freedom of ornamentation to be a release from natural processes. (p. 65)

Mathews suggests that Euro-Americans objectify their surroundings and separate themselves from nature and from their environment, which, in effect, cleaves them from their community. Such values are opposed to traditional Ojibway and Osage worldviews of belonging and balance.

Last, it is impossible to escape the value of holism in native cultures. Indians embrace an interconnectedness in life, what LaDuke (1993) describes as "reciprocal relations" and "cyclical thinking." She notes,

Cyclical thinking, common to most indigenous or land-based cultures and value systems is an understanding that the world, time, and all parts of the natural order flow in cycles. . . . Within this understanding is a clear sense of birth and rebirth, and a knowledge that what one does today will affect one in the future, on the return. . . . A second concept, reciprocal relations, defines the responsibility and ways of relating between humans and the ecosystem. Simply stated, the resources of the ecosystem—whether wild rice or deer—are, with few exceptions, recognized as animate and, as such, gifts from the Creator. . . . Within the practice of reciprocity is also an understanding that you take only what you need and leave the rest. (pp. 99-100)

In summary, traditional native ethics place high value on maintaining the balance between humans and environment. American Indian writers describe such values as the interdependence of people, animal, and plant life, in contrast to the European concept of the human species as "dominant over all species" (Great Lakes Indian Fish and Wildlife Commission, n.d.). Values form the nucleus of understanding how Indian communities manage their lives—as a whole rather than in chunks. However, such values— although embedded within native cultures—are descriptions, rather than predictions, of thinking and behavior. Sense of place, interconnectedness, reciprocal relationships, and the primacy of community together form an important foundation for native ethics, which are woven into the fabric of traditional Indian lives. These threads can be found in popular literature, scholarly writing, and Native American journalism.

The three tenets—sense of identity, of place, and of interconnectedness—emerge in native literature and arise from interactions with the Euro-American cultural system. But care must be taken to avoid treating each culture as distinct from one another. Too often, "tribal" is equated with "primitive," and Indian values are defined in atavistic terms that are "romantically beguiling but scientifically untenable" (McNickle, 1973/1979, p. 12). The challenge among native scholars is to remind critics that American Indian values continue to be negotiated within a broader cultural framework.

Ethical Implications for Communication

Indigenous or First People—who live all over the world—have rarely been credited for the contributions they have made to humanity as a whole and to many different cultures and religions. Their value systems were the bedrock from which civilizations emerged. Their communal traditions formed the backgrounds influencing the origins of religions, such as Buddhism, Christianity, and Islam. They are "first" in the sense that they represent a cultural heritage—preceding all others—which is often described as communitarian. One central question is this: How will indigenous people enrich the ethical consciousness and moral conscience of our individualistic age, and what contributions can First People make?

Native Americans as well as other First People are steeped in a reverence for the web of life. The web of life comprises both the natural and the sociocultural environments, all parts of a whole: interconnected, interdependent, and reciprocal. If one is injured, the other suffers. If natural resources are exploited, people are likely to be exploited as well.

The web of life, or the created order, is the basis for ethics of indigenous people. Life is more than individual lives. Life is the interconnectedness of individuals. They are first and foremost part of a community, with a place, a hearth, and land. As a community, they are part of the life of nature, its soil, water, and sky. Perhaps the most important ethical principle of American Indians is harmony or balance within the universe of being. Such harmony is achieved only by a reverence for life—all life in the created order. Communication ethics, therefore, is a reflection of the web of life. This, according to Native American ethics, is the proper role of communication: to cultivate and safeguard life. This is the paradigm that indigenous stories represent.

A second ethical principle emerges from the Native Americans' search for social identity. Indeed, our survival has been marked by resiliency in the face of political, economic, and social attempts at destruction and assimilation. Adaptation to tremendous change, however, has not extinguished our culture nor has Euro-American ideology engulfed and replaced native ethics. As scholars, we need to articulate these cultural dimensions and acknowledge the active resistance on the part of indigenous peoples to either resist external value systems or renegotiate their meanings. And although it may be true that Indian ethics arise from internal needs, identity, and community, such values are operationalized within an external context—through behavior and communication. Such interactions, by definition, occur within the vast framework of a multilayered and constructed reality. By necessity, Indian culture is dynamic and resilient.

All this must be viewed against the background of a long history of oppression, exploitation, acculturation, commodification, and near annihilation of our people. Still, the hegemonic discourse about Native Americans persists to this day. This discourse must be changed to one based on the genuine acknowledgment of American Indians as Others, with respectful acknowledgment of their very Otherness. This is a fundamental ethical principle of communications. And this principle, *a priori*, is the active recognition—through communication—of Others as beings with equal dignity. A second *a priori* principle is equally important: the active acceptance of Otherness as a unique human good. This should be the precondition of a renaissance of Native American culture, which is not only oriented to the past but also to the future, with a promise of myriad new cultural expressions.

There is, however, a third aspect in the act of acknowledging the Other. It is often forgotten that part of "Otherness" is the history of injury, trauma, and bewilderment. The recognition of this side of Otherness implies both coresponsibility and solidarity. Such acknowledgment has a liberating potential for all partners in the communication process. Then, the ethical principle of recognition of the Other leads to another principle of communication ethics: liberation. In acknowledging Others, we liberate ourselves from the fetters of denial and negation and rise to a new communicative freedom.

> Uncle Joe pokes his thumb at the picture, and explains how each man chose a path—one the traditional Osage way—while the other adopted the way of the white settlers. Joe grins and asks me, "who is to say which way is right?"

Acknowledgments

My thanks to Joe and Judy Neff, whose Osage stories enrich our lives. I am grateful to the editors, Clifford Christians and Michael Traber, for their support on the project and for comments on the chapter draft. Thanks also to Professor Sidner Larson for his insights and suggestions concerning native values, and for his generosity of time and spirit. My thoughts surrounding values arise from myriad discussions and arguments, most notably with David Sillars, who views the world through his own lens—one that reflects an unparalleled brilliance. Thanks, David.

References

Abourezk, James. (1977). *American Indian policy review commission.* Washington, DC: Government Printing Office.

Bad river raises issues of federal trust responsibility. (1990, Fall). *Masinaigan,* p. 14.

Berkhofer, Robert F., Jr. (1978). *White man's Indian: Images of the American Indian from Columbus to the present.* New York: Vintage.

Clifford, James. (1988). *The predicament of culture.* Cambridge, MA: Harvard University Press.

Coleman, Cynthia-Lou. (1994). *An examination of the relationship of structural pluralism, news role and source use with framing in the context of a community controversy.* Unpublished doctoral dissertation, University of Wisconsin, Madison.

Coleman, Cynthia-Lou. (1995). Science, technology and risk coverage of a community conflict. *Media, Culture and Society, 17,* 65-79.

Deloria, Vine, Jr. (1969). *Custer died for your sins.* New York: Macmillan.

Deloria, Vine, Jr. (1973). *God is red.* New York: Grosset & Dunlap.

Deloria, Vine, Jr. (1974). *The Indian affair.* New York: Friendship.

Deloria, Vine, Jr. (1979). *The metaphysics of modern existence.* San Francisco, CA: Harper & Row.

Great Lakes Indian Fish and Wildlife Commission. (n.d.). Brochure. (Available from author, P. O. Box 9, Odanah, WI, 54861)

Holm, Tom. (1992). Patriots and pawns: State use of American Indians in the military and the process of nativization in the United States. In M. Annette Jaimes (Ed.), *The state of native America* (pp. 345-370.) Boston, MA: South End.

Kewley, Mary Jo. (1990, July 16). Band opposes mine on spiritual grounds. *Wausau Daily Herald,* p. 4A.

Krupat, Arnold. (1993). Scholarship and Native American studies: A response to Daniel Littlefield, Jr. *American Studies, 34*(2), 81-101.

LaDuke, Winona. (1993). A society based on conquest cannot be sustained: Native peoples and the environmental crisis. In Richard Hofrichter (Ed.), *Toxic struggles: The theory and practice of environmental justice* (pp. 98-106). Philadelphia, PA: New Society.

Larson, Sidner. (1991-1992). Native American aesthetics: An attitude of relationship. *Melus, 17*(3), 53-67.

Mathews, John Joseph. (1988). *Sundown.* Norman: University of Oklahoma Press. (Original work published 1934)

Mead, George Herbert. (1962). *Mind, self, and society.* Chicago: University of Chicago Press.

McNickle, D'Arcy. (1979). *Native American tribalism: Indian survivals and renewals.* New York: Oxford University Press. (Original work published 1973)

McNickle, D'Arcy. (1993). *The surrounded.* Albuquerque: University of New Mexico Press. (Original work published 1936)

Mohawk, John. (1992). Looking for Columbus: Thoughts on the past, present and future of humanity. In M. Annette Jaimes (Ed.), *The state of native America* (pp. 439-444). Boston, MA: South End.

Nabokov, Peter. (Ed.). (1991). *Native American testimony.* New York: Penguin. (Original work published 1978)

Rose, Wendy. (1992). The great pretenders: Further reflections on whiteshamanism. In M. Annette Jaimes (Ed.), *The state of native America,* (pp. 403-21). Boston, MA: South End.

Rutlin, Terry. (1991, July 7). 400 protest against mine. *Wausau Daily Herald,* p. 1A.

Rutlin, Terry. (1991, July 23). Endangered species has a PR problem. *Wausau Daily Herald,* pp. 1, 2.

Steinberg, Stephen. (1989). *The ethnic myth: Race, ethnicity, and class in America.* Boston, MA: Beacon.

Svensson, Frances. (1973). *The ethnics in American politics: American Indians.* Minneapolis, MN: Burgess.

Treaty rights provide avenue for environmental protection: Tribes say firm no! to mining. (1990, Fall). *Masinaigan,* pp. 14-15.

Warrior, Robert Allen. (1995). *Tribal secrets: Recovering American Indian intellectual traditions.* Minneapolis: University of Minnesota Press.

Weatherford, Jack. (1988). *Indian givers: How the Indians of the Americas transformed the world.* New York: Crown.

PART III

Applications

CHAPTER 11

Communications, Hope, and Ethics

PEDRO GILBERTO GOMES

Three concepts are basic to human life, namely, communication, which renders social life possible; hope, which allows us to live in the utopia of a fairer society; and ethics, which judges and establishes norms for human behavior. Relating these three concepts in a coherent way is not always easy. But in social communication, the ethical dimension of human actions is at the same time reality and hope. Why?

First of all, because human beings are imbued with a moral conscience that determines their daily actions. This conscience results from complex social, familial, political, cultural, and religious contexts. Because human beings are moral by their very nature, media professionals can be expected to obey self-imposed principles such as justice, brotherhood-sisterhood, and reciprocity.

Despite our moral character, however, some specific questions are posed whenever we venture into the issue of communication ethics. Many consider morality a purely individual matter; from this perspective, no external

AUTHOR'S NOTE: This chapter was translated by Elvio Funck, Ph.D.

agent should ever tell a communications professional how to act. More-over, when norms involve the media, the first thing that comes to mind is a code of principles designed to control professional behavior. Such codes, however, are hardly ever obeyed (Gomes, 1989b, p. 11). Why? Because we typically assume that "morality is intrinsic to one's conscience and, there-fore, to life and experience"; and, if so, "codes, doctrines, authorities, and institutions" are secondary. "Good does not result from the proper appli-cation of theoretical norms; rather, it always results from an interaction involving the individual or individuals" (Bach, 1992, pp. 114-115).

The second consideration is methodological. How can the issue of ethics be approached without external interference, such as that of a legislator who dictates the rules for others to obey? And there are other questions also: How can the temptation of moralizing in a derogatory way be avoided? And, how is Manichaeism to be avoided, that is, how can we overcome the simplicity of the moral dictum "do good and avoid evil?"

Approaching ethics, therefore, does not necessarily involve, on the prac-tical level, defining whatever is good or evil in the behavior of media pro-fessionals. The concepts of good and evil have not yet been clearly and simply defined. It is not just a question of doing good and avoiding evil because nobody with a good conscience will do evil for evil's sake. The real problem is how to do good in the particular moment one is living (Gomes, 1989b, pp. 13-14).

Therefore, if a media professional is guilty of misconduct, the issue can-not be approached through court procedures or codes of professional ethics. A sophisticated law system, for assorted reasons, will never develop effec-tively the ethical conscience of media practitioners. Today's professionals react apprehensively to what may look like a set of norms impinging on their actions. Such a negative response became apparent in the Declaration of Talloires, which rejected every kind of code that might in any way regu-late the journalistic profession around the world.[1]

The Importance of
Universal Principles

The ethical and moral crisis now affecting society in general and the media in particular will not be eliminated by further sophistication of the judicial system (Gomes, 1989b, p. 11). The solution to this crisis involves basic changes that reside in the development of a moral and ethical con-science. Only such a fundamental revolution will allow media practitioners to be guided by self-imposed universal principles.

Here the issue of universal principles comes into focus. They lead us not only to such specific matters as liberation ethics arising from Latin American reality but also to the possibility of universal values that apply to everybody, whatever their creed, race, or social strata. On the issue of universal values in the Latin American context, Tony Mifsud (1988) states the following:

> The universe of values is none other than the humanizing horizon of the individual himself. Every human being is called to become a person, an individual. Such a call is imperative and mandatory, as it involves self-fulfillment. Values are frames of reference inside which the conditions and goals that allow a human being to become humanized are assigned or self-assigned. Therefore, values embrace both the subjective and the objective poles between which the individual grows and lives. (p. 94)

We must acknowledge, however, that not all values are on the same level. Between them is a gradation that takes into account the multiple and discrete dimensions of our individual personhood. Such gradations range from partial aspects, such as biological values, to ethical-religious ones. Ethical-religious values embrace human beings as a whole, rendering their lives both meaningful and purposeful (Mifsud, 1988, p. 96). In fact, when ethics in the Latin American context is discussed, ethical-religious values are the ones taken into account, even though it must be recognized that in Latin America, biological values are often denied. Food and water, clothing and shelter, and above all, the safety and security of family life are constantly being jeopardized in large segments of Latin American society.

When the necessary presence of ethical-religious values is recognized, the issue of developing a moral conscience is at stake. Such development starts from a situation of anomie and progresses from heteronomy to autonomy. Along this progressive journey, individuals develop their moral conscience and become aware of values (see Gomes, 1989b, p. 50). Lawrence Kohlberg (as cited in Mifsud, 1980), for example, proposed three levels and six progressive and consecutive stages in developing our moral sense.[2] His third level, the postconventional (autonomous or principle based), is particularly relevant to the problem of ethics in Latin America. At the final stage of this level, a person's orientation is provided by universal ethical principles. The self becomes distinct from social roles, and values are defined in terms of self-imposed principles of justice. Here is what Mifsud (1981) says about the moral conscience at this stage:

> Justice is defined by force of a decision made by the individual conscience. Such ethical principles, willingly assumed, rely on logical understanding, on universality and on stability. They are both abstract and ethical; they are not concrete moral norms, like the Ten Commandments. In essence, they are universal principles, having to do with justice, reciprocity, and the equality of human rights, as well as with the respect owed to every human being as a concrete individual. (p. 159)

Within this framework of moral development, justice is a fundamental concept, one that needs to be made more precise in the context of Latin America.

Justice and Injustice

> Justice is more clearly understood by those who suffer injustice. The principle of justice should not be understood as embracing every single individual's perspective. It would be fairer to say that this principle is limited to the perspective of those who are disadvantaged. . . . Justice, as an option, belongs to the ethical sphere; while involving the "where to" to of cosmo-vision; however, it also belongs in the sphere of metaethics. (Mifsud, 1980, p. 50)

In Latin America, justice in the context of injustice is of overriding significance. Justice as seen from the viewpoint of those who suffer injustice—of those who are exploited and oppressed—is the point from which we start and by which we can make relevant distinctions about media ethics.

Enrique Dussel (1986) provides an orientation to this topic. According to Dussel, established social morality can be distinguished from community ethics. Established social morality concerns the moral order established by the social system. From this perspective, everything contributing to the maintenance of the system is good. Morally acceptable actions are those that neither criticize nor attack the established order. Conversely, every action that aims to transform the established system is considered harmful and must, therefore, be opposed.

Community ethics, on the other hand, is transcendental and permanently criticizes the established system. Therefore, whereas the established social morality is particular and belongs to a well-defined social group, community ethics is universal. Its principles are basic for critiquing established social morality.

Dussel (1986) states that a system of liberating ethics implies a clear understanding of a particular situation requiring liberation. It must be recognized, however, that each situation claims to have its own morality and an assured conscience. "Wherever the established system of morality is in power, its practices and codes are considered to be good" (p. 43). The established system of morality, therefore, determines whatever is good or bad for its members. Those who conform to its rules and regulations are considered righteous. They never find fault with the system but adapt to it in everyday circumstances and obey its laws. Whoever seeks to substitute a new system—based on the ideals of justice and fraternity-sorority—is considered evil, unbalanced, a social outcast. "Society shapes or educates the moral conscience of its members according to criteria of the flesh" (p. 45), that is, according to criteria established by society itself, refusing any change. The moral conscience shaped in terms of such criteria will reprimand whoever does not abide by them and will never condemn the very system as perverse (see p. 45). "The moral conscience based on the principles of the established system fosters a safe and insensitive conscience vis-a-vis the practices of a system which it approves but which may, in its origins, be perverse and domineering" (p. 46).

Individuals oriented by universal principles transform the kingdom of evil that rules over the society in which they live. This refers specifically to the Latin American continent, which is organized and governed by oppressive and unfair norms and policies. When those who are sensitive enough to listen to the voice of the Other break with the kingdom of evil, an inversion takes place. The Other is the human being cheapened as non-human, compelled to remain silent, prevented from being a participant, and kept away from the decision-making process. The prophet transforms individuals who are poor, half-dead, destitute, and outcast into worthy human beings deserving to be heard and assisted (Dussel, 1986, p. 51).

For this transformation to be achieved, it is necessary, first of all, to listen attentively to the Others' voices, to their pleas for help, food, medicine, and for life itself. In fact, "listening to the Other's voice is exactly the same as having an ethical conscience" (Dussel, 1986, p. 51).

> Having a conscience is not so much applying principles to concrete situations
> but listening to the voice that speaks to me from beyond the system's horizon,
> which rises from the poor who claim the justice they are entitled to as their
> holy and absolute right as human beings. (p. 51)

As a consequence, ethics involves a journey toward the outside, a search
for and construction of a new order. Ethical human beings cannot conform
to structures that cause oppression, domination, and marginality. They have
been born inside a system, but they strive to transcend it, endeavoring to
create a new and fairer order.

Incorporating the perspective of the poor, of the destitute, and of the
outcast is fundamental for community ethics. It is absolutely necessary to
take sides with those who cannot count on the established social morality—structured as it is in the interests of the dominating classes. Those who
conform to the laws and regulations of the established system—perverse
and unfair as they may be—are situated on the second level of moral development, that is, oriented by law and order. They do nothing but abide
by and adapt to such laws and regulations; that is enough to give them a
safe conscience. Conversely, those who incorporate an ethical perspective
oriented by universal principles find fault with the established social model
and do their utmost to make it a fairer system.

If the distinction developed so far is applied to communication ethics, it
will be observed that quite a few of the ethical structures in communication
actually stem from the established moral system. Such structures are there
to preserve the system and to render it more efficient rather than to transform it. The ethical codes of the media, and the committees that try to
regulate propaganda, must be understood along these lines. Changes are
made with the sole purpose of smoothing out the rough edges of the system.
The deep roots of the system, however, are left untouched; they continue
to support the capitalist system, geared toward profit. Therefore, although
products that are hazardous to public health and commercials involving sex
and violence are banned, commercials advertising food in a starving society are not questioned. Likewise, commercials trying to sell mansions in a
homeless society and commercials of huge hospitals or schools in an illiterate society—or where many citizens die in the queues of the social security system—are not questioned either. The established social order, subordinated to a structure geared toward profit, will not tolerate the

questioning of its very foundations. Such questioning, however, can only take place if the system of oppression is seen as acts of aggression against the homeless, the starving, the diseased, the illiterate, and the outcast.

Community ethics, on the other hand, caters to the poor, to those who have no voice, no place, and no chance in today's society. It questions, therefore, every system that allows for people to be left on the margin of society and that defends a monopoly of the sources of information and communication. Community ethics as a universal concept sees the poor (in former days, the serfs and the slaves) as those forced to keep silent, deprived of human dignity, and turned into a political tool, into an object used to make a few wealthy people still more affluent. From this perspective, therefore, communication ethics questions the established social system and insists on transformations. However, those who shoulder such prophetlike responsibility are cursed and persecuted by those in power, including the mass media moguls.

If the issue of social justice is analyzed in this way, then the problem of media ethics assumes a different perspective. Instead of bringing radical transformation to the structure of social communication, codes of professional ethics are nothing but placebos that serve to justify our inertia in the face of the changes required in the media. Professionals who abide by such models—rather than by self-imposed universal principles—feel justified in doing so and never question their concrete actions. In this way, the system is perpetuated and multiplied, and the foundations on which it is built are never questioned.

Therefore, if community ethics takes up the case of the poor and listens to their claims—thus contributing to their social redemption and treating them as dignified human beings—the social morality controlling the field of communications does nothing but maintain the situation of oppression and at the same time, creating a false image of equality, justice, and tranquility. Instead of contributing to an exodus from slavery into the land of freedom, the established moral code in power allows for the oppressive system to be streamlined so that it may become more acceptable and less shocking. Rather than leaving the land of slavery, the oppressed remain there, expected to thank those in power for giving the poor and the destitute—the "non-humans" in our gullible and exploited Latin America—such privileges as food handouts and slum clearances.

Media Professionals

After the preceding considerations about community ethics and the established moral code, the media professional shall now be brought into focus (Gomes, 1989a, pp. 103ff). It is relatively easy to identify the fundamental values of communications and to describe how they are constantly jeopardized. However, when the media profession is faced with this reality, problems arise. There is an enormous gap between the theory (recognizing the crucial moral principles at stake) and the practice (living up to these principles). Such a gap is present wherever human beings are involved in communications.

The critical issue is not doing good and avoiding evil but rather making concrete decisions on how the good is to be accomplished. Of course, a code of ethics is not enough. Nor can the sheer law by itself bring about concrete moral practice. The decision to act circumspectly has to be made by professionals themselves, and from the way they act as human beings, they express a positive or negative view of oppression in contemporary society. Every moment, every different reality brings new challenges. Such challenges call professionals to take a concrete stand and adopt an ethical attitude.

In their daily activities, however, professionals are divided. Out of the sheer need to survive, they may have to adapt to the policies of whoever pays their wages and whose motives they are afraid to question. They feel, however, the appeal of the poor's conscience. It affects them powerfully whenever self-esteem and self-respect are denied, because both are inherent to every human being and cannot be simply overlooked. The issue of ethics in the area of communications, therefore, must be approached in such a way as not to jeopardize the professionals' need to survive and, at the same time, not to violate either their own consciences or that of their fellow humans.

As noted earlier, the established moral codes approach the issue in a too simplistic way. Norms and laws are structured in terms of class interests, and the moral fulfillment of the individual is achieved simply by submitting to such norms and laws. Whoever abides by the law is justified; whoever does not is condemned. The ethical legitimacy of laws is not to be questioned. This simplification of the issue, however, does not ensure professional fulfillment. Human beings—if fully developed—cannot find contentment in mere legal obedience. Their critical minds tell them clearly what is to be questioned and what laws need to be modified before they feel free to obey them.

One way to approach the problem is to envisage ethical issues—as far as media professionals are concerned—as "the art of the possible."[3]

As the art of the possible, politics awakens in today's conscience from the moment when humans start shaping society, based on projections toward a society that is still to be built. The problem of the possible in politics is not a new one. The problem becomes central, however, the very moment when societies begin to be shaped by criteria taken from certain social norms that allow us to project a society functioning in terms of an adequate and humane ordering of social relations (Hinkelammert, 1986, p. 11).

Hinkelammert (1986) derives this concept from the criticism of capitalist societies by Karl Marx and of socialist societies by Max Weber. Marx analyses capitalist society in terms of its feasibility and concludes that it is an absolutely impossible achievement. Therefore, he proposes that it be replaced by a socialist society. Marx's proposition is not based on ethical or moral grounds but simply on practical feasibility—a capitalist society just cannot survive. According to Marx, "rationality linked to values does not require transformation while rationality linked to purposes necessarily calls for transformation" (Hinkelammert, 1986, p. 13). This is why Hinkelammert states the following:

> Marx's discussion of the capitalist society which turns the political panorama and its realism into a discussion about the ranges of the possible and, therefore, of accomplished , politics, is not oriented primarily by ethics, but rather by a relation between means and ends. Before any ethical judgment can be made, we are faced with judgments of facts, which tell us that something can only be ethically mandatory if it is feasible. You do not have to do something if it is not possible for you to do it. This ancient postulate, which goes back to medieval scholasticism, is now applied to society itself. However, "having to" can only be followed by "being able to"; there is one alternative, and this alternative can also be the common denominator of a set of possible alternatives. The deciding issue here has to do with the polarization between the possible and impossible.
>
> In this case, Marx concludes: The limited criterion between the possible and the impossible is the criterion of how human life can be reproduced in a real and concrete way. A society which cannot speed up such reproduction is an impossible society. The only possible societies are those which adjust their structures to the requirements of reproduction in real life. (p. 13)

Max Weber uses the same reasoning to state that a socialist society is impossible, lacking feasibility.

As both capitalist and socialist societies still exist, it appears that we are in the presence of impossible societies. This is why Hinkelammert (1986) asks, "What sense does the thesis of the impossibility make if impossible societies have existed for centuries?" (p. 17). In distinguishing between what is possible and what is impossible, let us say that the impossible is less concerned with whatever is done and more with what we believe is being done. When we believe that what we are doing is something different from what is actually being accomplished, we are probably bungling whatever we are doing. What someone does is never impossible, but what one believes one is doing may very well be. This belief distorts and paralyzes the capacity of doing.

> Our will always aims at the impossible, because it aims at the best, whatever our criterion for best may be. It is by means of our imagination—but also by means of the concept of impossibility—that the milestone of the possible is discovered. Whoever is not daring enough to conceive the impossible will never discover the possible. What is possible results from submitting the impossible to the criterion of feasibility. (Hinkelammert, 1986, p. 17)

As far as communication ethics is concerned, the distinction between the possible and the impossible may well bring us closer to understanding the issue. The possible concerns the daily duties professionals have to perform in their jobs. The impossible is not what is feasible; rather, it is projected into the utopic horizon of a desirable ethical action. The possible has to do with the applicability of the ethical norms made relative by the contingencies of the moment. If media professionals accept the relativity of ethical norms, whereas at the same time projecting them toward the utopic ideal of a new society, they bring feasibility to their daily activities. This means that, in terms of communication ethics, we are in permanent quest at the level of the moral conscience. The sum total of our partial actions does not amount to the totality of the desired utopia. The daily quest for feasibility is a constant process toward a dream. The dream, however, never comes true, but it remains always on the horizon of the impossible. When individuals are doing something and believe they are doing something else, their capacity to act is paralyzed. That is, when individuals believe that their actions are absolute and definitive rather than relative, their creative capacity is blunted and they stop progressing toward the best for which their reason yearns.

This is why in their daily actions professional communicators always conceive the impossible and aim at it. Then, in their day-to-day work routines, they will little-by-little find out the "possible-reasonable" in terms of the needs and demands of the social class to which they belong. In their daily actions, they constantly try to submit the impossible to the criterion of feasibility. This is the only way—as far as I understand it—that media professionals can meet the demands of both their conscience and the need to survive professionally. They have to look far into the future—perhaps dreaming about impossible human accomplishments—and submit their dreams to the criterion of feasibility at every given moment. Such moments always differ, given the wide range of historical conditions in which media professionals live.

The "celebration of faith deep inside the liberating practices anticipates life in the ultimate utopia" and "this anticipated celebration allows us to discern the utopic dimension of the liberation practice itself" (Pablo, 1983, pp. 310-311). Likewise, the moral actions of communication professionals are imbued with an ultimate utopia of a perfect society and of the full development of the moral conscience. However, the celebration deep inside the liberating practice does not thoroughly reveal what such utopia may be nor what it may accomplish. Nor will the possible acts of professionals ever exhaust the ethical possibilities of daily life—just as the celebration anticipates life but does not exhaust the ultimate and possible utopia of people's liberation.

This is exactly why communication practitioners are called on to break away from established social codes—which support the wrongdoings of an unfair society—and to pursue the demands of liberating ethics. They question their own professional codes, lest they should risk justifying the system or just retouching it superficially. Reality, charged with ethics and appealing to justice and liberation, will motivate them professionally. Therefore, before getting familiar with new techniques, practices, and norms, they will have to develop their own consciences of reality and be open to challenges and summons. They will be constantly exercising a hermeneutics of reality, from which will follow the questioning of the system of oppression, and into which liberating ethical criteria will interject. Only then will they be committed to the true reality and to the people who mainly compose it, namely, the poor, the outcasts, those who are coerced into silence by an oppressive system. These very people will give them the energy and the motivation needed to act professionally.

Media professionals are not entirely responsible for the moral and ethical crisis that permeates the mass media enterprise; yet they cannot ease their share of responsibility altogether. The responsibility they are supposed to assume is their identification, in their daily activities, with the exploited class. Such identification will determine the utopia to be aimed at, as well as the contents of the impossible they will strive to reach—even though they will never reach it, for it is unattainable. To be sure, the impossible for the working class is different from the impossible for the classes that control material, symbolic, and cultural production. Full socialization of this production has become the people's utopia and the utopia of media professionals who identify with them. Partial conquests are steps toward a process that will never be completed in history and that is, therefore, a transcendental, metahistorical dream.

Conclusion

We cannot understand concrete reality without the quest for utopia that is in human nature. Those who give in to the unavoidable in their daily activities, refusing the possibility of dreams, will never successfully accomplish their day-by-day duties. It is only by keeping our eyes fixed on the horizon of utopia—where there is faith in an ethical life and in policies compatible with dignity and justice—that our present life becomes pregnant with meaning.

However, dreaming by oneself is not enough. The dream must be shared, and more and more people have to believe that it is a possible dream. Only then will it begin to come true. Helder Camara used to say that when someone dreams by oneself, that is just a dream; when several people share the same dream, it is the beginning of reality.[4] The dream of a perfect society is nourished in people's imaginations, which tell them that such a dream is possible and encourage them to engage their lives in trying to make it come true. Communicators are also called to engage in this pursuit. Rather than submit to professional norms, they should commit themselves to developing a moral conscience ruled by universal and self-imposed principles of justice, brotherhood-sisterhood, reciprocity, and human rights. In the utopian dimension of the acts of media professionals, we finally reach hope. We hope because we act ethically; we act ethically because we hope to develop a perfect society.

Notes

1. This declaration was signed by 60 institutions linked to the transnational system of information, including Agence France Press, Reuters, Associated Press, United Press International, World Committee for the Freedom of the Press, International Federation of Newspaper Managers, and Inter-American Press Institute. According to the *New York Times* (as quoted in the Declaração de Talloires, 1985),

> This meeting marks the first time that newsmen and radio-TV networks in the West and elsewhere in the free world, have presented a united front against the campaign waged by the Soviet block and by some countries of the Third World with the purpose of conferring upon UNESCO the authority to regulate the circulation of news and information around the world. (pp. 64-65)

2. The reference to Lawrence Kohlberg comes from Mifsud (1980).
3. This concept is developed by Hinkelammert (1986, pp. 11-21) when he writes about politics as the art of the possible.
4. This statement was made during the opening ceremony at the 1981 congress of the Union of Christian Communicators of Brazil, in Florianopolis. The conclusions were published in Soares, Fleuri, and Camara (1982).

References

Bach, Marcos. (1992). *Uma Nova Moral? O Fim do Sistema Tradicional.* Petrópolis, Brazil: Vozes.

Declaração de Talloires. (1985). *Chasqui, 1*(II época), 64-65.

Dussel, Enrique. (1986). *Ética Comunitária: Liberta o Pobre!* Petrópolis, Brazil: Vozes.

Gomes, Pedro Gilberto. (1989a). *Direito de Ser: A ética de Comunicação na América Latina.* São Paulo: Paulinas.

Gomes, Pedro Gilberto. (1989b). Ética de Comunicação e Comunicação ética. In *Ética da Comunicação* (pp. 11-14, LCC-Cadernos No. 4). São Paulo: Loyola/UCBC.

Hinkelammert, Franz J. (1986). *Crítica à Razão Utópica.* São Paulo: Paulinas.

Mifsud, Tony. (1980). *Desarrollo Moral Según Lawrence Kohlberg: Exposición y Valoración Desde la ética Cristiana.* Doctoral thesis, Universidad Pontifícia de Comillas, Facultade de Teologia, Madrid.

Mifsud, Tony. (1981). Una Perspectiva Psicólogica del Juicio Moral: Lawrence Kohlberg. *Teología y Vida* (Santiago de Chile), *23*(2), 149-167.

Mifsud, Tony. (1988). *Hacia una Moral Liberadora: Moral de Discernimiento* (Vol. 1, 2nd ed.). Santiago de Chile: Paulinas.

Pablo, Richard. (1983). Reflexion Teológica Sobre la Dimension Utopica de la Praxis. In Roul
    Vidales & Luis P. Rivera (Eds.), *La Esperanza en el Presente de América Latina*. San Jose,
    Costa Rica: Departamento Ecumenico de Investigacion.
Soares, Ismar de Oliveira, Fleuri, Reinaldo Matias, & Camara, Helder. (1982). *Juventude e
    Dominação Cultural*. São Paulo: Paulinas/UCBC.

CHAPTER 12

Communication Ethics
in a Changing Chinese Society

The Case of Taiwan

GEORGETTE WANG

*There can be no community without communication, and
the nature of any community will be strongly influenced by
the modes of communicative behavior found within it. . . . If
communication is allowed to degenerate, we risk a . . .
wide-ranging adverse effect.*

—C. Arthur (1989, p. 10)

In examining the role of communication, Chris Arthur (1989, pp. 10-12)
argues that communication in a community is like the water supply to an
ecology system. Its failure may lead to serious consequences, including
distorted pictures of events and relationships, thereby altering perceptions,
values, and behavior.

Although it cannot be emphasized too much that communication is fundamental to human society, looking from the other side of the argument,
communication—like water without the ecological system—becomes

meaningless outside of its sociocultural context. As Chu (1992) points out in discussing communication in Chinese society, both the form and content of communication are dictated by norms and values that at the same time dictate other aspects of the society. From a holistic perspective, political, economic, social, cultural, and communication factors are all important elements in one system. Because the interaction of these elements determines the course of development for the system as a whole, change in one will inevitably bring changes in others.

For the same reason, communication ethics may transcend time and space, but it is within a sociocultural context that codes of behavior are valued and observed. Therefore, when the norms and values that govern society shift, the weight these criteria carry and the way they are interpreted by the public and media professions also change.

Recent changes in Taiwan[1] offer a rare opportunity to examine the close relationship between communication ethics and societal values. Many of these changes—the birth of opposition parties, increasingly active social movements, and the collapse of decades-old political and sociocultural taboos—have far-reaching implications for the norms and rules that have governed this society and its patterns of communication as well. Through a critical examination of such transformations, the intricate relationship between ethical principles and their sociocultural context becomes crystallized. Only when this relationship is fully grasped will the discussion of communication ethics be meaningful.

Traditional Chinese Cultural Values

Despite calls for political independence from China, there has been little dispute about the Chinese cultural heritage in Taiwan, formed on the basis of Confucian teachings. For almost 2,500 years, the four principles and eight virtues (*se wei ba de*) laid down by Confucianism have guided Chinese society as criteria for moral judgments, of which *Li* (propriety) is the first on the list.

In its narrow sense, *Li* merely refers to the proper manners for people to interact with one another. One cannot, however, determine what manners are proper without knowing how interpersonal relations should be conducted. The propriety principle, therefore, not only calls for observing manners but underscores the importance of conducting human interaction in appropriate ways—those that are compatible with the roles individuals play in their respective social institutions. By embedding the rules of propriety in social life, "*Li* stands for a defense of the moral significance of the extant traditional forms of social order. *Li* is the principle that channels respect for each other and for the world, and regulates human nature" (Blackburn, 1994, p. 75).

In discussing the essential aspects of Chinese philosophies, Cheng (1983, p. 32) notes a principle that he describes as "part-whole interdetermination." According to Cheng, this principle asserts that everything belongs to a whole and nothing can be determined, evaluated, or understood without reference to it. Following this line of thinking, individuals are defined by the role they play in the society; interpersonal relations and interactions have to develop accordingly. Communication behavior as an aspect of human interaction is, therefore, deeply intertwined with the rubrics of society.

One phrase from the *Book of Zhou* (or *Zhou Shu*) has often been cited as proof of the importance placed on public opinion in ancient China: "Heaven sees through the seeing of the people; heaven hears through the hearing of the people" (Chu, 1974, p. 2). Emperors by themselves were not merely encouraged to listen to the people; their welfare was further demonstrated by the existence of magistrates-at-large in the ancient Chinese bureaucratic system. A position normally awarded only to those who were committed to justice and righteousness, the magistrates-at-large traveled about the country, seeking out injustices and collecting public opinion for the ruler.

Such practices, however, did not alter the fact that communication in Chinese society was basically one-way, following the vines of a hierarchical, paternalistic social structure. With the emphasis placed on propriety and group harmony instead of free exchange of ideas, the politically powerful were benign and virtuous when they listened to their people, but their power itself was not based on such virtues. If rulers did not want to listen, officers who typically came from the gentry class would risk their lives if they told the truth (Chu, 1992).[2] Similar patterns of communication characterized other social institutions, including families. More frequently than not, messages were sent from the ruler to the ruled, from the learned to the ignorant, from seniors to juniors, and from men to women. Confucianism laid down principles for conducting interpersonal relations that also dictated the mode of communication.

Because communication behavior is to be conducted following the same set of rules that govern Chinese society generally, it is almost impossible to breach communication standards without infringing on other rules as well. Therefore, disregarding the rules when communicating carries implications far beyond the act of communication itself. Communication that may trigger the "face" problem needs to be carefully managed or avoided altogether (Chu, 1992). For the same reason, confronting others—especially elders—with truth or disagreement cannot be regarded as merely an exchange of information or of viewpoints but as an impolite and rude gesture; it may lead to an unfavorable judgment of the person's manners and behavior. Under these circumstances, truth-telling is not merely an ethical issue but a high art.

In addition to communication restraints embedded in interpersonal relations, traditional Chinese cultural values—emphasizing modesty, humility, tolerance, and caution as essential ingredients of a "gentleman's" (*juin ze*) expressions—do not encourage eloquence and criticism or speaking out, even when interpersonal relations are not an issue. Criticism is not welcome because it indicates a lack of the tolerance necessary in maintaining group harmony. In addition, people are not entitled to criticize others if they cannot do as well as, or better than, what had been asked of others.

Closely associated with the emphasis on tolerance and modesty is a de-emphasis on skills in using words. Typical of such an attitude is a statement in Confucian teaching: "Those who are good with words and expressions are short of kindness in heart." Mencius (371-328 B.C.), the second most influential person in the Confucian tradition, was once compelled to admit that he did not like arguing; whenever it happened, he said he just did not have a choice. Given this cultural tradition, it is not surprising that expressing opinion policy is a difficult task for the Chinese. As a proverb says: "Disasters often come from one's mouth." Speaking out can easily tarnish one's image as a "true gentleman," trigger the "face" problem, offend others, and jeopardize interpersonal relations.

In modern times, freedom of expression is protected by the Constitution. However, until several years ago, many Chinese people would still feel the fear of saying something wrong in front of others, even when they were in a Western social context. A study conducted in the United States in 1977 discovered that Chinese students—along with many others from East Asian nations—showed greater reservations about speaking out in public as compared to their American counterparts (Wang, 1977).

Given this close integration of Chinese sociocultural values and communication practices, the relationship between ethical norms and the behavior of Chinese journalists can be better understood.

Communication Ethics and Sociocultural Values

Communications ethics consists of fundamental principles that validate codes of practice in communication. Although there has been no universal agreement as to what these principles are, a survey of the literature shows a high degree of consensus on the ethics of those in the communication profession (Belsey & Chadwick, 1992; Bohere, 1984; Traber, 1993). Among these common principles, truth-telling and fair and accurate reporting have been most frequently emphasized.

Adherence to truth is so important in accurately representing events or persons that the responsibility for telling the truth is placed on media professionals, not just on information sources. It takes a professional to bring truth to the public; very frequently, people whom journalists contact for information are reluctant to speak out. Bailey (1988, pp. 174-175), in his analysis of leadership, made the cynical remark that "no leader can survive as a leader without deceiving others." The history of the press tells us that one of journalism's greatest challenges has always been discovering and unveiling truth amid deceptive information, cover-ups, and pressure from people and institutions that wish to keep the public from knowing the truth.

Whereas barriers to truth-telling come from the outside world, the fairness principle guards against prejudices and biases from within professionals themselves. The decades-long debate over the possibility of genuine objectivity has left the question largely unsettled (Pang, 1994b). Despite cogent claims that human beings are born with subjective views due to everyone's unique background and experience, journalists of the 1990s generally insist that fair and objective reporting remains an important goal even if it is not completely possible.

The difficulties of achieving fairness lie in the complexity of the issues involved. Whereas biases from one's political, religious, social, and ethnic background are easier to detect, partiality stemming from the nature of news discourse itself has been emphasized of late. The criteria for news favoring social conflict, the bizarre, and the prominent (usually the typical powerful male elites) are ultimately distortions of reality and therefore of ethical concern. It is generally agreed that fairness in reporting can be achieved not by simply presenting arguments from all sides but by placing facts in context. However, contextual factors themselves include a wide range of values such as privacy, the public's right to know, and national security.

These and other principles—freedom, humaneness, and justice, for example—are upheld as codes of human behavior for the journalism profession in almost every nation. In Taiwan, a "Republic of China's Code of Press Ethics" was passed by the Press Council in 1974 (Lee, 1985). In this code, accuracy, objectivity, and fairness are given primary importance; also included are clauses on the protection of privacy. The code passed by the Press Council obviously borrowed its ideas from the West. In the strict and formal sense, there is no Chinese journalism ethics per se, but cultural factors, steeped in specific moral traditions, determine to a large extent the process of journalistic decision making.

Journalists know that they should always be loyal to the general public rather than to any particular individual or interest group. However, which professional values and ethical norms take priority in decision-making processes depends on many factors. As Christians, Fackler, and Rotzoll (1995) point out, different media may make entirely different decisions following the same set of ethical codes.[3] Contrary decisions are made because media workers have their own ways of prioritizing the norms of ethics; for one, protecting privacy may be the most important consideration, whereas for another, freedom of information is paramount. Such analyses allow for an in-depth understanding of how journalists make decisions about professional ethics but not why. As in all decision making, four groups of factors are essential in setting priorities in communication ethics, regardless of whether one is in the media profession or not. They not only set the background for moral reasoning but are present in every stage of the process.

1. *Sociocultural factors:* the nature of the political, economic, and social infrastructure, along with the dominant values and beliefs
2. *Organizational factors:* the tradition, goals, power structure, work ethics, and peer pressures of the organization in which individuals work
3. *Individual factors:* a person's values, beliefs, personality, education and professional training, and past experiences
4. *Situational factors:* given similar organizational or sociocultural factors, individuals may still behave differently because of the particular circumstances under which they have to make the decision.

Obiously, it is difficult to determine what factor is most important in making decisions about communication ethics; in each case, the weight that these factors carry may be different. They are interrelated and dialectic, for each contains elements that may work for and against the observation of ethical norms. Together, they interact to exert impact on the decision. As a result, when sociocultural values change, other factors will fluctuate as well.

As noted earlier, journalism ethics is rooted in Western culture and built around such fundamental concepts as freedom of expression, the right to know, protection of individual privacy, and equality of all human beings. These principles govern not just the behavior of media professionals but also the action of average citizens. If codes of ethics for media professionals are defined as journalism ethics, then ethical norms guiding the behavior of both journalists and average citizens should also be viewed as communication ethics. To Chinese media professionals, many codes of journalism ethics are foreign because the underlying principles of these codes are not found in traditional Chinese communication ethics.

Chinese communication ethics closely follows the codes of conduct for interpersonal interaction. In a culture that places greater importance on social institutions than on individuals, the idea of inborn human rights—including freedom of expression and the right to know—is alien. It is therefore not surprising that in the framework of Chinese society, certain principles of journalism ethics are being supported, whereas others are not. The individual right to access the media, for example, would be less readily acceptable than truth-telling. Because individuals are not encouraged to speak out in public, using the media to propagate one's ideas is almost unthinkable. Such behavior directly contradicts the Confucian definition of a "humble gentleman."

Protection of personal privacy is another example. With extended families dominating Chinese society for centuries, it is common for people to share things—from kitchen utensils to personal feelings—with those under the same roof. The necessity of having individual privacy is not only foreign but even difficult to comprehend. Also difficult to understand is the need to pay attention to the people at the grass roots in fair news reporting. In a feudalistic society, those who were junior, inferior, and ignorant were expected to obey and listen; it was only natural that they be placed at the receiving end of a one-way communication process.

Once social and cultural factors have been taken into consideration, it is easier to understand why journalists in some countries seem to consistently overlook certain principles of ethics while emphasizing others. The observance of journalism ethics in Taiwan reflects the drastic change in communication ethics as a result of the sociocultural transformation taking place.

Communication Ethics in Transition

When the earliest version of a newspaper dawned in China in the 18th century, it primarily served as a venue for important government announcements. Because China was plagued by war, poverty, and above all, a low literacy rate, newspapers were seen as publications by the gentry for their own class. This tradition was continued until well after the birth of the Republic in 1911.

It is important to note that during its course of development, Chinese newspapers have taken on quite different missions. During the 8-year Sino-Japanese war, they were used as instruments for national consolidation. However, in more peaceful days, the newspaper and later radio and television largely remained acquiescent institutions. These media either maintained harmonious relationships with the authorities—similar to what we have observed in Taiwan in the early days of the Nationalist rule—or became part of the government propaganda machine, as witnessed in China under Communist rule.

Up until the 1980s, press freedom was rather limited in Taiwan. In addition to censorship, a freeze was put on the number of newspapers and radio licenses, although all three broadcast television networks had—and still have—the government or the ruling party as their major shareholders. Jail sentences awaited those who dared to test the government's tolerance.

Aside from government control, the commitment to "harmonious relations" has a cultural overtone. Although there is no evidence that a paternalistic, hierarchical society necessarily breeds authoritarian control over the press, the traditional pattern of communication in a Chinese society could have facilitated or justified government control over the mass media, especially because the Chinese press was started by members of the gentry class. Although the gentry may not compromise truth for their own life, they may do so for "the good of the country," if so perceived.

At the time of political appeals for fighting Communism, national consolidation, and economic development, very few challenged the one-way, top-down pattern of communication in the first few decades of Nationalist rule in Taiwan. Although local elections were held, the absence of a strong opposition party made it difficult for genuine political competition to take place. For "the benefit and security of the country," the majority of journalists learned to cope with censorship and frequent instructions for reporting news events in certain ways. There were a few cases when journalists were arrested and jailed for alleged subversive activities. However, the press rarely stood up to or openly challenged government authority. It was no secret that the owners of the two largest privately owned newspaper conglomerates—the *United Daily News* and the *China Times*—were members of the Nationalist Central [Committee's] Standing Committee.

As a greater percentage of the population became literate and well-educated and general economic conditions improved, Taiwanese society became more heterogeneous and democratization more obvious. In 1988, the government announced the revocation of martial law, which brought a new era to Taiwan. This marked the beginning of party politics, constitutional reforms, and increasingly active social movements. President Lee Denghuey has described these changes as "a revolution without bloodshed" (Lin & Su, 1995, p. 4). The changes have not only removed barriers for democratizing society, they have had far-reaching influence on cultural norms and values. When members of the opposition party challenged the legality of the existing political infrastructure, they in fact launched an assault against an authority that had rarely been questioned before.[4] The attacks of the political authority, a strategy used by the opposition party, gradually eroded the cultural bond that kept people from voicing disagreement and discontent. Fueled by the lifting of martial law, social movements quickly became part of the daily routine. People suddenly discovered that they were free to stage a protest for any cause worth the effort. Together as groups, ordinary citizens managed to make news and gain access to the media that had normally been monopolized by the elites.

The impact was equally strong on media workers. They openly challenged interference with press freedom and professionalism. During the days of martial law, the press rarely opposed government controls. However, when people became rights conscious, so did journalists. Lee Yanchiou, the anchorwoman of one of Taiwan's three broadcast television networks, stunned the public by describing herself as a puppet, a government mouthpiece. In a televised speech after she won the "Best Anchor Award" at the Golden Bell Award Ceremony, Lee criticized the government for attempting to manipulate news reporting. Her bold gesture was followed by Fan Nien-hua, anchorwoman of another television network, who handed in her resignation after she had been given "instructions" to leave out a story on an opposition party. These actions of two television anchorwomen have not yet put an end to the government's attempt to control the last of its media stronghold, broadcast television. However, the outcry signifies the journalists' awakening consciousness of their rights and responsibilities.

On September 12, 1994, a march was held in Taipei on behalf of the journalists' right to professional autonomy. The group that calls itself the 912 Team was initially formed in reaction to the acquisition of the *Independence Daily* and *Independence Evening* newspapers by a seedy business conglomerate. They feared that their autonomy in editorial and professional matters would be infringed by the new owner. Thus, the staff requested that an agreement be signed to protect their interests. These efforts soon gained support from those working in other news media, and the movement quickly developed into an association advocating autonomy in the profession. It was recognized that journalists, like all other professional groups, had to take action if their rights were to be protected from pressures outside and within the news media. The formation of a journalists' association—or labor union, as some have advocated—may be the first step to ensure the ethical principle of freedom. For the first time in the history of journalism in Taiwan (and China), there is now an organized effort to guard against interferences with press freedom.

The increasing attention paid to the "people's voice" is another major change in the media scene following political reform. Already before martial law was lifted, there were debates among journalists whether they should remain a passive third party in a time of drastic change or take up the challenge of becoming social advocates and serving as spokespersons for the underprivileged. This attempt to redefine fair reporting was primarily a concern of the professional community. But when democratization took off, the situation developed quite differently.

Immediately after martial law in Taiwan was lifted, the freeze on the number of newspaper licenses and the number of pages of each newspaper was revoked. In response, almost all major newspapers redesigned their layout. Letters to the editor, which used to occupy no more than one-fifth of a page, were allocated a half or even a full page in the new formats.

Accused of monopolizing the radio spectrum, the government made a similar decision in 1994 for broadcasting by inviting applications for new licenses. In fact, the advent of communications technologies had already changed the face of the electronic media in Taiwan since the 1980s. Cable television networks, which were illegal before 1994, now offered up to 60 channels. For those who are not on cable networks, satellite television program have become readily accessible with a small dish on the rooftop.

The new and open channels of communication—together with the increasingly louder people's voice—contributed to the fall of the one-way, top-down communication pattern that had dominated Chinese society and communications since Confucianism laid down the rules for human interaction.

Taiwan's mayoral and gubernatorial elections in 1994 saw yet another breakthrough in using the electronic media. To advocate alternative political ideals and as acts of defiance, 14 underground radio stations began broadcasting in the time when the government opened applications for new radio licenses in 1994. In an attempt to lower production costs and to keep in touch with listeners, they soon found call-in programs the most popular attraction. A typical call-in program featured a host, sometimes with an invited guest, discussing issues arising from news events. Such radio talk shows quickly rose in popularity for at least two major reasons: First, the topics usually chosen for discussion were highly controversial; and second, because few of the hosts themselves had much professional training, their daring, down-to-earth style encouraged the normally silent listeners to speak out.

In less than a year, following the experiments of underground stations, licensed radio stations and television networks also began to produce programs of a similar nature. All of a sudden, everyone was using the airwaves to express his or her viewpoints. For a culture that used to teach its people to listen and obey, the change would have been unthinkable just a few years earlier.

Ethical Dilemmas

To those concerned with cultural and political influences on communication in Taiwan, recent changes have certainly been encouraging (Chu, 1992). These changes also have significant implications for the way communication ethics is interpreted and to what extent ethical principles are observed. Now when journalists rise to defend their professional autonomy, they are expected to be more accurate and fair with the truth. With the people's voice increasingly strong, the audience and reader have made it clear that they expect media coverage to present a balanced picture. However, there are developments in the media landscape of Taiwan that pose a series of new and fundamental ethical questions.

First, truth remains hidden behind an open forum of ideas. Although journalists are more conscious of internal and external control of information, truth is not necessarily more accessible. As society becomes heterogeneous and diversified, for each controversial issue, there may be several versions of the same story. When media workers are not motivated or lack adequate organizational support, the media become a mouthpiece for politicians, social activists, and diverse political groups. Audiences and readers now face the impossible task of making sense of the contradictory arguments, attacks, and counter-attacks.

This problem is especially pronounced during elections, when the news media are full of claims, accusations, promotional activities, and polling results from parties and candidates. As Pang (1994a) observes, so-called horse race reporting shows a lack of responsibility on the part of the media. After the 1994 election, a Taipei mayoral candidate who lost in the race sued reporters of a television network for spreading unsubstantiated claims by other candidates. He said the report had tipped the election outcome to his disadvantage. Although the court eventually ruled the journalists not guilty, the lawsuit was a warning to those engaging in horse race reporting.

Second, there are now diverse pressures on the media that make ethical conduct difficult. In an authoritarian society, the government is usually the major force impinging on freedom of expression. But in the process of democratization, average citizens quickly became rights conscious, forgetting the traditional emphasis on obligations. When new rules have not yet been fully established, this newly discovered, sometimes overblown, consciousness may act against press freedom. As a veteran reporter puts it, in the past, news editors had to deal with phone calls from the government; now they have to deal with phone calls, protests, and even harassment from all corners of society.

Third, boundaries are blurred between people's right to know, the right of media access, freedom of speech, and communication ethics. At first glance, this statement may seem to be contradictory, because an individual's right to know, freedom of speech, and communication ethics are different aspects of the same core concept; they support one another and are closely related. However, in times of drastic changes, certain norms and rules are promoted at the expense of others. Sometimes, it is no longer clear where the boundaries of different individual rights lie. Several incidents may exemplify the confusion that Taiwan journalists have encountered during a time of rapid social change.

People's Right to Know Versus Individual Privacy. Communication ethics may at times call for withholding information under certain circumstances to protect the privacy of an individual. Because individual privacy has never been an issue in the collective Chinese society, violation of this right has hardly attracted attention in the past. But when the people's right to know becomes the ultimate concern of media practitioners—or in some cases, an excuse for politicians to further their own purposes—the individual's right to privacy is literally trampled underfoot. During the 1994 election campaign, announcing the names, addresses, and telephone numbers of certain persons—and in some cases, even the names of the schools their children attended—became a favorite strategy of call-in radio programs for mobilizing the audiences to boycott or protest the decisions, opinions, or behavior of various people. Many who suffered the loss of their privacy were government officials and legislators, but average citizens were not exempted. It is easy to point out that certain information should be withheld to protect individual privacy, but no one seems to be sure where the boundary lies.

Press Freedom Versus Public Order. Press freedom, like all other human freedoms, is not unconditional. Should it include the right to mobilize an audience for action? This controversy was triggered by call-in radio programs and the government staging a large-scale crackdown against underground radio stations in response. Interestingly, the reason given for the government's action was not merely because these stations had no license but also because they used their programs to gather crowds for specific purposes. In the eyes of the government, this was a threat to public order.

If press freedom is not unconditional, then what are the conditions involved? Are gatherings of crowds in themselves a threat to public order? Should a call-in program take responsibility for the behavior of the crowd if it only announced the time and place of the gathering? What if it begins to give instructions as to how a crowd should act?

Right to Media Access Versus Trial by the Press. With increasing awareness of people's right to access the media, a wider section of the population may be represented in them. Does this mean that everyone has the same right?

The question was triggered by the arrest of a fugitive who was one of Taiwan's most wanted criminals. Two reporters from one of Taiwan's largest private newspapers were interviewing the criminal before the police arrived. The reporters were not charged with legal offenses; however, their action stirred debate about whether they had violated ethical standards (Pang, 1994c). The two reporters claimed they had to keep the police at bay because journalists had to protect their sources. Moreover, they argued, even criminals had the right to tell their side of the story. This defense was found unacceptable by many in the community, but they reacted mainly against the positive way the criminal was depicted in the stories filed by the two reporters. If, however, the criminal were not depicted as a hero, would such an interview be acceptable? And if criminals are not to have the right to tell their side of the story—for fear of the press intruding on a fair trial—are there others who should also be denied the right of media access? Who should they be and who is to make the decision?

These are a few examples of the ethical dilemmas that the media have faced in Taiwan. Today's media are by no means free from political manipulation or commercial pressure; instead of government control, all major political parties now own different media. Nevertheless, democratization of the political system and new ways of participation have turned a traditionally silent majority into an outspoken and rights-conscious people.

Conclusions

Social scientists have long realized that different cultures nurture different values. Even in China and Taiwan—societies that share the same cultural heritage—significant value differences were found after 40 years of independent development (Wang, Chu, Chung, & Chi, 1992). Such differences, however, are not and cannot be total. Values in different cultures can therefore be visualized as partly overlapping circles. Within each culture, some values are unique, but there are also values shared with others. As societies develop and interchange and communication across cultures intensifies, the overlapping parts expand.

When China came under Western influence by the end of the Chin Dynasty in the 19th century, the merits of modernization—including scientific and technological development and democratization of the political system—were becoming clear. It was also obvious that certain traditional values contradicted Western values that were basic to the concept of a modern democratic society. By the early 20th century, China was at a crossroads, trying to determine whether to westernize completely and thus deemphasize, if not reject, its ancient cultural tradition.

To the present-day Chinese, the issue is no longer relevant because it has become apparent that total westernization is neither possible nor desirable. However, partial westernization did take place in the process of social development in Taiwan, and the adoption of a democratic political system has become a major task. The authoritarian, feudal-imperial political system that existed in China for thousands of years was toppled in the 1911 revolution, but Taiwan did not really have a chance to become democratic until opposition parties were allowed to compete in free elections in 1988. When it did take place, changes in one sphere of the society soon led to changes in others. As Mandler (1993) points out, "values are mostly schema dependent and schemas are developed primarily in the social context" (p. 253).

Social changes not only stimulate value changes, but new and different social institutions also enhance different subsets of values (Rokeach, 1973). Because campaigning in elections requires communication skills to propagate one's own ideals and attack opponents, the first principles to be challenged were the Confucian teachings that have a direct bearing on communication behavior: modesty, tolerance, and a negative attitude toward eloquence.

So far, people are still trying to keep a balance between old and new values. In Taiwan, blunt verbal attacks are not unusual among politicians nowadays. However, such attacks on someone senior in the same community would still be seen as rude and offensive to the whole community. The overall changes that have taken place not only shed new light on the way the Chinese have communicated for centuries but underscore the importance of social and cultural factors in the articulation of communication ethics. Media professionals have been prompted to reexamine their role, reshuffle their priorities of values and norms, and redefine the meaning of ethical principles. Above all, it is now clear to media professionals that ethical behavior has become much more complex and, indeed, more taxing in the new democratic dispensation. In the sea change that has occurred in Taiwan since 1988, a number of observations can be made that might be of general relevance to societies in similar sociopolitical situations.

The first, and perhaps the least expected change, is the public's attitude toward the mass media. A public sphere in which citizens and pressure groups can have a public voice was created when the government yielded some of its erstwhile all-pervasive influence to the citizens and their media. People are beginning to act as an authentic public, with both positive and negative implications with regard to communication ethics.

The emergence of a public sphere brought freedom of communication and active participation in public affairs from all walks of life. Largely unfettered public communication now has a chance to help create a public ethics committed to a common good in which all the people have a stake. The challenge to Taiwanese civil society is to orchestrate these diverse voices toward a search for, and articulation of, a common good for all people. In this sense, the "part-whole indetermination" of ancient Chinese philosophy still holds true: Every citizen, and all the different groups of citizens, belong to the whole of society and cannot be relegated to the margins.

There are nonetheless some troubling developments generated by the birth of this fledgling public sphere. As the examples given have illustrated, the "right way"—according to the judgment of a certain segment of the public—is the indiscriminate invasion of privacy. The right of privacy is a human value that may not be sacrificed to political interests or sensationalism; if so, it amounts to people's exploitation and is thus humanly debasing. Also disturbing to media professionals is the audience's insistence on the "right way" being "my way." With the strong emphasis on rights—which received little attention in the past for cultural and political reasons—ethical considerations, such as respecting individual lives and opinions, tolerance, and the traditional concept of *Li,* run the risk of being swept aside. But even with such drastic changes in attitudes and values, the emergence of the public sphere has not yet been able to help override the political and commercial motives of media owners. The question is whether the public's ethical consciousness toward the media, still in its beginnings, will develop further. Will people become genuinely co-responsible partners of the media?

Second, truth-telling as an ethical norm continues, in traditional Chinese fashion, to be also an art. It is still the old art of showing respect for people, above all to senior citizens and those genuinely serving the community in leadership positions. But with the multiplicity and diversity of public voices, the quest for truth demands new forms of truth-telling. There is a need for new criteria for evaluating truth claims, new methods of detecting a measure of consensus in public communication. The hallowed certainties of the past that the government-controlled media used to proclaim may no longer be desirable. But the public expects the mass media to provide some solid pointers about the state of the nation: the country's economy, the people's safety and security, the health of the natural environment, and, above all, the country's future course. During times of rapid social change, the public expects the voices of chaos and the voices of order to be some-what balanced, if only tenuously. Public reassurance is a basic need of all societies; therefore, one of the ethical responsibilities of public communi-cation is to convey at least a measure of certainty about life-in-common, a certainty that must be based on truth. Truth, ultimately, is about the certain-ties of life, without which humans seem unable to function properly.

Truth, therefore, has a much wider horizon than accuracy of objectivity by which journalists often define it. Truth should lead to genuine under-standing, including the understanding of the forces of social change. Com-prehensive understanding tries to make sense of the world, or create mean-ing, which is an all-pervasive concept. Meaning, based on truth, is part of the ordered universe. Both modern and ancient Chinese societies would concur with this.

Last, in spite of the confusion that Taiwan's political and communication revolutions have stirred up, orderly and peaceful lives— probably the most universal and practical goal among most people and nations—remain highly desirable for those living on the island. Media-invoked violence in Parliament,[5] harsh language in call-in programs, and aggressive measures in seeking media access may be necessary approaches to break away from traditional cultural and political taboos. However, these are to be viewed as symptoms of a transition period, a transition from an authoritarian to a truly democratic society in which order will be restored with respect of each other and tolerance toward different views and opinions. Whether modern or traditional, Chinese or Western, the values and ethical norms that best promote and uphold life's contentedness—or even happiness—are likely to be the most universal human values of all.

Notes

1. The island of Taiwan, smaller in territory than Switzerland, is just 98 miles from the coast of mainland China. From 1895 to 1945, Taiwan was under Japanese occupation. It emerged from World War II as one of Asia's poorest countries but is now one of the richest in the region, with a population of about 21 million. Chiang Kai-shek led his defeated nationalist army from mainland China to Taiwan in 1949 where he reestablished the Republic of China, claiming that his government was the sole legitimate authority in China. China, in turn, has regarded Taiwan as a renegade province. When the People's Republic of China was admitted to the United Nations in 1971, Taiwan was expelled. In 1979, the U.S. withdrew diplomatic recognition and ended the mutual defense treaty. Shortly after Chiang Kai-shek's government had moved to Taiwan in 1949, martial law was imposed and no new opposition parties were allowed. In 1988, martial law was lifted and Taiwan began to embrace democracy.

2. In Chinese history, the gentry class maintained a close relationship with the rulers. Through national examinations, the imperial court selected from the gentry the best talents for its bureaucratic system. They were expected to be loyal to the ruler but nonetheless just and truthful intellectuals.

3. They build their analysis on the Potter Box of moral decision making in which four steps are crucial: definition of the situation, identification of values, appeal to ethical principles, and choosing loyalties.

4. To support its claim as the sole legitimate government of China after its retreat from the China mainland, the Nationalist Government, now based in Taipei, extended the term of the legislators who had been elected from all over China back in the 1940s until after the constitutional reform in 1991.

5. With broadcast television in the hands of the government, opposition party members in parliament have found an effective way to attract media attention by staging dramatic spectacles in parliamentary sessions, which frequently end in violence.

References

Arthur, Chris. (1989, October). Learning to be responsible for the media environment [Special issue]. *Media Development, 36,* 10-12.

Bailey, F. G. (1988). *Humbuggery and manipulation: The art of leadership.* Ithaca, NY: Cornell University Press.

Belsey, Andrew, & Chadwick, Ruth. (Eds.). (1992). *Ethical issues in journalism and the media.* London: Routledge.

Blackburn, Simon. (1994). *The Oxford dictionary of philosophy.* Oxford, UK: Oxford University Press.

Bohere, G. (1984). *Profession: Journalist.* Geneva: International Labour Office.

Cheng, Chung-ying. (1983). Chinese philosophy and recent communication theory. *Media Development, 30*(1), 30-34.

Christians, Clifford G., Fackler, Mark, & Rotzoll, Kim B. (1995). *Media ethics: Cases and moral reasoning* (4th ed.). New York: Longman.

Chu, Chuan-yu. (1974). *A history of the development of public opinion and press freedom in China.* Taipei: Zhenqzhonn Bookstore.

Chu, Leonard L. (1992, June). *The right to communicate in Chinese society: Cultural and political factors.* Paper presented at the Conference on the Right to Communicate, Shatin, Hong Kong.

Lee, Jan. (1985). *Communication law.* Taipei: National Chengchi University, Graduate School of Journalism.

Lin, Lin-wen, & Su, Wei-rong. (1995, February 28). Enhancing group harmony and establishing the "new Taiwanese" concept. *United Daily News,* p. 4.

Mandler, George. (1993). Approaches to a psychology of value. In Michael Hechter, Lynn Nadel, & Richard E. Michod (Eds.), *The origins of values* (pp. 229-260). New York: Aldine De Gruyter.

Pang, Ka-fat. (1994a, April 14). Horse-race reporting also fashionable in Taiwan. *Xin Daily,* p. 33.

Pang, Ka-fat. (1994b). *Objectivity in news reporting.* Taipei: San Min.

Pang, Ka-fat. (1994c, November 4). Sensationalism in Taiwan newspapers. *Xin Daily,* p. 32.

Rokeach, Milton. (1973). *The nature of human values.* New York: Free Press.

Traber, Michael. (1993). Communication ethics. In G. Gerbner, H. Mowlana, & K. Nordenstreng (Eds.), *The global media debate: Its rise, fall and renewal* (pp. 151-158). Norwood, NJ: Ablex.

Wang, Georgette. (1977, May). *Opinion expression.* Paper presented at the annual conference of the International Communication Association, Berlin.

Wang, Georgette, Chu, Godwin C., Chung, Wei-wen, & Chi, Jin-yao. (1992). *A comparative study of values in Taiwan and China.* Unpublished research report. Taipei, Taiwan: National Science Council.

CHAPTER 13

Japanese-Style Communication in a New Global Age

HIDEO TAKEICHI

Culture is the bedrock of all forms of communication. Senders and receivers, as constituent members of a society, share the values embedded in the cultural interchanges within that society. The media, as cultural products, receive their vitality from the values they share with society as a whole.

As in all countries, Japanese interpersonal and mass mediated communications reflect the cultural values of Japanese society. As the Japanese interact in everyday life, however, they do not realize the media's influence on them. Like fish swimming in water, not knowing what water really is, the Japanese are submerged in a media environment but are unaware of its influence. Human beings tend to think that their normal methods of communication are a matter of course. But if someone distances himself or herself from Japan, distinctively Japanese patterns of communication come into view. To compare communication patterns with those of other cultures, we need to take a fresh look at our own daily communication routines to reevaluate them.[1]

Traditional forms of Japanese communication emphasize harmony, meaning peace and good relations with people in one's immediate surroundings. Because Japan is a small, cramped country of 123 million people, instead of strongly asserting their views and wishes, people think it is better to suppress their own impulses, desires, and opinions and make compromises with others.

This tendency to value harmony benefits society, of course, but it has some negative aspects as well. In the process of emphasizing group harmony, the rights of individuals are of secondary importance. Japanese tend to look down on the plight and rights of the weak, and many problems of journalistic ethics have arisen in relation to this issue. In addition, despite the fact that international communication is being pursued along with the globalization of the economy, the idea of group harmony prevails only within the boundaries of Japan. The realization is still weak that communication transcends different cultures and encompasses the whole earth. In short, Japanese traditional communication has had its own meaning and significance but fails to cope sufficiently with the problems of internationalization. It is necessary for the Japanese to strive for a new harmonious communication to be realized from a global viewpoint.

Thus, the ethics of communication is a great challenge for a Japan facing a new age. The Japanese must fashion a new type of communication that is not closed in by its national borders but aims at a communication of love between fellow human beings and transcends the differences of nationality and culture.

Japanese Patterns of Communication

A restrained attitude is one of the most distinctive patterns of Japanese communication. Not speaking on impulse has come to be respected. Especially in the past, people who spoke a lot were looked down on. Talkative people were thought to be reckless. In a business organization, especially in the case of new employees, people who insist strongly on their own ways of doing things are disliked; they are thought to be impudent and are even ridiculed. In a group, someone who says something that violates the unwritten rules and tacit agreements of the group is considered a troublemaker or even an eccentric.

The underlying values are those that prize the goal of the group above everything else. To achieve what the group is aiming for, the members more or less suppress their opinions and are patient. One begins to gain individual existence only when the group prospers. When someone is committed to the company's goals and spends all his or her energy to achieve them, then company personnel are supposed to experience their deepest *raison d'etre*.

For the sake of the group, especially for its harmony and prosperity, working together is certainly desirable. For the economic growth of a business enterprise, for developing the nation's cities and towns, group harmony is certainly beneficial. Since the Meiji era and through the decade of high-speed economic growth, this trend has become even stronger.

In the Japanese environment, it is easy to achieve group cohesion. Even though a small fraction of the population is made up of ethnic minorities such as the Ainu, on the whole, and especially when compared to the United States, Japan is a highly homogeneous society. Religion, language, and cultural background are generally held in common. It is therefore a society in which people can communicate and understand each other easily and with a limited amount of words.

The social anthropologist Edward T. Hall (1977) calls Japan a "high context" society (p. 68; cf. 1969, 1973). In fact, the ability to understand each other's feelings without exchanging words is looked on as the high art of communication in Japan. Someone who cannot quickly and accurately grasp the others' true feelings and unspoken thoughts is criticized as a poor observer or even as dim-witted. When borrowing money or an object from another, it is, for example, embarrassing to explicitly ask for it. To deduce exactly what the speaker is requesting, before hearing all the details and circumstances, is considered to be part of politeness.

Kakuei Tanaka, the former Prime Minister who had to retreat from the front of the political stage—due to the Lockheed scandal and to illness—was called "a man with a head like a computer." A self-educated person who did not even have a high school education, Tanaka, before even hearing the details of a lobby's petition, would rattle them off in machine-gun fashion, "I got it. I got it." It seems that he was so perceptive and quick-witted that he could understand what people wanted to say in an instant.

In Japan, husbands and wives do not often exchange words between themselves. This is a predominant feature of past traditions. In present times, a lord-of-the-manor husband with a silent, obedient wife has become rare. In modern Japan, however, there is a nostalgic longing for the silent communication of the past. For example, the popular novels of Kuniko Mukouda, which center around a 1930s middle-class family in Tokyo, are still selling and have been made into television dramas many times over.[2] In these heart-warming dramas, people are able to understand one another without saying very much. Mukouda's books have captured the Japanese heart of wordless communication.

In the Japanese language, the subject of the sentence is sometimes omitted. If one says simply *onaka ga suita* ("the stomach is empty"), no one really knows who is hungry. Theoretically, it could mean "I am hungry" or "you are hungry" or "we are hungry." By itself, the sentence only indicates that someone's stomach is empty. But in Japanese communication, this sentence is easily understood by the circumstances; it usually means, "my stomach is empty." Japanese communication is like a Chinese watercolor (*suiboku*) in which the scenery is deliberately not drawn in great detail; some parts of the picture are intentionally shrouded in clouds and mist.

Of the movies made in Japan after World War II, those of Yasujiro Ozu, who directed films such as *Tokyo Story,* sketched in detail the daily life of Japan's middle class. In his films, there are many scenes in which families communicate faintly and only dimly perceive each other's feelings. The words are few, but their meanings are vast. If viewers criticize this kind of communication, they have not fully understood it. Viewers themselves must actively take part in the dialogue of the film. Japanese sympathetic communication (*sassuru*) is, in great part, a form of communication that struggles to preserve the harmony between speakers and listeners.

Japanese patterns of communication are also evident in the mass media. One major way in which the Japanese media differ from their Western counterparts is their system of lifelong employment. The majority of Japanese journalists work until they retire in the company where they began. They are able to settle down and tackle their jobs without worrying about where they will work next.

Individual journalists usually collect data when working on a story, but when there are major events, it is common for Japanese journalists to work in teams to gather information. For example, when writing a series of articles on economic tensions between the United States and Japan, the foreign bureau, the political department, the economic department, photography, and the local departments will each provide reporters and cover the story from various angles. Whereas it is impossible to cover it all by oneself, a team can expect to produce complete and detailed reports. Overseas reporters are mobilized as well, but it is not unusual for reporters from Japan to be dispatched to join the overseas group if a series of articles is planned.

In these ways, a communication of harmony continues to function not only between individuals but in the media as well. This is an inherited, traditional way of communication that has yielded some good results.

Why should patterns of communication evolve in which individuals suppress their own desires and ambitions and give priority to the welfare of the group? This is common not only to Japan but is shared with many countries in Southeast Asia. It is probably due to the fact that for a long time, Japan and Southeast Asia have been agricultural societies. Unlike the constantly moving nomadic tribes, agricultural people are rooted in the land, their lives revolving around the cultivation of crops. In this situation, the spirit of group harmony is more than a lifestyle; it is an absolute necessity. In Japan, where nearly 70% of the land is mountainous terrain, a great many people have had to live on the limited flatland. Furthermore, for making a living by working the paddy fields, the entire community had to be cooperative. Even bringing water to the fields had to be done jointly. If one household stubbornly opposed the day's schedule, water from the higher fields could not flow down to the lower ones. And if the water stopped halfway, planting rice became impossible.

Generation after generation, life in this natural environment came to place more importance on the logic of the group and its well-being rather than giving priority to individuals. Those who opposed the group's interest were socially ostracized—except for funerals, their relations with other villagers were completely cut off. Without communicating with other villagers, they endured a solitary, isolated existence. With such harsh social punishment, it would be much easier to suppress one's own assertions and desires and follow the same line as everyone else.

Problems With Traditional Communication

Traditional forms of communication that put the value of the group above that of the individual have their good sides. But they also have negative consequences. The latter are evident in the low respect for individual human rights and in what might be called the patriotic imperative of the Japanese mass media.

Apathy Toward Human Rights

The first negative aspect that arises from making the logic of the group the first and most important consideration is a tendency to look lightly on the individual's situation. In Japan, the degree of concern about human rights is generally low. Certain parts of the press lack consideration for those in weak positions. Also, defamation of character and invasion of privacy have recently become serious problems. In addition, there are many cases in the media, specifically in advertising, where the representation of women is discriminatory and sexist.

In situations that might cause the harmony of the group to crumble, people refrain from conclusively pursuing the responsibility of those involved. Instead of making the issues clear, things are left in a perpetual gray haze. There is a tendency to make matters of responsibility vague and blurred. As a result, it is likely that the damages awarded to a person who has suffered injury are often left unspecified.

Criticism against individuals who deviate from the norm is severe as well. Nowadays, in Japanese grade schools and junior high schools, the problem of bullying has become very serious. When everybody complies with the rules, he or she is safe; but when individuals do something different, they are harassed into conformity. Sometimes, grade school pupils even commit suicide to protest against those who bullied them.

When the norms in a group are strong, people outside who are not obeying the group's norms tend to be excluded. This tendency can be seen in the Japanese mass media. There is not a single law suppressing freedom of speech in Japan. However, freedom of speech is voluntarily curtailed. Particularly, the spirit of criticism toward governmental powers is weak. Insisting that government officials be responsible only occurs on a superficial level. Instances of self-censorship by the press are frequent. It is now more important for readers to check what is not written rather than what is. Political reporters tend to have a feeling of solidarity with the politicians they meet regularly. The critical spirit of reporters when dealing with public problems is often diluted. Such dull political reporting was especially characteristic during the rule of the Liberal Democratic Party from 1955 to 1993.

The weekly photographic magazines, sports newspapers, and some television shows have a particular disregard for the rights of citizens. These media are aiming to increase sales or ratings through sensational journalism. The breach of ethics by weekly photo magazines has become atrocious. They peer into the personal lives of the famous and violate their rights of privacy.[3] Using actual names in reporting proves the factuality of what is reported, but depending on times and circumstances, it can injure people's rights. When the first test-tube baby was successfully born in Japan, one of the famous national newspapers, the *Mainichi Shimbun* (October 14, 1983, evening edition), ignored the mother's request that a pseudonym be used; it reported her real name instead. The newspaper contended that they did so because "it was such good news for women unable to bear children." However, the newspaper did not consider the plea for anonymity from this woman living in a rural community who had undergone the surgery.

Another national newspaper, *The Asahi Shimbun* (April 20, 1989, evening edition), reported on the so-called "phony coral reef defacing" incident. A photographic article showed the initials "K.Y." carved onto a beautiful reef in the sea at Iriomote Island, off the main coast of Okinawa. The article asked belligerently, "Who is this K.Y.?" As an environmental campaign article, readers widely praised it. However, soon afterwards, it became apparent that the criminal responsible for the graffiti was none other than the newspaper's photographer who had taken the picture. Readers were disgusted and shocked by the reporter's lack of morals. He had deceived them and then screamed, "Who is the criminal?" For them, the ethics of journalism had been completely lost. In a similar case, a television production company making a program on organized crime deliberately staged a violent scene to get more vivid footage. This episode not only raised the public's ire but it also brought severe warnings from the police.

An example of the sheer lack of ethical will power is in cigarette advertising. In the United States and elsewhere, there are loud calls for a complete ban of tobacco advertising in the media. In Japan, cigarette commercials are not banned even on television. For 1 or 2 seconds within a commercial, the watcher is cautioned, "Smoking causes loss of health, so be careful not to smoke too much." Except for this mild warning, everything else is left in a do-as-you-please state.

Pornographic comic books aimed at children have also become a problem in the last few years. There are scenes of incest, prostitution, rape, and other violent sexual acts. In short, they have made sexuality into a commodity to be sold. As it transforms women into male tools, there is an uproar that children may imitate what they have seen and read. Among the pay telephone services available, several are sexually explicit. Some underage children have been using these sex services, and this has caused a great commotion. Even in video games, sexually graphic descriptions and suggestive images have increased. When juveniles play such games, they might be affected negatively. Local governments are now at work drafting ordinances to regulate these forms of exploitation that violate human dignity.

In at least one area involving human rights, the situation has recently improved. The practice of reporting the names of suspect offenders without clarifying their legal positions has been abandoned. Since December 1989, almost all Japanese newspapers and television stations no longer simply report the names of those involved in crime stories without clarifying exactly where they stand with the law. As a general rule, the word *suspect* is now attached to the names of those involved in a crime before the courts have acted. If names are printed in the papers or mentioned on TV at the arrest stage, the impression is given that the persons identified are criminals. In the past 10 years, there are numerous examples of homicide cases in which it became clear that the suspect had been framed, but mass media practices ignored the plight of the accused.

The privacy of individuals who become objects of the news media is invaded for no other reason than the media's logic of boosting sales. Japanese society still does not sufficiently respect individual rights. Aggressive media workers have little regard for the people on whom they report. They are not treated as individuals with their own characters. Without being aware of it, Japan is an anonymous society where the individual face cannot be seen.

Peace Within and Without

A second negative aspect stemming from traditional Japanese communication aimed at group harmony concentrates only on the inner group and shows little concern for outsiders. The Japanese are satisfied merely with harmony within their own circles. When looked at from a wider perspective, Japanese communication patterns are closed and discriminatory toward other countries and cultures. The Japanese themselves seem to be unaware of this. Communication for harmony should include the larger context, indeed the world, yet the Japanese show little leadership in this respect.

Japan has caused trade frictions with America, Europe, and other Asian countries. With each passing year, the problem has intensified, especially regarding the United States. Trade problems first arose over textiles, then over television, automobiles, and steel, and spread further to agricultural goods. Now, it is no longer simply manufactured goods but intellectual property rights, patents, and copyrights.

One reason for these problems is the cohesiveness of the Japanese mentality. Trade frictions are not simply economic or political struggles but involve cultural and value-oriented differences. Compromise is needed on both sides. But as far as the Japanese side goes, it is no longer good enough for Japan to think only of its own prosperity. As its economic activities keep expanding, for example, Japan has reached a point where protection of the environment around the globe must be taken seriously. Not just the prosperity and the environment of one's own country should be considered but the wherewithal and coexistence of all of Asia and of the entire world.

In general, the Japanese mass media are highly protective of their own country. For example, a Malaysian court found a subsidiary of a Japanese chemical corporation guilty of neglecting to regulate the flow of toxic materials, which damaged the health of the Malaysian citizens (*Asahi Shimbun,* August 11, 1992, morning edition). Japanese environmental protection groups and lawyers supported this decision, but the Japanese media reported very little about the evolution of the case. For this reason, Japanese readers and viewers had the impression that the court's decision was suddenly handed down. The Japanese media should not only raise ethical problems internally but also question the ethical implications of Japan's foreign trade and manufacturing.

There is a Japanese proverb, *tabi no haji wa kakisute,* which literally says, "away from home, one tends to throw away one's shame." It means that persons who behave ethically within their own country may suddenly abandon their ethics when separated from their daily life and neighborhood. The media should not make the same mistake. They have ethical responsibilities not only within their own country but to other countries as well.

Future Directions

In which directions will Japanese communication develop in the future? At the very least, Japan's traditional communication seeking group harmony ought to be developed into a new form adapted to the age of international or global communication. For this to happen, the Japanese media must learn to respect other people's points of view, breaking out of their prevailing ethnocentrism.

Shedding the Closed-Society Mentality

The Japanese people should challenge the mentality of insider's communication. There is a need to transcend national borders and national profits and cultivate a viewpoint that considers others rather than only oneself. If someone thinks exclusively of the prosperity and profit of his or her own country, the aim of inclusiveness can never be realized. Communication that transcends borders and aims at the realization of human progress for all is the only social goal that is defensible for the future. Governments are bound by their countries' self-interest. They are thus poor players in the international arena of ethics. Only journalists, educators, and religious leaders who possess a consciousness that reaches beyond national profit can promote the ethics of global communication.

Communication, and ethics of communication, that match the new era must also be considered from the others' point of view and not just from one's own. A revolution in thinking is necessary to correct the Japanese media's ethical stance. Harmonious reporting benefiting Japan alone widens the communication gap between countries and will pose further problems for effective intercultural communication. The ethical task of Japanese public communication is to apply its concept of harmony to the international and intercultural levels.

It is essential that the mass media raise the public's consciousness of global issues that affect all human beings. These issues include the rapid degradation of the environment and the quests for international justice and global peace. Journalists should become global reporters who are not bound by national interests. Such reporting calls for a global ethics of communication.

Eliminating Ethnocentrism

The next step in the development of communication fit for the new age is the elimination of ethnocentrism. It is important to be proud of the values and culture of the society to which one belongs. But if we are unable or unwilling to recognize any value systems other than our own, global communication cannot function without impunity. There is a need to respect other countries and to aim at international exchanges that go beyond the boundaries of state and government. It is very important for media practitioners, while strengthening their self-awareness, to make every attempt to appreciate and establish contacts with different cultures.

It is not easy to shed or redirect an ethnocentric attitude. The Japanese have acquired it through centuries of being immersed in their own social and cultural milieu. Likewise, the mass media are cultural products of a particular society or community. Thus, the media cannot function nor survive without taking into consideration the social values and traditions of the people they are supposed to serve.

The mass media also have a tendency to claim that they serve the national interest first and foremost, over and beyond other considerations. The year 1995 marked the 50th anniversary of the end of World War II. Japanese and U.S. newspapers ran articles and commentaries on whether dropping atomic bombs on Hiroshima and Nagasaki was justified or not. Many U.S. newspapers, such as the *Washington Post* (February 10, 1995) and the *New York Times* (March 23, 1995), reported that President Truman's decision was justified because it hastened the end of the war and prevented additional U.S. casualties.

Japanese newspapers reported extensively on President Clinton's comments supporting Truman's policy. They also gave prominence to the uneasy, if not negative, reactions of high officials of the Japanese government. Similarly, the *Asahi Shimbun* (April 14, 1995) carried reports published in U.S. newspapers about the atomic bombs. The Japanese press did not express their own opinions but merely translated articles from the U.S. press. This clearly implied that the Japanese still think that using atomic bombs was not justified, because it caused the death and injuries of thousands of Japanese civilians.

Fifty years after the war, a wide gap still exists between the U.S. press and the Japanese over their historical evaluation of the bombing of Hiroshima and Nagasaki. How can people better grasp the full meaning of these events after carefully considering the differing viewpoints? How can people find a way to reach a total understanding of the real meanings of atomic destruction, an understanding that goes beyond personal grief and national interest?

It is difficult to find a satisfactory answer to such questions. Nonetheless, we must continue to work for it. And in the process of seeking an answer, personal biases should not cloud our reasoning; they should not prevent us from moving closer to a more objective way of perceiving and looking at things. If we cannot allow ourselves to be detached from personal prejudices and preferences, it is naive to expect that we can reach a commonality in seeing things. In a global age, each country's people and mass media cannot communicate if they allow themselves to be bound by indigenous social values only.

The word *communication* derives from the Latin word *communis,* which means "in common." Communication is about sharing what each one holds dear, that is, sharing between God and humans and among ourselves. Such sharing is the spirit of communication. In other words, the real essence of communication is love.

If one possesses the spirit of love, with a little modesty, one can learn from others. Learning from one another is something that should be carried out within every country through many channels. It is not sufficient to exchange diplomatic documents between governments. Intercultural reciprocity should take place on the grassroots level, among people in everyday life, bringing alive communication from many angles so that with humble hearts we can truly learn from one another. In Japan, this important task has hardly begun.

Japan must once more reevaluate and rectify its traditional patterns of communication and achieve a wider, more encompassing, truly global understanding of communication. This is the foundation of communication ethics in modern Japanese society. And it is also the ethical mentality that holds values in common with the entire world.

Conclusion

After these critical reflections on communication patterns and practices in Japan and the need for a new communication ethics, it may be useful to apply Japan's own ethical principles to the project of universal human values.

The principle of *harmony* can be interpreted ultimately as a quest for mutual understanding, sharing, and genuine conviviality. Harmony is a communitarian value; its horizon is a community living in peace. Peaceful communities can only be established and made to flourish by communications that express and strengthen social bonds, recognizing the dignity of the community and of all its members. It should also imply the concept of freedom, because no community can be in a state of harmony if some of its members or sections of the community are repressed and relegated to silence.

Thus, in spite of all the problems connected with the current Japanese principle of harmonious communication, the ethical core value it enshrines can be of universal significance. Is not one of the very goals of interpersonal communication the establishment of honest and harmonious relationships? And could this principle not be applied to the whole complex world of the mass media? This would, however, presuppose that harmony is reappraised and reevaluated as an ethical principle, taking into account the intricate web of communication that exists between different peoples, nations, and cultures. Genuine harmony is never exclusive but always inclusive.

Another principle discussed has been *group solidarity*. It is a difficult, perhaps alienating concept for people steeped in cultures that glorify individualism. It also has serious drawbacks, as seen, regarding individual human rights. And it can cause untold miseries for people who dare to step out of line and refuse to conform. But it also has redeeming features.

Solidarity as an ethical principle means more than submission to a group. It can become an active movement that shapes communication and the mass media in a positive way. Solidarity encapsulates the process leading towards unity with others, thus creating a movement of common concerns. The natural environment is one such concern. Another is the vision of a global human family living in mutual cooperation and peace. But the most important form of solidarity is a commitment to justice. The first mark of civility, and for that matter of a civilization that deserves the name, is a special concern for the weak. This group includes the physically dependent, that is, mainly, the very young and the very old. It includes people without social and economic power, as, for example, refugees who are merely, and sometimes hardly, tolerated. The weak may also mean members of minorities, be they ethnic, religious, or social. Genuine solidarity is also concerned with women's rights and the powerlessness that they encounter in almost every sphere in life.

What then started with the narrow concept of group solidarity can be enlarged to fit, as it were, the real world needs of today—not only in Japan but on a global scale.

Out of harmony and solidarity grows a third principle, that of *affinity* or *empathy*. Empathy from a Japanese perspective is a feeling for people, an active familiarity with human nature and the human condition. Empathy, it was pointed out, makes it sometimes superfluous to use words—as in the relationship between husband and wife or in the family in general.

Affinity is an emotional quality that is the result of mutual acceptance and trust. In the realm of social communication, it is the mutual confidence between senders and receivers of messages, and such confidence is based on truthfulness. Western analyses of the Japanese way of "saving face" are generally widely off the mark. Saving face does not mean deception but is grounded in a type of respect for the other that can best be expressed as affinity.

Affinity and empathy should not be restricted to Japanese culture but should be developed into an ethical principle of communication, above all, in intercultural and international communication. It means more than truthfulness. It means genuine concern for the other, all others. It is as much a feeling as it is a norm. Earlier, it has been called the spirit of love.

These three ethical principles, developed from a critical reading of Japanese communication patterns, admittedly have a utopian dimension. But only a utopian vision can free us from the narrow constraints of the Japanese mass media and break down the ethnocentric barriers that characterize communication around the world.

Notes

1. The perspectives outlined in this chapter are elaborated in Ashihara (1992); Barnland (1989); Beasley (1990); Casmir (1991); Christopher (1993); Condon and Saito (1974); Edelstein, Bowes, and Harsel (1978); Gudykunst (1993); Kim (1981); Lebra and Lebra (1986); Nakane (1973); and Varley (1973).

2. Some famous novels of Kumiko Mukouda are *A Un* [*Brief but Deep Communication*] and *Chichi no Wabijo* [*Father's Letter of Apology*].

3. In Japan, there are hardly any sensational newspapers among general dailies, but some sports papers, photo magazines, and weekly magazines are highly sensational.

References

Ashihara, Yoshinobu. (1992). *The hidden order.* Tokyo: Kondansha International.

Barnland, Dean C. (1989). *Communicative styles of Japanese and Americans.* Belmont, CA: Wadsworth.

Beasley, William G. (1990). *The rise of modern Japan.* Tokyo: Charles E. Tuttle.

Casmir, Fred L. (Ed.). (1991). *Communication in development.* Norwood, NJ: Ablex.

Christopher, Robert C. (1993). *The Japanese mind.* Tokyo: Charles E. Tuttle.

Condon, John C., & Saito, Mitsuko. (1974). *Intercultural encounters with Japan.* Tokyo: Simul Press.

Edelstein, Alex S., Bowes, John E., & Harsel, Sheldon M. (Eds.). (1978). *Information societies: Comparing the Japanese and American experiences.* Seattle: University of Washington, School of Communications, International Communication Center.

Gudykunst, William B. (Ed.). (1993). *Communication in Japan and the United States.* New York: State University of New York Press.

Hall, Edward T. (1977). *Beyond culture.* Garden City, NY: Anchor.

Kim, Young C. (1981). *Japanese journalists and their world.* Charlottesville: University Press of Virginia.

Lebra, T. S., & Lebra, W. P. (1986). *Japanese culture and behavior.* Honolulu: University of Hawaii Press.

Nakane, Chie. (1973). *Japanese society.* Tokyo: Charles E. Tuttle.

Varley, Paul. (1973). *Japanese culture: A short history.* Tokyo: Charles E. Tuttle.

CHAPTER 14

Vagaries of Time and Place

Media Ethics in Poland

KAROL JAKUBOWICZ

In the 1980s, Polish dissidents coined a slogan. "There can be no freedom without solidarity." The Communist government came back with a different slogan, emblazoned on a banner stretched across the Central Committee building, "There can be no freedom without responsibility." Today, in the media and elsewhere, there is lots of freedom but limited solidarity and precious little responsibility.

This chapter provides a brief overview of the ongoing debate in Poland over the norms and values of journalism and the media. It forms part of a much larger struggle over the norms and values of Polish society in general.

Great Expectations (1980-1989)

The Solidarity revolution of 1980 was more about dignity and values than anything else. Ever since, the Poles—media practitioners among them—have wrestled with the question of what value system to recognize and follow. The question could not be more urgent. The rapid change triggered by the revolution has involved a wholesale revamping of the social, political, and economic system. In its wake, the old way of life has disintegrated, being replaced slowly and painfully by a new one.

The birth of Solidarity was a direct consequence of the crisis of the late 1970s. In the sphere of social consciousness, the crisis had caused widespread feelings of deprivation, anomie, and alienation (Sztompka, 1982) as well as "frustration in the face of . . . violations of [the] principles of democracy and social justice. . . . The sense of dignity of large social groups, including particularly the workers, was undermined" (Nowak, 1988, p. 44). Striking workers, "motivated by . . . dignity and honor much more than by material needs" (Król, 1981, p. 11), formulated demands that they saw, in part, as a "rehabilitation of their rights, the restitution of accepted values, recognized as an integral part of their culture, customs and morals" (Wójcicki, 1981, p. 101). Accordingly, the process leading to the birth of Solidarity was also "a profound moral experience; . . . moral values also became categories of understanding and ordering reality" (Staniszkis, 1983, pp. 357-358). The axiological consensus uniting those active in the movement can be represented as shown in Table 14.1.

After the birth of Solidarity, many journalists working in the official media sought to atone in some way for their role in perpetuating the Communist system and for serving as its propaganda arm. They sought to regain credibility, in part by reasserting the need to observe scrupulously the journalistic code of conduct. The emergency congress called by the Association of Polish Journalists (which soon became a staunch ally of Solidarity)— with the intention of reassessing the role of the profession in the new social and political situation—made this clear through its resolution in October 1980:

> By enforcing observance of the norms of journalistic ethics by each and every member, the Association will create an important guarantee of the proper functioning of the media of social communication in Poland. Violation of these norms is not just an individual matter for a particular journalist; it is an offense against the whole profession, its status and credibility. The Congress puts the authorities of the Association under an obligation to the membership[1] in terms of . . . observing the journalistic code of conduct, and at the same time to review the body of norms which regulate the rights and obligations of journalists. These norms should be updated and submitted to a general debate within the

TABLE 14.1 Axiological Foundations of the Solidarity Movement

Manifestation of Crisis in Social Consciousness	*Values and Ideals Espoused by Solidarity in Response to Crisis*
Deprivation	Justice, equality
Anomie	Truth, rule of law, rationality, discipline
Alienation ·	Democracy, representation, creativity, dignity
	Patriotism

profession and in society in general, as in the last instance it is public opinion which is empowered to supervise their observance. (O znaczeniu środków komunikacji społecznej, n.d., pp. 42-43)

Solidarity soon began developing some ideas on the fundamental principles for reforming the media system. Among them were freedom of speech; social, political, and cultural pluralism and a purity of world views in the media; truth; the right to communicate; communication as empowerment; subjectivity (in the sense of mastery over one's own fate, of being a subject and not an object); and socialization of the media (meaning direct societal supervision of the media and media accountability to society). It was to have been a system of participatory communication, involving structural guarantees of social feedback, access to, and participation in, media activities. The Solidarity approach was akin to proposals by Williams (1968) and Keane (1991) to use public funds and public institutions to ensure positive freedom to communicate for all groups in society.

McQuail's (1992) proposal that a set of basic communication values—freedom, justice-equality, and order-solidarity—serve as a framework of principles for media assessment is apropos to our analysis. In these terms, the main features of media systems based on those values can be reconstructed, as shown in Table 14.2.

Clearly, the system of social communication proposed by Solidarity was to have been grounded in the basic communication values of equality-justice, with important consequences for the way the media operated. As Jean Cohen (1993) has pointed out,

The legitimacy of the public sphere is tied up with its potential for *inclusion*, and the existence of the public sphere as the central context of democratic

TABLE 14.2   Media Systems as Defined by Their Underlying
Communication Values

Features of Media System	Basic Values		
	Freedom	*Justice-Equality*	*Order-Solidarity*[2]
Goal	Unrestricted freedom of communication	Equal access to media, cohesion, fair reflection in media of society in all its diversity	Increasing commonality and sharing of outlook and experience
Main mechanism	Market	Public intervention to ensure equality in communication	Centralized command system
Underlying philosophy	Market driven, exclusion, negative freedom of speech	Inclusion, democracy, positive freedom of speech (right to communicate)	Political exclusion, hegemony, homogenization
Communicators	Everyone with the means to do so	All social groups	Only "approved" voices

access calls for programs of inclusion. . . . Thus the formal legal guarantees
(legal rights) together with mechanisms for facilitating of *equality of access
to the public sphere* . . . become all the more important in relationship to a
functioning public sphere. (p. 7, italics added)

Accordingly, the earlier-mentioned emergency congress of the Association
of Polish Journalists passed a resolution that read in part,

> The Congress expresses the hope that the coming political change will bring
> about the development of the system of social communication. This means
> both a rise in the print-runs of newspapers, and the future mushrooming of
> local newspapers, and of radio and television stations, which is imperative for
> processes of social integration, and breaking through the centralization of
> cultural and social life in Poland. . . . The Congress also expresses the hope
> that all major segments of society will obtain a chance fully to express their
> views by means of their own dailies and periodicals, with print-runs commen-
> surate with the social demand for them. Today this refers primarily to the press
> of the new trade union movement, as well as the press of political movements
> other than the Polish United Workers' Party, to the Catholic press and that of

other denominations. (O znaczeniu środków komunikacji społecznej, n.d., p. 43)

This approach remained at the core of Solidarity's stance on social communication until the end of the 1980s. At the 1989 Round Table conference, Solidarity obtained the Communist government's acceptance of the document summing up the debate on the media and expressing exactly that approach:

> The media of social communication, irrespective of their political or religious orientation, should . . . express social opinions and the views and proposals of all political and other movements, taking into account also the views and opinions which they do not share. The parties recognize as justified the aspirations of all new actors of social and political life to publish their own newspapers. This is an inalienable aspect of trade unions and political and social pluralism. (*Sprawozdanie z prac,* 1989, pp. 1-2).

This entire approach had much in common with Brecht's (1967) original call for radio to serve as a medium of communication rather than distribution, with Enzensberger's (1974) concept of the emancipatory use of the media, and with the program of democratic participation outlined by Groombridge (1972). It was born out of a distrust of the official media and the journalists working for them. Accordingly, it was based on a view of communication as interaction, rather than as a one-way, top-down flow of messages. It called for the deprofessionalization of the media and put stress on social access and participation. Calls for socialization of the broadcast media were justified by paraphrasing Talleyrand: Broadcasting is much too serious a thing to be left to professional broadcasters.

The debate over the media necessarily concentrated on analyzing the weaknesses and failings of the official media in their roles as propagandistic mouthpieces of the system. However, a positive program regarding the values and norms on which media operations should be based can also be deduced from that debate. The fundamental value was that of truthfulness—in the media and in life in general.[3] The 1981 Congress of Solidarity committed itself to a struggle against lies and falsehood in all areas of life and declared that "society wants to live in truth and has a right to do so" (*Statut,* 1981, p. 5). Other norms and values underscored by the 1981 Congress are typical of community and alternative media, with their stress on popular empowerment by means of communication, involvement in the life of the community, commitment to social action, and so forth (Downing, 1984; Jankowski, 1988; Jankowski, Prehn, & Stappers, 1992).

This approach is strongly reminiscent of what Denis McQuail (1994, pp. 131-132) recognizes as the democratic-participant media theory, one of the normative theories of the press. James Curran (1991) calls it the "radical democratic perspective of the media" in which "the media are viewed as a complex articulation of vertical, horizontal and diagonal channels of communication between individuals, groups and power structures," and should be defined as "assisting the equitable negotiation or arbitration of competing interests through democratic processes" (pp. 30-31).

This radical democratic perspective of the media involved a certain view of society and the media's role in it. Curran (1991) presents it this way (see Table 14.3).

This approach assumes that the media should be a countervailing agency serving to redress the imbalance of power in society and compensating for the inferior resources and skills of subordinate groups. In this view, the media should help subordinate groups to advocate their interests by comparison with dominant groups, serving as a channel of communication within the group and as a vehicle for the group's participation in social discourse as a whole. This approach is often associated with partisan or investigative styles of journalism; however, as a means of intragroup and intergroup communication, the media were understood to have a role in enabling adjustments to social norms and in interpersonal relationships.

Even before views similar to these were being advanced in the Solidarity-inspired debate over the system of social communication, a large-scale *samizdat* industry of dissident, underground media had emerged (Jakubowicz, 1990a). Their ideological commitment, strident language, and role in promoting opposition to the system—as well as their help in organizing the dissident movement—resulted in a situation where the Leninist definition of journalists as "mass propagandists, agitators and organizers" could well be applied to them.

This was even more true when martial law was imposed in December 1981, and the underground press became the focus of opposition to it. Practically the entire official press was suspended for a time, a purge of "disloyal" journalists was conducted, and strict censorship was reimposed. Some time afterward, the Association of Polish Journalists was first suspended and then disbanded by order of the authorities. The Association of

TABLE 14.3 Democratic Perspective of the Media

Aspect of Media System	*Seen as*
Public sphere	Public arena of contest
Political role of media	Representation-counterpoise
Media system	Controlled market
Journalistic norm	Adversarial
Entertainment	Society communing with itself
Reform	By means of public intervention

SOURCE: Adapted from Curran (1991).

the Journalists of the Polish People's Republic took its place, formed by reporters loyal to the martial law government.[4]

At that time, leaders of the Association of Polish Journalists sought again to reaffirm the importance of scrupulously observing the journalistic code of conduct, clearly believing that the obligation to tell the truth was incompatible with toeing the official line and engaging in propaganda to support martial law. In March 1982, they issued an appeal to journalists, stating in part,

> We feel duty-bound to recall that the Journalistic Code of Conduct remains in force and no-one can relieve anyone from the obligation to observe it. Let the realization that one day all actions will be judged in its light serve as a warning to those who believe that the time of contempt for honor and journalistic reliability will last forever. ("Do członków," 1989, p. 175)

Later, they issued another document, seeking to spell out explicitly the norms and values binding on journalists in the official media under those very special circumstances of martial law. The document stated that journalists working for the official media could continue to do so if they could write as before; if they could not but were forced to work by economic necessity, they should not allow themselves to be forced to "praise martial law or seek to persuade their audience that everything was all right" ("Zasady postępowania dziennikarzy," 1989, p. 186) The document went on:

> If you praise and support martial law and seek to win public acceptance for it, if you attack those who cannot defend themselves, if you publish false or

tendentious information, if you consciously do anything that serves to weaken the spirit of solidarity of the Polish people—then be sure that you will lose face and your good name in the eyes of your audience. What is more, you will put at risk the good name of your colleagues and the entire profession. Do not be surprised if one day you will have to suffer the consequences. (p. 186)

The document formulated some do's and don'ts for journalists, including the following:

Sign everything you write, no pseudonyms or initials; in this way, unsigned texts, or those with unrecognizable bylines, will advertise their dishonesty for all to see.

If you have taken the place in an editorial office of someone who does not want to, or cannot, hold the job at this time, be doubly careful to avoid embarrassment and putting yourself in an equivocal situation; add collegial loyalty to your list of principles.

Do not try to persuade people who refuse to cooperate with your medium to drop their boycott.

If you are making good money, share some of it with those whom martial law has denied the opportunity to practice their profession.

Select a newspaper, radio, or television program and keep a record of how it observes the code of conduct and these principles. Pass the documentation on to someone you can trust.

If you have no choice and are forced by economic necessity to join an organization whose activities run counter to our credibility, or work for a medium generally recognized as untrustworthy, write a statement explaining the circumstances, get two people to witness it, and deposit it with someone with an impeccable reputation. In the future, this will protect your reputation and membership in good standing in our profession.

With time, the system of norms and values characteristic of the official media themselves changed to some extent. Due to *glasnost* (Jakubowicz, 1990b), the government recognized the loss of its information monopoly after 1987. The reason for this, in part, was the emergence of a pluralistic media system—due to the spread of dissident publications, easy access to satellite television, and an end to jamming foreign Polish-language radio stations. The government realized that these changed circumstances required a new information and propaganda system capable of "stealing the opposition's thunder" (Jakubowicz, 1991). That involved a degree of liberalization, more openness and truthfulness in reporting, though the fundamental nature of the media system and the subordination of the media and journalists to the goals of the political system remained unchanged (Jakubowicz, 1989; Pisarek, 1989).

A Rude Awakening (1989-1995)

After the creation of a Solidarity-led government in Poland in September 1989, many of the ideas about the desired shape of social communication once proclaimed by Solidarity were now quietly dropped. In fact, they fell by the wayside along with the entire somewhat visionary concept of the proposed new system of social organization as a "self-governing common-wealth." Instead of seeking to develop a "third way"—a social-democratic system combining the best features of socialism and capitalism—the new government rather unexpectedly adopted a liberal, free-market approach.[5] Accordingly, in place of building a new system of social communication embodying the basic value of justice-equality, they came much closer to basing it on the value of freedom. In other words, they adopted the market model with only a few elements of a public policy model. In addition, whatever public policy it contained served not so much to guarantee the right to communicate for everyone but for the government and the major political forces. The new political elites tended to use the media—especially the broadcast media—to further the goals of their political program, just as the Communists had done for their own purposes. They justified this by pointing out that they, at least, had a democratic mandate to govern.[6]

The differences that were once artificially suppressed by the efforts of the Communist state to create an appearance of united support for the regime now exploded into an infinite variety of political parties. Poland has some 270 political parties today. Their emergence was spurred by the ideological confusion of Polish society and its search for an answer to the intractable problems of the transition period. As a result, what has emerged in Poland and elsewhere in the region is not the civil society that had been the dream of the dissidents but a political society where the continuous struggle for power politicizes everything and creates very little social space for the functioning of a free public sphere. Moreover, public opinion is still unable to call politicians and the authorities to account, which means that when the media try to perform the watchdog function, politicians can shrug them off and continue much as before. All this lends substance to the view advanced by Splichal (1994) that Central and Eastern Europe have seen so far, by and large, the "Italianization of the media" (pp. 145-146), that is, the development of a media system traditionally associated with Italy, in which (a) the media are under strong state control, (b) the media show partisanship toward political causes or organizations, (c) the media and political elites show a strong degree of integration, and (d) there is no consolidated and shared professional ethic among media practitioners. Italianization is particularly true of the broadcast media—especially state or public service broadcast organizations—which are under intense political pressure and find it particularly difficult to distance themselves from the world of party politics.

Journalists are not without blame in this somewhat disappointing turn of events. In many cases, they lack the skills to provide audiences with the information needed to assess developments and government policies. They also reject calls to improve their professional skills. As a result, their work tends to express mainly their own views and fails to articulate the needs, interests and opinions of huge segments of society. Any criticism of their performance is rejected on the grounds that it infringes on the freedom of the press and their own freedom of speech.

What is more, media practitioners—who still have vivid and painful memories of censorship and what used to be called "manual steering" of the media by the authorities—usually reject any talk of responsibility out of hand. This leads to a lack of accountability and promotes a distorted notion of professionalism—understood as a defensive occupational ideology, based on the rejection of anybody's claim to judge or influence the performance of journalistic functions. Journalists are suspicious of all forms of public regulation of the media and insist on unrestricted freedom—often as a way of covering a multitude of sins.

One such sin is political bias. This is a heritage from the past, both of old guard journalists once employed by the official media and of the new guard writing for dissident media. Many journalists regard freedom of speech as freedom to express their own views and biases. They define themselves as guardians or leaders of society, called (by virtue of their superior access to information and understanding) to be in the forefront of political developments. The view of journalism as politics conducted by other means dies hard.

Another sin consists in currying favor with the public, demonstrating courage and independence by attacking the authorities. The media's often quite vicious treatment of the new governments has arguably been a factor in promoting a mood of disillusionment in the general public and creating a sense of anticlimax, with predictable political consequences.

The often cutthroat competition among newspapers and periodicals adds another, familiar element to all this—the willingness of publishers, editors, and journalists to employ the entire arsenal of the yellow press and scandal sheets to boost sales.

In short, it could be said that too few Polish journalists know the difference between freedom and license. The result is repeated calls in Poland (as in other Central and Eastern European countries) for a return to communication ethics as a means of curing the ills of contemporary Polish journalism. In fact, what is needed is the professionalization of broadcasters and journalists in general, both in the sense of raising journalistic standards and of collective professionalization. Regarding the latter, the profession needs to develop a service ideal. As an autonomous group, they should serve the public and not the authorities or some ideology. Journalists must redefine themselves as nonpartisan, impartial interpreters of social reality; their self-understanding as propaganda tools must be replaced by providers of competently collected and written information.

There is recent evidence that this process has begun. Polish journalists are shaking off resentments of the past (born out of the divisions and differences among them dating back to martial law and driven by the profoundly different experiences of those who had worked for the official or for the underground media under the Communist system). They are beginning to realize that they need to constitute a united force in dealing with both employers and the authorities. They are also beginning to appreciate the merits of self-regulation as a way of preventing external regulation. This may be a first step toward professionalization as understood here.

Moreover, there is now—for the first time since the end of martial law in Poland—some form of dialogue and cooperation among all journalistic associations and unions. This has led to the joint adoption of what had been called the "Ethical Charter of the Media." Intended to be applied by owners and publishers as well as working journalists, this short document proclaims that in the pursuit of their professional duties, they will be guided by principles of truth, objectivity, separation of information and comment, integrity, respect and tolerance, primacy of the good of the audience, and freedom and responsibility.[7]

Also, a new journalistic code of conduct is being developed.[8] It is a more extensive document, seeking to redefine the journalistic profession in the light of changes unfolding in Poland generally and on the media scene in particular. The draft of this new code consists of five chapters: "General Principles," "The Ethical and Professional Obligations of Journalists," "Journalists and their Employers," "Journalists and their Colleagues," and "Final Provisions."

The "General Principles" section encourages the professionalization of journalists. To this end, it defines journalism as a profession serving society at large. The idea is to set journalists apart from the owners and publishers, by pointing to potentially different goals pursued by the two groups: profit, self-interest, or political goals on the part of at least some owners and public service on the part of journalists. Defining journalists as professionals also implies that they should be guided by their own service ideal and professional ethics, even if this sometimes puts them on a collision course with their employers.

The journalists' basic obligation is defined as searching for the truth and their main obligation as enabling everyone to take advantage of the public's right to receive true, full, and impartial information. It is emphasized that unless people understand the situation around them fully enough to form their own judgments, they cannot meaningfully take part in public debate. Journalists are obligated to protect the independence and credibility of their profession as well as freedom of speech and media pluralism.

Journalists' ethical and professional obligations are defined in much the same terms as in other codes of conduct. The chapter on relations with employers stresses the journalists' responsibility to consciously choose and accept the editorial line of the medium they work for and still retain the right to voice their own views. At the same time, it encourages journalists to refuse assignments that run counter to their fundamental convictions, norms of professional ethics, or the law.

The chapter on relations with colleagues emphasizes, in part, the journalist's obligation to protect the good name of the profession, observe professional solidarity, and assist colleagues in need.

Thus, the "new" journalistic code of ethics returns to a fairly classical view of the journalistic profession. The major reason is the state of confusion and alienation prevailing in Polish society—bordering in some cases on anomie. Beset by what has been called "transformation neurosis" (Frentzel-Zagórska, 1994), many people are facing an axiological and psychological crisis resulting from (a) a sense of anticlimax, of dashed hopes, and a need to face a reality completely different from what they had expected; and (b) their disability fundamentally to readjust their system of values, as required by the changing social, economic, and political circumstances.

On this second issue, a neoliberal, free-market social and economic system clearly corresponds to a totally different mindset and system of values than the former authoritarian system. Before 1989, the survival strategy adopted by many people involved an attitude of acquired helplessness and passivity. This was a way of dealing with an acute feeling of inability to control events, thus shifting responsibility for their lives to the state, and a propensity to grumble as a method of relieving stress (Titkow, 1993). Now, such attitudes prevent them from using the opportunities offered by business and the free market. A newborn generation of businessmen and yuppies make journalists an object of ridicule, and instead of encouraging them to adopt new values and attitudes, the press clings to its accustomed traditions, unable to cope with change.

Research into changes in social consciousness conducted in 1991 to 1992 (Reykowski, 1993) showed that certain social strata (the uneducated, unemployed, elderly, and so forth) ran counter to changes in the social system as a whole (see Table 14.4).

In light of this, journalists have recognized that they have contributed to the feeling of anticlimax and disillusionment by failing to abide by the ideal of social communication they had formulated. They admit they have added to the confusion and disorientation of large segments of society by neglecting their professional obligation to provide impartial information and analysis of the process of transformation. What is more, many journalists—no longer sure they know what path the country should follow—have lost a sense of mission and moral responsibility for providing leadership to the general public. Once external circumstances made that possible, most journalists began to withdraw from the trenches of political battle and returned to a more narrowly defined concept of journalism as reflected in the new code of ethics now being developed.

TABLE 14.4 Changes in Social Consciousness, 1991-1992

Views and Attitudes Required by Social Change	Views and Attitudes Gaining in Popularity
Right-wing views	Left-wing views
Individualism	Collectivism
Democracy	Authoritarian views

Conclusion

In the space of 15 years, Polish media and journalists have gone through a number of quite different philosophies of media operation and systems of norms and values underlying the practice of journalism. Those philosophies were, in part, a response to external circumstances that shaped the media system and affected the practice of journalism. During this period, various groups of journalists oriented their work to the pursuit of quite different goals, as well as to change those goals and values over time.

As far as the official Communist media are concerned, the driving force was mostly conformism and cynical, resigned, or skeptical accommodation. Many journalists accepted, of necessity, a role as propagandists, at the same time welcoming any sign of liberalization as a chance to evade the restrictions that usually applied.[9] However, conviction about the norms and values of journalistic practice was the driving force of change in the underground media and among, first of all, the dissidents and, since 1989, among people working in free media.

The moot question here is whether journalism should indeed be conviction driven. By subordinating their work to the promotion of social and political change, journalists must necessarily opt for an advocacy-oriented and campaigning style of writing, bordering at times on propaganda. As has been noted, these journalists fit the Leninist concept of mass propagandists, agitators, and organizers much better than those working for the official Communist media and were indeed much more effective in performing these functions. The goal, however, lies in the search for a middle way between professionalized journalism and the ambiguous, laissez-faire attitude adopted by many Polish journalists in recent years.

As we have seen, media views on the kind of journalism Poland needs have changed radically, just as the circumstances in which the media operate and the situation in the country in general have changed over the past 15 years. Clearly, the self-definition of journalists and their view of the nature of their job are determined by the particularities of the time and place in which journalists operate. Yet there is no escape from the timeless and universal principle of truthfulness, both in the sense of accurate, fair, and comprehensive reporting and in honoring the wish and the right of society "to live in truth."

During the period of great expectations and also the rude awakening, the discussion could have been enriched by looking beyond journalism conventions and codes to ethical principles cross-culturally. The Solidarity revolution probed deeply into issues of human dignity and social justice. To the extent that a wide-ranging understanding of basic human values can be included in public debates of this magnitude, a civil society would have had a better chance of emerging rather than a political society continually struggling over power. Journalists risk becoming entrapped in power structures unless they are constantly concerned about the distribution and, above all, the just dispensation of authority and power.

Occasioned by the new ethical charter and code of ethics, Polish journalists are rediscovering generally accepted norms of professionalism and are rededicating themselves to the observance of these values. Professionalism, however, is more than the acquisition of journalistic competence. It is part of a professional culture, defining the characteristics of a profession, and enshrining specific values, such as the ethos of public service. Cultivating a professional culture requires as much sociopolitical vision as it requires skills. Rather than settling into journalistic conventions too easily, professional journalists should thus continue to evaluate professional norms in the context of such universal principles as truth telling, free expression, and justice. They thereby learn to genuinely serve the public interest. Perhaps, then, even in a volatile political situation, an understanding of the third way can come into its own.

Notes

1. Many members of the Association had been stalwarts of the party press and propagandists on behalf of the Communist system, which may explain the desire to purge the Association of such members. In any event, no such vetting procedure was conducted.

2. Of course, order-solidarity is an ambiguous basic value of communication. It could develop naturally, with media helping build a social consensus based on common views. It is

interpreted here as the goal of a policy of domination and ideological synchronization serving the perpetuation of a totalitarian or authoritarian system.

3. Truthfulness, of course, is one of the so-called global universals of media ethics; see Cooper (1989).

4. This new Association adopted its own code of conduct, which was closely based on that of the Association of Polish Journalists. For an English translation of this code, see Pisarek (1989), Appendix 1.

5. This switch shocked at least some people at the top. Karol Modzelewski, one of the legendary leaders of the Polish dissident movement, writes in the Autumn of 1993,

> I still cannot get over the ease with which elites emerging out of the workers' movement did an about-turn. . . . This effortless transformation of unionists into liberals attests to a lack of, or rather a waning of loyalty to the social constituency of the movement. . . . That makes me ashamed. And that is why I am in the opposition.

6. This trend in Poland, of course, is not unique. Based on the experience of various countries where the political scene is volatile, the media are generally used to further the goals of the government or a particular party rather than serving the public interest. To this end, politicians seek to gain privileged access to air time and to the press practically on demand. Elites of all ideological persuasions are clearly determined to make sure that the political clout they have won, thanks to popular support, translates into running or overseeing (or both) broadcasting and access to air time. These circumstances make it difficult for the media to evolve as they should.

7. The Association of Catholic Journalists demanded that the Charter also contain clauses obliging media practitioners to respect national culture and tradition, national and religious feelings, and to refrain from corrupting and depraving the audience (with pornography and so forth). It was agreed that these principles would be incorporated into the new journalistic code of conduct.

8. In fact, both the Association of Journalists of the Republic of Poland (so renamed from the Association of Journalists of the Polish People's Republic) and the Association of Polish Journalists (reinstated after 1989) recognize and seek to enforce their codes of conduct, which are quite similar in terms of their ethical content. However, these principles are little known to the new generation of journalists who have usually refrained from joining either of the two associations. In any case, a need is felt to create a document that will address the issues in the language of today and will take account of the new situation in Polish journalism.

9. For an account of the attitudes of journalists working for the official Polish media in the 1980s, see Jakubowicz (1992).

References

Brecht, Bertolt. (1967). Der Rundfunk als Kommunikationsapparat. In B. Brecht's *Gesammelte Werke in 20 Bänden* (Vol. 18). Frankfurt: Subrkamp.

Cohen, Jean L. (1993, June 19-21). *The public sphere, the media and civil society.* Paper presented at the Conference on the Development of Rights of Access to the Media, Institute for Constitutional and Legislative Policy, Central European University, Budapest.

Cooper, Thomas. (1989). Global universals: In search of common ground. In Thomas Cooper (Ed.), *Communication ethics and global change* (pp. 20-39). White Plains, NY: Longman.

Curran, James. (1991). Rethinking the media as a public sphere. In Peter Dahlgreen & Colin Sparks (Eds.), *Communication and citizenship: Journalism and the public sphere in the new media age* (pp. 27-52). London: Routledge.

Do członków Stowarzyszenia Dziennikarzy Polskich. (1989). *Most, 21,* 174-175.

Downing, John. (1984). *Radical media: The political experience of alternative communication.* Boston, MA: South End Press.

Enzensberger, Hans Magnus. (1974). *Palaver: Politische Überlegungen.* Frankfurt: Suhrkamp Verlag.

Frentzel-Zagórska, J. (1994). Demokracja, elity polityczne i nerwica transformacyjna. *Kultura i Społeczeństwo, 4,* 41-59.

Groombridge, B. (1972). *Television and the people: A programme for democratic participation.* Harmondsworth, UK: Penguin.

Jakubowicz, Karol. (1989). Media ethics in Poland. In Thomas Cooper (Ed.), *Communication ethics and global change* (pp. 100-108). White Plains, NY: Longman.

Jakubowicz, Karol. (1990a). Solidarity and media reform in Poland. *European Journal of Communication, 5*(23), 333-354.

Jakubowicz, Karol. (1990b). Between communism and post-communism: How many varieties of glasnost? In Slavko Splichal, J. Hochheimer, & Karol Jakubowicz (Eds.), *Democratization and the media: An east-west dialogue* (pp. 40-55). Ljubljana, Slovenia: University of Ljubljana Press.

Jakubowicz, Karol. (1991). Musical chairs? The three public spheres of Poland. In Peter Dahlgren & Colin Sparks (Eds.), *Communication and citizenship: Journalism and the public sphere in the new media age* (pp. 155-175). London: Routledge.

Jakubowicz, Karol. (1992). From party propaganda to corporate speech: Polish journalism in search of a new identity. *Journal of Communication, 42*(3), 64-73.

Jankowski, N. (1988). *Community television in Amsterdam.* Amsterdam: University of Amsterdam Press.

Jankowski, N., Prehn, O., & Stappers, J. (1992). *The people's voice: Local radio and television in Europe.* London: John Libbey.

Keane, J. (1991). *The media and democracy.* Cambridge, UK: Polity.

Król, M. (1981). O "Tezach" kilka uwag krytycznych. *Tygodnik Solidarność, 11,* 11.

McQuail, Denis. (1992). *Media performance: Mass communication and the public interest.* London: Sage.

McQuail, Denis. (1994). *Mass communication theory.* London: Sage.

Modzelewski, K. (1993, September 3). Lojalność wobec nieznajomych, *Gazeta Wyborcza.*

Nowak, Stefan. (1988). Społeczeństwo Polskie drugiej połowy lat osiemdziesiątych (Próba diagnozy stanu świadomości społecznej). *Studia Socjologiczne, 1,* 23-55.

O znaczeniu środków komunikacji społecznej w Polsce i roli SDP w ich rozwoju. (n.d.). *Stenogram nadzwyczajnego zjazdu delegatów Stowarzyszenia Dziennikarzy Polskich.* Warsaw: Mimeo.

Pisarek, Walery. (1989). European socialist countries. In Kaarle Nordenstreng & Hifzi Topuz (Eds), *Journalist: Status, right and responsibilities* (pp. 97-135). Prague: International Organization of Journalists.

Reykowski, J. (1993). Zmiany systemowe a mentalność polskiego społeczeństwa. In J. Reykowski (Ed.), *Wartości i postawy Polaków a zmiany systemowe: Szkice z psychologii politycznej* (pp. 9-48). Warsaw: Polska Akademia Nauk.

Splichal, Slavko. (1994). *Media beyond socialism: Theory and practice in east-central Europe.* Boulder, CO: Westview.

Sprawozdanie z prac Podzespołu ds. Środków Masowego Przekazu. (1989). Warsaw: Mimeo.

Staniszkis, Jadwiga. (1983). "Solidarność" jako związek zawodowy i ruch społeczny. In W. Morawski (Ed.), *Demokracja i gospodarka* (pp. 331-374). Warsaw: Uniwersytet Warszawski.

Statut: Uchwala Programowa z Aneksem, Dokumenty Zjazdu. (1981). Gdańsk: Biuro Informacji Prasowej.

Sztompka, Piotr. (1982). Dynamika ruchu odnowy w świetle teorii zachowania zbiorowego. *Studia Socjologiczne, 3-4,* 69-93.

Titkow, A. (1993). *Stress i życie spoleczne: Polskie doświadczenia.* Warsaw: PIW.

Williams, Raymond. (1968). *Communications.* Harmondsworth, UK: Penguin.

Wójcicki, K. (1981). The reconstruction of society. *Telos, 47,* 98-112.

Zasady postępowania dziennikarzy na czas stanu wojennego. (1989). *Most, 21,* 186-187.

CHAPTER 15

Accepting the Other

On the Ethics of Intercultural
Communication in Ethnographic Film

KEYAN G. TOMASELLI
ARNOLD SHEPPERSON

The question of ideology is generally missing from discussions of ethics. Whereas all people have acquired the language skills to query their specific cultural experience (Shepperson, 1995), the ways in which these same skills can be used to justify oppression or exploitation are crucial to the concept of ideology. In this sense, then, ideology is a set of symbolic practices by which one limited group appropriates the terms of a pregiven signifying grid, used by others to make sense of their worlds, to obscure their oppression or exploitation. The discursive orderings and legitimation of the norms by which the stronger social groups at a particular historical juncture privilege certain kinds of social and professional practices as "normal, natural and the way things should be," are ideologically supportive of the material power (juridical, economic, military) necessary to retain or reproduce the relations of superordination and subordination.

This deployment of symbolic capacity is related to the issue of one group of people maintaining (an)other group(s) in relationships of tutelage. Ideology, therefore, has the communicative nature of a strong rhetoric. The norms governing the relations between professional strata and other social groupings can be interpreted as double standards (Heller, 1984, 1987). These relations are not co-ordinate but superordinate and subordinate. Typically, such asymmetrical power relations are not fully understood in the concrete and local circumstances of a communication encounter, and as a result, the consequences of such encounters are not always recognized.

This chapter begins by looking at visual anthropologists and ethnographic filmmaking in terms of the asymmetry of power between professionals and those who are studied. As a communicative practice, ethnographic film can be seen as a definitive form of multicultural encounter and intercultural communication. For any context to qualify as intercultural, there must be a clear problematization of the dual or multiple cultures between which such communication occurs. We identify at least four potential cultures in the business of producing and exhibiting ethnographic films; this makes the field a good candidate with which to confront the issue of normative pluralism.

The minimum number of cultures in an ethnographic film's communicative encounter with humanity are (a) the subject community, (b) the film crew as a community, (c) the academic community (students as well as academic researchers and teachers), and (d) the wider film/video viewing audience. In the nature of ethnographic—and for that matter, all documentary—film, it is possible that these four communities are not temporally coextensive with each other. As an artifact, film can outlast its producers, subjects, and original audiences. However, given that the great body of ethnographic film production has emerged in recent years, for the most part, the original communities involved in the majority of ethnographic film encounters are still around. (We acknowledge exceptions such as Clifford Abrahams, whose case is discussed later.) They are, generally, 20th century people confronting the problems of the contemporary era. Since the 1950s, all participating communities in the ethnographic film context have inhabited a modern world. This temporal-historical condition brings the topics of this chapter into a special perspective: the peculiar way in which modern conditions have relativized normative thinking. Put differently, the existence of multigenerational communities in modern nation-states—and clashes between both communities and generations—have given rise to a plurality of normative frameworks.

On a wider scale than the discipline of visual anthropology but still within the confines of the academy, Katherine Namuddu and J. M. Sibry Tapsoba (1993) have drawn attention to the persistence of outdated paradigms in the formation of donor policy regarding aid for African educational institutions. Their point is that "much cultural evidence about how various societies have attempted to transform themselves . . . has been ignored." This ignorance has arisen from "misconceptions regarding the kind of development" necessary for "undeveloped" peoples (p. 26). The formulation of this lack of development can be connected with the images constructed of indigenous peoples in the materials from which experts gained their knowledge about the societies who were to "benefit" from such policies.

Wider issues emerge in a concrete global situation in which communicating knowledge about other peoples reproduces the dependence of one group on the power of another. One of these issues is the way in which the "knowledge" (professionally produced information) encoded in such films becomes a resource for reproducing or extending the relations of tutelage.

We trace the emergence of the ideological critique of ethnographic film as a precursor to an analysis of what might properly constitute a basic normative framework for this practice as an emblem of intercultural and multicultural communication in general. Our theoretical context for this framework is derived, with some modification, from Agnes Heller's (1987) contrast between the conceptions of static and dynamic justice. We will highlight the static nature of professional ethics in communication. We then examine dynamic alternatives that focus on the participation of all parties to an ethnographic film encounter. Having examined several ethnographic filmmakers whose practices have evolved in response to the sociopolitical critique of their practice, we extend the concept of dynamic justice to sociopolitical aspects of the wider multicultural communication context. Our conclusion indicates that locating the protonorms of multicultural communication in the realm of dynamic justice complements the roles of ethics and morality in institutional and personal activity.

Academic Myths and Racism

With the rise of 20th century intellectualism (Gramsci, 1970; Pirsig, 1992), academia has become, in many instances, the myth-making process where factories called universities shape knowledge in terms of dominant paradigms. These paradigms could be thought of as modern forms of myth. As such, they formalize sets of ideas, assumptions, and conclusions that reflect broader social and political consensus about the ways in which people, processes, events, conditions, and situations are to be understood during particular historical conjunctures. Within such broader discursive networks and global media, particular ways of seeing are popularized in terms of pregiven (often racist) frames of reference or paradigms.

The debate over how social scientists should label Bushmen, for example, reached a crescendo in 1990, with accusations and counteraccusations of racism, opportunism, and insensitivity consuming hundreds of pages in books and journals (see, e.g., Gordon, 1990a, 1992; Wiley, 1982; Wilmsen, 1989; Wilmsen & Denbow, 1990). Those so named were less concerned than those arguing about naming; they rarely perceived the consequences of having been stereotyped themselves. This is more a comment on the way anthropological perspectives of culture have been taught than of what the original ethnographers and filmmakers intended. The debate is one of several that reflect the wider questioning of relationships between Western academies and first peoples of the non-Western world.

Received interpretations are only questioned during times of crisis and rapid transition. Sometimes, such questioning can take a lifetime to occur, and the case of documentary filmmaker John Marshall is instructive. Marshall's film, *The Hunters* (1956)—product of the Marshall family's seminal ethnographic work on the !Kung completed in the 1950s—was crucial in popularizing Western views of the Bushmen (Ruby, 1993). Picturing them as isolated hunter-gatherers in pristine primitiveness, the film has an almost poetic quality. This characteristic is complemented with an empathetic narration linking the hunting activities shown with a mythical reconstruction of cultural values long lost to industrial societies.

Up to the early 1980s, no less than 40 American distributors ensured that *The Hunters* was shown more than any other film on Africa. Given its academic status, the film became a metonym both for the whole of Africa and for hunter-gatherer societies in general. As David Wiley (1982) puts it,

> A film intended to be a factual "documentary" becomes one of the few films concerning Africa seen by American students and serves to confirm the negative and unbalanced stereotypes of the continent and its peoples. The customs of this group, constituting a minuscule minority of Africa's population, are viewed as "Africa in microcosm" by too many North Americans without significantly balancing alternative views of the continent. (p. xix)

The San comprised less than 0.01% of the total African population in the 1950s,[1] and this film conceals the Marshalls' own filmed evidence of !Kung San social linkages with other societies or how and why these "hunters" came to the Kalahari Desert in the first place.

The Hunters is more illustrative of the dominant anthropological paradigm of the 1950s and 1960s than of the Bushmen themselves. As such, the film's academic popularity is an index of the wide acceptance of aspects of the "primitive" cultures paradigm inherited from 19th-century adoptions of the work of the 16th-century philosophers. Indeed, *The Hunters* demonstrates the art of anthropological restoration: Because Marshall could not find any suitably "wild Bushmen" (Gordon, 1990b), so he reconstructed without acknowledgement an ethnographic present in terms of the dominant theoretical Western image of a "stone-age" people-caught-in-time. This lifestyle, however, was rapidly disappearing in all but academic textbooks (some still being used in the 1990s) and films.

A film made for Granada television in Britain, Terence Turner's *The Kayapo: Out of the Forest* (1989), shows how these warriors-turned-videomakers took on big capital and the Brazilian state in defending their territory. This film, however, conceals the relationships that developed between anthropologist Turner and certain of the Kayapo communities. He does not explain how and why they so easily adopted small-format video technology in making their case to government and World Bank officials and others involved in "developing" the rain forests (see Ogan, 1989; Turner, 1990). James Faris (1992) points out that the Kayapo are not equal partners with news-photographers and that video technology notwithstanding, they enter the world media at an irreparable disadvantage in terms of power, access, and follow-through. Nevertheless, a degree of self-empowerment is evident in the film and in the Kayapo's campaign to prevent the funding of the dams that would have flooded the region in which they, the Yanomami, and others, were living.

However, other unanswered questions are implied in Turner's narration with regard to the nature of the Kayapo's relations with neighboring groups living in the same area. Very little information is available on whether and how films and TV series have been screened to the subject communities themselves. We need to know how they reacted to the films. An important scene in *Kayapo,* for example, shows their delegation filming the generators of a hydroelectric plant; at no stage does Turner discuss with them why they filmed these machines and not something else. Similarly, one never finds out what the delegation had to say to their communities about what had been filmed and why. Did they understand what had happened? What were the implications for their communities and for those with whom they interact? What is the subject community's relations with the government of the territory they inhabit, and so on?

Received View of the Other

When anthropologists are not talking to other anthropologists, they are talking to Western television audiences through series such as British Granada TV's *Disappearing World,* National Geographic films, and numerous other documentaries that dominate the world's airwaves. These productions, mainly commercially driven, often suppress unpalatable situations, cultural alienation, and the debilitating effects of social contamination and Western tourism. They tend to preserve the beauty and exoticness of the Other in conformity with the dictates of the received view that the Other must necessarily be untouched by modernity if it is to warrant the audience's attention.

At the same time, the presence of anthropologists and filmmakers among these communities has actually given rise to a whole economy of aesthetics absorbed from previous encounters. Subjects have been known to take on new personas, invent lost tribal traditions, and even make up grunting languages to satisfy the a priori needs of filmmakers, journalists, and tourists. Awareness of this situation has led anthropologists to begin questioning the inherited wisdom of their discipline. With the benefit of hindsight provided by Thomas Kuhn, practitioners are conscious of a paradigm change in their field.

Marshall's *The Hunters* is of immense value in discussions of ideology in social science. It also indicates how certain scientific paradigms about the Other become entrenched as stereotypes in the popular imagination, migrating from anthropological documentary to slapstick fiction such as *The Gods Must be Crazy* (1980) and its sequel released in 1990. Yet the experience of Marshall indicates that practitioners can also bring to the academy an uneasiness about the ways in which their paradigm has served to reproduce an ideology in terms of which the Other is subordinated (economically, politically, and epistemologically).

Given the relative primitiveness of documentary film theory at that time, Marshall can be forgiven his media restorations of the 1950s. The almost total lack of ethnographic film theory through which to develop a production methodology was another impediment, and the absence of ethical guidelines was only addressed much later by himself and others. However, Marshall *was* one of the first to adopt the new cinéma vérité methodologies that encouraged people to speak for themselves without interruption. To his credit, later films such as *N!ai: Story of a !Kung Woman* (1980) implicitly responded to this kind of criticism, as did *The !Kung San: Resettlement* (1988) and *Pull Ourselves Up or Die Out* (1985). These films offer extremely uncomfortable scenes of San social disintegration, drunkenness, and cultural alienation. They engage viewers at an emotional level not normally achieved by anthropologist filmmakers.

In 1990, Marshall began to publicly question his ethics in making films on the !Kung. His semiautobiography is a self-critique of how his early film making was a projection of his own fantasies and how his later work aimed to reduce these personal projections onto others. Marshall's more recent films were designed to raise funds for Bushmen development projects. Instead of seeing audiences as commoditized target markets, Marshall's Documentary Educational Resources (DER)—which distributes anthropological films made all over the world—tries to stay in touch with its viewers to overcome the producer alienation that normally results from mass distribution. Regarding other productions, it is to Granada TV's credit that it has many films that neither construct the Other in terms of difference nor suppress political issues. *The War of the Gods* (1971), for example, makes direct comparisons between a South American Indian religious ritual and an Anglican communion in England.

Documentary filmmakers have begun to use their productions to draw attention to how the subjects see the anthropologists. In the American Pub-

lic Broadcasting System's *Anthropology on Trial* (1983), for example, a
Big Man among the Kawelka considers himself the professor. He tells the
camera that the anthropologist arrived on his island without knowledge and
that it was this clueless immigrant who was his student. The same program
reveals the dismay felt by the subjects of anthropology at their objectifica-
tion in Margaret Mead's books and films and how this resulted in a loss of
control over the meaning of their lives and cultures (see Ehrenreich, 1985).

Norms and Exhibition

The controversy dealt with here arises from a complex set of conflicting
normative demands. On the one hand, there is the professional requirement
that a visual anthropologist or ethnographic filmmaker ought to observe
certain standards of objectivity. These criteria relate to the distance maintained between the filmmaker as subject and the filmed communities as
objects of knowledge. On the other hand, there are public norms of decency,
in terms of which the showing of certain animal sacrifices filmed during a
ritual will offend the norms of public taste in a viewing community.

Yet a thornier issue has arisen, about which passionate discussion (even
vituperative polemic) is conducted. This is the question of the duties of
filmmakers toward the communities filmed in pursuit of their profession
and the rights of these peoples to control the knowledge and benefits ac-
cruing from film, books, or photographs made of their worlds. Even images
that aim to challenge ways of seeing the Other are all too often rearticulated
by their viewers into the centuries-old negative and racist stereotypes and
discourses through which most people encounter or make the Other.

But there is a further, related, issue: the nonanthroplogical use of studies
derived from the "objective" images of ethnographic film. In the reigning
global atmosphere of power economics, the use as means of filmed subjects
to justify inequity in the form of ethnotourism—or to justify the eradication
of cultural practices on the grounds that they are counterproductive in an
industrial context—can lead to policies that border on genocide.

There is, furthermore, the vexing question of copyright, rarely raised in
the academic literature. Most films vest copyright with the producer or
anthropologist. But what about the films' subjects? Because they have no
control over the filmmakers, this does not mean that they should have no
control over how the films are used. Because the subjects are ostensibly

themselves the content, without which the film could not be made, why are the subjects denied copyright? Is this even discussed with them? Conversely, where subjects do demand monetary or other kinds of returns, surely these questions affect anthropological interpretation. Why, for example, did the filmmakers of *The Trobriand Islanders* conceal the negotiations over payment on that film?

Suppressing this sort of information may ensure continuing access to the anthropologist's tribe. But by not explaining these relationships and what they mean in the modern world, it also massages corruption or distortions of political processes caused by cash economies. In contrast, the brutal honesty of *N!ai* reveals the social ravages her film star status caused her group. However, only in 1990 did Marshall publicly admit that he paid N!ai R10 (US$14) a day while she worked on that film. In contrast, the makers of *Clifford Abrahams* (1984) made it quite clear at the start of the video that the down-and-out, drug-addicted Clifford would be paid for his services and that he would benefit from future earnings of the production. But Abrahams never really understood the crew's intention of making a video to try to visualize the usually hidden structural processes that made him what he is. Payment simply fed his drug and alcohol habit and he died within a few years of its production.

Consideration of these effects on the people and communities imaged on the films and TV are often forgotten when scholars return to the academy, the TV production company, or media institution. Their subjects, the objects of study, the human raw material without which anthropology and sociology could not survive, have to get on with their lives—or perhaps pick up the pieces—after the observers have left.

Finished films could be argued to serve the function of popularizing knowledge to television audiences and students. But these are essentially two different audiences. Broadcasters tend to construct the former group as passive, consumerist, uncritical, and largely demanding of gloss and entertainment. Their programming is developed (by and large) on the assumption that the understanding of reality by TV viewers is mainly in terms of media and advertising stereotypes. Students, hopefully, are more knowledgeable and critical, able to respond intelligently to supposedly open-ended ethnographic records. This distinction between audiences raises the question of appropriate content. Films that contain scenes and dialogue considered to be an invasion of privacy in the filmmaker's culture might also be considered as such by the films' subjects. This is especially true if the subjects are made aware of the nature of film-video distribution and the kinds of audiences that might see films in which they are depicted. One wonders how often subjects are informed about such issues.

The subjects or observed are disempowered in most, if not all, contemporary academic-production-financial-legal relationships. Frequently, copyright serves as the ultimate means whereby transnational capital ensures its continued capacity for making money. In general, the present situation regarding the wider use of images of the Other can be said to reproduce the relationship between the developed and developing worlds. The dominant discourse dichotomizes mature and primitive forms of human existence. However, crucially, the images are seen as essentially neutral, as information rather than ideology. What viewers make of these images is largely assumed to be a function of the medium and the programming within which the images are distributed. Academically, they are considered part of the theory of the history of the human race; commercially, the images entertain or inform viewers or both and vie for ratings. It is this kind of ideology that also sees audiences as consumers.

Exhibition and the Critique of Ideology

Not all ethnographic filmmakers unquestioningly presume that their work will be commoditized. In addition to Marshall's DER, for example, some university-based video crews that worked with anti-apartheid organizations in South Africa purposefully refused to copyright their productions. The images and sounds encoded were considered by both video makers and the subject-participants to belong to the people. They are drawn from, and hence belong to, the collective popular memory.[2] As Costas Criticos and Tim Quinlan (1991) explain with regard to *Hanging Up the Nets: The Bay Fishing Community,* the community itself decided to whom the video should be distributed and what to do with the income from the video's sale to Natal schools and other purchasers.

Through his !Kung Bushmen Foundation, Marshall facilitated resistance by the Namibian San to the South African government's destruction of this group politically, culturally, economically, and socially. Instead of standing by helplessly, Marshall eventually acted; he avoided the kind of accusation that Survival International (1990) leveled against an unnamed academic who made his career and lots of money through his books and films on the besieged Yanomamo Indians of Brazil.

So far, our discussion has considered several problematic aspects of the paradigm style of intercultural communication. However, the work of Marshall with the !Kung and other San groups, Turner with the Kayapo, and Eric Michaels' media interventions with regard to Australian Aboriginals (see O'Regan, 1990), go beyond mere ethnography and anthropology. They indicate a political responsibility that anthropologists and the film/video makers who work with them should demonstrate. These responses capture several contradictions that can be extended to the general nature of communication in a multicultural context. Specifically, these examples help to elucidate the genesis of a new approach to communication ethics that can accommodate the immense contradictions of the contemporary world. But elaborating this new approach to communication ethics in a modern multicultural environment cannot begin until the existing ideological structure has been clarified.

There are strong rhetorics that attempt to subsume, if not suppress, the plurality of cultures and communities. Where concrete forms of communication between social groupings or cultures exist, there are questions that cannot be answered unambiguously by recourse to the standard paradigm. The intellectual resources of the age make more than one kind of answer possible. This also means that norms and values are subject to review. Specifically, the potential exists for a dynamic approach to normative activities—even if constrained by strong rhetorics valorizing influence and profit.

Reformulating the ethical environment in which communication can take place among the many parts of the modern whole begins with realizing that the plurality of cultural groups shares the world. Many groups might insist that their forms of life resist some aspect of modernity, but they nonetheless do not seek to be removed from all contact with others. Instead, they try to reproduce themselves under terms and conditions over which they have a greater element of control. From our point of view, as academics in film and cultural studies, the confusion of normative systems can be overcome by basing the communication between groups on global criteria derived from what is common among all responses to totalizing ideologies: people's articulated needs for *freedom* and their demand for the protection of *life* and the improvement of *life chances*.

Norms and Culture

Agnes Heller (1987) considers freedom and life chances the basic common value ideas in systems of dynamic justice. The modern age, she points out, faces a peculiar tension over formal and traditional approaches to the idea of justice.[3] Traditional norms of justice are inherited as complete bodies of concrete norms and rules; formal justice appeals to unchanging transcendental imperatives that by their very abstractness exclude the particularity of persons and cultures. On the other hand, modernity rejects tradition as a basis of judgment. As Shepperson (1995) puts it, "the founding tradition of the modern age is that tradition is bunk" (p. 80). Consequently, the inherent dissatisfaction between generations engendered by this disparity makes it almost an obligation for successor generations to question the values of their predecessors (Heller, 1984; Heller & Fehêr, 1988). Heller develops this notion further, basing her conception of dynamic justice on the ongoing possibility that those who inherit a situation in the modern world will at some stage challenge the values they encountered within the context of growth.

The contemporary environment for all the conflicting and contradictory cultural voices is nonetheless one in which the social and material achievements and failures of the modern age are present. Heller's approach squarely confronts this condition. She insists that something else cannot emerge unless people begin by consciously acting within the world they occupy. They cannot wait on a different order, because by doing so, people set themselves up to have something potentially just as bad imposed on them. Heller therefore contextualizes almost all her work within an appraisal critical of modern thought, though nonetheless rooted in it.

The present situation goes beyond a critique of the intellectual context of the Cold War. Much has been made of the fact that the postmodern era is marked by the collapse of attempts to subsume all sociopolitical activity under either capitalist or socialist political economies. However, this condition was a specific manifestation not of the modern project itself but of the confusions generated by the actual achievement of the potential of the modern era: the standoff between two superpowers with the nuclear capacity to terminate humanity's existence. In the period since the Iron Curtain rusted away, it has become apparent that the Cold War's rigid ideological division of the world masked many other developments. Not least of these, Heller (1976, 1984, 1987) points out, has been the consequence of economic theory to elide the differences between human Need (the capitalization is hers) and necessity or interest. She is consistently critical of sociological attempts to collapse the human category of Need into the scientific and logical category (or mode) of Necessity. In her earliest work (1976), and in all subsequent writing, she draws attention to the fact that modernity has realized a plurality of needs and that this plurality is a definitive characteristic of the modern human condition. Heller rejects the dismissal of utopian thought. In the absence of a critical vision—rooted in their actual contemporary circumstances—of what kind of future human beings can achieve by their own conscious efforts, people will continue to be the objects of totalizing minorities constituted around issues of sectional interest and not real need (Heller, 1984, 1992; Heller & Féher, 1988).

People's being-in-the-world is both future and past oriented. People come to understand both because of where they come from and because of their potential to decide where they want to go (they can visualize a better circumstance). That many people, if not most, seem not to have decided or to have recognized their historicity is every bit as much a holdover of premodern traditions of hierarchy sedimented in institutions as it is of the necessary or causal relation between social and personal conditions (Heller, 1987, 1992).

On the issue of norms, rules, and values, Heller's work draws on two principal philosophical traditions. On the one hand, she locates herself firmly in Aristotle's legacy. She insists that the proper activity of philosophy is trying to engage human questions about human action. Heller distances herself from any suggestion that it is philosophy's business to produce "philosophies of everything" that will provide the final answer to every possible question. On the other hand, she does not reject anti-Aristotelian sources *tout court*. Despite her recognition of Kant as an arch-transcendentalist, she nonetheless gives him due recognition for his "substantive formula of the categorical imperative. If he had formulated nothing else, Kant would remain the greatest genius of modern philosophy" (Heller, 1992, p. 105).

Heller's reformulation of Kant's injunction is central: "Act in such a way that you will always treat humanity, whether in your own person or in the person of any other, never simply as a means, but always at the same time as an end" (as quoted in Paton, 1948, p. 91). Her claim to be a radical theorist (sociologist, philosopher) is based on her consistent reference to the thwarting of human potential inherent in the modern human condition, by its continued justification of constituting humans as means to the ends of others. Her approach to dynamic justice arrives at the Kantian practical imperative by accepting an irrational basis to the formal idea of justice.

The problem of right action in philosophy, as she sees it, has been dogged by the fact that its justification can take on two mutually exclusive yet logically coherent forms. In terms of pure logic, it is possible to prove both that it is better to suffer an injustice rather than commit one and better to commit an injustice than to suffer one. Socrates could not convince Trasymachos that the former attitude is superior to the latter, and, for Heller (1987), the issue comes down to the least rational of mechanisms for choosing. One must, she says, wager that it is better to suffer an injustice than to commit one (p. 70). This essentially negative formulation of the righteous person makes it possible for Heller to further distinguish between Kant's universalist (categorical imperative) and specific (substantive or practical imperative) ethics. The latter combined with a commitment to the wager of righteousness forms the basis for evaluating the justice of concrete attitudes in existing human environments and thereby minimizes the need to fall back on a static formal system. This fits in with Heller's view that the humanist legacy of the modern age can be recovered in action and at the same time give direction to individual actions in a pluralist world.

Communication and the Talents of Modernity

Our observation that people frame opposition to their social and political conditions in terms of the value ideas of freedom and life is to some extent derived from Heller (1984). For her, freedom becomes concretized in the Kantian means-end formulation: People who are means to the ends of others are not free. The value of life concerns the ways in which social arrangements promote, inhibit, or are indifferent to the potential for persons to raise their endowments into talents. In the context of ethnographic film, there is reason to conclude that people's freedom is limited by this form of communication between cultures. Looking at the ways in which subject communities have developed a dependence on specific paradigms brought to their worlds over time by anthropologists and filmmakers, we can also conclude that these interchanges have limited the range of talents into which people can raise their endowments.

Heller (1987) has identified two fundamental kinds of talent that are rewarded in the modern world: making money and maneuvering between institutions. Contemporary mass communications practice relies heavily on practitioners' ability to demonstrate the former (making money), whereas a review of academic communication suggests that anthropologists succeed or fail on their ability to demonstrate competence in the latter (maneuvering between institutions). However, the question remains as to how communication between cultures benefits subject communities both as ends-in-themselves and in terms of the plurality of talents they can aspire to develop.

In the realm of dynamic justice, Heller shows that the limitations placed on people by the valorization of these two classes of talent introduces a kind of censorship on the ways people can achieve recognition by their peers and the wider community (Heller, 1987). Among the possible talents that do not usually gain monetary or political recognition, Heller (1987) gives as examples such "non-rational propensities . . . as a sensitivity to mystical experience, the ability of self-abandon, a sense of humor, creative energies, and so on" (p. 312). Ability in these kinds of propensities tends to be marginalized by the necessity for those who possess them to succeed monetarily or politically. For our purposes here, communication as a talent becomes limited by the necessity for practitioners to succeed at making money or maneuvering between institutions. Other kinds of communicative action fail to reap the rewards (riches, power, or both) that accrue to the recognized communications practices of the modern world. One need only review the pressure being placed on public broadcasting, for example, or the commoditization of religious broadcasting to recognize that these practices only get noticed when their ownership or management can both satisfy the demands of particular constituencies and generate taxable profits.

In practice, this censorship of talents has two serious consequences. First, the limits placed by this restriction of people's life chances also serve to relegate those who are talented in other ways to the margins of society. What this means is that on a global scale, the dominant approach to organized communications practice to some extent reproduces Foucault's (1970) interpretation of the marginalization of deviance in industrial society. Cultures that define themselves on other kinds of talent (or on a greater range of talents) are constrained either to marginal status as far as they fail to profit or build power bases on these talents, or they have to restructure their practices (cultural and social) to make money or gain leverage (or both) by doing them.

In the second place, the marginalization of ways of life not based on making money is extended into the political marginalization of communities based on other lifestyles. In those bodies (such as the United Nations) in which the needs and interests of the global community are supposed to be represented, talents other than those of maneuvering between institutions are not recognized by those who presently dispose of global power. Put differently, the power to do good inherent in the material accomplishments of the modern age is negated by the strong rhetoric of those whose power is based on the combination of this potential with the limited talents of making money and horse trading between institutions.

Our review of visual anthropology and ethnographic filmmaking may seem too narrow a base on which to discuss other kinds of communication between cultures or at least communication in an environment that contains a plurality of cultures. But the discussion so far has indicated that certain consequences of these practices have relevance in a wider context. In the next section, we will prepare for our conclusion by first looking at the general relevance of talents in a pluralistic communications context. This will form the basis for discussing our preference for values of justice instead of morality as protonorms for communication.

Thereafter, we will examine the context of freedom in terms of means-end relationships to clarify our wariness about traditional Western ethics as a basis for these protonorms. We have to stress again that this does not dismiss moral and ethical thought but arises from an appreciation that these two fields have spheres of application that are proper to other kinds of human relationships. Indeed, it is the substance of our conclusion that an approach through dynamic justice complements mainstream ethical approaches in the modern environment of multicultural communication.

Contesting and Censorship of Communicative Talent

So far, we have examined the case for locating the protonorms of multicultural communication within the sphere of dynamic justice. Little has been said of the connection between such protonorms and classical evaluative spheres, such as ethics and morality. Indeed, Heller (1987) has stressed that although justice, morals, and ethics cannot be seen in isolation, collapsing them together in the modern world has contradictory outcomes. Following her approach, we agree that the modern age has made it possible for moral norms to be challenged as new generations encounter different situations unforeseen by their predecessors. But this challenge has largely to do with norms of decent conduct (Heller, 1992) and thus refers more readily to how persons act or fail to act. Similarly, the ethical issue of how social groups or institutions ought to relate to each other refers to entities that are constituted around specific activities, behaviors, or functions in a broader sociological environment (Heller, 1987).

In the contemporary age, in which the global condition embodies the accomplishments and contradictions of all phases of the modern era, communication between cultures becomes problematic if viewed strictly from ethical and moral perspectives. Yet these points of view are relevant, as the example of ethnographic film and visual anthropology has indicated. Marshall, Michaels, Turner, and others have challenged the norms and rules (embodied in paradigms) of their institutional activity and as individuals can be said to have done so from a moral standpoint.

On the one hand, that such knowledge can be communicated at all is part of the technological accomplishments of the modern age; on the other, the conflicts arising from the limitations imposed by the talents of modernity summarizes an important contradiction. Communication of this kind is necessary if the relationships between ways of life are to be free of conflict. Yet the power associated with three centuries of developing economic and political talents is based on the historical experience of generations within one limited way of life. The inward specificity of this evolution has given rise to the idea that the practices and institutions of modern communication more or less coincide. This sociological interpretation, although it excludes the personal dimension of morality, permits norms and rules of communication to be formalized as ethical codes of conduct.

In the context of communication between different ways of life about different ways of life, the differences themselves are institutionalized as knowledge of the Other. Other beliefs, other economies, other reproductive arrangements, and so on are categories and classifications based on the historical containment of the early development of the modern era within the confines of Western Europe. Yet the political and economic outcome of this development has been the extension of modernity to the whole globe, a condition formally recognized in bodies such as the United Nations and the World Trade Organization. The practical extension of this formal system into the subject communities of anthropology and ethnographic film negates their status as Other.

We thus come to the crux of our problem: The contemporary professional context of communications, exemplified by ethnographic film in terms of multicultural encounters, is an institutionalized activity. It is rooted in a tradition of treating others as means and it demands that the Others' talents conform to the preconceived notions of ways in which the Other has been characterized. However, people such as Marshall, Turner, and Michaels have shown how professional communication practices between different ways of life can begin to overcome the ideological nature of scientific paradigms.

The Present as Beginning the Way Forward

African philosophers such as Valentin Y. Mudimbe (1988), in analyzing the possibility of an African philosophy of knowledge, concluded that Western anthropology is essentially ethnocentric. Anthropology's very object of study has been the intellectual construction of an Other from non-African perspectives. Western social science's analysis of the Other derived from early European intellectual imperatives that made a fetish of difference and the exotic (Foucault, 1970). Methodologies from within this set of intellectual imperatives have imposed ways of describing Others, using the differences between the signifying grids of the Same and the Other to discredit or suppress the way these Others preferred to describe themselves.

These discourses stem in significant part from the way 18th-century and 19th-century thinkers appropriated the record left by 16th-century ethnographers (Foucault, 1970; Toulmin, 1990). Encountering these Renaissance tales of exotic differences, the differences were in turn categorized in various ways as Otherness. Linnaeus's 18th-century concepts of genetics, when coupled to ideas of progress and evolution, created the discursive possibility for the emergence of anthropology. As a discourse, anthropology was historicized as the "history of mankind" in precisely this evolutionist and geneticist context, projecting images of "primitive" peoples in terms of the (imperialist) colonial academic agenda. These agendas were often driven less by a thirst for knowledge than for the academic, social, and missionary careerism of many of the individuals who practiced it.

The strong rhetoric of scientific paradigms derives its authority from the long selective tradition of interpretations with which the dilemmas of the modern age have been dismissed as irrational. By basing the activity of communication on one or an other paradigm or on strong rhetoric—statistical, physical, or sociological—institutions have essentially eliminated the classical ethical problem of how to live the Good Life. Codes of conduct, based on and justified through these paradigms, are rules. Practitioners are thought to perform ethically when they follow these professional codes and by doing so conscientiously, they avoid the irrational choices inherent in the concept of justice. In other words, institutional codes of ethics are constructed in ways that make proper professional behavior *adiaphoric*. Professionals who do the job by the book should not, in theory, encounter any dilemma of morality in which two courses of action present themselves such that choosing to follow either would entail violating the moral maxim under which the other course is defined.

These dilemmas arise in communicative contexts where practitioners as persons have to decide whether concrete academic-professional goals have to be subordinated to an equally pressing but far less certain goal. For us, as for Heller, an example of such a goal is the achievement of the radical project: the best possible sociopolitical world. It is possible, and even necessary, to define this question in terms of morality or ethics.[4]

In moral terms, the definition is relevant insofar as individual practitioners must choose to act in one way or another. Ethically, practitioners can raise the issue with respect to the actual relations that obtain or ought to obtain between their specific institutions and the wider sociopolitical environment. But the patently inequitable relations between global social groupings—for example, those between developed and developing nations or between women and men—are only partially addressed within these individual and institutional concerns. We suggest that the values of dynamic justice serve the function of basic norms for inter-cultural and multicultural communicative action.

In this context, freedom is a value idea rooted in the critique of inequitable modern relations of production, reproduction, and distribution (Honderich, 1987). In communicative terms, therefore, freedom can be seen as a protonorm insofar as the consequences of communicative action alleviate people's tutelage in means-ends relationships. Similarly, the justice-value of life serves as a protonorm insofar as the consequences of a communicative encounter can be intended to promote a plurality of ways in which people's endowments can be raised into talents.

In the wider context of communication generally, the values of dynamic justice permit challenges to other kinds of paradigm approaches. As an example, the widely studied field of mass communication comes under some pressure if the practice is analyzed with reference to the assumptions underlying the concept of "mass." The essentially mechanical notion of mass communication retains credibility because of the strong rhetoric of sociological paradigms premised on the historical experience of the modern age. Yet the conditions of the modern world indicate that mass society no longer exists, if ever it did. The classes of classical sociology have changed, and researchers find a growing multiplicity of finite social groups or clusters instead. What is more, these smaller social groups globally tend to reject the idea that there is a single communication form that serves all possible personal, social, and political needs.

Under these conditions, static norms of communicative practice must necessarily fail to satisfy the needs of any group (except the one that formulates such norms). The realization in the modern world of the plurality that emerged during the 16th-century European Renaissance has taken on forms proper to the contradictions of the present. The idea of dynamic justice helps prevent a recurrence now of one of the main reasons the first phase of the modern age failed. It avoids the static systems of tradition that the Renaissance inherited as a model for morality and justice. Furthermore, the value ideas of freedom and life provide simple and readily applicable maxims against which to evaluate the communicative relations between social groups.

The best possible sociopolitical world, the utopia of radical dynamic justice, is not present on a global stage. On the other hand, the examples provided by Marshall, Michaels, and Turner, among others, indicates that a variety of communicative actions are possible that can accommodate the cultural plurality of the world. One of the real problems in the contemporary normative context of communication—that is to say, the potential incommensurability of the normative systems of cultures in the modern world—can be addressed if the basic value ideas of dynamic justice, freedom, and life, become adopted as protonorms for communication in this environment. Indeed, we believe that these value ideas can be used as the basis for maxims that (a) eliminate means-ends relations of tutelage between groups and individuals and (b) widen the ways in which people's endowments can be raised into talents. In so doing, professional communications practice can reaffirm the original humanist project of modernity, thereby taking the first step in humanity's path beyond the modern age.

Notes

1. *The Hunters* retained this dominance until the early 1980s when *The Gods Must be Crazy* (1980) was released in the United States in 1983. This film is now screened in colleges and universities across the U.S. in Third World cinema courses, anthropology, and even in literature programs that include film components. This film is presented by academics in terms of both critical and positive perspectives.

2. The evolution of one such video is discussed by Lazarus and Tomaselli (1989); for other examples, see Scott (1994).

3. Hereafter, we distinguish three phases of modernity. We derive these from interpretations of the work of Heller (1983) and Hannah Arendt (1958). Briefly, the modern *age* begins with the Renaissance challenge to medieval ecclesiasticism and its associated traditions; the modern *era* encompasses the periods commonly known as the Enlightenment and the Industrial Revolution; and the modern *world* refers to the contemporary condition. We do not intend to deny that there is a crisis of modern thought. Instead, we argue from the position that the present time is not so much postmodern but caught in the death throes of an era. However, it would be premature to proclaim the date and time of birth of the new age. We are too much in the middle of events.

4. The ethical is distinguished from the moral in the following way: Ethics refers to the field of human activity in the social-institutional realm, whereas morality deals with the individual person's attitudes, propensities, or inclinations to act in certain ways. Ethics is thus essentially the "theory of acceptable behavior" of persons in their everyday activity as members of public or social bodies. The criteria of ethics are generally rules of correct or incorrect conduct. Morality can be seen, in contrast, as the "theory of conscience" in the light of which one's acts can be judged as good or evil according to the norms of a given community.

References

Arendt, Hannah. (1958). *The human condition.* Chicago: University of Chicago Press.

Asch, Tim. (1979). Making a film record of the Yanomamo Indians of Southern Venezuela. *Perspectives of Film, 2,* 4-9.

Criticos, C., & Quinlan, T. (1991, Spring). Putting education and anthropology to work: Community video and ethnographic documentation in South Africa. *CVA Review,* pp. 49-53.

Ehrenreich, J. (1985). Anthropology on trial. *American Anthropologist, 87,* 218-221.

Faris, James. (1992). Anthropological transparency: Film, representation, and politics. In P. I. Crawford & D. Turton (Eds.), *Film as ethnography* (pp. 171-181). London: Manchester University Press.

Feldman, Seth. (1977). Viewer, viewing, viewed: A critique of subject-generated documentary. *Journal of the University Film Association, 29*(4), 23-38.

Foucault, Michel. (1970). *The order of things.* London: RKP.

Gordon, Rob. (1990a, February/May). Kicking up a Kalahari storm. *Southern African Review of Books,* pp. 18-19.

Gordon, Rob. (1990b, Spring). People of the Great Sandface: People of the great white lie? *CVA Review,* pp. 30-33.

Gordon, Rob. (1991). Buschmannschwarmerei in Südafrika. In R. Kapfer, W. Petermann, & R. Thoms (Eds.), *Jäger und Gejagte: John Marshall und Seine Filme* (pp. 165-179). Munich: Trickster Verlag.

Gordon, Rob. (1992). *The Bushmen myth and the making of a Namibian underclass.* Boulder, CO: Westview.

Gramsci, Antonio. (1970). *Selections from the prison notebooks* (Trans., Q. Hoare & N. G. Smith). London: Lawrence & Wishart.

Heller, Agnes. (1976). *The theory of need in Marx.* London: Routledge & Kegan Paul.

Heller, Agnes. (1983). *A theory of history.* Oxford, UK: Basil Blackwell.

Heller, Agnes. (1984). *A radical philosophy.* Oxford, UK: Basil Blackwell.

Heller, Agnes. (1987). *Beyond justice.* Oxford, UK: Basil Blackwell.

Heller, Agnes. (1992). *A philosophy of morals.* Oxford, UK: Basil Blackwell.

Heller, Agnes, & Fehér, F. (1988). *The postmodern political condition.* Cambridge, UK: Polity.

Honderich, T. (1987). *Violence for equality: Inquiries in political philosophy.* London: Routledge.

Lazarus, Alison, & Tomaselli, Keyan G. (1989). Participatory video: Problems, prospects and a case study. *Group Media Journal, 8*(1), 10-15.

Mudimbe, Valentin Y. (1988). *The invention of Africa: Gnosis, philosophy and the order of knowledge.* Bloomington: Indiana University Press.

Namuddu, Katherine, & Tapsoba, J. M. Silbry. (1993). *The status of educational research and policy analysis in sub-Saharan Africa.* Ottawa, Canada: Development Research Centre.

Ogan, Christine. (1989). Video's great advantage: Decentralized control of technology. *Media Development, 36*(4), 2-5.

O'Regan, Tom. (1990). Communication and tradition: Essays after Eric Michaels [Special issue]. *Continuum: An Australian Journal of the Media, 3*(2).

Paton, H. J. (1948). *The moral law: Kant's groundwork of the metaphysic of morals.* London: Hutchinson.

Pirsig, R. M. (1992). *Lila: An inquiry into morals.* New York: Free Press.

Ruby, J. (Ed.). (1993). *The cinema of John Marshall.* Philadelphia: Harwood.

Scott, Chuck. (1994). *The Lesotho video herders project.* Aarhus, Denmark: Intervention.

Senft, G. (1987). Nanam'sa Bwena—Gutes Denken. Eine ethnolinguistsche Fallstuddie uber eine Dorfversammlung auf den Trobriand Inseln. *Zeit schrift fur Ethnologie, 112,* 191-222.

Shepperson, Arnold. (1994). Tits'n'buns: Film and the appropriation of the human body. *Visual Anthropology, 6,* 395-400.

Shepperson, Arnold. (1995). *On the social interpretation of cultural experience: Reflections on Raymond Williams's early cultural writings (1958-1963).* Master's thesis, University of Natal, Durban, South Africa.

Survival International. (1990). *Yanomami.* London: Author.

Tomaselli, Keyan G., Williams, Alan, Steenveld, Lynette, & Tomaselli, Ruth E. (1986). *Myth, race and power: South Africans imaged on film and TV.* Bellville, South Africa: Anthropos.

Toulmin, Stephen. (1990). *Cosmopolis: The hidden agenda of modernity.* New York: Free Press.

Turner, Terence. (1990, Spring). Visual media, cultural politics, and anthropological practice: Some implications of recent uses of film and video among the Kayapo of Brazil. *CVA Review,* pp. 8-13.

Ucko, P. (1987). *Academic freedom and apartheid: The story of the World Archaeological Congress.* London: Peter Duckworth.

Wiley, David, with Cancel, R., Pflugrad, D., Elkiss, T. H., & Campbell, A. (1982). *Africa on film and videotape 1960-1981.* East Lansing: Michigan State University, African Studies Center.

Williams, Raymond. (1963). *The long revolution.* Harmondsworth, UK: Pelican.

Williams, Raymond. (1983). *Keywords.* London, Fontana.

Wilmsen, Edwin. (1989). *Land filled with flies: A political economy of the Kalahari.* Chicago: University of Chicago Press.

Wilmsen, Edwin. (1991a, Spring). Comments on Paul John Myburgh's *People of the Great Sandface. CVA Review,* p. 60.

Wilmsen, Edwin. (1991b). Die Dokumentation war ein Vermachtnis. In R. Kapfer, W. Petermann, & R. Thomas (Eds.), *Jäger und Gejagte: John Marshall und Seine Filme* (pp. 80-102). Munich: Trickster Verlag.

Wilmsen, Edwin, & Denbow, J. R. (1990). Paradigmatic history of San-speaking peoples and current attempts at revision. *Current Anthropology, 31*(5), 489-524.

CHAPTER 16

Women, Welfare, and the United States Media

ROBIN ANDERSEN

On a segment of ABC's *PrimeTime Live* (February 16, 1995), host Diane Sawyer featured a group of teenage mothers receiving Aid to Families with Dependent Children (AFDC): "To many people, these girls are Public Enemy No. 1." Addressing them directly, she continued, "You know, a tax payer at home will say, 'Why should I pay for your mistakes?'" Poor, unmarried teen mothers were similarly singled out by *Newsweek* columnist Jonathan Alter (1994) as the root of "every threat to the fabric of this country" (p. 41). Themes of guilt and shame were constructed by Alter and Wingert (1995) in another *Newsweek* cover story on February 6, 1995. Poor young women were compared to "drunk drivers" and the writers claimed that "the public is game for a little humiliation" (p. 24). This discourse illustrates the degree to which the media have followed the agenda set by public officials promoting what they call "welfare reform."

A study done by Fairness and Accuracy in Reporting (FAIR) surveyed the sources used in the media coverage of the welfare debate from December 1, 1994, to February 24, 1995 (cited in Flanders & Jackson, 1995). The study found that Representative E. Clay Shaw, Jr., of Florida, the chair of the House subcommittee that drafted the "Personal Responsibility Act," was the single most influential voice in the media debate on welfare. Shaw, who describes welfare as a system that pampers the poor, logged in with the most media appearances—a total of 37. The FAIR study (Flanders & Jackson, 1995) quotes a *New York Times* article (February 10, 1995) by David Rosenbaum announcing that personal responsibility had achieved political consensus: "Politicians and scholars from all points of the political compass agree . . . that, as Representative E. Clay Shaw, Jr. said today, [the welfare system has] 'destroyed responsibility, diminished personal dignity and created economic disincentives that bar people from success' " (p. 14).

Whereas the press has followed the lead of certain elected officials on the issue of welfare—allowing them to set the agenda as well as the parameters of debate—news stories have gone further. Indeed, the rhetoric of "the enemy," along with themes of guilt, blame, and even public humiliation, are now prominent features of media discussions of welfare recipients. Poor women, especially those of color, have been vilified in stories across the media spectrum. From talk radio diatribes, to television investigations of welfare fraud, to background profiles on poverty by the papers of record, poor mothers have been stereotyped as irresponsible, immoral, child-abusing, drug-addicted deviants who drain public finances and violate the public trust.

This chapter will examine the language of vilification used to depict poor women who receive AFDC. Its various manifestations will be evaluated within the broader context of theoretical formulations that seek to position media discourse within an ethical perspective. The welfare rhetoric in the U.S. media provides a disturbing case of discursive practice but one that illuminates pivotal sites at which an ethical perspective would be capable of promoting the goals of democratic participation, social and economic justice, and ultimately, the basic human rights to dignity and fairness.

This chapter first traces the traditional formulations from which ethical perspectives on media discourse have been drawn. Enlightenment ideals of public participation based on information and uninhibited public debate serve as the foundation for U.S. conceptualizations of the media's role in a democratic society. Freedom of the press has been viewed as a means to guarantee full and open public debate, long considered a necessity for democratic practice and one that allows a wide range of issues of common concern to be resolved in the public interest. The need for a broadly defined, uninhibited public discourse has led some to argue for an ethics of media pluralism (Barney, 1986). Although these principles remain cogent and indispensable to democratic practice, it will be argued that such traditional conceptions need to be augmented, expanded, and in some cases, critically reexamined.

Regarding the Enlightenment model of media practice and citizen participation, it is necessary to carefully consider two key principles that serve as its foundation. First, language has been traditionally defined in operational terms as primarily information exchange. In the marketplace of ideas, more is always better, regardless of the speech acts employed, the narratives constructed, or the visual associations depicted. Such assumptions need to be reassessed in light of current formulations that posit that language is far more than information. Rather, language is the primary way in which we understand the world, define ourselves and others, and formulate judgments based on modes of discourse that contain significations over and above their information content. Therefore, an ethical evaluation of media discourse must consider the types of speech acts employed and the narrative constructions of exclusion that dehumanize the poor and present women and minorities as Other.

The second assumption underpinning the traditional model of democratic media practice is the concept of citizenship. Citizen participation in public debate assumes that rational judgment and reasoned deliberation will have an impact on social practice. It also assumes that fairness, equality, and unbiased evaluation will be brought to bear on discursive practices within the civic arena. However, such a formulation of citizenship cannot explain the acceptance of bias nor the effectiveness of media vilification and dehumanization. What makes the public gravitate to "explanations" that blame women, the poor, and minorities for present global economic transformations affecting the standard of living of most U.S. citizens? This question requires that the conception of citizenship be contextualized within the broader discursive practices of the symbolic environment. Citizenship implies subjectivity, and acknowledging that subjectivity is in large part discursively formed helps account for the efficacy of bias. It also allows us to postulate effective ethical practices intended to mitigate such undemocratic phenomena.

In developing a discursive ethics of media discourse, this chapter will draw on Jürgen Habermas's formulation of the public sphere and Nancy

Fraser's modification of the Habermasian model. Cooper (1991), following Foucault (1984a), has offered an ethics of resistance, from which key elements will be retrieved for evaluating contemporary American discursive practice.

When considering the need for a discursive ethics, Cooper (1991) observes that ethics is concerned with "what relationships we *ought* to have with ourselves and others" (p. 24). Language as the means through which we communicate with each other and as a society is therefore a pivotal site for ethical concern: "Ethics is related to communication because when we communicate, we reveal ourselves and constitute ourselves in terms of others" (p. 24). Thus, the establishment of social belonging, through language, ultimately determines how members of society will be considered, valued, and treated.

The changing contours of public debate, media formats, and participatory practices make clear the need for ethical protonorms to undergird public sphere discourse. A discursive ethics will be formulated that considers the modes of communication used to construct visual and verbal narratives (how something is said also signifies). An ethical approach asserting fundamental imperatives of human dignity also considers the way in which individuals and members of subordinate social groups are regarded in communication discourse. The assumed subjectivities of those who engage in dialogue and those who are asked to accept such messages will also be considered.

Section 1 summarizes the media coverage of welfare, describes the depictions of welfare recipients, and indicates the sources called on to articulate the debate. Media coverage is evaluated according to the traditional Enlightenment model of ethical media practice and democratic participation.

Section 2 expands the discussion on media ethics to consider the modes of communication, the language evoked, and the types of narratives employed in media accounts of welfare recipients. Such considerations require an expanded theoretical model able to shed light on the discursive formation of social identity, bias, and such practices as scapegoating. Current conceptions of the public sphere and the public interest will be reevaluated in light of the lack of participatory equality existent in media discourse.

Finally, key foundational principles or protonorms are proposed. Media coverage of the welfare debate demonstrates the need to articulate ethical solutions to the media's dehumanizing language, narratives, and visual cues that ultimately discourage human empathy and democratic practice. Establishing ethical parameters for public-sphere debate will enhance democratic discursive practice and further the goals of democracy based on human dignity, acceptance of the other, and a commitment to the marginalized.

Media Coverage of Mothers on Welfare

Media coverage of women who receive AFDC falls far short of presenting either a diverse image, a multiplicity of voices, or a full and uninhibited debate on the issue of welfare. Numerous influential accounts in the media present poor women as "welfare cheats" and abusive mothers who refuse to work because of a lack of "personal responsibility."

Williams (1995) cites a flurry of press reports about one Boston woman named Clarabel Ventura, charged with "abusing her four-year-old son by plunging his hands into boiling water." Press accounts described her as a crack-addicted neglectful mother who "sent her children out in the projects alone after midnight, knocking on doors to beg for food, cigarettes and money"[1] (pp. 1159-1160). Such behavior was linked to the fact that she received welfare benefits. She was living in a rent-subsidized apartment and receiving AFDC, food stamps, and benefits from the Women and Infant Children Program. An article that ran in the *Boston Herald* the day after the story broke was titled "Welfare Gone Wrong."[2] The journalist used the case to generalize, painting a stereotypical picture of the welfare mother: "Alcohol and/or cocaine addicted, living in hell-holes with a handful of babies; women abandoned by one man, then another, by their families long ago. Women, abused and neglected themselves, who hit 14 or 16 and begin creating abused and neglected carbon-copies of themselves" (Hutchinson, 1994, p. 5).

After four days of investigating the Ventura family, the *Boston Globe* (Sennott, 1994b) ran a lengthy "background" article. Clarabel's mother, Eulalia, had come from a village in Puerto Rico in 1968. She had 17 children, virtually none of whom had a full-time job. Many of the grandchildren and great-grandchildren had applied for welfare themselves. The reporter informed taxpayers that they could spend as much as $1 million on public assistance for this one family alone. On February 21, 1994, another story by the *Boston Herald* (Carr, 1994) was titled, "Ventura Family Tree Sinks Roots in Rich Welfare Soil." It offered more sweeping generalizations about welfare: "Every day there's a different welfare horror story" (p. 8).

Williams (1995) summarizes the stereotype of welfare mothers as irresponsible:

> This mother is usually African-American (and increasingly Latina). She has many children, is not a "productive" member of the labor force, and does not share the ideals of mainstream Americans. Variations on this theme include unmarried teen pregnancy, drug use, child abuse or neglect, failure to ensure children's attendance at school or adequate medical care. (p. 1163)

Indeed, such irresponsibility is typically presented as a consequence of their receiving welfare benefits. Another study documenting news reports of welfare mothers showed that the same myths were consistently perpetuated. Nahata (1992) found that the average welfare recipient is described as a "black, unwed, unemployed, teenage mother of several children, living in the inner city" (p. 18).

Public Perception

Focus group research on attitudes toward the welfare system demonstrates that public perceptions of welfare recipients conform to media imaging but are contrary to empirical data. Male professionals participating in a Denver focus group believed that welfare recipients "will be on welfare the rest of their lives. Their kids are destined for it. It is self-perpetuating."[3] In one national phone survey, 82% agreed that the majority of welfare recipients would "never get off welfare." Another 83% thought that many people receiving benefits were not entitled to them.[4] Perceptions conformed to stereotypes that welfare mothers have many children, are lazy and African American, are living well on taxpayers' money, and frequently defraud the system. In addition, "A poll of 1994 voters found that one out of five believed that welfare was *the largest* federal government expense, larger even than defense" (Sklar, 1995, p. 53).

In one focus group study, respondents were surprised when they learned that the facts contradicted their perceptions. Contrary to the singular discourse on welfare mothers, they are a diverse group of people. The average woman on AFDC is white. She has 1.9 children, which is fewer than the average woman not on AFDC.[5] The average recipient receives welfare for 18 months, usually beginning after a precipitating event, such as desertion by a husband or boyfriend or an unexpected pregnancy. Only 7% to 15% stay on welfare for 8 consecutive years, and less than 10% are considered "chronic" recipients. No evidence indicates an increased "dependency" on welfare in recent times. One study (Duncan & Hill, 1988) that traced young women who grew up on welfare found that 64% received no welfare as young adults.

No evidence whatsoever supports the assertion that AFDC encourages out-of-wedlock births. In fact, southern states have higher rates of unwed pregnancies but lower benefits. Fewer than 8% of AFDC recipients are under 20 years of age. Childbearing by unmarried women cuts across class, age, and education. Two-thirds of all women who give birth outside of marriage are not living below the poverty line. The vast majority are white, adult women. Most AFDC recipients do not neglect or abuse their children. As Williams (1995) puts it, "Welfare is not an inner-city, long-term, inter-generational, teenage-pregnancy problem" (pp. 1189-1190).

Those intent on cutting entitlements to the poor portray AFDC as a major drain on public funds, when in fact it accounts for only 1% of the federal budget.[6] And in 1994, states spent only 2% of their revenues on AFDC.

The Economic Void

One of the most disturbing aspects of welfare coverage in the U.S. media has been the near total failure to contextualize the debate within a broader discussion of economics. Social entitlements to the poor are being cut at the state and federal levels, reducing benefits that already fall far below the poverty line. At the same time, an increasing number of U.S. citizens are joining the ranks of the poor. Job losses within both white-collar and blue-collar industries have created a falling standard of living for most U.S. citizens. Over the last decade, corporate management strategies have consistently cut labor costs to increase profit margins.[7] "The growing impact of job-cutting is increasingly evident in national statistics. Wages are falling as a percentage of national income, while profits are rising" (Uchitelle, 1993, p. D3). In her bestselling book, *The Overworked American*, Juliet Schor (1992) confirms that the decline in wages has been "a phenomenon of the last 10 years" (p. 109). Even as figures indicate an economic "recovery" since 1991, "there have been broad-based wage reductions during the recovery . . . for both blue and white collar men" (Herbert, 1993, p. A23).[8] And even in the face of the general trend toward increased productivity, "the average real (inflation-adjusted) weekly earnings of production and nonsupervisory private sector workers crashed 16% between 1973 and 1993—falling below 1967 levels" (Sklar, 1995, p. 50).[9]

Corporate "job-shedding" creates falling income levels and a shrinking middle class by concentrating wealth in fewer hands; it impoverishes increasing numbers of U.S. citizens. "Economic inequality is now so extreme that the richest one percent of U.S. citizen families have nearly as much wealth as the entire bottom 95 percent" (Sklar, 1995, p. 49). The gap between the rich and the poor in Manhattan, New York, is worse than in Guatemala. The United States now has the highest level of income concentration of the other Western industrial nations.[10] As wealth flows upward in America, one out of four children is born into poverty.

Such economic statistics are doled out in a piecemeal fashion in media discourse and always delinked from the welfare debate. Media stories featuring welfare recipients consistently avoid the impact of such economic trends on the poverty rate. The themes of personal responsibility and replacing welfare with "workfare" assert that the poor could join the work force if only they were not so lazy. There is no room in the discourse of personal responsibility to illuminate the powerful barriers that keep young mothers from working. Missing from media discussions are welfare policy alternatives that take into consideration the need for day care, and health benefits, and a raise in minimum wage (see Bergmann & Hartmann, 1995; Polakow, 1995). The FAIR study found that such "alternatives were virtually never given a space to be heard" (Flanders & Jackson, 1995, p. 15).

Perceptions and Public Policy

The selective repetition of anecdotal stories of welfare mothers shapes public perception of welfare recipients and informs the public debate. "The mainstream media's failure to present a clear and unmistakable counter-image, or to present the entire story of welfare, only encourages and legitimizes an equally unidimensional, biased response from society" (Williams, 1995, pp. 1163-1164).

The stereotypical images, the loss of a multiplicity of voices, and the lack of economic context generate particular attitudes that lead to unjust and ineffective public policies. Such a truncated spectrum of debate results in "a rigid and narrowly defined, rather than comprehensive and nuanced, welfare policy that is unresponsive to the needs of the vast majority of mothers receiving welfare" (Williams, 1995, p. 1191). Narrowly focused media discourse serves to justify policy decisions designed to reduce family assistance programs. For example, the numerous press accounts of the Ventura family corresponded with the approval of a floor amendment in the Massachusetts Senate terminating most AFDC benefits after 2 years.

A misinformed public engages in faulty judgments that lead to inappropriate public policies. Fundamental preconditions for democratic pluralism require full information and public debate. The value of the Enlightenment model of public information as a precondition for citizen participation is apparent. Critically assessing the speech acts themselves, however, draws out the analysis by amplifying the criteria for evaluating such discursive practice. How has the language of vilification affected public debate, perceptions, and policies? Considering public discourse from an ethical perspective will expand our understanding of the effectiveness of discursive practices that shape public perceptions.

Subjectivity, Citizenship, and the Public Sphere

Arguing for a discursive ethics requires a reassessment of the traditional view of information and its uses. One must begin by asking the basic question of what it means to be human, living "in the house of language" as Heidegger put it. According to Kovel (1995),

> The differentiating point which distinguishes the subjectivity of humanity from that of nature is not consciousness as such, but self-consciousness, that is, the formation of an internally organized subject, or self, that endows itself and the object world with qualities. (p. 5)

Self-consciously regarding oneself and others and giving the world meaning through signification constitutes the very definition of humanity.

> The distinguishing feature of human self-consciousness is the interposition of language. Language is not to be seen as an instrumentality here, that is, as the pragmatics of information exchange (though it includes this): rather as the signified and potentially conscious emergence of an inner, imaginary world created by the self and through which it moves. (Kovel, 1995, p. 5)

The relationship between language and subjectivity is the key to participating in public life. Discursive participation entails "simultaneously constructing and expressing one's cultural identity through idiom and style" (Fraser, 1993, p. 16). Indeed, language provides the means to speak in one's own voice. Such a definition of language amplifies the essentially pragmatic conception of communication as information exchange, a construction characteristic of Enlightenment thinking and of Habermas's rationally ordered public sphere.

An alternative view asserts that communication practice actively takes part in the construction of subjectivity. In this sense, we can speak of a discursively formed subject, one contextualized within the larger environment of public discourse. In this context, language functions to give form and meaning to self-identity and the construction of self and other. Subjectivity is thus socially positioned, enabling social interaction and a sense of belonging. Therefore, communication practices must not be evaluated merely from the point of view of information content. If we take discursive subjectivity seriously, we must also assess the ways in which discursive practice frames individual subjectivities within the larger social environment. This brings ethical questions to the fore.

Constructing Women and the Poor as Other

The depictions of poor young women on welfare are narrative constructions of exclusion that assign subjective sensibilities to welfare recipients. As Williams (1995) points out, "The image of an AFDC recipient as happy, healthy, or proud is unacceptable" (p. 1167). Heroic young mothers who struggle under the worst hardships are not featured in media narratives. Indeed, representations of deviants or hopeless victims are preferred over attitudes of struggle and determination. For example, an editorial column in the *Boston Globe* titled "Welfare Mothers With an Attitude" denigrated one young mother who asserted "I'm a natural at motherhood. It's my job" (Goodman, 1992, p. 19). Shame-filled, hopeless, or depressed are the only affective states considered acceptable in media discourse.

Welfare mothers who go to school, who do not use drugs or abuse their children, more closely exemplify the average recipient, but those women's stories do not fit media narratives foregrounding themes of blame and guilt. Such themes are essential for portraying welfare recipients as the dehumanized Other, beyond the bounds of social emulation and inclusion.

Welfare mothers are not rendered in the language of shared humanity; rather the audience is invited to view such displays of poverty as aberrations. Presented as Other, drained of the language of belonging, a subjectivity deserving of emotional emulation is impossible. The poor may be victims, but they are not portrayed as innocent. Their suffering exists on the other side of the thematic divide of personal responsibility. Their poverty results from immoral actions, irresponsibility, or some other personal flaw not part of the viewer's lexicon of experience.

Absent from the media are narratives of belonging and inclusion. As content analysis demonstrates, welfare mothers are not allowed to bear witness to their lives and struggles. Only 10% of media sources are recipients themselves, and their voices are most often used to confirm asserted stereotypes (Flanders & Jackson, 1995). Lacking is a view of poverty experienced from the perspective of the recipients' social position. Indeed, the media provide only the distanced view of the spectator. The lack of emotional emulation turns that view into voyeurism.

"Nowhere is there any recognition that the media's insistence that welfare mothers are deviant is itself destructive" (Williams, 1995, p. 1194). Demeaning media narratives construct degrading social identities for poor mothers. To validate herself in the face of such imagery of who society says she is, the welfare mother must tell herself that she is different. She must "other" herself, assuming a position outside and distinct from the social group (with the corresponding set of shared political interests) to which she belongs. In doing so, she must "affirm that the vast majority of welfare recipients do indeed fit the negative image harbored in our collective unconscious" (p. 1194).

Foucault's ethics of resistance and Fraser's (1993) views on the formation of subjectivity in relation to power are relevant here. Much public discourse revolves around defining people's needs, especially for the poor. Fraser asserts that individuals and subordinated groups must resist social and bureaucratic categorization. Public policy is dominated by experts engaging in technical reasoning, and along the way, social identities are also constructed and assigned. "The people whose needs are in question are repositioned. They become individual 'cases' rather than members of social groups or participants in social movements" (Fraser, 1989, p. 174).

But when welfare mothers and support groups resist such labels and organize to advance their own interests, the media often portray such actions as harmful to their own cause. One article asserted, for example, that "protesters demanding to testify in one hearing had alienated legislators" (Aucion, 1994, p. 27).

An ethics of media pluralism enjoins the media to incorporate more discourse into the public debate, and more inclusiveness is indeed necessary. Advancing a discursive ethics should qualify and critically evaluate the narrative themes and discursive practices employed. There is little information content in vilification, public humiliation, and dehumanized narratives of exclusion. Ethical media practice depends on a foundation of such protonorms as human dignity, respect for others, and solidarity with the oppressed. Indeed, dehumanized depictions foster bias and preclude a more authentic discourse capable of explaining issues of economics, poverty, and social policy. Selecting narratives to illustrate themes of blame and guilt block alternative stories of courage and struggle.

Rational Discourse and Associational Subtexts

Another aspect of media practice to be considered from an ethical perspective are the media narratives. Stereotyping consists of repeating selected images to the exclusion of others. Media analysis demonstrates that the dominant media image of the welfare mother is (a) very young and (b) African American and Latina. The FAIR study confirmed that "when the age of welfare recipients was given, they were generally 17, 18 or 19 years old—even though only six percent of mothers who receive AFDC are younger than 20" (Flanders & Jackson, 1995, p. 15). When ABC's *PrimeTime Live* (September 17, 1994) "investigated" welfare fraud, the women featured on the program were virtually all Black and Latina. The fraud investigator felt compelled to mention, however, that the majority of welfare defrauders in reality are nonminorities and come from the middle class (see Cabrero-Sud, 1994). Such images not only perpetuate misleading information about welfare recipients, they serve to vilify young minority women. Such stereotyping creates the impression that all young mothers of color are deviant. Such practices that present a "partial totality" mystify the process of actual social and economic forces and lead to scapegoating.

Textual association (both visual and verbal) is another common strategy used to construct media stories about welfare. Visual images tied to the welfare issue become iconographic references that, through repetition, come to be received as explanation. Welfare recipients are characterized as women who abuse and neglect their children. ABC's *World News Tonight*

(June 14, 1995) tied visual footage of a family living in urban squalor to the discussion of welfare. "Here's an example of the problem. When police found 19 children living in squalor in a Chicago apartment last winter, it was a shocking symbol of all that is wrong with the system. Their mothers received more than $5,000 a month in welfare."

Visual juxtapositions create associational subtexts. These associations become the commonsense understanding of the issue. This powerful symbolic rubric frames public discussion and reinforces received messages. Within the welfare debate, associational symbols have proven to be more influential than rational discourse, even at the policy level. Many congressional debates open with such anecdotal symbolic stories.[11] Another illustration of this point, in the rare cases when alternative examples of welfare mothers are presented, they are easily discounted as anomalies. They become exceptions to the rule (Williams, 1995, pp. 1165-1166).[12] And in *Mandate for Change*—the Democratic Leadership Council blueprint for the Clinton presidency—one reference to age is included in the chapter "Replacing Welfare with Work, the "15-year-old welfare mother with a new baby." As Sklar (1995) observes, "In reality, *0.1 percent* of mothers receiving AFDC are 15 or younger, and *less than four percent* are 18 or younger" (p. 54). Another report from the White House Working Group on the Family, as quoted in Williams (1995), demonstrates how the media and policy makers alike can no longer separate mythic constructions from the facts.

> Statistical evidence does not prove those suppositions [that welfare benefits are an incentive to bear children]; and yet, even the most casual observer of public assistance programs understands there is indeed some relationship between availability of welfare and the inclination of many young women to bear fatherless children. (p. 1174)

The mythic constructions of welfare recipients through association and visual construction represents one of the most difficult challenges to a discursive ethics. As women's rights advocate Francis Fox Piven commented, "I am struck by how little evidence matters in talk about welfare" (Flanders & Jackson, 1995, p. 16). Indeed, in the instance of welfare policy, the loss of discursive truth and reasoned deliberation has threatened the very foundation of democratic practice. It calls into question fundamental assumptions about the nature of citizenship and the efficacy of reasoned public discourse.

Citizenship, Judgment, and Bias

One of the most compelling yet problematic aspects of democratic participation is the concept of citizenship itself. Ethical discussions of rhetoric and political communication in U.S. society have long been shaped by an instrumental view of democratic participation derived from the Enlightenment. "The Enlightenment approach to politics furnishes ethical standards such as rationality, choice, democratic procedure and democratic values as the yardsticks" by which communication acts are measured (Cooper, 1991, p. 24). In this view, the citizen takes center stage, as the actor whose participation is vital to a model of democratic governance. Citizen participation is based on the assumption that individuals are capable of choice; and that choice is based, in turn, on a set of rational criteria from which sound judgments can be made. For democracy to endure, individual autonomy and participation are essential.

As Barney (1986) argues, the public's ability to make correct decisions is a basic premise of the legal structure built around the First and Fourteenth Amendments: "Judgment skills are a critical factor, but their role awaits another discussion" (p. 62). A discussion of judgment is indeed necessary here. A purely "rational" model of reasoned judgment does not provide the tools for evaluating public discourse and media formulations in general but especially for the type of discourse now common to the welfare debate. Understanding that the formation of subjectivity takes place in a discursive environment can help account for the perpetuation of prejudice that serves to maintain and justify antidemocratic practices. As Johnnie Tillmon (as quoted in Williams, 1995), leader of the welfare rights movement, observes,

> People still believe that old lie that AFDC mothers keep on having kids to get a bigger welfare check. On the average, another baby means another $35 a month—barely enough for food and clothing. There are a lot of other lies that male society tells about welfare mothers: that AFDC mothers are immoral . . . lazy, misuse their welfare checks, spend it all on booze, and are stupid and incompetent. If people are willing to believe these lies, it's partly because they're just special versions of the lies that society tells about all women. (p. 1167, supranote 47)

To be effective, the dehumanizing, biased, and ultimately irrational media constructions of poor women must resonate with the public. And indeed they do. A large segment of the public gravitates to such images to validate its own race and gender perceptions that are perpetuated, at least in part, for broader social and political purposes. The acceptance of racial and gender bias "allows the public to devalue and distance themselves from poor women, and encourages politicians to develop policy based on gender, race, and class stereotypes" (Williams, 1995, p. 1191).

The discourse of otherness appeals to prejudice, bias, and fear of those deemed distinct from ourselves. An Enlightenment model of singularly rational actors (be they individuals or elected officials) cannot explain or critique current discursive practice. Nor can it account for the acceptance of mythic "explanations," even when they run counter to empirical evidence. If we take seriously the discursive formation of subjectivity, it leads to an ethical imperative to avoid the dehumanizing discursive practices and media depictions that promote antidemocratic social forces.

The Public Sphere Reassessed

At this point, it is instructive to return to the model of the public sphere that has achieved academic popularity through Jürgen Habermas. The model postulates inclusion and equality as essential to public participation. In this light, we must ask if women can be treated equitably within the public sphere given the discursive practices that characterize the welfare debate. One of the most striking findings of the FAIR study was how male-dominated the welfare debate had become. "Of sources whose gender could be identified, 71 percent (608 sources) were male—discussing policy proposals that will disproportionately affect women" (Flanders & Jackson, 1995, p. 14).[13] Most politicians are male, and those sources were most often allowed to comment. Numerous women's rights activists and policy analysts have formulated alternative proposals for an effective welfare policy. However, they have been excluded from the debate.

Fraser (1993) questions the validity of the assertion that citizens will be able to participate equally in the public sphere regardless of their socioeconomic and sociosexual status. She argues that the notion of bracketing status distinctions to engage in public discourse is untenable in stratified societies because the public sphere is pervaded by the same structural relations of domination and subordination that exist in the wider social organization. "In stratified societies, unequally empowered social groups tend to develop unequally valued cultural styles" (p. 11). Recognizing difference in cultural styles accorded unequal social status results in devaluing subordinate points of view. Subordinates acquiesce and their needs are compromised because their forms of expression lack cultural legitimacy. As we have seen, access to the media by poor women is restricted, but when they are allowed to speak, their discursive style is indeed devalued. In addition, the visual construction of poverty is often portrayed as the fault of those willing to live in such conditions.[14]

After arguing that discursive equality is not possible within the broader context of social inequality, Fraser advances a different formulation of the public sphere model. Instead of positing a singular model of public discourse, one in which subordinated groups are not heard, Fraser (1993, p. 14) offers an alternative model of multiple publics, referred to as "subaltern counterpublics." Historically, such counterpublics existed and developed along with the bourgeois public sphere proposed by Habermas.

The historiography of Ryan and others demonstrates that the bourgeois public was never *the* public. On the contrary, virtually contemporaneous with the bourgeois public, there arose a host of competing counterpublics, including nationalist publics, popular peasant publics, elite women's publics, and working-class publics (Fraser, 1993, p. 7).

In fact, the bourgeois public sphere arose as a distinct arena of public discourse, displacing an older elite culture and providing legitimacy to the formations of the rising bourgeois class. The new discursive practices and ethos carried with them markers of distinction from "the various popular and plebeian strata it aspired to rule" (Fraser, 1993, p. 6). Joan Landes (1988) observed that most prominent among those distinctions were gender differences. Landes (1988)—describing the formation of the republic public sphere in France—notes that a discursive practice was constructed in direct opposition to the more woman-friendly salon style that became stigmatized as artificial, effeminate, and aristocratic. The new republican practices were defined in contrast as rational, virtuous, and manly. "In this way, masculinist gender constructions were built into the very concept of the republican public sphere" (Fraser, 1993, p. 5).

Because of the historical roots of exclusion by gender and class, and the disadvantage to subordinated groups in contemporary public discourse, Fraser presents a postbourgeois public sphere model based on multicultural and gender diversity. No longer conceived of as singular, Fraser asserts that now, as in the past, a variety of counterpublic discursive arenas actually compose the public sphere. She argues that a multiplicity of parallel discursive arenas provides spaces for dissent and discussion, where members of subordinated groups, "invent and circulate counterdiscourses, so as to formulate oppositional interpretations of their identities, interests, and needs" (Fraser, 1993, p. 14). As an example, she cites the late-20th-century U.S. feminist movement as a subaltern counterpublic, with its "variegated array of journals, bookstores, publishing companies, film and video distribution networks, lecture series, research centers, academic programs, conferences, conventions, festivals, and local meeting places" (p. 14). Such arenas have allowed women to theorize, define, and express their needs, social positions, and identities, "thereby reducing, although not eliminating, the extent of our disadvantage in official public spheres" (p. 15).

Using such participatory arenas for debate and discussion, "women have invented new terms for describing social reality, including 'sexism,' 'the double shift,' 'sexual harassment,' and 'marital, date, and acquaintance rape' " (Fraser, 1993, pp. 14-15). In addition to women's counterpublics, which Fraser defines as egalitarian and democratic, she acknowledges that other antidemocratic counterpublics also exist.

Antidemocratic Counterpublics

Not all counterpublics are virtuous. Some of them are explicitly antidemocratic and antiegalitarian. Even so, according to Fraser (1993), "these counterpublics emerge in response to exclusions within dominant publics [and they therefore] help expand discursive space" (p. 15). For Fraser, "widening discursive contestation is in fact a good thing in stratified societies" (p. 15). But the counterpublics provoked by hot talk on hate radio demonstrate the opposite. On such programs, the homeless are derided, women are labeled *feminazis,* and teen mothers are animal-like "breeders" with no sense of shared humanity. When it presents subordinated groups as Other, hate radio denies their basic right to human dignity. Even though hate radio is a counterforum to the dominant public sphere, it does not expand discursive space. Hate radio functions in contemporary United States to narrow debate. When the hosts of hate radio blame women, the poor, and minorities for the country's ills, they further obscure the systemic economic and political reasons for the social decline they so profitably exploit. It is not enough to be simply reactive as a method of "expanding discursive space."

In fact, the relationship between such counterpublics and the broader public sphere is, in most cases, not one of contestation at all. The discursive foundation for radio hot talk was firmly set in place by mainstream media discourse. Take for example, the rhetoric of right-wing radio host Rush Limbaugh (1992), "The poor in this country are the biggest piglets at the mother pig and her nipples. The poor feed off the largesse of this government and they give nothing back. Nothing" (p. 41).[15] Such language is only a little further down a continuum of dehumanized, gendered media images that serve to discredit government entitlements to poor women.

Hot talk is often an open attempt to annihilate the social identities of groups targeted. Much of hate radio is formatted with "nonguested confrontation." The lack of an actually existing subject facilitates the construction of Otherness. "The host is free to pontificate, entertain and intimidate to his heart's content—with no guests and only a few heavily screened callers to challenge whatever he might say" (Talbot, 1995, p. 42).

The impact of such polemics on our relationships with ourselves and others is socially destructive. Cooper (1991), following Foucault, explains that "for the polemicist, the game consists in abolishing the partner" rather than "recognizing him as a subject with a right to speak" (p. 38). For example, Foucault (1984b) characterizes the polemicist as the opposite of a participant in dialogue and asks,

> Has anyone ever seen a new idea come out of a polemic? One gesticulates: anathemas, excommunications, condemnations, battles, victories, and defeats are no more than ways of speaking after all. And yet in the order of discourse, they are also ways of acting that are not without consequences. (pp. 382-383)

Such polemical discourse pushes the broader media dialogue toward more titillating and extreme positions to compete for audiences.

The polemical discourse of Otherness facilitates the assignment of blame to subordinated groups. It deflects discussion away from global economic transformations and corporate practices that have accelerated unemployment and a falling standard of living for working-class white men (the group that composes the largest segment of the counterpublic for hate radio).

Arguing from another perspective, Condit (1987) asserts that warlike discourse is not so threatening, because ultimately the public explanation for actions must always be expressible in the form of the common interest. But the aggressive dehumanizing discourse of scapegoating is most often justified in terms that appeal to the general good. Cutting state, federal, and municipal budgets is done with rhetorical flourish in the interest of every taxpaying citizen. Withholding social entitlements from poor mothers of color is justified by appealing to the larger public interest. Therefore, for democratic practice, the common good must be defined to include subordinated members. The language of dehumanization and blame prevents such inclusion. It also mystifies actual economic and political practices. In doing so, the incendiary discourse of hate radio works against the common good by directing public efforts away from real political solutions to social problems.

The political discussions and social sentiment in favor of cutting social entitlements to poor women (instead of cutting various corporate welfare programs, for example)[16] are not done in an inclusive or egalitarian discursive environment. Such harsh public actions targeting subordinated groups require a polemical discourse that dehumanizes minority members, women, and the poor. The language of exclusion denies basic human dignity and social belonging and justifies policies that worsen their social and economic situations. And the articulation of public interest is in fact part of that configuration. Polemics is a necessary prerequisite for political actions against subordinated groups. Discursive dehumanization is essential for the maintenance of stratification and social inequality and as such is a pivotal site for establishing an ethical perspective.

According to Fraser (1993), at some point, multiple publics must come together in interpublic discourse, within "a more comprehensive arena in which members of different, more limited publics talk across lines of cultural diversity" (p. 17). The public sphere, then, is a sphere in which diverse groups with well-developed values, rhetorics, and styles talk to one another, wherein not bracketing their differences but recognizing them. Fraser posits the possibility of such a multicultural discourse, as "not in principle impossible" (p. 17). But she offers few thoughts on how such communication could be achieved, other then to say it would require "multicultural literacy" (pp. 17-18).

The Need for a Discursive Ethics

It is precisely the ethical approach to discursive practice that is at issue with the notion of multicultural literacy. An ethical perspective, one that values human dignity and embraces difference without designating Otherness, would allow groups to find common interests and bonds. Fraser (1993) calls for theorizing the contestatory interaction of different publics to "identify the mechanisms that render some of them subordinate to others" (p. 18). Certainly, the language, themes, and narrative constructions that dehumanize the poor, women, and minorities can be defined as communicative mechanisms that render some subordinate to others. The need for a discursive ethics that recognizes the common humanity of those at the bottom of stratified societies ought to be underscored. Indeed, the recognition that they are members of publics, and that they are socially connected members of the human family, must be a basic premise for ethical literacy. Such a perspective would counter the increasingly common discursive practice of stigmatizing poor women as deviant individuals outside our shared humanity.

Fraser (1993), among other theorists, is critical of liberal political theory in general and the prevalent assumption that a democratic form of political life can be organized while leaving in place the "socioeconomic and sociosexual structures that generate systemic inequalities" (p. 12). Ultimately, she rejects as idealistic the contention that social inequality can be bracketed and argues that "it is a necessary condition for participatory parity that systemic social inequalities be eliminated" (p. 12).

Certainly, abolishing social and economic inequality is the ultimate purpose, and critical theorizing generally seeks to find pathways in democratic practice intended to reach that goal. But without actively asserting the need for the precondition of discursive parity, how will it be possible to find the pathways to achieve equality? In other words, how can social injustice be eliminated given an entrenched media environment that facilitates the maintenance of structural inequality through dehumanization, blame, and hate? In actually existing U.S. democracy, the mass media serve as the broad public sphere, the space Fraser has defined as interpublic discourse. Therefore, a discursive ethics (in Fraser's terms, multicultural literacy) of media practice is essential.

For the discourse of scapegoating to resonate at a particular historical moment, two basic preconditions must be at play in public discourse: a restricted media environment and the discourse of dehumanization. First, information available to the public to understand actual economic and political practices must be restricted. This is indeed the case in the U.S. media. During the last two decades, a succession of media mergers has taken place. From Capitol Cities-ABC-Disney to the Time-Warner-Turner mergers, each was progressively larger, each setting yet another historical precedent. Presently, less than 20 corporations control the vast media industry. It comes as no surprise that during the same time corporate ownership and control of the media took place, information critical of corporate America has become harder to find on the news agenda.[17] Increased commercial influences from marketing and advertising strategies have also served to weaken independent coverage critical of economic practices and corporate activities (see Andersen, 1995). Such economic censorship has resulted in the piecemeal reporting of economic data and corporate practices, delinked from a broader framework of understanding. Fulfilling the mandate for a broad, uninhibited, and inclusive public discourse—in that sense, part of the Enlightenment model—remains an essential goal. Also, broadening the spectrum of representation both for policy discussions as well as for welfare recipients would help alleviate the present injustice and imbalance.

The loss of media diversity creates public anxiety and sets the stage for scapegoating. In place of knowledge about the economic contradictions of capitalist democracy, subordinated groups are blamed for economic decline through dehumanized depictions. The media, especially hate radio demagogues, provide easy "explanations" to a set of complex and confusing problems. Such explanations serve to maintain current economic and political structures in the face of increasing hardship for the majority. As Sklar (1995) points out, "the military budget continues consuming resources at Cold War levels, while programs to invest in people, infrastructure, and the environment are sacrificed" (p. 50). But such persuasive justifications require the demonization of the "non-people," the discursive construction of "otherness." A discursive ethics requires expanding Enlightenment conceptions of language and citizenship. No longer conceived only as the rational exchange of information in the public sphere, language is understood as part of the discursive formation of subjectivity. Formulating discursive subjectivity questions the assumption of rationality, both regarding information and citizenship. It provides an ethical approach able to address issues of stereotyping and visual association, dehumanization, and polemical discourse.

Given this formulation, communication must be viewed as a focal point for ethical concern. The contours of public debate must be guided by a discursive ethical practice able to confer basic human dignity on all members of society. Such an ethical protonorm would allow democratic participation and deliberation to flourish in U.S. democratic society.

Ethical Protonorms

The media coverage of welfare recipients and the welfare debate amounts to some sort of symbolic "cleansing" of U.S. society. Young mothers of color are paraded like the "enemies" of society and treated like a sore on the body politic that should be removed. The problematic moral consequences of dehumanization become even more serious if the mass media's role as social legitimizer is taken into consideration. If lies, prejudice, and even hate are uttered publicly, and, as it were, in a media chorus, the public is likely to adopt the same attitudes and display similar behavior. Such a discursive context reinforces a public sensibility in which dehumanization is encouraged and therefore amplified.

Once the very humanity of socially marginalized groups is denigrated, the ethical problems become staggering. No patchwork media reform movement can substantially change the situation. It shows a gaping moral void that needs to be filled with three fundamental principles of ethical reasoning, namely, respect for human dignity, acceptance of the Other, and active solidarity with the weak and vulnerable.

Human dignity is a quality of life that is accorded or denied intersubjectively. It is based on the axiomatic principle that each human being has intrinsic value. This value is unaffected by class, status, or achievement, let alone gender, race, or age. Humans have dignity because of their very being, because of life itself, which is never a means but always an end in its own terms.

Intersubjectivity makes life specifically human. No ontological understanding of the human being is possible outside the web of relationships with others. The role of language in establishing those relationships is fundamental. Thus, the concept of human dignity is intimately related to communication practice as a way of confirming life-in-common. Human dignity therefore exists collectively and includes the right to belong and participate, as well as the right to be acknowledged with respect in public dialogue.

Speaking of rights, however, typically obscures the notion of dignity. Rights are normally minimally defined and seen as primarily pertaining to individuals. Human dignity, in contrast, envisions life in its social context, as an interdependent web of community relationships. Therefore, all acts of exclusion and excommunication—including symbolic media practices—are contrary to the principle of human dignity. Regaining the sense of human dignity is a momentous ethical project but one well worth the effort.

The public discourse regarding single mothers receiving welfare benefits raises another fundamental issue: the existence of Others, and the acceptance (or lack of it) of their otherness. If human dignity refers to life-in-common, it must be realized that all communities and societies are characterized by diversity. There are the obvious biological differences of male-female, young-old, and black-white pigmentation of skin that are apparent to the naked eye; other more subtle distinctions are associated with class and culture. Human dignity must be acknowledged—that is, socially recognized—in the diversity of a community or society.

Media stereotypes present a formidable obstacle to the acceptance of a multifarious world. Media portrayals of mythic middle-class values, assiduously associated with whiteness, establishes a "social cosmology" that divides the world between us and them (Galtung, 1986). Thus, once again, those groups that do not fit into the social cosmology of the dominant are marginalized, ignored, or vilified. The ethics of intercultural discourse aims at reversing this trend. It is based on the conscious acknowledgment (presupposing knowledge and knowing) of Others as different yet fully accepting them in all their differences as persons. Those with whom one might not have a natural affinity are not to be merely tolerated but radically affirmed. The affirmation of the Other contains and constitutes a new liberating potential of life-in-common for all (Kovel, 1991).

Human dignity and the affirmation of the Other presuppose an active solidarity with those groups of people who count little or nothing in social life, including the life of the mass media. Again, the media have an inherent ethical problem in this respect. On the one hand, according to professional rules and news criteria, those in power (mostly white males) constitute reliable news sources. On the other hand, the glamorous and wealthy are predominantly the "stars" of entertainment, sports, and the glitzy world of product promotion—now the very fabric of TV itself. The poor, the marginalized, the weak and vulnerable are relegated to the (symbolic) gutters of street crime; drug abuse; and unsavory, overcrowded, urban tenements. Such visuals most often contextualize single mothers on welfare.

The litmus test of any civilization, past or present, is how it deals with the weak and vulnerable members of society. The term "civil society" is only superficially about the creation of a public sphere or an interpublic discourse. On a deeper level, civil society concerns the public's conscience and its expression. Civil society consists in essence of social movements that aim at improving social life for all but particularly for those at society's margins.

All civilized societies assume in principle that those in authority and power—that is, government and its institutions—have the sacred duty to ameliorate social and economic inequalities. If that assumption is nullified, civilization has lost its sense of justice. Thus the ethical project before civil society and its public voices is nothing less than regaining society's very heart.

The analysis of the public discourse about welfare recipients in the United States, with its concentration on single mothers of African American or Latino origin, and the ethical questions resulting from this discourse need to be put into a wider perspective. Women on welfare are just one— albeit new and dramatic—manifestation of a general tendency in U.S. media representations. This trend has been analyzed since 1969 by the Cultural Indicators' Project of the Annenberg School for Communications at the University of Pennsylvania. This research has identified "heroes and villains" and "winners and losers" on prime-time television:

> A disproportionate number of ill-fated characters comes from the ranks of poor, Latino and foreign men, and both old and young Afro-Americans, and poor women. At the bottom of Fate's "pecking order" are characters portrayed as old women and mentally ill, perpetuating stigma of the most dangerous kind. . . . The world of television seems to be frozen in a time-warp of obsolete and damaging representations. (Gerbner, 1994, pp. 43-44)

Television projects a power structure that is based on gender, class, ethnicity, age, and disability. Morally, it is a problem of denial and of social annihilation. The tacit implication is that such people should not exist. The dehumanized narratives of exclusion symbolically annihilate poor young mothers as the flawed victims for whom all hope is lost.

Every discourse begins and ends with the question, discourse for what? Discourse ethics is based on three pillars or ethical protonorms: the realization of human dignity for all; the acceptance of the Other as one of us; and the active commitment to, and solidarity with, those at the margins of society.

Notes

1. See Sennott (1994a); cited in Williams (1995).

2. The article also noted that Ventura was pregnant with her seventh child and that it was "unknown whether the baby was fathered by one of the four men with whom she already had children."

3. Study cited in Williams (1995, p. 1172, supra note 69).

4. Peter D. Hart Research Associates (1993), "A National Survey of Voter Attitudes Toward Poverty and Welfare Reform T19," cited in Williams (1995, p. 1172, supra note 69).

5. The average AFDC family size dropped 28% since 1969, and 72.7% of all AFDC families have 2 children or less. Many thanks to Kim Christensen, an expert on the political economy of women, for my understanding of this topic.

6. In fact, in real economic terms, AFDC benefits have fallen by 43% since 1970.

7. The front page of *The New York Times* carried Proctor and Gamble's announcement "to eliminate 13,000 jobs during a year of record earnings" (Uchitelle, 1993, p. A1). Explaining that in the current economic climate it was impossible to raise prices to keep profits high, workers would have to be eliminated. The action "called attention to a surprising aspect of America's job crisis: Profitable companies with booming sales are shedding jobs" (Uchitelle, 1993, p. A1). Proctor and Gamble illustrate a practice that has become daily regimen at many profitable U.S. companies. General Electric, for example, beginning in 1981, laid off 25% of its work force, over 100,000 employees. As Lee and Solomon (1990) observed, "these cutbacks occurred at a time when the company was earning record profits" (p. 77).

8. Throughout the 1980s, higher-paying manufacturing jobs were replaced with low wage and part-time positions. Job loss is now considered permanent, not temporary, and the number of job openings available to an unemployed worker has declined by 37% since 1984 (Uchitelle, 1993, p. D3).

9. U.S. economic disparity is exemplified by the income inequality between U.S. CEOs and workers. The average CEO "earned" as much as 41 factory workers in 1960. By 1992, it took 157 factory workers to make what is paid the average corporate executive.

10. On April 17, 1995, another front page article in *The New York Times* announced, "Gap in Wealth in U.S. Called Highest in West" (Nasar, 1992, p. A1).

11. For example,

> Governor Weld of Massachusetts sent copies of news reports about the Ventura Family to all legislators to underscore the need for welfare reform. A few months later, speaking to a conservative Washington think tank, he began a keynote address to proposing welfare cuts with the Ventura story. (Quoted in Williams, 1995, p. 1188)

12. When Massachusetts State Representative Marjorie Clapprood testified before a Joint Committee on Human Services describing her experience as a child whose mother received AFDC on her behalf, it did not resonate and was giving little media fanfare.

13. Not counting welfare recipients, 77% of the sources were men.

14. For example, Williams (1995, p. 1165, supra note 36) cites a case in which images of garbage and clutter strewn about the apartment of one welfare family were accompanied by text proclaiming that they lived like animals. The chaos and mess, however, was largely due to police activity.

15. During his many hours on the air on a variety of radio and TV programs, Limbaugh has used this metaphor over and over with a few variations, including calling for the replacement of the eagle as the national mascot with a huge sow that has a lot of nipples and a bunch of fat little piglets hanging on them.

16. In a rare editorial (published after Republicans won the U.S. congress in 1994), *Business Week,* as quoted in Sklar (1995), noted that "Western Republican senators hollered about the millions in the crime bill that went to midnight basketball. . . . But they defend the tens of billions that subsidize ranching, mining, and lumbering every year" (pp. 53-54).

17. This relationship is demonstrated by Professor Carl Jensen's (1993) ongoing Project Censored. The majority of the top 25 censored news stories for 1992 dealt with issues critical of corporate practices. Through restricted coverage of corporate practices and malfeasance, from toxic dumping, to the blackout of news about the electric car, journalists and editors have pulled away from their historical role of keeping big business accountable to the public.

References

Alter, Jonathan. (1994, December 12). The name of the game is shame. *Newsweek,* p. 41.

Alter, Jonathan, & Wingert, Pat. (1995, February 6). The return of shame. *Newsweek,* pp. 21-24.

Andersen, Robin. (1995). *Consumer culture and TV programming.* Boulder, CO: Westview.

Aucion, Don. (1994, June 2). Religious leaders urge senate to reject welfare benefits cuts. *Boston Globe,* p. 27.

Barney, Ralph. (1986). The journalist and a pluralistic society: An ethical approach. In Deni Elliott (Ed.), *Responsible journalism* (pp. 60-80). London: Sage.

Bergmann, Barbara, & Hartmann, Heidi. (1995, May 1). A program to help working parents. *The Nation, 260*(17), 592-595.

Cabreros-Sud, Veena. (1994, November/December). News flash: Poor mothers on crime spree! *EXTRA!, 6*(7) 12-13.

Carr, Howie. (1994, February 21). Ventura family tree sinks roots in rich welfare soil. *Boston Herald,* p. 8.

Condit, Celeste Michelle. (1987). Crafting virtue: The rhetorical construction of public morality. *Quarterly Journal of Speech, 73,* 79-97.

Cooper, Martha. (1991). Ethical dimensions of political advocacy from a postmodern perspective. In Robert E. Denton, Jr., (Ed.), *Ethical dimensions of political communication* (pp. 23-47). New York: Praeger.

Duncan, Greg, & Hill, Martha. (1988, January). Welfare dependence within and across generations. *Science,* 467-469.

Flanders, Laura, & Janine Jackson. (1995, May/June). Public enemy no. 1? *EXTRA!, 8*(3), 13-16.

Foucault, Michel. (1984a). On the genealogy of ethics: An overview of work in progress. In Paul Rabinow (Ed.), *The Foucault reader* (pp. 340-372). New York: Pantheon.

Foucault, Michel. (1984b). *Polemics, politics, and problemization.* In Paul Robinow (Ed.), *The Foucault reader* (pp. 381-390). New York: Pantheon.

Fraser, Nancy. (1989). *Unruly practices: Power, discourse and gender in contemporary social theory.* Minneapolis: University of Minnesota Press.

Fraser, Nancy. (1993). Rethinking the public sphere: A contribution to the critique of actually existing democracy. In Bruce Robbins (Ed.), *The phantom public sphere* (pp. 1-32). Minneapolis: University of Minnesota Press.

Galtung, Johan. (l986). Social communication and global problems. In Philip Lee (Ed.), *Communication for all* (pp. 3-l5). Maryknoll, NY: Orbis.

Gerbner, George. (1994). Women and minorities on TV: A study of casting and fate. *Media Development, 41*(2), 38-44.

Goodman, Ellen. (1992, April 16). Welfare mothers with an attitude. *Boston Globe,* p. 19.

Herbert, Bob. (1993, September 8). No job, no dream. *The New York Times,* p. A23.

Hutchinson, Bill. (1994, February 15). Welfare gone wrong. *Boston Herald,* pp. 5-6.

Jensen, Carl. (1993). *Censored: The news that didn't make it and why.* Chapel Hill, NC: Shelburne.

Kovel, Joel. (1991). *History and spirit: An inquiry into the philosophy of liberation.* Boston: Beacon.

Kovel, Joel. (1995, May). *Ecological Marxism and dialectic.* Paper presented at Cultural Studies Seminar, Fordham University, Bronx, New York.

Landes, Joan. (1988). *Women and the public sphere in the age of the French Revolution.* Ithaca, NY: Cornell University Press.

Lee, Martin A., & Solomon, Norman. (1990). *Unreliable sources: A guide to detecting bias in news media.* New York: Carol.

Limbaugh, Rush. (1992). *The way things ought to be.* New York: Pocket Star.

Nahata, Renu. (1992, July/August). Too many kids and too much money: Persistent media myths about welfare. *EXTRA!, 5*(5), 18.

Nasar, Sylvia. (1992, March 5). The 1980s: A very good time for the very rich. *New York Times,* pp. A1, D24.

Polakow, Valerie. (1995, May 1). On a tightrope without a net. *The Nation, 260*(17), 590-592.

Schor, Juliet. (1992). *The overworked American.* New York: Basic Books.

Sennott, Charles M. (1994a, February 16). Abuse suspect fought drugs, other woes. *Boston Globe,* p. 18.

Sennott, Charles M. (1994b, February 20). Finding four generations sustained by welfare. *Boston Globe,* pp. 1, 46.

Sklar, Holly. (1995, May). The snake oil of scapegoating. *Z Magazine, 8*(5), 49-56.

Talbot, Stephen. (1995, June). Wizard of ooze. *Mother Jones,* pp. 41-43.

Uchitelle, Louis. (1993, July 26). Strong companies are joining trend to eliminate jobs. *The New York Times,* pp. A1, D3.

Williams, Lucy. (1995, June). Race, rat bites and unfit mothers: How media discourse informs the welfare legislation debate. *Fordham Urban Law Journal, 22*(4), 1159-1196.

Conclusion: An Ethics of Communication Worthy of Human Beings

MICHAEL TRABER

One of the characteristics of the preceding chapters is their grounding in human nature and personhood. Their arguments are based on genuine humanism—in the sense that the very essence of human created-ness defines the horizon of people's moral stance. To be human is being moral; to be moral is being human. Morality means conduct befitting human beings.

A second feature of this book's approach to communication ethics is its social dimension. Humans are social beings. They cannot but be members of communities and societies. The good life of the individual cannot, ultimately, be realized unless it is at least intended or envisaged for all members of a society. The good life, therefore, encompasses a vision of the good society.[1] Communication ethics always envisages social justice.

A third theme that runs through most chapters of this book is the question of freedom in solidarity. Freedom, an essential attribute of the human being, encounters in communication the freedom of others. Without the acknowledgment of mutual freedom, no genuine communication is possible. Communicative freedom, however, can only blossom in solidarity: that is, in an attitude of responsibility for each other. The claim of unassailable freedom in universal solidarity is one of the most vexing questions in contemporary ethical discourse.

Fourth, the cross-cultural approach is the hallmark of this book. It attempts to situate ethical protonorms of communication in different, particularly non-Western, cultures. This approach, however, is not ethnographic but philosophical. It asks, how do different cultures reveal such protonorms about communication and, more important, how are these norms connected to the nature of human beings?

These four insights emerging from the chapters of this book should not be seen as a summary of their contents. The rich and variegated understanding of ethical protonorms of different cultures cannot possibly be summed up in a few pages. The four themes merely highlight the central arguments in the debate about a communication ethics that is based on universal human values.

The four themes shall now be discussed in turn. But teasing out the essence of the arguments is one thing. Analyzing them in terms of their applicability to real-life world practice is another. The ultimate test of the validity of ethical protonorms lies in their relevance for practical principles that can guide everyday human interaction, including the purposeful interactions of mass communication practitioners and their counterparts, mass media users.

Communications Befitting Human Beings

Until around the middle of the 18th century, communication was a comparatively straightforward matter. The communities to which people belonged were geographically circumscribed, and the print media—books and newspapers—were the prerogative of the elite. The technical means of electronic communication had not yet been developed. Communication ethics has reflected this situation; it has been confined principally to interpersonal communication.

The world of interpersonal face-to-face communication, as distinct from the mass media, is depicted in several chapters of this book. Thus, the question arises whether interpersonal communication is a solid enough base on which to construct a communication ethics for the modern world of mass media. When lying is seen as unnatural, as evidenced by the bodily reaction that can be measured by a lie detector, is it then reasonable to assume that broadcasters or advertising copy writers also blush when telling lies? As Jürgen Wilke (1992) points out,

> [That] mass communication is mostly indirect and one-way communication is of structural importance. Although forms of two-way communication have increased, journalists and audiences are largely separated from each other. This also has consequences for the journalists' professional ethics. People feel less bound to persons they do not know personally. . . . Therefore, mass communication needs a form of ethics that is still applicable even if certain effects on the audience cannot be observed directly. (pp. 4-5)

The contributors to this book argue that when humans engage in their most natural and most essential activity, communication, certain ethical principles are nonnegotiable. This position assumes that mass communication is first and foremost communication rather than a media product. When media are seen primarily as commodities for sale, similar to sugar and soap, they surreptitiously escape the field of moral judgment. Coupled with this widespread trend of commoditizing of the media (Hamelink, 1994, pp. 7-9), audiences are relegated into passivity. As Raboy and Dagenais (1992) observe,

> Can we claim that "being there" through the eye of the camera (as in Beijing, and so forth) provides meaningful information, usable in the exercise of democratic citizenship? For local populations perhaps. If publics were to be informed of pending political choices, rather than after the fact, their intervention could perhaps influence these choices. As it is, we are allowed to see only that which we can no longer do more than absorb. This is consumerism in its purest form. (p. 60)

There is a further assumption behind the consumerist view of the mass media, namely, that they are value-free. This is constantly suggested by reference to consumer choice. The moral burden, as it were, is then put on audiences, whereas the media go scot-free: they are only offering choices. It may be worth recalling that the large-scale study by the National Institute for Mental Health (1982), combining more than 2,500 research projects, concluded that U.S. television is indeed a source of values. U.S. television, and most television elsewhere, is steeped in values that are ideologically determined, as Robin Andersen's chapter illustrates.

Regardless of these truly de-moralizing trends, there is no escape from the fact that communications, both interpersonal and mass mediated, are human actions and therefore, like all other human actions, subject to ethical norms. But acting is not the same as doing. Journalists, for example, use technical know-how in the construction of stories; they use journalistic techniques. As such, techniques belong to the realm of doing, like the work of all other artisans. But if journalistic techniques are developed in ways that condition and co-determine the contents of the messages, they become part of acting, that is, part of the intended interaction with others. The so-called professional criteria for news (timeliness, conflict, importance of persons, and so forth) are examples of this. They may serve as a quick reference guide for the selection of news and are therefore techniques. But at the same time, they select the situations worthy of reporting (conflicts, accidents) and choose VIPs as the prime social actors, often to the exclusion of others (mainly women, children, and manual laborers). Thus, the willfully chosen "criteria" of news are not merely techniques but indeed part of human actions.

Communications as human actions are grounded in the very nature of human beings, or the *humanum*. What distinguishes human beings from other animals is their ability to use language. Aristotle already made the distinction between sound and language. Whereas other animals may utter sounds to express pain or lust, only humans possess language that they use "to tell each other what is good and bad, and what is just and unjust" (*Politics* I,2 1253a 16; see also Pfürtner, 1992, p. 39). Language then is essential for the *humanum,* containing, as it does, the potential for a full development of human nature, both for individuals and groups or communities.

Language makes relationships possible. Relationships are based on the exchange of experiences, of joys and anxieties, of hopes and fears, of commitments and admissions of failure. Such sharing includes information about the world we live in, which is usually presented in story form. But communication is always more than just information. In the stories we tell each other about the world in which we live, we participate in the lives of others. Not all communication, however, is life enhancing. There is communication that de-humanizes. The task of ethics is to reflect on, and subject to reason, the life-enhancing and dehumanizing acts of communications, both interpersonal and mass mediated.

The acknowledgment through communication of a person's human dignity is minimally defined by laws in most, if not all, cultures. Each person is entitled to a good reputation or honor. Any statement, hint, or suggestion that a person's character is disreputable or his or her behavior dishonorable are subject to laws covering defamation and slander. An ethical protonorm, namely human dignity, has been translated into a legal framework with practically universal application.

Similarly, most countries have laws prohibiting, to various degrees, the publication or exposure in public of sexual acts that are likely to offend the public. Obscenity laws intend to protect against abuse what is most personal and private in peoples' lives, their sexual intimacies. But more fundamentally, they aim at safeguarding, again minimally, the respect owed to all women, men, and children by virtue of their human dignity.

These examples, however, also illustrate the ethical dilemmas of our time. Libel cases now center on the cost of litigation rather than the restoration of a person's reputation. The media, not merely the lawyers, are partly to blame for this. As the University of Iowa study on libel and the press shows (see Christians, Ferré, & Fackler, 1993, pp. 73-74), many plaintiffs originally wanted an apology or correction by the media. When the media refused that, they contacted a lawyer. The question of compensation then takes over, and the moral dimension of a person's injured reputation moves backstage.

Similarly, pornography Many magazine editors and media proprietors are pushing the pornographic pose and content to the limit, testing what might still be permissible under the law. They totally miss the point about human dignity nor are they concerned about the likely offense to the public. Obscenity laws can therefore be counterproductive. Rather than stopping violations of human dignity, which is their ultimate raison d'être, various media have become obsessed by sexuality. The dignity of women and men is now under sustained media attack.

These examples show that laws, to say the least, are unsatisfactory guides to morally appropriate behavior. Ethics allows for no shortcuts. Ethical principles are either grasped and acknowledged in full for what they are and meant to be, or they turn into moral charades, adding insult to injury.

Communication Ethics Is Social Ethics

Communication is by definition oriented toward others; it is an intersubjective, dialogic process. And mass communications, by virtue of their public roles, are a public service that is essential to the community and society of which they are part. The MacBride Report (*Many Voices, One World,* MacBride, 1980, p. 34) compares communication with the nervous system. If the nervous system breaks down, proper coordination in the body is no longer possible, pain is no longer registered, the body becomes dysfunctional. Communications in modern democratic societies play a similar role: When public communications fall below a certain minimum level, societies start disintegrating. According to Selbourne (1994), communication is "the only means to maintain the discourse between citizens without which the civic bond itself is mute" (p. 212). Selbourne explains:

> When the excessive power of particular interest in the control and dissemination of information is able, in free pursuit of such interest, to impose upon the sovereign civic order systematic falsehood, or values which degrade the citizen who receives such information, the civic order, under its duty of self-protection and protection of the citizen, is obligated to prevent such abuse. (p. 213)

For Selbourne (1994), "civic order is both ethically and historically prior to the state, whose interests the latter must serve: and the moral status of the citizen-body and its collective power greater than that of the state, however armed" (p. 90). When communication's role in society and the moral status of civil society are interpreted in such a way, communication ethics takes on a new profile. Individual ethics that is concerned with principles that guide individual actions and refer to questions of personal choice is unable to cope with mass mediated communication. One of the problems of communication ethics is that considerably more attention has been given to individual than to social ethics. This has meant that many institutional practices of the mass media have not been subjected to as critical an ethical discernment as have individual practices. Social ethics develops principles that guide institutional and societal morality and refer to issues of social policy.

A social ethic of communication is the very opposite of the economic-industrial rationality that is commonly applied to the mass media—the pursuit of profit, technological efficiency and effectiveness, and competition in the economic marketplace. In contrast, social ethics of communication is based on a *social* rationale or raison d'être, of the mass media:

- They are primarily a service to their publics, to which they are ultimately accountable;
- They are holistic, relating to the whole person in the whole community and the whole of society, treating audiences as people rather than objects; and
- They are committed to social justice, which means exposing injustices and cultivating active solidarity with the marginalized and disadvantaged sectors of society.

Social ethics, among other things, is concerned with the mass media as institutions and communication as part of social systems. One of the arguments frequently advanced against communication ethics is that the mass media are not guided by persons who can make independent choices and take autonomous actions. Instead, they operate as an intricate network of interrelated roles and functions for the sake of an integrated process. The media are therefore considered institutional systems beyond the reach of individual morality (see, e.g., Saxer, 1992).

Boventer (1986) comes to the conclusion that "journalism functions largely as a self-sufficient and self-centered organizational structure . . . which is reminiscent of feudalism rather than democracy" (p. 253). Feudalism refers to the media's relationships with the power elites. "They agree upon their mutual interests without being held responsible for them" (p. 254).

We therefore have to distinguish between the mass media's institutional working procedures and their systems of power in a societal context. The first, as explained earlier, belongs to the realm of techniques, the second to the sphere of morality; but both are interconnected. Social ethics subjects mass media systems to moral reasoning in so far as they address their publics, that is, as acts of communication. It is the relational rather than the technical aspects of media enterprises that are the concern of ethics. In addition, social ethics scrutinizes the mass media about the type of society that they project, often implicitly. If they hold up a mirror of society in which, for example, the weak and vulnerable hardly exist, or in which women have no say, or where money is the highest good, then moral choices about society have been made. These choices are translated into policy decisions. And such decisions are made by policy makers. It is precisely in the field of policy making that the protonorms of communication ethics are crucial.

Based on principles that consider being-in-community as essentially human, social ethics aims at the transformation of society. "The theory of media ethics that we advocate . . . makes transformative social change the end. . . . It gives priority to civic transformation as the press's occupational norm" (Christians et al., 1993, p. 14). Social ethics, therefore, gives the media a new meaning and allots them a central place in society. This cannot be dismissed as advocacy journalism. It flows directly from the duty that the mass media owe their communities and societies. This duty, however, implies dialogue. Rather than proposing a sociopolitical program of action, the media are to tease out the views of their audiences on the type of society in which they want to live and the type of social order they hope to bequeath to their children. Christians et al. (1993) call them normative communities:

> Nurturing communitarian citizenship entails, at a minimum, a journalism committed to justice, covenant and empowerment. Authentic communities are marked by justice; in strong democracies, courageous talk is mobilized into action. Covenant bonds rather than contractual calculations make genuine community possible. In normative communities, citizens are empowered for social transformation, not merely freed from external constraints, as classical liberalism insisted. (p. 14)

Social ethics does not abrogate or suspend individual ethics. Media workers, together or alone, still make dozens of moral decisions every day. But these decisions assume added weight and importance if judged from the vantage point of social ethics.

Persons in Solidarity

Humans as social beings are meant to be with and for others. But humans are also persons, and as such are autonomous. Personhood signals the independent self and its freedom.[2]

Human freedom is axiological. It needs no proof. It is part of life experience and can only be reflected on. Reflection reveals that freedom is an integral part of human nature and thus a precondition for humans to be moral beings. Freedom makes all specifically *human* actions possible, including communications. It includes the possibility of self-determination and self-development. But the self that is to be developed directs us back to human nature. The rationale for freedom is to become more truly human and humane. Freedom is both part of being human and of becoming humane. "The range of choice open to the individual is not the decisive factor in determining the degree of human freedom, but *what* can be chosen and what *is* chosen by the individual" (Marcuse, 1968, p. 23).

In determining the object of choice, one should remember that humans are not born free. Humans take their places in already existing relationships, family relations included. Humans therefore encounter other freedoms, that is, the freedom of others. Freedom must accept other freedoms unconditionally rather than merely tolerating them. Freedom must seek out, and intentionally open up to, other freedoms. In brief, freedom is not oriented toward objects of desire but toward people. Only in the free encounter with others can genuine freedom be experienced.

The unconditional acknowledgment of the other's freedom takes place in symbolic structures. They are made up of stories, images, signs, laws, religions, and work practices that, taken together, are called culture. This symbol structure can enhance or limit freedom. Therefore, those who use the symbols have a duty to create and cultivate conditions whereby the freedom of all is commonly acknowledged and enhanced.

Communicative freedom always implies solidarity, a solidarity that is universal, that is, extends to all people and peoples. The reason for this does not lie in the fact that the present generation understands the interconnections between peoples in one world. Here, the concept of universality is based on the fundamental equality of all human beings and their identical claims to freedom. In the context of specific sociopolitical conditions, the abstract concept of universal solidarity becomes quite concrete. It is, above all, solidarity with those whose freedom has been taken away, or seriously diminished, thus rendering them less than human. In these cases, solidarity becomes, as it were, operational, that is, transforms itself into concrete communicative actions. Commenting on the work of Emmanuel Levinas, Christians (1995) describes this ethical transformation:

> In responding to the Other's need, the baseline for justice is established across the human race. Ethics is no longer a vassal of philosophical speculation, but is rooted in human existence. We seize our moral obligation and existential condition simultaneously. (p. 88)

Solidarity then is not so much a feeling as a particular way of being. The concept expresses

a sense of togetherness with others, a unity of interest . . . fighting together for an idea, an interest, for mutual help.

   Like all forms of communication, solidarity is of course situation-bound. It takes place within determined concrete conditions. In short, one is in solidarity with other people and subjects about a matter, in a situation. (Thomassen, 1985, p. 143)

If active solidarity means participating in the lives of those whom society has relegated to the gutters and ghettos, it also implies joint suffering and remembrance. Both suffering and remembering are existential. They connect past with present, they ascertain the causes of injustice and the scope of suffering, they are marked by the physical and symbolic annihilations of past and present, they are aware of guilt and call for repentance and restitution. Solidarity has an anamnestic quality. If solidarity of remembrance is used selectively, it contradicts itself. Anamnestic solidarity can only be applied universally.

Solidarity is also anticipatory; it is oriented toward generations still unborn. At a time when the consequences of science and technology can hardly be foreseen, when rearmament and militarist competition show no sign of abetting—despite rhetoric to the contrary and at a time when few dare to predict the future of basic social institutions such as the family or the future availability of natural resources due to the exploitation of the physical environment—at such times, a feeling of insecurity is spreading that generates fear of the future. Anticipatory solidarity, instead, aims at generating hope. It anticipates a world in which humane conditions for all prevail. It is engaged in the building and rebuilding of social and political structures that can best promote justice for all. Hope in the future and hope for all is the hallmark of universal solidarity.

Ultimately, solidarity is similar to love.

It is exclusively occasioned by the other person (or persons), and calculation of thought involving personal advantage ruins it. . . . It is unconditional respect of the other person(s). . . . It has an ethical definitiveness. It is a giving of oneself that is so unreserved that it excludes cognition and evaluation of the other person(s). And finally, it is an anonymous, suprapersonal force in our life that emerges as an undeserved gift—or grace. (Thomassen, 1985, p. 145)

Obviously, love entails much more than solidarity. But both love and solidarity are steeped in freedom and express an essential human condition, altruism. Altruism means to be directed toward the other. Like love, it is reciprocal. And both love and solidarity are a force for liberation—of self and other.

Universal Values in Different Cultures

A unique feature of this book is the recognition that ours is a multicultural world. This is not just a statement of fact but implicitly of values. Different cultures are the heritage of humankind and form a kaleidoscope through which we can look at human nature. What is essentially human can only be retrieved culturally, that is, by empathetic discernment and analysis of the culturally conditioned *humanum*. Any talk about universal values is meaningless unless they are culturally validated.

But culture can also become an ideology. The most widespread cultural ideology is that of the "superiority" of the Caucasian race, the apex of which supposedly are the Anglo-Saxon people of the North Atlantic. In Egypt, Sudan, and other parts of Africa, cultural ideology defends and makes "respectable" the genital mutilation of girls. Cultural ideologies, cutting across almost all nations, have dictated gender relationships and are invoked to justify the suppression of women. Cultural ideology had led to ethnic cleansing and, at its worst, to genocide.

One of the merits of the international human rights debate has been the exposure of cultural differences in the approach to rights. The most obvious difference lies in the very definition of human rights. In some cultures, only an individual can have rights, whereas in others, the emphasis is on group, community, and other collective rights. International human rights conferences have also highlighted the tensions between the "is" and the ethical "ought to be." There is a growing consensus that certain universal standards for the social accordance of human dignity must be upheld, regardless of cultural differences.

The debate about ethics and culture has brought to the fore the realization that personhood transcends all cultures. This is, in fact, the ground of ethics. Personhood implies the capacity of free choice, the ability to reflect and argue rationally, and the endowment of its inner and intrinsic worth. Personhood thus brings together freedom, rationality, and equality in dignity, all of which are ethically definitive characteristics of human beings. As to personhood's transcendence of culture, Fleischacker (1994) sums up the argument as follows:

> Morality concerns what people should do as people, rather than as Ibos, Italians, whites, Blacks, women, men or other subsets of people. Presumably, this claim derives in part from the overriding importance we attach to what we call "morality," on the assumption that what all people should do will naturally trump, in cases of conflict, what this or that subset of people should do. Above all, however, it points out a deep connection between the use of the word "moral" and the use of the word "person." For the universalist, that connection is immediate and clear: the moral "should" always applies to persons and never to types of persons. Most human groups with which we are familiar have a conception of how all human beings should behave, which may coincide with, or more probably will run alongside, their conception of what their members, in particular, should do. If the group believes that all people should do precisely as it does, we can call their entire code of behavior "morality." If not, we reserve the term for that part of the code they do universalize, and call the rest "manners," "folkways," "ritual," or the like. (p. 8)

The second ontologically constituting element of human nature, community, has already been discussed. What is at stake here, however, are the ways in which communities are organized in different cultures and the value systems that are relevant to them. The preceding case studies from Asia, Africa, and Native America are essentially communitarian, and their value systems are based on a communitarian ethics. But they also show a transitional character: Communitarian value systems are under assault by the assertion of individualism. In spite of this historical process—which is largely due to the spread of Western education and Western mass media—the communitarians have not lost the intellectual argument. There is indeed a counterweighing trend led by three intellectual movements: critical or cultural studies, feminist theory, and a new type of applied ethics (Christians, 1991, pp. 15-21). All three trends are represented in this book. Names associated with the first are Arens, Christians, Elliot, and Pasquali. Feminist theory is the framework of Robin Andersen's and Deni Elliott's chapters. Gomes, Jakubowicz, Takeichi, Tomaselli and Shepperson, and Wang show, albeit from widely different perspectives, that the journalistic profession has an intrinsically moral character. These chapters on applied ethics put functions and performance of media on an ethical scale and try to redefine the media's fundamental purpose.

The communitarian rationale is substantiated in several chapters of this book. Communication ethics is based on a definition of human nature that conceives of humans as members of a community. This does not simply mean that the community is supreme and that individuals have to subordinate themselves to it. It does, however, mean that there is a moral commitment to community, aiming at both civic order and civic transformation. Communication guided by communitarian social ethics provides a sense of certainty and direction rather than leaving community members in ambiguity and fear of chaos.

A precondition for being-in-community is truth-telling. Conviviality is only possible on the assumption that people are telling the truth, whereby mutual trust is possible. Both truth and trust are expressed in different ways across cultures. But truth-telling nevertheless remains the foundation on which relationships are maintained and cultivated. The protonorm of truth-telling is unchallenged by any culture. But as Dietmar Mieth's chapter shows, the application of this norm can be complex.

The communitarian principles of social ethics further locate communication in the field of social justice. No genuine conviviality is possible when social conditions persist that disrespect, marginalize, and oppress certain groups or sectors of the community. The mass media fail in their moral duty if they disregard this problem. But beyond that, solidarity means an active engagement in the struggle for a more just and more equitable social order, both nationally and internationally. The protonorm of universal solidarity is, therefore, derived from the very nature of social being. However, the ways in which the struggle for social justice is waged depends on situations, circumstances, and the demands of culture.

Just about everybody seems to agree with the ethical protonorm of human dignity, and yet our daily experiences—including mass mediated experiences—attest to the contrary practice. Why do people torture, maim, and kill—to single out just the grossest violations—when they are universally convinced that humans have a dignity of their own? Peter Berger (1979) addresses this paradox by referring, perhaps typically, to atrocities committed in non-Western countries.

> When we condemn the horrors inflicted on the people of Cambodia by [the Pol Pot] government, we need not do so by reference to Western values alone. Cambodia is a Buddhist country, and it is Buddhism that has as its highest moral tenet the "respect for all sentient beings." Similarly, the atroci-

ties inflicted on the Chinese people in the course of various Maoist experiments, such as the physical extermination of entire classes of the population or the separation of children from their parents, are not just violations of Western notions of morality; . . . rather, they are violations of the entire corpus of ethics of the Chinese tradition, which holds, among other things, that government should be "human-hearted" and that "filial piety" is one of the highest human goods. And if we pass moral judgment on a Muslim ruler . . . for acts of cruelty, we may do so, not alone in the name of the Judeo-Christian tradition, but in the name of the ethical core of Islam itself: every call to prayer, from every minaret from the Maghreb to Java, begins with an invocation of God who is *al-rahman al-rahim,* whose nature is to be compassionate and who has compassion, and who commands men to be compassionate also. (pp. 9-10)

There seem to be two reasons for the divergence between principle and practice. The first is the arrogance of state power with its monopoly of force. Governments or self-proclaimed quasi-governments abuse their powers of punishment and thus wantonly injure life. The second explanation is more subtle. Human dignity means that the human being is always an end in itself and never a means. Humans cannot become instruments for something else. When they are used, they are abused. In using others, we render them less than human. The argument of the ethnic cleansers and torturers is indeed that their victims are subhuman and therefore not deserving of respect or compassion.

This paradox can also be explained in terms of communication: When dialogue stops, violence starts. Violence is the ultimate failure of communication, both interpersonal and intergroup. If human beings refuse to enter into, or continue to maintain, a communicative relationship, that is, when the other is no longer considered an equal partner and when intersubjectivity wanes or disappears, humans condition themselves for using violence. Thus, every interpersonal and intergroup conflict can be analyzed in terms of its faulty communicative structure.

An ethical framework for human dignity is grounded in a universal culture of respect for life, which in turn is based on core values from many different and specific understandings of human dignity. Respect for life is unconditional and fundamental. It is not tied to achievement, age, gender, race, or class. It is life itself that is respectworthy. Although human life has a dignity of its own, as life, it is part of the web of life. It cannot be detached from animal life or plant life. The dignity of the created order must be affirmed in its totality.

All affirmation of human dignity takes place through various modes of communication: through intrapersonal reflections and interpersonal and social communications. As the mass media are an important source of meanings for many people, they contribute to our understanding of human dignity and respect for life. When their images and messages rob people of their dignity, we do not remain unaffected. The way they describe and depict acts of violence—from street crime to wars—are of special relevance. They disclose what life is worth and how human dignity is valued or devalued.

Conclusion

When speaking about universal human values, we do not use the word *universal* in a Kantian or even Habermasian sense. Nor do we think that universal values could be cross-culturally empirically verified. We are not dealing with a scientific or pseudoscientific generalization. The evidence that emerges from the chapters of this book is of a different nature. The chapters demonstrate that certain ethical protonorms—above all, truth-telling, commitment to justice, freedom in solidarity, and respect for human dignity—are validated as core values in communications in different cultures. These values are called universal not just because they hold true cross culturally; in fact, there may be cultures or there might be future cultures where such evidence is spurious. The universality of these values is beyond culture. It is rooted ontologically in the nature of human beings. It is by virtue of what it means to be human that these values are universal.

This implies another observation, namely, that regardless of culture, all human beings share the same nature. This is not an assumption but an observation that is self-evident. In the search for ethical universals, we are thus not primarily concerned with anthropology as a social science but with anthropology as a philosophical discipline. We are in search of the ultimate and unconditional characteristics of human life from which the meaning of human actions can be derived. Communication is one such act. It qualifies the entire human being.

Notes

1. *The Good Society* is the title of a forthcoming book of John Kenneth Galbraith. When asked what it would be like to live in a good society, Galbraith explained:

> To summarize: everybody has a sense of personal security, a basic income, basic health care, basic protection against unemployment, and we have a tolerant attitude toward immigration. We see the enormous importance of education, not purely in technical terms, but as a way of deepening the enjoyment of life. And going on to a sense of responsibility in the rich countries for what is happening in the poor countries. (*The Independent,* London, January 8, 1996, p. 11).

2. Here I am partly following the reflections of Thomas Pröpper (1995).

References

Berger, Peter. (1979). Are human rights universal? In Barry Rubin & Elizabeth Spiro (Eds.), *Human rights and U.S. foreign policy* (pp. 6-24). Boulder, CO: Westview.

Boventer, Hermann. (1986). New media: The morality of freedom and political education. *Communication, 9,* 247-269.

Christians, Clifford G. (1991). Communication ethics [Special issue]. *Communication research trends, 11*(4), pp. 1-31.

Christians, Clifford G. (1995). Communication ethics as the basis of genuine democracy. In Philip Lee (Ed.), *The democratization of communication* (pp. 75-91). Cardiff: University of Wales Press.

Christians, Clifford G., Ferré, John P., & Fackler, P. Mark. (1993). *Good news. Social ethics and the press.* New York: Oxford University Press.

Fleischacker, Samuel. (1994). *The ethics of culture.* Ithaca, NY: Cornell University Press.

Hamelink, Cees J. (1994). *Trends in world communication: On disempowerment and self-empowerment.* Malaysia: Southbound.

MacBride, Sean. (1980). *Many voices, one world* (Report by the International Commission for the Study of Communication Problems). New York: Unipub.

Marcuse, Herbert. (1968). *One dimensional man.* London: Sphere.

National Institute for Mental Health. (1982). *Television and behavior: Ten years of scientific progress and implications for the eighties.* Rockville, MD: U.S. Department of Health and Human Services.

Pfürtner, Stephan H. (1992). Zum Ethos offentlicher Kommunikation. In Adrian Holdereggger (Ed.), *Ethik der Medienkommunikation: Grundlagen* (pp. 17-50). Freiburg-Schweiz: Universitätsverlag.

Pröpper, Thomas. (1995). Autonomie und Solidarität: Begründungsprobleme sozielethischer Verpflichtung. In Edmund Arens (Ed.), *Anerkennung der Anderen: Eine Theologische Grunddimension interkultureller Kommunikation* (pp. 95-112). Freiburg, Germany: Herder.

Raboy, Marc, & Dagenais, Bernard. (1992). *Media, crisis and democracy: Mass communication and the disruption of social order.* London: Sage.

Saxer, Ulrich. (1992). Journalistische Ethik im elekronischen Zeitalter—eine Chimäre? In Adrian Holderegger (Ed.), *Ethik der Medienkommunikation: Grundlagen* (pp. 105-119). Freiburg, Germany: Herder.

Selbourne, David. (1994). *The principle of duty: An essay on the foundations of the civic order.* London: Sinclair-Stevenson.

Thomassen, Niels. (1985). *Communicative ethics in theory and practice.* London: Macmillan.

Wilke, Jürgen. (1992, August). *Professional ethics in journalism training.* Paper presented at the conference of the International Association of Mass Communication Research, Guarujá, Brazil.

Suggested Reading

Abourezk, James. (1977). *American Indian policy review commission*. Washington, DC: Government Printing Office.

Adams, Robert Merrihew. (1993). Religious ethics in a pluralistic society. In Gene Outka & John P. Reeder, Jr. (Eds.), *Prospects for a common morality* (pp. 93-113). Princeton, NJ: Princeton University Press.

Ahmad, Khurshid. (1976). *Islam: Its meaning and message*. London: The Islamic Foundation.

Alexy, Robert. (1978). Eine Theorie des Praktischen Diskurses. In Willy Oelmüller (Ed.), *Normenbegründung—Normendurchsetzung* (pp. 22-58). Paderborn, Germany: Schöningh.

Alexy, Robert. (1986). *Theorie der Grundrechte*. Frankfurt am Main: Suhrkamp.

Alter, Jonathan. (1994, December 12). The name of the game is shame. *Newsweek,* p. 41.

Alter, Jonathan, & Wingert, Pat. (1995, February 6). The return of shame. *Newsweek,* pp. 21-24.

Andersen, Robin. (1995). *Consumer culture and TV programming*. Boulder, CO: Westview.

Apel, Karl-Otto. (1973). *Transformation der Philosophie* (Vol. 2). Frankfurt am Main: Suhrkamp.

Apel, Karl-Otto. (1980). The a priori of the communication community and the foundations of ethics: The problem of a rational foundation of ethics in the scientific age. In *Towards a transformation of philosophy* (Trans., G. Adley & D. Frisby, pp. 225-300) [The International Library of Phenomenology and Moral Sciences]. London: Routledge & Kegan Paul.

Apel, Karl-Otto. (1980). *Towards a transformation of philosophy* (Trans., G. Adley & D. Frisby) [The International Library of Phenomenology and Moral Sciences]. London: Routledge & Kegan Paul.

Apel, Karl-Otto. (1987). Fallibilismus, Konsenstheorie der Wahrheit und Letztbegründung. In Forum für Philosophie Bad Homburg (Ed.), *Philosophie und Begründung* (pp. 116-211). Frankfurt am Main: Suhrkamp.

Apel, Karl-Otto. (1988). *Diskurs und Verantwortung: Das Problem des Übergangs zur postkonventionellen Moral*. Frankfurt am Main: Suhrkamp.

Apel, Karl-Otto. (1989). Normative Begründung der "Kritischen Theorie" durch Rekurs auf lebensweltliche Sittlichkeit? Ein transzendentalpragmatisch orientierter Versuch, mit Habermas gegen Habermas zu denken. In A. Honneth et al. (Eds.), *Zwischenbetrachtungen im Prozess der Aufklärung: Jürgen Habermas zum 60. Geburtstag* (pp. 15-65). Frankfurt am Main: Suhrkamp.

Apel, Karl-Otto. (1993). Das Anliegen des angloamerikanischen "Kommunitarismus" in der Sicht der Diskursethik. In M. Brumlik & H. Brunkhorst (Eds.), *Gemeinschaft und Gerechtigkeit* (pp. 149-172). Frankfurt am Main: Suhrkamp.

Apel, Karl-Otto. (1994a). C. S. Peirce and Post-Tarskian truth. In E. Mendieta (Ed.), *Selected essays: Vol. 1. Towards a transcendental semiotics* (pp. 175-206). Atlantic Highlands, NJ: Humanities Press.

Apel, Karl-Otto. (1994b). *Selected essays: Vol. 1. Towards a transcendental semiotics* (Ed., E. Mendieta). Atlantic Highlands, NJ: Humanities Press.

Apel, Karl-Otto. (1996). *Selected essays: Vol. 2. Ethics and the theory of rationality.* Atlantic Highlands, NJ: Humanities Press.

Apel, Karl-Otto, & Kettner, M. (Eds.). (1992). Diskursethik vor der Problematik von Recht und Politik: Können die Rationalitätsdifferenzen zwischen Moralität, Recht und Politik selbst noch durch die Diskursethik normativ-rational gerechtfertigt Werden? In K.-O. Apel & M. Kettner (Eds.), *Zur Anwendung der Diskursethik in Politik. Recht und Wissenschaft* (pp. 29-61). Frankfurt am Main: Suhrkamp.

Arab League. (1978). *Charter of Arab media.* Cairo: Arab League Press.

Arendt, Hannah. (1958). *The human condition.* Chicago: University of Chicago Press.

Arendt, Hannah. (1967). *Wahrheit und Lüge in der Politik.* Munich-Zürich: Piper Verlag.

Arens, Edmund. (1994). *The logic of pragmatic thinking: From Peirce to Habermas* (Trans., D. Smith). Atlantic Highlands, NJ: Humanities Press.

Arens, Edmund. (1995). *Christopraxis: A theology of action* (Trans., J. Hoffmeyer). Minneapolis, MN: Fortress.

Aristotle. (1942). *Nicomachean ethics* (Trans., W. D. Ross). London: Oxford University Press.

Aristotle. (1952). *Eudemian ethics* (Trans., H. Rackham). London: William Heinemann.

Armouti, M. (1982). *Communication development and society.* Irbid, Jordan: Yarmouk University Press.

Arnowitz, Stanley, & Giroux, Henry A. (1991). *Postmodern education: Politics, culture, and social criticism.* Minneapolis: University of Minnesota Press.

Arthur, Chris. (1989, October). Learning to be responsible for the media environment [Special issue]. *Media Development, 36,* 10-12.

Asch, Tim. (1979). Making a film record of the Yanomamo Indians of Southern Venezuela. *Perspectives of Film, 2,* 4-9.

Ashihara, Yoshinobu. (1992). *The hidden order.* Tokyo: Kondansha International.

Aucion, Don. (1994, June 2). Religious leaders urge senate to reject welfare benefits cuts. *Boston Globe,* p. 21.

Augustinus, Aurelius. (1953). *Die Lüge und Gegen die Lüge* (Ed., Paul Keseling). Würzburg: Augustinius Verlag.

Bailey, F. G. (1988). *Humbuggery and manipulation: The art of leadership.* Ithaca, NY: Cornell University Press.

Barney, Ralph. (1986). The journalist and a pluralistic society: An ethical approach. In Deni Elliott (Ed.), *Responsible journalism* (pp. 60-80). London: Sage.

Barnland, Dean C. (1989). *Communicative styles of Japanese and Americans.* Belmont, CA: Wadsworth.

Barroso, Pofirio. (Ed.). (1984). *Códigos Deontológicos de los Medios de Comunicación.* Madrid: Ed. Paulinas.

Baudrillard, Jean. (1983). *Simulations* (Trans., P. Foss, P. Patton, & P. Beitchman). New York: Semiotext(e).

Beasley, William G. (1990). *The rise of modern Japan.* Tokyo: Charles E. Tuttle.

Belsey, Andrew, & Chadwick, Ruth. (Eds.). (1992). *Ethical issues in journalism and the media.* London: Routledge.

Benhabib, Seyla. (1986). *Critique, norm, and utopia: A study of the foundations of critical theory.* New York: Columbia University Press.

Benhabib, Seyla. (1992). *Situating the self: Gender, community and postmodernism in contemporary ethics.* Cambridge, UK: Polity.

Benhabib, Seyla, & Dallamayr, Fred. (1990). *The communicative ethics controversy.* Cambridge, MA: MIT Press.

Berger, Peter. (1979). Are human rights universal?: In Barry Rubin & Elizabeth Spiro (Eds.), *Human rights and U.S. foreign policy* (pp. 6-24). Boulder, CO: Westview.

Bergmann, Barbara, & Hartmann, Heidi. (1995, May 1). A program to help working parents. *The Nation, 260* (17): 592-595.

Berkhofer, Robert F., Jr. (1978). *White man's Indian: Images of the American Indian from Columbus to the present.* New York: Vintage.

Bernstein, Richard J. (1986). *Philosophical profiles: Essays in a pragmatic mode.* Philadelphia: University of Pennsylvania Press.

Bien, Günther. (1900). Lüge. In *Historisches Wörterbuch der Philosophie* (pp. 533-544) (Vol. 5). Basel: Schwabe Verlag.

Blackburn, Simon. (1994). *The Oxford dictionary of philosophy.* Oxford, UK: Oxford University Press.

Bohere, G. (1984). *Profession: Journalist.* Geneva: International Labour Office.

Bok, Sissela. (1979). *Lying: Moral choice in public and private life.* New York: Random House Vintage Books.

Bok, Sissela. (1986). *Lügen: Vom täglichen Zwang zur Unaufrichtigkeit.* Hamburg: Rowohlt Verlag.

Bonhoeffer, Dietrich. (1977). *Ethics* (Ed., E. Bethge, 10th ed.). Munich: Kaiser Verlag.

Boventer, Hermann. (1986). New media: The morality of freedom and political education. *Communication, 9,* 247-269.

Boyd, Douglas. (1993). *Broadcasting in the Arab world: A survey of radio and television in the Middle East.* Philadelphia: Temple University Press.

Breckenridge, Carol A., & van der Veer, Peter. (1994). *Orientalism and the postcolonial predicament.* Delphi: Oxford University Press.

Brown, W. Norman. (1970). *Man in universe: Some continuities in Indian Thought.* Berkeley: University of California Press.

Buber, Martin. (1965). *Between man and man* (Trans., Ronald G. Smith). New York: Macmillan.

Buber, Martin. (1970). *I and thou [Ich und Du]* (Trans., Walter Kaufmann). New York: Scribner.

Büchele, Herwig. (1982). *Politik wider die Lüge: Zur Ethik der Öffentlichkeit.* Vienna: Europa Verlag.

Cabreros-Sud, Veena. (1994, November/December). News flash: Poor mothers on crime spree! *EXTRA!, 6*(7), 12-13.

Calhoun, C. (Ed.). (1992). *Habermas and the public sphere* [Studies in Contemporary German Social Thought]. Cambridge, MA: MIT Press.

Cámara, Helder. (1970). *Espiral de Violencia.* Barcelona: Herder.

Carr, Howie. (1994, February 21). Ventura family tree sinks roots in rich welfare soil. *Boston Herald,* p. 8.

Casmir, Fred L. (Ed.). (1991). *Communication in development.* Norwood, NJ: Ablex.

Cassirer, Ernst. (1951). *The philosophy of the enlightenment.* Princeton, NJ: Princeton University Press.

Chase, Kenneth R. (1994, May). *Rethinking rhetoric in the face of the other.* Paper presented at the Third National Communication Ethics Conference, Gull Lake, Michigan.

Cheng, Chung-ying. (1983). Chinese philosophy and recent communication theory. *Media Development, 30*(1), 30-34.

Christians, Clifford G. (1986) Reporting and the oppressed. In Deni Elliott (Ed.), *Responsible journalism* (pp. 109-30). London: Sage.

Christians, Clifford G. (1991). Communication ethics [Special issue]. *Communication research trends, 11*(4), 1-31.

Christians, Clifford G. (1995). The problem of universals in communication ethics. *Javnost [The Public], 2*(2), 59-69.

Christians, Clifford G. (1995). Communication ethics as the basis of genuine democracy. In Philip Lee (Ed.), *The democratization of communication* (pp. 75-91). Cardiff: University of Wales Press.

Christians, Clifford G., Fackler, Mark, & Rotzoll, Kim B. (1995). *Media ethics: Cases and moral reasoning* (4th ed.). New York: Longman.

Christians, Clifford G., Ferré, John P., & Fackler, P. Mark. (1993). *Good news: Social ethics and the press.* New York: Oxford University Press.

Christopher, Robert C. (1993). *The Japanese mind.* Tokyo: Charles E. Tuttle.

Chu, Chuan-yu. (1974). *A history of the development of public opinion and press freedom in China.* Taipei: Zhenqzhonn Bookstore.

Chu, Leonard L. (1992, June). *The right to communicate in Chinese society: Cultural and political factors.* Paper presented at the Conference on the Right to Communicate. Shatin, Hong Kong.

Clifford, James. (1988). *The predicament of culture.* Cambridge, MA: Harvard University Press.

Cohen, Jean L. (1993, June 19-21). *The public sphere, the media and civil society.* Paper presented at the Conference on the Development of Rights of Access to the Media, Institute for Constitutional and Legislative Policy, Central European University, Budapest.

Cohen, Jean L., & Arato, A. (1992). *Civil society and political theory* [Studies in Contemporary German Social Thought]. Cambridge, MA: MIT Press.

Coleman, Cynthia-Lou. (1994). *An examination of the relationship of structural pluralism, news role and source use with framing in the context of a community controversy.* Unpublished doctoral dissertation. University of Wisconsin, Madison.

Coleman, Cynthia-Lou. (1995). Science, technology and risk coverage of a community conflict. *Media, Culture and Society, 17,* 65-79.

Condit, Celeste Michelle. (1987). Crafting virtue: The rhetorical construction of public morality. *Quarterly Journal of Speech, 73,* 79-97.

Condon, John C., & Salto, Mitsuko. (1974). *Intercultural encounters with Japan.* Tokyo: Simul.

Cooper, Marc. (1995, April 10). The paranoid style. *The Nation, 260*(14), 486-492.

Cooper, Martha. (1991). Ethical dimensions of political advocacy from a postmodern perspective. In Robert E. Denton, Jr. (Ed.), *Ethical dimensions of political communication* (pp. 23-47). New York: Praeger.

Cooper, Thomas. (1989). Global universals: In search of common ground. In Thomas Cooper (Ed.), *Communication ethics and global change* (pp. 20-39). White Plains, NY: Longman.

Cooper, Thomas W. (1994). Communion and communication: Learning from the Shuswap. *Critical Studies in Mass Communication, 11*(4), 327-345.

Corn, David. (1995, May 15). Playing with fire. *The Nation, 260*(19), 657-658.
Coward, Harold G., Lipner, Julius J., & Young, Katherine K. (1989). *Hindu ethics.* Albany: State University of New York Press.
Craemar, Otto. (1933). *Die Christliche Wahrhaftigkeitsforderung und die Frage ihrer Begründung und Begrenzung.* Dresden: Unqelenk Verlag.
Crawford, S. Cromwell. (1974). *The evolution of Hindu ethical ideals.* Calcutta: Firma K. L. Mukhopadhyay.
Crawford, S. Cromwell. (1995). *Dilemmas of life and death: Hindu ethics in a North American context.* Albany: State University of New York Press.
Creel, Austin B. (1977). *Dharma in Hindu ethics.* Columbia, MO: South Asia Books.
Criticos, C., & Quinlan, T. (1991, Spring). Putting education and anthropology to work: Community video and ethnographic documentation in South Africa. *CVA Review,* pp. 49-53.
Curran, James. (1991). Rethinking the media as a public sphere. In Peter Dahlgreen & Colin Sparks (Eds.), *Communication and citizenship: Journalism and the public sphere in the new media age* (pp. 27-52). London: Routledge.
Cushman, Donald P. (1989). Interpersonal communication within a rules theoretic position. In S. S. King (Ed.), *Human communication as a field of study: Selected contemporary views* (pp. 88-94). Albany: State University of New York Press.
Deloria, Vine, Jr. (1969). *Custer died for your sins.* New York: Macmillan.
Deloria, Vine, Jr. (1973). *God is red.* New York: Grosset & Dunlap.
Deloria, Vine, Jr. (1974). *The Indian affair.* New York: Friendship.
Deloria, Vine, Jr. (1979). *The metaphysics of modern existence.* San Francisco, CA: Harper & Row.
Derrida, Jacques. (1984). Deconstruction and the other. In R. Kearney (Ed.), *Dialogues with contemporary continental thinkers: The phenomenological heritage.* Manchester, UK: Manchester University Press.
Do Czlonków Stowarzyszenia Dziennikarzy Polskich. (1989). *Most, 21,* 174-175.
Donagan, Alan. (1977). *Theory of morality.* Chicago: University of Chicago Press.
Doniger, Wendy, & Smith, Brian K. (Eds.). (1991). *Laws of Manu.* New Delhi: Penguin.
Downing, John. (1984). *Radical media: The political experience of alternative communication.* Boston, MA: South End.
Duncan, Greg, & Hill, Martha. (1988, January). Welfare dependence within and across generations. *Science,* pp. 467-469.
Dussel, Enrique. (1979). *Filosofia de la liberación Latinoamericana.* Bogotá: Nueva América.
Eco, Umberto (1967). *La Strategia de la Ilusion.* Barcelona: Ed. Lumen.
Edelstein, Alex S., Bowes, John E., & Harsel, Sheldon M. (Eds.). (1978). *Information societies: Comparing the Japanese and American Experiences.* Seattle: University of Washington, School of Communications, International Communication Center.
Eggensberger, Thomas, & Engel, Ulrich. (Eds.). (1995). *Recherche zwischen Hochscholastik und Postmoderne* (Vol. 9). Mainz, Germany: Walterberger Studien, Philosophische Reihe, Grünewald Verlag.
Ehrenreich, J. (1985). Anthropology on trial. *American Anthropologist, 87,* 218-221.
Ellul, Jacques. (1980). *The technological system* (Trans., J. Neugroschel). New York: Continuum.
Ellul, Jacques. (1989). *What I believe* (Trans., G. W. Bromiley). London: Marshall Morgan & Scott.
Engberg-Pedersen, Troels. (1983). *Aristotle's theory of moral insight.* Oxford, UK: Clarendon.
Enzensberger, Hans Magnus. (1974). *Palaver: Politische Überlegungen.* Frankfurt: Suhrkamp Verlag.

Falkenberg, Gabriel. (1982). *Lügen: Grundzüge einer Theorie sprachlicher Täuschung.* Tübingen: Niemeyer Verlag.

Faris, James. (1992). Anthropological transparency: Film, representation, and politics. In P. I. Crawford & D. Turton (Eds.), *Film as ethnography* (pp. 171-181). London: Manchester University Press.

Farley, Margaret A. (1993). Feminism and universal morality. In Gene Outka & John P. Reeder, Jr. (Eds.), *Prospects for a common morality.* Princeton, NJ: Princeton University Press.

Farrell, Thomas B. (1993). *Norms of rhetorical culture.* New Haven, CT: Yale University Press.

Fasching, Darrell. (1992). *Narrative theology after Auschwitz: From alienation to ethics.* Minneapolis, MN: Fortress.

Fasching, Darrell. (1993). *The ethical challenge of Auschwitz and Hiroshima.* Albany: State University of New York Press.

Fasching, Darrell. (1995, January). Response to Peter Haas. *The Ellul Forum, 14,* p. 15.

Feldman, Seth. (1977). Viewer, viewing, viewed: A critique of subject-generated documentary. *Journal of the University Film Association, 29*(4), 23-38.

Ferry, J. M. (1987). *Habermas: L'Éthique de la Communication.* Paris: Presses Universitaires de France.

Flanders, Laura, & Jackson, Janine. (1995, May/June). Public enemy no.1? *EXTRA!, 8*(3), 13-16.

Fleischacker, Samuel. (1994). *The ethics of culture.* Ithaca, NY: Cornell University Press.

Forecasting International. (1994). *America's future: 74 trends.* Bethesda, MD: World Future Society.

Fornet-Betancourt, R. (Ed.). (1990). *Ethik und Befreiung.* Aachen, Germany: Verlag der Augustinus Buchhandlung.

Fornet-Betancourt, R. (Ed.). (1992). *Diskursethik oder Befreiungsethik?* Aachen, Germany: Verlag der Augustinus Buchhandlung.

Fornet-Betancourt, R. (Ed.). (1993). *Die Diskursethik und ihre latinamerikanische Kritik.* Aachen, Germany: Verlag der Augustinus Buchhandlung.

Fornet-Betancourt, R. (Ed.). (1994). *Konvergenz oder Divergenz? Eine Bilanz des Gesprächs zwischen Diskursethik und Befreiungsethik.* Aachen, Germany: Verlag der Augustinus Buchhandlung.

Forst, R. (1994). *Kontexte der Gerechtigkeit: Politische Philosophie jenseits von Liberalismus und Kommunitarismus.* Frankfurt am Main: Suhrkamp.

Foucault, Michel. (1973). *The order of things.* New York: Vintage.

Foucault, Michel. (1984). On the genealogy of ethics. An overview of work in progress. In Paul Rabinow (Ed.), *The Foucault reader* (pp. 340-372). New York: Pantheon.

Foucault, Michel. (1984). *Polemics, politics, and problemization.* In Paul Robinow (Ed.), *The Foucault reader* (pp. 381-390). New York: Pantheon.

Fraser, Nancy. (1989). *Unruly practices: Power, discourse and gender in contemporary social theory.* Minneapolis: University of Minnesota Press.

Fraser, Nancy. (1993). Rethinking the public sphere: A contribution to the critique of actually existing democracy. In Bruce Robbins (Ed.), *The phantom public sphere* (pp. 1-32). Minneapolis: University of Minnesota Press.

Freire, Paulo. (1970). *Pedagogy of the oppressed* (Trans., Myra B. Ramos). New York: Continuum. (Original work published 1968)

Freire, Paulo. (1973). *Education for Critical Consciousness.* New York: Continuum. (Original work published 1969)

Frentzel-Zagórska, J. (1994). Demokracja, Elity Polityczne i Nerwica Transformacynja. *Kultura i Spoleczenstwo, 4,* 41-59.

Gadamer, Hans-Georg. (1975). *Truth and Method [Wahrheit und Methode]* (Trans., G. Barden & J. Cumming). New York: Seabury. (Original work published 1965)

Galilei, Galileo. (1970). *Dialogo Sopra i due Massimi Sistemi del Mondo.* Turin: Einaudi.

Galtung, Johan (1986). Social communication and global problems. In Philip Lee (Ed.), *Communication for all* (pp. 3-15). Maryknoll, NY: Orbis.

Gandhi, Mohandas C. (1948). *The story of my experiments with truth.* New York: Public Affairs Press.

Gasiet, Seev. (1980). *Eine Theorie der Bedürfnisse.* Frankfurt: Campus Verlag.

Geisman, Georg, & Oberer, Hariulf. (Eds.). (1986). *Kant und das Recht der Lüge.* Würzburg: Verlag Königshausen and Neumann.

Gelfand, Michael. (1973). *The genuine Shona: Survival values of an African culture.* Gweru, Zimbabwe: Mambo.

Gerbner, George. (1994). Women and minorities on TV: A study of casting and fate. *Media Development, 41*(2), 38-44.

Gerwith, Alan. (1978). *Reason and morality.* Chicago: University of Chicago Press.

González, Jorge Alejandro. (1983, August). Cultura(s) Popular(es) Hoy. *Comunicacion y Cultura* (UAM-Mexico) *10,* 7-30.

Goodman, Ellen. (1992, April 16). Welfare mothers with an attitude. *Boston Globe,* p. 19.

Gordon, Rob. (1990a, February/May). Kicking up a Kalahari storm. *Southern African Review of Books,* 18-19.

Gordon, Rob. (1990b, Spring). People of the great sandface: People of the great white lie? *CVA Review,* 30-33.

Gordon, Rob. (1991). Buschmannschwarmerei in Südafrika. In R. Kapfer, W. Petermann, & R. Thoms (Eds.), *Jäger und Gejagte: John Marshall und Seine Filme* (pp. 165-179). Munich: Trickster Verlag.

Gordon, Rob. (1992). *The Bushmen myth and the making of a Namibian underclass.* Boulder, CO: Westview.

Government of India. (1958). *The collected works of Mahatma Gandhi* (Vol. 53, appendix 3). Delhi: Ministry of Information and Broadcasting, Publications Division.

Govinda Das, Buba. (1947). *Hindu ethics: Principles of Hindu religio-social regeneration.* Madras: G. A. Natesan.

Gramsci, Antonio. (1970). *Selections from the prison notebooks* (Trans., Q.Hoare & N. G. Smith). London: Lawrence & Wishart.

Groombridge, B. (1972). *Television and the people: A programme for democratic participation.* Harmondsworth, UK: Penguin.

Gudykunst, William B. (Ed.). (1993). *Communication in Japan and the United States.* New York: State University of New York Press.

Gudykunst, William B., & Antonio, P. S. (1993). Approaches to the study of communication in Japan and the United States. In W. B.Gudykunst (Ed.), *Communication in Japan and the United States* (pp. 18-48). Albany: State University of New York Press.

Günther, K. (1988). *Der Sinn für Angemessenheit.* Frankfurt am Main: Suhrkamp.

Habermas, Jürgen. (1975). *Legitimation crisis* (Trans., T. McCarthy). Boston: Beacon.

Habermas, Jürgen. (1979). What is universal pragmatics? In *Communication and the Evolution of Society* (pp. 1-68) (Trans., T. McCarthy). Boston: Beacon.

Habermas, Jürgen. (1983). *Moralbewusstsein und kommunikatives Handeln.* Frankfurt am Main: Suhrkamp.

Habermas, Jürgen. (1984). *Aspekte der Handlungsrationalität.* In *Vorstudien und Ergänzungen zur Theorie des kommunikativen Handelns* (pp. 441-472). Frankfurt am Main: Suhrkamp.

Habermas, Jürgen. (1984). Erläuterungen zum Begriff des kommunikativen Handelns. In *Vorstudien und Ergänzungen zur Theorie des kommunikativen Handelns* (pp. 571-606). Frankfurt am Main: Suhrkamp.

Habermas, Jürgen. (1984). *Theory of communicative action: Vol. 1. Reason and the rationalization of society* (Trans., T. McCarthy). Boston: Beacon.

Habermas, Jürgen. (1984). Wahrheitstheorien. In *Vorstudien und Ergänzungen zur Theorie des kommunikativen Handelns* (pp. 127-183). Frankfurt am Main: Suhrkamp.

Habermas, Jürgen. (1987). *Theory of communicative action: Vol. 2. Lifeworld and system: A critique of functionalist reason* (Trans., T. McCarthy). Boston: Beacon.

Habermas, Jürgen. (1989). *The structural transformation of the public sphere: An inquiry into a category of bourgeois society* (Trans., T. Burger & F. Lawrence) [Studies in Contemporary German Social Thought]. Cambridge, MA: MIT Press.

Habermas, Jürgen. (1990a). Discourse ethics: Notes on a program of philosophical justification. In *Moral consciousness and communicative action* (Trans., C. Lenhardt & S. Weber Nicholsen, pp. 43-115) [Studies in Contemporary German Social Thought]. Cambridge, MA: MIT Press.

Habermas, Jürgen. (1990b). *Moral consciousness and communicative action* (Trans., C. Lenhardt & S. Weber Nicholsen) [Studies in Contemporary German Social Thought]. Cambridge, MA: MIT Press.

Habermas, Jürgen. (1990c). *Strukturwandel der Öffentlichkeit: Untersuchungen zu einer Kategorie der bürgerlichen Gesellschaft* (Rev. ed.). Frankfurt am Main: Suhrkamp.

Habermas, Jürgen. (1991). Treffen Hegels Einwände gegen Kant auch auf die Diskursethik zu? In *Erläuterungen zur Diskursethik* (pp. 9-30). Frankfurt am Main: Suhrkamp.

Habermas, Jürgen. (1992). *Faktizität und Geltung: Beiträge zur Diskurstheorie des Rechts und des demokratischen Rechtsstaats.* Frankfurt am Main: Suhrkamp.

Habermas, Jürgen. (1993a). *Justification and application: Remarks on discourse ethics* (Trans., C. Cronin) [Studies in Contemporary German Social Thought]. Cambridge, MA: MIT Press.

Habermas, Jürgen. (1993b). On the pragmatic, the ethical, and the moral employments of practical reason. In *Justification and application: Remarks on discourse ethics* (Trans., C. Cronin) (pp. 1-17) [Studies in Contemporary German Social Thought]. Cambridge, MA: MIT Press.

Habermas, Jürgen. (1993c). Remarks on discourse ethics. In *Justification and application: Remarks on discourse ethics* (Trans., C. Cronin) (pp. 19-111) [Studies in Contemporary German Social Thought]. Cambridge, MA: MIT Press.

Halbfass, Wilhelm. (1988). *India and Europe: An essay in understanding.* Albany: State University of New York Press.

Halbfass, Wilhelm. (1991). *Tradition and reflection: Explorations in Indian thought.* Albany: State University of New York Press.

Hall, Edward T. (1969). *The hidden dimension.* Garden City, NY: Doubleday.

Hall, Edward T. (1973). *The silent language.* Garden City, NY: Anchor.

Hall, Edward T. (1977). *Beyond culture.* Garden City, NY: Anchor.

Hamelink, Cees J. (1983). *Cultural autonomy in global communications: Planning national information policy.* New York: Longman.

Hamelink, Cees J. (1994). *Trends in world communication: On disempowerment and self-empowerment.* Malaysia: Southbound.

Hardgrave, Robert, Jr., & Kochanek, Stanley A. (1993). *India government and politics in a developing nation.* Orlando, FL: Harcourt Brace Jovanovich.

Havel, Václav. (1989). *Living in truth* (Ed., Jan Vladislav). London: Faber & Faber.

Havel, Václav. (1994, August 1). Post-modernism: The search for universal laws. *Vital Speeches of the Day, 60*(20), 613-615.

Held, David. (1980). *Introduction to critical theory: Horkheimer to Habermas.* Berkeley: University of California Press.

Heller, Agnes. (1976). *The theory of need in Marx.* London: Routledge & Kegan Paul.

Heller, Agnes. (1983). *A theory of history.* Oxford, UK: Basil Blackwell.

Heller, Agnes. (1984). *A radical philosophy.* Oxford, UK: Basil Blackwell.

Heller, Agnes. (1987). *Beyond justice.* Oxford, UK: Basil Blackwell.

Heller, Agnes. (1992). *A philosophy of morals.* Oxford, UK: Basil Blackwell.

Heller, Agnes, & Fehér, F. (1988). *The postmodern political condition.* Cambridge, UK: Polity.

Henrici, Peter. (1983, March). Towards an anthropological philosophy of communication. *Communication Resource, 1,* pp. 1-4.

Herbert, Bob. (1993, September 8). No job, no dream. *The New York Times,* p. A23.

Herman, A.L. (1991). *A brief introduction to Hinduism: Religion, philosophy and ways of liberation.* Boulder, CO: Westview.

Holderegger, A. (1992). Einführung: Ethik in der Mediengesellschaft. In A. Holderegger (Ed.), *Ethik der Medienkommunikation.* Freiburg-Schweiz: Universitätsverlag.

Holm, Tom. (1992). Patriots and pawns: State use of American Indians in the military and the process of nativization in the United States. In M. Annette Jaimes (Ed.), *The state of Native America* (pp. 345-370.). Boston, MA: South End.

Holmes, Robert L. (1993). Ethical relativism. In his *Basic moral philosophy* (pp. 19-42). Belmont, CA: Wadsworth.

Honderich, T. (1987). *Violence for equality: Inquiries in political philosophy.* London: Routledge.

Honneth, Axel. (1986). Diskursethik und implizites Gerechtigkeitskonzept. In W. Kuhlmann (Ed.), *Moralität und Sittlichkeit.* Frankfurt am Main: Suhrkamp.

Hopkins, E. Washburn. (1924). *Ethics of India.* New Haven, CT: Yale University Press.

Hulteng, John. (1981). *Playing it straight: A practical discussion of the ethical principles of the American Society of Newspaper Editors.* Old Saybrook, CT: Globe Pequot.

Hume, David. (1739). *Treatise of human nature.* London: J. Noon.

Hume, David. (1963). *Enquiries concerning the human understanding and concerning the principles of morals.* Oxford, UK: Clarendon Press. (Original work published 1748 and 1751)

Hutchinson, Bill. (1994, February 15). Welfare gone wrong. *Boston Herald,* pp. 5-6.

Hutchinson, D. S. (1986). *The virtues of Aristotle.* London: Routledge & Kegan Paul.

Idowu, Bolaji E. (1962). *Olodumare—God in Yoruba belief.* London: Longmans.

Ingram, D. (1990). *Critical theory and philosophy.* New York: Paragon House.

Islamic Countries Association. (1980). *Charter of Islamic media.* Mecca, Saudi Arabia: Islamic Countries Association.

Ivans, Molly. (1995, June). Lyin' bully. *Mother Jones,* p. 36.

Jaafar, Mohammad. (1978). *Philosophical and ethical studies.* Cairo: Dar Al Uloum Bookshop.

Jackson, Janine. (1993, April/May). Who gets to talk? *EXTRA!, 6*(3), 14-17.

Jakubowicz, Karol. (1989). Media ethics in Poland. In Thomas Cooper (Ed.), *Communication ethics and global change* (pp. 100-108). White Plains, NY: Longman.

Jakubowicz, Karol. (1990). Solidarity and media reform in Poland. *European Journal of Communication, 5*(23), 333-354.

Jakubowicz, Karol. (1990). Between communism and post-communism: How many varieties of glasnost? In Slavko Splichal, J. Hochheimer, & Karol Jakubowicz (Eds.), *Democrati-*

zation and the media: An East-West dialogue (pp. 40-55). Ljubljana, Slovenia: University of Ljubljana Press.

Jakubowicz, Karol. (1991). Musical chairs? The three public spheres of Poland. In Peter Dahlgren & Colin Sparks (Eds.), *Communication and citizenship: Journalism and the public sphere in the new media age* (pp. 155-175). London: Routledge.

Jakubowicz, Karol. (1992). From party propaganda to corporate speech: Polish journalism in search of a new identity. *Journal of Communication, 42*(3), 64-73.

Jahn, Janheinz. (1961). *Muntu: An outline of neo-African culture.* London: Faber & Faber.

Jankowski, N. (1988). *Community television in Amsterdam.* Amsterdam: University of Amsterdam Press.

Jankowski, N., Prehn, O., & Stappers, J. (1992). *The people's voice: Local radio and television in Europe.* London: John Libbey.

Jay, M. (1973). *The dialectical imagination: A history of the Frankfurt school and the institute of social research 1923-1950.* Boston: Little, Brown.

Jeffrey, Patricia. (1979). *Indian Women in Purdah.* London: Zed.

Jensen, Carl. (1993). *Censored: The news that didn't make it and why.* Chapel Hill, NC: Shelburne.

Jhingran, Saral. (1989). *Aspects of Hindu morality.* Delhi: Motilal Banasidass.

Johnstone, Christopher L. (1993, November). *Ontological vision as ground for communication ethics: A response to the challenge of postmodernism.* Paper presented at convention of the Speech Communication Association, Miami, Florida.

Jonas, Hans. (1984). *The Imperative of Responsibility* [Macht oder Ohnmacht der Subjektivität? Das lieb-Seele Problem im Vorfeld des Prinzips Verantwortung]. Chicago: University of Chicago Press.

Jordan Ministry of Information. (1993). *Jordan press and publications law.* Amman: Jordan Ministry of Information.

Jorgensen, Leslie. (1995, March/April). AM armies. *EXTRA!, 8*(2), 20-22.

Juusela, Pauli. (1991). *Journalistic codes of ethics in the CSCE countries.* Tampere, Finland: University of Tampere, Department of Journalism and Mass Communication Publications, Series B.

Kant, Immanuel. (1968). *Die Metaphysik der Sitten* (Ed., Karl Vorländer). Hamburg: Meiner Verlag.

Kant, Immanuel. (1986). *Über ein vermeintes Recht: Aus Menschenliebe zu Lügen.* Würzburg: Verlag Königshausen und Neumann.

Kant, Immanuel. (1990). *Eine Vorlesung uber Ethik* (Ed., Gerd Gerhardt). Frankfurt: Fischer-Taschenbuch-Verlag.

Kasoma, Francis P. (1994). *Journalism ethics in Africa.* Nairobi, Kenya: African Council for Communication Education.

Kausch, K. (1988). *Kulturindustrie und Populärkultur: Kritische Theorie der Massenmedien.* Frankfurt am Main: Suhrkamp.

Keane, J. (1991). *The media and democracy.* Cambridge, UK: Polity.

Kepnes, Steven. (1991). *Buber's hermeneutic philosophy and narrative theology.* Bloomington: Indiana University Press.

Kewley, Mary Jo. (1990, July 16). Band opposes mine on spiritual grounds. *Wausau Daily Herald,* p. 4A.

Khadduri, Majid. (1984). *The Islamic conception of justice.* Baltimore, MD: John Hopkins University Press.

Khan, Benjamin. (1965). *The concept of dharma in Valmiki Ramayana.* New Delhi: Munshi Ram Manohar Lal.

Kidder, Rushworth M. (1994). *Shared values in a troubled world.* San Francisco: Jossey-Bass.

Kim, Young C. (1981). *Japanese journalists and their world.* Charlottesville: University Press of Virginia.

King, Winston L. (1946). *Buddhism and Christianity: Some bridges of understanding.* Philadelphia, PA: The Westminster Press.

Kishwar, Madhu, & Ruth, Vanita. (1984). *In search of answers: Indian Women's voices from Manushi.* London: Zed.

Kissling, C. (1990). Die Theorie des kommunikativen Handelns in Diskussion. *Freiburger Zeitschrift für Philosophie und Theologie, 37,* 233-252.

Klein, Alexander. (1989). Quoted in Stuart Henry, "Deception." In *International Encyclopedia of Communication* (pp. 459-462) New York: Oxford University Press.

Kovel, Joel. (1991). *History and spirit: An inquiry into the philosophy of liberation.* Boston: Beacon.

Kovel, Joel. (1995, May). *Ecological Marxism and dialectic.* Paper presented at Fordham University, Cultural Studies Seminar, Bronx, New York.

Kramer, Hans. (1992). *Integrative Ethik.* Frankfurt: Suhrkamp Verlag.

Krishna, Daya. (1991). *Indian philosophy: A counter perspective.* New York: Oxford University Press.

Król, M. (1981). O "Tezach" Kilka Uwag Krytycznych. *Tygodnik Solidarnoność, 11,* 11.

Krupat, Arnold. (1993). Scholarship and Native American studies: A response to Daniel Littlefield, Jr. *American Studies, 34*(2), 81-101.

Küng, Hans. (1991). *Global responsibility: In search of a new world ethic* (Trans., John Bowden). London: SCM.

LaDuke, Winona. (1993). A society based on conquest cannot be sustained: Native peoples and the environmental crisis. In Richard Hofrichter (Ed.), *Toxic struggles: The theory and practice of environmental justice* (pp. 98-106). Philadelphia, PA: New Society.

Lacy, Creighton. (1965). *The conscience of India.* San Francisco, CA: Holt, Rinehart & Winston.

Landes, Joan. (1988). *Women and the public sphere in the age of the French revolution.* Ithaca, NY: Cornell University Press.

Larson, Gerald J. (1995). *India's agony over religion.* Albany: State University of New York Press.

Larson, Gerald, & Deutsch, Eliot. (Eds.). (1988). *Interpreting across boundaries: New essays in comparative philosophy.* Princeton, NJ: Princeton University Press.

Larson, Sidney. (1991-1992). Native American aesthetics: An attitude of relationship. *Melus, 17*(3), 53-67.

Lazarus, Alison, & Tomaselli, Keyan G. (1989). Participatory video: Problems, prospects and a case study. *Group Media Journal, 8*(1), 10-15.

Lebra, T. S., & Lebra, W. P. (1986). *Japanese culture and behavior.* Honolulu: University of Hawaii Press.

Lee, Jan. (1985). *Communication law.* Taipei: National Chengchi University, Graduate School of Journalism.

Lee, Martin A., & Solomon, Norman. (1990). *Unreliable sources: A guide to detecting bias in news media.* New York: Carol.

Lee, Philip. (Ed.). (1986). *Communication for all: The church and the new world information and communication order.* Maryknoll, NY: Orbis.

Lesch, W. (1992). Unparteilichkeit und Anwaltsfunktion: Anmerkungen zu einem Dauerkonflikt der theologischen Ethik. *Stimmen der Zeit, 210,* 257-270.

Lesch, W. (1994). Theologische Ethik als Handlungstheorie. In E. Arens (Ed.), *Gottesrede—Glaubenspraxis: Perspektiven theologischer Handlungstheorie* (pp. 89-109). Darmstadt: Wissenschaftliche Buchgesellschaft.

Levinas, Emmanuel. (1979). *Totality and infinity.* The Hague, Netherlands: Martinus Nijhoff.

Levinas, Emmanuel. (1981). *Otherwise than being or essence.* The Hague, Netherlands: Martinus Nijhoff.

Levinas, Emmanuel. (1985). *Ethics and infinity: Conversations with Philippe Nemo* (Trans., R. A. Cohen). Pittsburgh, PA: Duquesne University Press.

Lichtenberg, J. (1990). *Democracy and the mass media.* Cambridge, UK: Cambridge University Press.

Limbaugh, Rush. (1992). *The way things ought to be.* New York: Pocket Star.

Lin, Lin-wen, & Su, Wei-rong. (1995, February 28). Enhancing group harmony and establishing the "New Taiwanese" concept. *United Daily News,* p. 4.

Lotz, J. B. (1963, Winter). Person and ontology [Person und Ontologie]. *Philosophy Today, 7,* 279-297. [reprinted from *Scholastik, 38*(3), 335-360]

Lopez, Donald S. (Ed.). (1995). *Religion of India in practice.* Princeton, NJ: Princeton University Press.

MacArthur, J. R. (1993). *Second front: Censorship and propaganda in the Gulf war.* Berkeley: University of California Press.

MacBride, Sean. (1980). *Many voices, one world: Report by the International Commission for the Study of Communication Problems.* Paris: UNESCO.

Makunike, E. C. (Ed.). (1973). *Christian press in Africa: Voice of human concern.* Lusaka, Zambia: Multimedia.

Mandler, George. (1993). Approaches to a psychology of value. In Michael Hechter, Lynn Nadel, & Richard E. Michod (Eds.), *The origins of values* (pp. 229-260). New York: Aldine De Gruyter.

Mann, Thomas. (1977). *Versuch über Tschechov: Ausgewählte Essays.* Frankfurt: S. Fischer Verlag.

Marcuse, Herbert. (1968). *One dimensional man.* London: Sphere.

Marshall, John. (1993). *The cinema of John Marshall* (Ed., J. Ruby). Philadelphia, PA: Harwood.

Martín-Barbero, Jesús. (1991). Etica y cultura. In *Colombia, Una Casa Para Todos: Debate Etico* (pp. 151-157). Santafé de Bogotá: Antropos.

Mathews, John Joseph. (1988). *Sundown.* Norman: University of Oklahoma Press. (Original work published 1934)

Mbiti, John S. (1969). *African religions and philosophy.* London: Heineman.

McNickle, D'Arcy. (1979). *Native American tribalism: Indian survivals and renewals.* New York: Oxford University Press. (Original work published 1973)

McNickle, D'Arcy. (1993). *The surrounded.* Albuquerque: University of New Mexico Press. (Original work published 1936)

McQuail, Denis. (1992). *Media performance: Mass communication and the public interest.* London: Sage.

McQuail, Denis. (1994). *Mass communication theory.* London: Sage.

Mead, George Herbert. (1962). *Mind, self, and society.* Chicago: University of Chicago Press.

Mejía Quintana, Oscar, & Tickner, Arlene. (1992). *Cultura y Democracia en América Latina: Elementos para Una Reinteopretación de la Cultura y la Historia Latinoamericanas.* Bogotá: M & T Editores/Tercer Mundo.

Merrill, John C. (1975). Ethics and journalism. In J. C. Merrill & R. Barney (Eds.), *Ethics and the press: Readings in mass media morality* (pp. 8-17). New York: Hastings.

Mieth, Dietmar. (1984). Wahrhaftigkeit-Aufrichtigkeit-Glaubwürdigkeit: Die Idee einer ethischen Kultur der Politik. In *Die neuen Tugenden* (pp. 154-169). Düsseldorf: Patmos Verlag.

Mieth, Dietmar. (1989). Warum das Lügen so schön ist: Eine Anleitung zu den feineren Formen der Unmoral. *Orientierung* (Zurich), *53*, 73-75.

Misra, K. P. & Gangal, S. C. (1981). *Gandhi and the contemporary world*. Delhi: Chanakya.

Modzelewski, K. (1993, September 3). Lojalność Wobec Nieznajomych, *Gazeta Wyborcza*.

Moemeka, Andrew A. (1981). *Local radio: Community education for development*. Zaria, Nigeria: Ahmadu Bello University Press.

Moemeka, Andrew A. (1984). Socio-cultural environment of communication in traditional/ rural Nigeria: An ethnographic exploration. In *Communicatio Socialis Yearbook, 3,* 41-56. Indore, India: Satprakashan Sanchar Kendra.

Moemeka, Andrew A. (1989). Communication and African culture: A sociological analysis. In S. K. T. Boafo (Ed.), *Communication and culture: African perspectives* (pp. 1-10). Nairobi, Kenya: WACC-African Region.

Moemeka, Andrew A. (1993). *Development (social change) communication: Building understanding and creating participation*. New York: McGraw-Hill.

Moemeka, Andrew A. (1994, April 29-May 1). *Socio-cultural dimensions of leadership in Africa*. Paper presented at the Global Majority Retreat, Rocky Hills, Connecticut.

Moemeka, Andrew A. (1996). Interpersonal communication in communalistic societies. In W. B. Gudykunst, S. Ting-Toomey, & T. Nishida (Eds.), *Communication in personal relationships across cultures* (pp. 197-216). Thousand Oaks, CA: Sage.

Moemeka, Andrew A., & Kasoma, Francis P. (1994). Journalism ethics in Africa: An aversion to deontology? In Francis P. Kasoma (Ed.), *Journalism ethics in Africa* (pp. 38-50). Nairobi, Kenya: African Council for Communication Education.

Mohawk, John. (1992). Looking for Columbus: Thoughts on the past, present and future of humanity. In M. Annette Jaimes (Ed.), *The state of Native America* (pp. 439-444). Boston, MA: South End.

Morris, Charles. (1938). *Foundation of the theory of signs*. Chicago: University of Chicago Press.

Mowlana, Mohamad. (1989). Communication ethics and the Islamic tradition. In Thomas Cooper (Ed.), *Communication ethics and global change* (pp. 137-147). New York: Longman.

Mudimbe, Valentin Y. (1988). *The invention of Africa: Gnosis, philosophy and the order of knowledge*. Bloomington: Indiana University Press.

Müller, Gregor. (1962). *Die Wahrhaftigkeitspflicht und die Problematik der Lüge*. Freiburg-Basel-Vienna: Herder Verlag.

Nabokov, Peter. (Ed.). (1991). *Native American testimony*. New York: Penguin. (Original work published 1978)

Nahata, Renu. (1992, July/August). Too many kids and too much money: Persistent media myths about welfare. *EXTRA!, 5*(5), 18.

Nakane, Chie. (1973). *Japanese society*. Tokyo: Charles E. Tuttle.

Namuddu, Katherine, & Tapsoba, J. M. Silbry. (1993). *The status of educational research and policy analysis in sub-Saharan Africa*. Ottawa, Canada: Development Research Centre.

Nandy, Ashis. (1983). *The intimate enemy: Loss and recovery of self under colonialism*. New York: Oxford University Press.

Nandy, Ashis. (1995). *The savage Freud and other essays*. New York: Oxford University Press.

Naqvi, Syed Nawab. (1981). *Ethics and economics: An Islamic synthesis*. Leicester, UK: The Islamic Foundation.

Nasar, Sylvia. (1992, March 5). The 1980s: A very good time for the very rich. *New York Times,* pp. A1, D24.

Niranjana, Tejaswini, Sudhir, P., & Dhareshwar, Vivek. (1993). *Interrogating modernity: Culture and colonialism in India.* Calcutta: Seagull.

Noddings, Nel. (1984). *Caring: A feminine approach to ethics and moral education.* Berkeley: University of California Press.

Nordenstreng, Kaarle. (1984). *The mass media declaration of UNESCO.* Norwood, NJ: Ablex.

Nordenstreng, Kaarle. (1989). Professionalism in transition: Journalistic ethics. In Thomas W. Cooper (Ed.), *Communication ethics and global change* (pp. 277-283). New York: Longman.

Nordenstreng, Kaarle, & Topuz, Hifzi. (Eds.). (1989). *Journalist: Status, rights and responsibilities.* Prague: International Order of Journalists.

Nowak, Stefan. (1988). Spoleczeństwo Polskie Drugiej Polowy Lat Osiemdziesiatych (Próba Diagnozy Stanu Świadomości Spolecznej). *Studia Socjologiczne, 1,* 23-55.

O'Regan, Tom. (1990). Communication and tradition: Essays after Eric Michaels [Special issue]. *Continuum: An Australian Journal of the Media, 3*(2).

O Znaczeniu Środków Komunikacji Spolecznej w Polsce i Roli SDP w Ich Rozwoju (n.d.). *Stenogram Nadzwyczajnego Zjazdu Delegatow Stowarzyszenia Dziennikarzy Polskich.* Warsaw: Mimeo.

Ogan, Christine. (1989). Video's great advantage: Decentralized control of technology. *Media Development, 36*(4), 2-5.

Okediji, Ola. (1970). *Sociology of the Yoruba.* Ibadan, Nigeria: University Press.

Okigbo, Charles. (1994). Towards a theory of indecency in news reporting. In Francis P. Kasoma (Ed.), *Journalism ethics in Africa* (pp. 71-87). Nairobi, Kenya: African Council for Communication Education.

Okigbo, Charles. (1995). *Communication in Africa: Toward a normative theory.* Unpublished Manuscript.

Oliver, Robert Tarbell. (1971). *Communication and culture in ancient India and China.* Syracuse, NY: Syracuse University Press.

Olthuis, James H. (in press). Face-to-face: Ethical asymmetry or the symmetry of mutuality? In James H. Olthuis (Ed.), *Knowing other-wise* (pp. 134-164). New York: Fordham University Press.

Oommen, T. K. (1995). *Alien concepts and South Asian reality.* New Delhi: Sage.

Outka, Gene, & Reeder, John P., Jr. (1993). *Prospects for a common morality.* Princeton, NJ: Princeton University Press.

Pang, Ka-fat. (1994, April 14). Horse-race reporting also fashionable in Taiwan. *Xin Daily,* p. 33.

Pang, Ka-fat. (1994). *Objectivity in news reporting.* Taipei: San Min.

Pang, Ka-fat. (1994, November 4). Sensationalism in Taiwan newspapers. *Xin Daily,* p. 32.

Pasquali, Antonio. (1974). *Comprender la Comunicación.* Caracas: Monte Avila.

Paton, H. J. (1948). *The moral law: Kant's groundwork of the metaphysic of morals.* London: Hutchinson.

Paul, Ellen F., Miller, Fred D., & Paul, Jeffrey. (Eds.). (1994). *Cultural pluralism and moral knowledge.* Cambridge, UK: Cambridge University Press.

Peukert, Helmut. (1981). Universal solidarity as the goal of communication. *Media Development, 28*(4), 10-12.

Peukert, Helmut. (1984). *Science, action, and fundamental theology: Toward a theology of communicative action* (Trans., J. Bohman) [Studies in Contemporary German Social Thought]. Cambridge, MA: MIT Press.

Pfürtner, Stephan H. (1992). Zum Ethos öffentlicher Kommunikation. In Adrian Holdereggger (Ed.), *Ethik der Medienkommunikation: Grundlagen* (pp. 17-50). Freiburg-Schweiz: Universitätsverlag.

Pirsig, R. M. (1992). *Lila: An inquiry into morals.* New York: The Free Press.

Pisarek, Walery. (1989). European socialist countries. In Kaarle Nordenstreng & Hifzi Topuz (Eds), *Journalist: Status, right and responsibilities* (pp. 97-135). Prague: International Organization of Journalists.

Polakow, Valerie. (1995, May 1). On a tightrope without a net. *The Nation, 260* (17), 590-592.

Polanyi, Michael. (1966). *The tacit dimension.* Garden City, NY: Doubleday.

Popper, Karl. (1994). *La Télévision: Un Danger pour la Démocratie.* Paris: Anatolia.

Postman, Neil. (1986). *Amusing ourselves to death: Public discourse in the age of show business.* New York: Penguin.

Pratt, Cornelius B. (1994). Journalism ethics and the new communication technology in Africa. In Francis P. Kasoma (Ed.), *Journalism ethics in Africa* (pp. 51-69). Nairobi, Kenya: African Council for Communication Education.

Pröpper, Thomas. (1995). Autonomie und Solidarität: Begründungsprobleme sozielethischer Verpflichtung. In Edmund Arens (Ed.), *Anerkennung der Anderen: Eine Theologische Grunddimension interkultureller Kommunikation* (pp. 95-112). Freiburg/Basel/Wien: Herder.

Putnam, Hilary. (1975). *Philosophical papers: Vol. 2. Mind, language and reality.* Cambridge, UK: Cambridge University Press.

Qaradawi, Yusuf. (n.d.). *The lawful and the prohibited in Islam* (Trans. Kemal El-Helbawy, M. Moinuddin Siddiqui, & Syed Shukry). Indianapolis, IN: American Trust.

Raboy, Marc, & Dagenais, Bernard. (1992). *Media, crisis and democracy: Mass communication and the disruption of social order.* London: Sage.

Radhakrishnan, S. (1989). *Indian philosophy.* New York: Oxford University Press.

Radwan, Zeinab. (1993). *Islam in the heart of contemporary times.* Dubai, UAE: Dar Al Qir'a Li' Jamee'.

Rauch, Jonathan. (1995, May). In defense of prejudice: Why incendiary speech must be protected. *Harper's, 290,* 37-46.

Rehg, W. (1994). *Insight and solidarity: The discourse ethics of Jürgen Habermas.* Berkeley: University of California Press.

Rendall, Steven, Naureckas, Jim, & Cohen, Jeff. (1995). *The way things aren't: Rush Limbaugh's reign of error.* New York: The New Press.

Reykowski, J. (1993). Zmiany Systemowe a Mentalność Polskiego Społeczeństwa. In J. Reykowski (Ed.), *Wartości i Podstawy Polaków a Zmiany Systemowe: Szkice z Psyscholo-gii Polity Cznej* (pp. 9-48). Warsaw: Polska Akademia Nauk.

Richman, Paula. (1991). *Many Ramayanas: The diversity of a narrative tradition in south Asia.* Oxford, UK: Oxford University Press.

Ricoeur, Paul. (1960). The antinomy of human reality and the problem of philosophical anthropology (Trans., D. O'Connor). *Il Pensiero, 5,* 273-290.

Ricoeur, Paul. (1986). *Ethics and culture.* Paris: Seuil.

Ricoeur, Paul. (1990). *Soi Même Comme un Autre.* Paris: Seuil.

Rödel, U., Frankenberg, G., & Dubiel, H. (1989). *Die demokratische Frage.* Frankfurt am Main: Suhrkamp.

Roderick, R. (1986). *Habermas and the foundations of critical theory.* New York: St. Martin's.

Rokeach, Milton. (1973). *The nature of human values.* New York: The Free Press.

Rose, Wendy. (1992). The great pretenders: Further reflections on whiteshamanism. In M. Annette Jaimes (Ed.), *The state of Native America,* (pp. 403-421). Boston, MA: South End.

Rutlin, Terry. (1991, July 7). 400 protest against mine. *Wausau Daily Herald,* p. 1A.

Rutlin, Terry. (1991, July 23). Endangered species has a PR problem. *Wausau Daily Herald,* pp. 1, 2.

Said, Edward W. (1978). *Orientalism.* New York: Vintage.

Said, Edward W. (1993). *Culture and imperialism.* New York: Knopf.

Saxer, Ulrich. (1992). Journalistische Ethik im elekronischen Zeitalter—eine Chimäre? In Adrian Holderegger (Ed.), *Ethik der medienkommunikation: Grundlagen* (pp. 105-119). Freiburg-Schweiz: Universitätsverlag.

Scannone, Juan Carlos. (1984, April-June). La Medisción Histórica de los Valores: Aporte Desde la Perspective y la Experiencia Latinoamericanas. *Cuadernos de Filosofia LatinoAmericana, 19,* 32-48.

Schacht, Richard. (1990, Fall). Philosophical anthropology: What, why and how. *Philosophy and Phenomenological Research, 50,* 155-176.

Scheler, Max F. (1962). *Man's place in nature* (Trans., Hans Meyerhoff). New York: Noonday. (Original work published 1928)

Schlick, Moritz. (1949). Is there a factual *a priori*? In H. Feigl & W. Sellers (Eds.), *Readings in philosophical analysis* (pp. 277-285). New York: Appleton-Century Crofts.

Schlick, Moritz. (1992). The future of philosophy. In Richard M. Rorty (Ed.), *The linguistic turn: Essays in philosophical method* (pp. 43-53). Chicago: University of Chicago Press.

Schmucler, Héctor. (1983, August). Interrogantes Sobre lo Popular. *Comunicación y Cultura* (UAM-Mexico), *10,* 3-5.

Schmucler, Héctor, & Pasquali, Antonio. (1987). Comunicación y Cultura. In Rafael Roncogliolo (Ed.), *Comunicación y Desarrollo* (pp. 169-186). Lima: Instituto para América Latina.

Schor, Juliet. (1992). *The overworked American.* New York: Basic Books.

Scott, Chuck. (1994). *The Lesotho video herders project.* Aarhus, Denmark: Intervention.

Selbourne, David. (1994). *The principle of duty: An essay on the foundations of the civic order.* London: Sinclair-Stevenson.

Sen, Amartiya. (1993, April 8). The threats to secular India. *New York Times Book Review.*

Senft, G. (1987). Nanam'sa Bwena—Gutes Denken. Eine ethnolinguistische Fallstudie über eine Dorfversammlung auf den Trobriand Inseln. *Zeit schrift fur Ethnologie, 112,* 191-222.

Sennott, Charles M. (1994, February 16). Abuse suspect fought drugs, other woes. *Boston Globe,* p. 18.

Sennott, Charles M. (1994, February 20). Finding four generations sustained by welfare. *Boston Globe,* pp. 1, 46.

Shepperson, Arnold. (1994). Tits'n' buns: Film and the appropriation of the human body. *Visual Anthropology, 6,* 395-400.

Shepperson, Arnold. (1995). *On the social interpretation of cultural experience: Reflections on Raymond Williams's early cultural writings (1958-1963).* Master's thesis, University of Natal, Durban, South Africa

Sklar, Holly. (1995, May). The snake oil of scapegoating. *Z Magazine, 8*(5), 49-56.

Splichal, Slavko. (1994). *Media beyond socialism: Theory and practice in East-Central Europe.* Boulder, CO: Westview.

Sprawozdanie z Prac Podzespolu ds. Środków Masowego Przekazu. (1989). Warsaw: Mimeo.

Staniszkis, Jadwiga. (1983). "Solidarność" Jako Zwiazek Zawodowy i Ruch Spoleczny. In W. Morawski (Ed.), *Demokracja i Gospodarka* (pp. 331-374). Warsaw: Uniwersytet Warszawski.

Stanley, Manfred. (1978). *The technological conscience: Survival and dignity in an age of expertise.* Chicago: University of Chicago Press.

Statut: Uchwala Programowa z Aneksem, Dokumenty Zjazdu. (1981). Gdańsk: Biuro Informacji Prasowej.

Steigleder, Klaus. (1992). *Die Begründung moralishen Sollens: Ethik in den Wissenschaften* (Vol. 5). Tübingen: Attempto Verlag.

Steinberg, Stephen. (1989). *The ethnic myth: Race, ethnicity and class in America.* Boston, MA: Beacon.

Stout, Jeffrey. (1993). On having a morality in common. In Gene Outka & John P. Reeder, Jr. (Eds.), *Prospects for a common morality* (pp. 215-232). Princeton, NJ: Princeton University Press.

Subhi, Ahmad M. (1969). *Ethical philosophy in Islamic thought.* Cairo: Dar Al Maaraef.

Suleri, Sara. (1882). *The rhetoric of English India.* Chicago: University of Chicago Press.

Svensson, Frances. (1973). *The ethnics in American politics: American Indians.* Minneapolis, MN: Burgess.

Sztompka, Piotr. (1982). Dynamika Ruchu Odnowy w Świetle Teorii Zachowania Zbiorowego. *Studia Socjologiczne, 3-4,* 69-93.

Talbot, Stephen. (1995, June). Wizard of ooze. *Mother Jones,* pp. 41-43.

Tahtinen, Unto. (1976). *Ahimsa: Non-violence in Indian tradition.* London: Rider.

Tannenbaum, P. H. (Ed.). (1980). *The entertainment functions of television.* Hillsdale, NJ: Lawrence Erlbaum.

Taylor, Paul W. (1963). The ethnocentric fallacy. *The Monist, 47*(4), 563-584.

Theunissen, Michael. (1984). *The other: Studies in the social ontology of Husserl, Heidegger, Sartre, and Buber* (Trans., C. Macann). Cambridge, MA: MIT Press.

Thomassen, Niels. (1985). *Communicative ethics in theory and practice.* London: Macmillan.

Thompson, J. B. (1990). *Ideology and modern culture.* Stanford, CA: Stanford University Press.

Titkow, A. (1993). *Stress i Zycie Spoleczne: Polskie Doświadczenia.* Warsaw: PIW.

Tomaselli, Keyan G., Williams, Alan, Steenveld, Lynette, & Tomaselli, Ruth E. (1986). *Myth, race and power: South Africans imaged on film and TV.* Bellville, South Africa: Anthropos.

Toulmin, Stephen. (1972). *Human understanding.* Oxford, UK: Oxford University Press.

Toulmin, Stephen. (1990). *Cosmopolis: The hidden agenda of modernity.* New York: The Free Press.

Traber, Michael. (1993). Communication ethics. In G. Gerbner, H. Mowlana, & K. Nordenstreng (Eds.), *The global media debate: Its rise, fall and renewal* (pp. 151-158). Norwood, NJ: Ablex.

Traber, Michael, & Nordenstreng, Kaarle. (1992). *Few voices, many worlds.* London: World Association of Christian Communication.

Turner, Terence. (1990, Spring). Visual media, cultural politics, and anthropological practice: Some implications of recent uses of film and video among the Kayapo of Brazil. *CVA Review,* 8-13.

Uchitelle, Louis. (1993, July 26). Strong companies are joining trend to eliminate jobs. *The New York Times,* pp. A1, D3.

Ucko, P. (1987). *Academic freedom and apartheid: The story of the world archaeological congress.* London: Peter Duckworth.

Varley, Paul. (1973). *Japanese culture: A short history.* Tokyo: Charles E. Tuttle.

Verene, Donald P. (1976). Vico's science of imagination: Universals and the philosophy of symbolic forms. In G. Tagliacozzo & D. P. Verene (Eds.), *Giambattista Vico's science of humanity* (pp. 285-317). Baltimore, MD: Johns Hopkins University Press.

Vico, Giambattista B. (1801). *Principi di una Scienza Nuova* (3 vols.). Milano: Dalla Tipo. (Original work published 1725)

Vico, Giambattista B. (1948). *The new science of G. Vico* (Trans., T. G. Bergin & M. H. Fisch). Ithaca, NY: Cornell University Press.

Waddy, Chris. (1982). *The Muslim mind.* London: Longman.

Walli, Koshelya. (1974). *The conception of ahimsa in Indian thought.* Varanasi, India: Bharata Manisha.

Wang, Georgette. (1977, May). *Opinion expression.* Paper presented at the annual conference of the International Communication Association, Berlin.

Wang, Georgette, Chu, Godwin C., Chung, Wei-wen, & Chi, Jin-yao. (1992). *A comparative study of values in Taiwan and China.* Unpublished research report. Taipei, Taiwan: National Science Council.

Warrior, Robert Allen. (1995). *Tribal secrets: Recovering American Indian intellectual traditions.* Minneapolis, MN: University of Minnesota Press.

Weatherford, Jack. (1988). *Indian givers: How the Indians of the Americas transformed the world.* New York: Crown.

Welch, Sharon. (1985). *Communities of resistance and solidarity: A feminist theology of liberation.* Maryknoll, NY: Orbis.

White, Morton G. (1981). *What is and what ought to be done.* New York: Oxford University Press.

Wiley, David, with Cancel, R., Pflugrad, D., Elkiss, T. H., & Campbell, A. (1982). *Africa on film and videotape 1960-1981.* East Lansing: Michigan State University, African Studies Center.

Wilke, Jürgen. (1992, August). *Professional ethics in journalism training.* Paper presented at the conference of the International Association of Mass Communication Research, Guarujá, Brazil.

Williams, Lucy. (1995, June). Race, rat bites and unfit mothers: How media discourse informs the welfare legislation debate. *Fordham Urban Law Journal, 22*(4), 1159-1196.

Williams, Raymond. (1963). *The long revolution.* Harmondsworth, UK: Pelican.

Williams, Raymond. (1968). *Communications.* Harmondsworth, UK: Penguin.

Williams, Raymond. (1983). *Keywords.* London: Fontana.

Wilmsen, Edwin. (1989). *Land filled with flies: A political economy of the Kalahari.* Chicago: University of Chicago Press.

Wilmsen, Edwin. (1991, Spring). Comments on Paul John Myburgh's *People of the Great Sandface. CVA Review,* p. 60.

Wilmsen, Edwin. (1991). Die Dokumentation war ein Vermächtnis. In R. Kapfer, W. Petermann, & R. Thomas (Eds.), *Jäger und Gejagte: John Marshall und Seine Filme* (pp. 80-102). Munich: Trickster Verlag.

Wilmsen, Edwin, & Denbow, J. R. (1990). Paradigmatic history of San-speaking peoples and current attempts at revision. *Current Anthropology, 31*(5), 489-524.

Wittgenstein, Ludwig. (1953). *Philosophical investigations.* Oxford, UK: Basil Blackwell.

Wittgenstein, Ludwig. (1956). *Remarks on the foundation of mathematics.* Oxford, UK: Basil Blackwell.

Wójcicki, K. (1981). The reconstruction of society. *Telos, 47,* 98-112.

Wold, Astri Heen. (Ed.). (1993). *The dialogical alternative: Towards a theory of language and mind.* Oslo: Scandinavian University Press.

Wolf, Jean-Claude. (1988). Kant und Schopenhauer über die Lüge. *Zeitschrift für Didaktik der Philosophie, 10,* 69-80.

Wolf, Jean-Claude. (1993). *Wahrheit und Lüge.* Unpublished manuscript.

Wong, David B. (1984). *Moral relativity.* Berkeley: University of California Press.

Wyschogrod, Edith. (1990). *Saints and postmodernism.* Chicago: University of Chicago Press.

Yoshikawa, Muneo J. (1988). Cross-cultural adaptation and perceptual development. In Y. Y. Kim & W. B. Gudykunst (Eds.), *Cross-cultural adaptation: Current approaches* (pp. 140-148). Newbury Park, CA: Sage.
Zasady Postepowania Dziennikarzy Na Czas Stanu Wojennego. (1989). *Most, 21,* 186-187.

Index

ABC, 300, 311
Abourezk, J., 199
Adams, R. M., 20
Adenauer, Konrad, 88
African communalistic society,
    171-172
  communication in, 172
  criticism of communication ethics of,
    186-189
  culturally regulated communication in,
    172-173
  See also African philosophical
    principles
African mass media:
  as government watchdogs, 187
  government ownership of, 187
  journalists, 190
  nation building and, 191
  socioeconomic development and, 191
African philosophical principles, 183, 185
  goals of, 173
  government and, 187-188
  likute, 191
  religion as a way of life, 173, 182-183,
    188
  respect for old age, 173, 181-182, 185,
    188
  sanctity of authority, 173, 179-181, 185,
    188
  supremacy of the community, 173,
    174-176, 188

  value of the individual, 173, 176-179,
    183, 188
Ahmad, K., 108, 112
Alexy, R., 54
Alter, J., 300
Alternative media, 39
American Public Broadcasting System,
  283-284
Andersen, R., 320
Anthropocentric morality, 42
Antonio, P. S., 184
Apel, Karl-Otto, 42, 46, 47, 48, 49, 53, 55,
  56, 60, 63
  discourse ethics of, x
Arab communicators:
  Arab-Islamic morality and, 120-123
  defense of Islam and, 121, 122-123
  honor and, 121
  responsibility and, 121-122
Arab Gulf Cooperation Council, TV charter
  of, 122
Arab-Islamic codes of ethics, 121
Arab-Islamic justice:
  as social equilibrium, 115-117
  principles of, 117
  through communication, 125
Arab-Islamic morality:
  Allah and, 107, 110, 124
  concept of dignity in, 111
  dimensions of, 106-109
  faith-centered, 107-108

About the Contributors

Robin Andersen, PhD, is Associate Professor and Chair of the Department of Communication and Media Studies at New York's Fordham University. Her research interests include the informational media and their impact on public opinion, the social and political impact of television, and the influence of advertising and media marketing on popular culture. She is the author of the book *Consumer Culture and TV Programming,* and has published in such scholarly journals as *The Media Reader, Journalism and Popular Culture, Media Culture and Society, Latin American Perspectives, Social Text, EXTRA!* and *The Humanist.* She has also produced radio and video documentaries and continues to work with WFUV radio 90.7 FM at Fordham University.

Edmund Arens studied philosophy and theology at the Universities of Münster and Frankfurt, Germany. He is author of *The Logic of Pragmatic Thinking: From Peirce to Habermas* (1994) and of *Christopraxis: A Theology of Action* (1995). He is also the author of several books in German, among them *Kommunikative Handlungen: Die paradigmatische Bedeutung der Gleichnisse Jesu für eine Handlungstheorie* (1982), and *Bezeugen und Bekennen: Elementare Handlungen des Glaubens* (1989). He has edited several books, including *Habermas und die Theologie* (1989) and *Anerkennung der Andern: Eine theologische Gunddimension interkultureller Kommunikation* (1995). He currently holds the chair of Fundamental Theology at Hochschule Luzern, in Lucerne, Switzerland.

Muhammad I. Ayish is Associate Professor of Communication at the Department of Mass Communication, the United Arab Emirates University, United Arab Emirates. He obtained his PhD in international broadcast communication from the University of Minnesota in 1986. His research interests are in international and Arab communication, especially broadcasting. His published research is in Arabic and in English, appearing in such journals as *Gazette, Abhath Al Yarmouk, Journal of Broadcasting and Electronic Media, European Journal of Communication, Media Development, Middle Eastern Studies,* and *Mass Media in the Middle East.*

Anantha Sudhaker Babbili is Professor and Chair of the Department of Journalism and Media Studies at Texas Christian University. He is on the guest faculty of Mexico's Universidad de las Americas, the United Kingdom's Oxford University and Regent's College, and India's Osmania University and the University of Hyderabad. He speaks several Indian languages, including his Dravidian and Sanskrit-based mother tongue, Telugu, as well as Hindi and Urdu. He holds an MA in journalism from the University of Oklahoma, and a PhD in mass communication from the University of Iowa. He has published numerous book chapters and essays in such journals as *Codigos, Interaction, Newspaper Research Journal, International Third World Studies Journal and Review, Media, Culture and Society, Journal of Communication Inquiry,* and *Journalism Quarterly.* He is the co-author of the British Film Institute study, *Bosnia by Television.*

Clifford G. Christians is Research Professor of Communications and Director, Institute of Communications Research at the University of Illinois, Urbana. He is the coauthor of the third edition of *Responsibility in Mass Communication; Jacques Ellul: Interpretive Essays; Media Ethics: Cases and Moral Reasoning* (four editions), and *Good News: Social Ethics and the Press.* He was the editor of *Critical Studies in Mass Communications,* serves on the editorial boards of the *Journal of Mass Media Ethics, Media Development,* and the *Journal of Ethics, Law and Society,* and he is an advising editor for *Media Ethics Update.* He has presented research papers and addresses on communication ethics in 20 countries.

Cynthia-Lou Coleman, PhD, pursues research related to health and risk communication and is particularly interested in how these issues affect Native Americans. She also studies how social values are constructed in the mainstream and advocacy press. An enrolled member of the Osage nation, she teaches communication theory, research methods, and public relations at the School of Journalism and Communication, University of Oregon at Eugene.

Deni Elliott is Professor of Ethics at the University of Montana and Director of the Practical Ethics Center there. She served 5 years as the first director for the Institute at Dartmouth. Her work in applied ethics spans the fields of education, journalism, science, and policy. Her works include edited and coauthored books, video documentaries, book chapters and articles for the academic press, magazine articles for the trade press, and newspaper pieces for the popular press.

Pedro Gilberto Gomes, PhD, is Titular Professor and the Director of the Center for Communication at the Universidade do Vale do Rio dos Sinos (Unisinos), São Leopoldo, Brazil. He also directs the MA program in Semiotics at the same university. He is President of ACIESTI (Association Catholique Internationale des Enseignants des Sciences Techniques de l'Information). He is the author of *Direito de Ser: A Ética da Comunicação na América Latina* (1989); *O Journalismo Alternativo no Projeto Popular* (1990); *A Comunicação Cristã em Tempos de Repressão* (1995); and Televisão e Audiência: Aspectos Quantitativos e Qualitativos, in *Cadernos de Comunicação,* No. 1, 1996.

Karol Jakubowicz is Lecturer at the Institute of Journalism, University of Warsaw. He is also Chief Expert for the National Broadcasting Council of Poland and holds the position of Deputy Chairman, Supervisory Board, Polish Television Ltd. He received his MA in English and PhD in media studies from the University of Warsaw. His research interests include media and broadcasting policy, comparative broadcasting systems, transformation of broadcasting systems, and the role of the media in social change. He has published widely on these subjects in Poland and internationally.

Dietmar Mieth is Professor of Theological Ethics at the University of Tübingen and Director of the Center for Ethics in the Sciences and Humanities at the same university. He is also Speaker for the European Network for Biomedical Ethics, member of the Group of Advisers for the "Ethical Implications of Biotechnology" at the European Community in

Brussels, and a member of the Foundation for the Journal *Concilium*. He has written about lies and lying in his book *Die Neuen Tugenden* (1984) and he has published 20 books on such subjects as the mystics, experimental ethics, narrative ethics, social ethics, and bioethics.

Andrew Azukaego Moemeka is Professor of Communication at the Central Connecticut State University, New Britain, Connecticut. A native of Obamkpa, Nigeria, he has a PhD in communication-sociology (New York), MS (Edinburgh), and BA (Lagos). He was Associate Professor of Mass Communication at the University of Lagos until 1992; since 1993, his publications include *Local Radio: Community Education for Development* (1981); *Reporters Handbook: An Introduction to Journalism* (1989); and *Development (Social Change) Communication: Creating Participation and Building Understanding* (1993). He is the editor of *Communicating for Development: A New Pan-Disciplinary Perspective* (1994).

Antonio Pasquali taught philosophy and communications at the Central University of Venezuela, Caracas. From 1984 to 1986, he was Assistant Director General of UNESCO, responsible for the communication sector; and from 1986 to 1990, UNESCO's Coordinator for Latin America. In 1974, he chaired the National Commission for a "Venezuelan Radio and Television Public Service" (Proyecto Ratelve). He is the author of *Comunicación y Cultura de Masas* (1962), *Sociologia e Comunicaçao* (1970), *Comprender la Comunicación* (1974), *La Comunicación Cercenada (1990),* and *El Orden Reina* (1992).

Gabriel Jaime Perez is Dean of the Communication School at Javeriana University, Bogotá, Colombia, where he heads the UNESCO Chair of Social Communication and teaches communication ethics. He has managed the Javeriana Radio Station (1979-1983), the Communication School's Department of Expression (1984-1988), the Graduate Program in Communication Research, and the Latin-American Course of Communication for Pastors (1989-1995). He has an MA in philosophy and theology and is currently working on a PhD thesis in communication ethics.

Haydar Badawi Sadig is Assistant Professor at the Department of Mass Communication, United Arab Emirates University, The United Arab Emirates. He obtained his PhD in mass communication from Ohio University in 1992. His research interests are in communication law and international communication.

Arnold Shepperson holds a research appointment in the Centre for Cultural and Media Studies, University of Natal, Durban, South Africa. He has published on semiotics, communication, and visual anthropology. He was formerly an electrician and draughtsman in the South African mining industry, an experience on which his continuing interest in cross-cultural encounters in economic and civil affairs is based.

Hideo Takeichi is Professor in the Department of Journalism at Sophia University in Tokyo. He worked for the *Yomiuri Shimbun* newspaper for 10 years, and was a Fulbright visiting scholar at the University of Missouri in 1980. His main fields of interest are international and intercultural communication, the history and development of American journalism, and communication law and ethics. He is the author (in Japanese) of *Fathers and Children: The Future of Communication* (1981) and *Comparative History of Newspapers in Japan and the United States* (1984). In Japanese, he coauthored *Introduction to Mass Communication* (1982) and *An Introduction to the American Mind* (1985). He has jointly translated several books from English into Japanese, among them works of Denis McQuail.

Keyan G. Tomaselli is Director and Professor in the Centre for Cultural and Media Studies of the University of Natal, Durban. He is the editor of the journal *Critical Arts: A Journal for Cultural Studies,* and author of *The Cinema of Apartheid* (1988).

Michael Traber studied philosophy and theology in Switzerland and communications in New York (Fordham and New York University, PhD in 1961). He worked as a journalist and book publisher in Zimbabwe and taught journalism in Zambia. From 1978 to 1995, he was on the staff of the World Association for Christian Communication in London. His last post was Director of Studies and Publications. He also edited the international journal *Media Development* from 1976-1995. He has written (in German) three books on Africa, numerous book chapters on communication ethics, and on the New World Information and Communication Order (NWICO). Among his edited books is *The Myth of the Information Society* (Sage, 1986).

Georgette Wang is Professor in the Department of Journalism, National Chengchi University in Taipei, Taiwan. She received her PhD from Southern Illinois University in 1977. She worked at the Communication Institute of the East-West Center in Honolulu and taught at universities in Taiwan and Hong Kong. Her major English publications are *Continuity and Change in Communication Systems,* coedited with Wimal Dissanayake (1984); *Information Society,* coauthored with Herbert S. Dordick (Sage, 1993); and *Treading Different Paths: Informatization in Asia* (1994).